*Social History of Africa*
# "WE WERE ALL SLAVES"

**Recent Titles in**
**Social History of Africa Series**
*Series Editors: Allen Isaacman and Jean Allman*

# "WE WERE ALL SLAVES"

## AFRICAN MINERS, CULTURE, AND RESISTANCE AT THE ENUGU GOVERNMENT COLLIERY

Carolyn A. Brown

HEINEMANN
Portsmouth, NH

JAMES CURREY
Oxford

DAVID PHILIP
Cape Town

Heinemann
A division of Reed Elsevier Inc.
361 Hanover Street
Portsmouth, NH 03801-3912

James Currey Ltd.
73 Botley Road
Oxford OX2 0BS
United Kingdom

David Philip Publishers
An Imprint of New Africa Books
  (Pty) Ltd.
P. O. Box 46962
Glosderry 7702
Cape Town, South Africa

www.heinemann.com

Offices and agents throughout the world

ISBN 0-325-07007-5   (Heinemann cloth)
ISBN 0-325-07006-7   (Heinemann paper)
ISBN 0-85255-684-5   (James Currey cloth)
ISBN 0-85255-634-9   (James Currey paper)

British Library Cataloguing in Publication Data is available upon request.

**Library of Congress Cataloging-in-Publication Data**

Brown, Carolyn A. 1944–
"We were all slaves" : African miners, culture, and resistance at the Enugu government
  colliery / Carolyn A. Brown.
      p.   cm. — (Social history of Africa, ISSN 1099-8098)
    Includes bibliographical references and index.
    ISBN 0-325-07007-5 (alk. paper) — ISBN 0-325-07006-7 (pbk. : alk. paper)
    1. Coal miners—Nigeria—Enugu—History.   2. Strikes and
lockouts—Miners—Nigeria—Enugu.   3. Coal mines and mining—Nigeria—
Enugu—History.   I. Title.   II. Series.
HD8039.M6152 N63   2003
331.7'622334'0966949—dc21          2001051630

Cover design by Gail Ivaksa

Cover photo: Sculpture of the 1949 Iva Valley Shooting Incident.

Printed in the United States of America on acid-free paper

07  06  05  04  03  SB  1 2 3 4 5 6 7 8 9

*I dedicate this book to my parents, the Rev. Henry B. and Gertrude P. Mitchell. They have both instilled in me an understanding of the importance of the struggle for social justice. It is this commitment to social justice that led me to this study of the coal miners of Nigeria. Although today their industry is but a ghost of its past importance to Nigeria, West Africa, and Britain, I hope that this book commemorates their role in the labor history of Africa. I similarly dedicate this book to them.*

Stretched out on their sides, they were picking away harder than ever, with only one idea in their heads: to make up a large total of tubs. In this desperate fight for such hard-earned gain, everything else faded into insignificance. They no longer noticed the water running down them and making their limbs swell, the cramps from unnatural postures, the stiffening darkness in which they were blanched like plants in a cellar.... Like moles burrowing under the weight of the earth, without a breath of air in their burning lungs, they went picking away.

—Émile Zola, *Germinal*, London, 1954.

# CONTENTS

# ILLUSTRATIONS

## DIAGRAMS AND TABLES

## GRAPHS

# ACKNOWLEDGMENTS

I have had the support—both moral and material—of many individuals and institutions throughout the years during which I researched this book. First, I would like to mention how I came to study this coal mine. In the early seventies I became interested in labor history and was particularly fascinated by miners. However, because of apartheid and being an African-American, I was unable to study the most important mines in Africa's political economy—the gold mines of South Africa. I wrote to a friend, Walter Rodney, about my interest and he suggested that I read Émile Zola's *Germinal*, to get a sense of the material conditions of coal mining and mentioned that no one had worked on the Enugu coal mines in southeastern Nigeria. Walter's death was a devastating personal loss at a time when the Caribbean movement was at its peak and many times his presence is still felt in the current debates about slavery and the slave trade, concerns over which his shadow still towers. It was Walter who mentioned the shooting of demonstrating coal miners in November 1949, a date which many call the "birth date" of Nigerian nationalism. This incident, the Iva Valley Shooting and concluding chapter of this book, was a constant presence in all my interviews in Enugu.

The field work for this project was conducted after the Nigerian Civil War in which many documents, both held personally and in the archives, were destroyed. However, these were available to both David Smock and Agwu Akpala, two scholars who had done the bulk of their research before the War and both generously shared their notes and personal documents with me. Dr. Akpala was an important source of referrals for people to meet in Nigeria and was extremely helpful in explaining the technicalities of mining as well as the complex system of industrial relations in force for the latter part of the industry's history.

The coal industry's history is very interwoven with that of the town of Enugu and the immediate environs. For that reason it was quite easy to locate excellent informants and, in many cases, to speak with the very people discussed in the volumes of documents found in the Public Records Office, Kew Gardens. This allowed me to have more than one perspective on a specific event. There are so many,

many people in Nigeria upon whom I have relied in working through the various phases of this project that it is difficult (and risky), to give specific names. My assistants, Matthew Nwabueze and Charles Ugoji, both of Akpakwume, Udi, devised a strategy for identifying informants. We went to Udi Siding paymaster on the day when pensioners were paid. They then trekked into the villages to schedule appointments. I conducted a series of open-ended interviews that helped me to flesh out the image of these proud working men from the representations in the archives. Raphael Ani, General Manager of the Nigerian Coal Corporation, arranged interviews and accommodations near the company's headquarters and the archives.

I wish to thank the many coal miners and other colliery personnel who allowed me to interview them and share their personal records. Many of them made difficult arrangements to meet with me on my various visits to Nigeria. Although many had lost their documents and personal mementos, their personal recollections and the many hours that they spent speaking with me allowed me to compensate for this vacuum. My most useful informants were the individual workers who created the industry's militant reputation and transformed, with their vision of the future and the "modern," both the city of Enugu and the adjacent countryside. To capture their spirit I went deep into the mines, watched how they worked and their demeanor, and ventured into their homes, in the villages, labor camps, and other areas of Enugu. These were men like Samuel Aneke of Obinagu, Udi, my first interview, who was among the first men to work in the mines. His memories of the "Fluenza" epidemic helped me to date his age and his description of the British invasion moved me to attempt to characterize the horror of what we historians dryly call "colonial transformation." Others, like Peter and Alice Afemufuna, a coal miner and wife who was a leader of the women's demonstration at the coal mines, described the events that led up to the 1949 crisis and gave me some insight into the terms under which miners' wives mobilized.

Others were more prominent and were cited in the archival record: Chief Nwafor Chukwani, C.C. Onoh, Eze Ozogwu, Augustine Ude, Charles Morris, Joseph Okpokwu, Isaiah Ojiyi, Josiah Agu, B.U. Anyasodo, and Emmanuel Okafor, who was wounded in the 1949 shooting. They had personal libraries that were destroyed during the war but they spent hours speaking with me to help reconstruct events.

I would also like to thank the Crown Agents for permission to use their rich trove of photographs taken during the construction of the Eastern Branch of the Nigerian Railway and the Udi Coalfields. These are the only remaining photographs of the early mines and I have tried to use them liberally to give this narrative a more human dimension. I have taken these pictures to the Nigerian National Archives, Enugu, where they can be available to other researchers. I would like to thank Chief U.O.A. Esse, director of these archives, and his staff for alerting me to relevant documents on the last phase of this project. Mr. Esse is an indomitable spirit who has worked tirelessly, despite the difficult conditions pertaining in his archive, to produce volumes of finders' aids and guides that truly facilitate the researcher's task. I would also like to thank Mr. Anayo Enechukwu of the Enugu Historical Documentation Center.

Documents on the colliery were scattered through a number of record groups in the Public Records Office and among other archives in England. For the British Trades Union Congress records, I would like to thank the Modern Records Project of Warwick University, Coventry. The staff of the Colonial Records Project, Rhodes House, Oxford University, Royal Commonwealth Society, British Library of Political and Economic Science, London School of Economics all helped me use personal papers, field notes, letters, and other memorabilia of various colonial civil servants and officials. Because the industry was a parastal, I often found these records full of anecdotal references to the colliery.

The project was generously supported by a number of research grants. In its initial stages, the research was supported by the now defunct Ford Foundation Program for African Americans Conducting Fieldwork in Africa and the Middle East. This program, which supported a generation of African-American Africanist scholars and activists, enabled me to divide a year between England and Nigeria. This was my first trip to Africa and without it I could not have supported field work in Africa. I also had several research grants from the City University of New York Research Foundation and a post-doctoral fellowship from the American Council of Learned Societies and the Social Science Research Council. These grants allowed me to refine my understanding of the way the colliery impacted upon a form of indigenous slavery in the early decades of the century, an important component of the social history of the industry's regional role. I also held a two-year Presidential Postdoctoral Fellowship from the University of California, during which I was based at the University of California Berkeley. The Stanford–University of California Joint Program on African Studies provided an excellent context for the testing of interpretations and Michael Watts, Richard Roberts, and Pearl Alice Marsh were wonderful colleagues always willing to read my work.

Most recently, I received support from the American Philosophical Society, and the National Endowment of the Humanities at the Schomburg Center for Research in Black Culture of the New York Public Library. These grants, while largely used for research on another project on the city of Enugu, did allow me to collect several additional interviews that are incorporated in the latter part of this book. For this phase of the project Anayo Enechukwu, Director of the Enugu Historical Documentation Bureau, has been a key person in completing the final interviews in Iva Valley Camp, one of the earliest coal labor camps.

I would like to thank Marcia Wright, who has been with me during the years that this project has evolved. She encouraged me during the confusing days when, fresh home from the field, I was totally overwhelmed with the material and had not a clue what to make of it. Marcia diligently read my various drafts, made concrete suggestions and always encouraged me to overcome the many obstacles in my path. I thank Rutgers University which supported several leaves of absence that allowed me to refine my analysis and to collect additional material and my colleagues in the history department who listened to numerous versions of segments of this project. These colleagues at Rutgers created an intellectual environment that encouraged me to probe deeper into my data. The strength of gender studies at Rutgers encouraged me to identify the role of gender in the rich systems of self-construction that so motivated Enugu's coal laborers.

The title for this book came from an interview in the South Nkanu village of Obiofia, Akegbe-Ugwu (5 August 1986), an area with a large and militant ex-slave (*Ohu*) population. When I asked if there were any salves working in the Enugu Government Colliery one person said "We Were All *Awbia* to the Europeans." I thought this was an excellent title for a book that describes the dialectics of the colonial workplace.

The term *Awbia*, meaning "stranger," was adopted as the name of slaves following a series of violent confrontations between freeborn and slave in the South Nkanu area. As a result the erstwhile slaves got the government to declare the term slave—*Ohu*—illegal and to require the name *Awbia* to be used. Today this name is still used, but, of course, everyone knows the origins of this group.

Finally, I thank my family, my children, Dedan Anderson, Haydee C. Brown, and Kathia Brown, who for a great part of their lives have "lived with" the Enugu coal miners, and their fathers Sam Anderson and Humberto Brown. Quite importantly, I thank my parents, the Rev. Henry B. Mitchell and Gertrude P. Mitchell, for always encouraging me with this book and understanding the complex elements of my obsession with Africa and its history.

# African Workers and European Theories: The Enugu Coal Miners and West African Labor History

On 18 November 1949 police fired on a group of miners engaged in a sit-in at the Iva Valley mine of Enugu Government Colliery in southeastern Nigeria, killing twenty-one miners and injuring several hundred. Additional fatalities occurred during protest demonstrations led by radical nationalists in eastern Nigeria's major cities of Calabar, Aba, Onitsha, Port Harcourt, and Enugu. The shooting riveted the Colonial Office and opened Labor to attacks in Parliament over the pace and nature of political change in Nigeria as well as the state's conduct towards its own African workers. From the standpoint of the state, a policy designed to insulate the labor movement from political radicalism, thereby creating "depoliticized" trade unions, backfired. The subsequent urban riots involved a very dangerous alliance that the state had worked assiduously to avoid. Radical nationalists, some espousing Marxist rhetoric, led the urban working class, casual workers, the unemployed, and disaffected indigenous traders to take over the streets. In the ensuing violence they attacked the buildings of European expatriate firms and opened the possibility of a general insurrection.

In some cities the police could restore order only after pitched battles in the streets against mobs of market "boys" and unemployed men. On the political front the tragedy forced a temporary alliance among the contending nationalist groups who formed a new coalition, the National Emergency Committee, that temporarily papered over the deep regional divisions in their fragmenting movement. A similar rapprochement occurred in the national trade union movement, itself fragmented by Cold War ideologies and battles, with the formation of the National Labour Committee. Both coalitions hurried to Enugu to investigate the incident and to serve as self-proclaimed mediators and representatives for the miners in the investigation that followed. The incident became a dramatic illustration of the abuses of British colonialism in popular memory, and the dead miners became icons for a national narrative of the birth of the independent state.

For the miners, the shooting was a shocking departure from the state's usual pattern of conflict resolution in the industry. Enugu workers saw the shooting as a betrayal occurring on the heels of a war in which they had agreed to make sustained and heroic sacrifices. It was even more incongruous to the men who had expected the state to recognize them as loyal state employees simply demanding "fair" and "just" treatment from their government/employers.

Normally the state's response to the workers' protest was largely accommodative. Previous unrest led to the deployment of state officials to investigate, followed by some type of wage adjustment or improvement in conditions. This was undoubtedly because of the industry's parastal status and the colliery's industrial conflicts were automatically thrust into the political arena of Parliamentary politics. During World War II the Colonial Office was especially preoccupied to represent the colonial state as an enlightened paternalistic power, especially with an industry whose metropolitan workers were so problematic at home. To this end it launched a series of social and labor reforms that attempted to co-opt the colonial labor movement into the ideological and organizational structures being used in the United Kingdom—industrial relations procedures, compulsory arbitration, joint concilliation, and controlled trade unions. These reforms opened new areas of contention which frequently erupted into work disputes in the postwar period.[1]

As was the case with many postwar labor conflicts at colliery, the 1949 dispute arose over conflicting interpretations of a recently introduced law, which in this case was against casual labor. This was a time of considerable political uncertainty—the Cold War—when state officials were debating the need for and forms of political reform. But in the meantime, they repressed every type of political or industrial action that appeared to threaten the process. They knew that they wanted African workers to form "responsible" trade unions and to behave as "respectable" workers, but they were not quite sure how to achieve what they wanted nor to identify it when they saw it. They had yet to determine their ability to direct and control the complex and rapidly changing political environment that accompanied decolonization. Many government officials were imprisoned by their own myopic visions of colonial order and its mythologies. But even the most "enlightened" agent, the Labour Party, was determined to prevent "political unionism" despite the contradiction in its own genesis. By an ironic twist of fate, it was Labour that would prove most violently repressive against colonial workers.

The state's assumption that the struggles of parastal workers could be depoliticized was naïve and was but another example of their misreading the sophistication of their workers. The explicitly political ways that the state had itself conceived African labor encouraged these colliery workers to grasp the connections between their industrial problems and the state. Government officials and colonial chiefs were involved in the recruitment and control of labor. Each strike, which was a confrontation between labor and the state, drew the immediate attention of many layers of the state from the local district officer to the Colonial Office.

Finally, martyrdom has not generated scholarly interest in the colliery workers within the historiography of African labor. The incident is mentioned in every political history of Nigeria, but with the exception of a seminal article by Agwu Akpala,[2] no scholars have moved beyond the incident to study these workers in their own right. There are two other monographs but each focuses on a specific period of the history or on the problems confronting management.[3] There are no monographs on the subject. This paucity of studies is symbolic of the historical obfuscation which has burdened the colliery's labor movement in the more than eighty years of its existence.

## CONTINUITIES BETWEEN COLONIAL AND METROPOLITAN LABOR: AFRICAN "CITIZENS" OF THE "COUNTRY OF COAL"

On its most fundamental level this book seeks to rescue the history of Nigerian colliery workers from its absorption by nationalist historiography. In this respect it is a case study of a key group of colonial workers. But on the other hand it uses this history as a prism to examine both changes in colonial labor policy and in the evolving consciousness of African men employed in colonial industries. One emphatic thread runs throughout the narrative—that the history of these men must be contextualized within the international historiography of coal miners' narratives. Most of the miners were of the Igbo-speaking ethnic group, one of Nigeria's three major populations and dominant group in southeastern Nigeria, east of the Niger River. These miners were a profoundly self-conscious sector of West Africa's working class, sharply aware of their position within the regional economy. They were a key sector of the colonial working class positioned in the enclave economy of West Africa. Their coal fueled the railways of West Africa, produced electricity in eastern Nigeria's cities, bunkered the ships that plied its coasts, and powered the steam engines that mined tin in northern Nigeria. These were the only coal mines in West Africa and Britain's first experiment with a nationalized coal industry, both factors having a profound influence on the course of the industry's history.[4]

Throughout the period covered by this study, Enugu's miners had a well-deserved reputation as West Africa's most belligerent working class. This militance, sharpened by their work traditions, gave them an autonomy in the workplace and encouraged pride in their skill and their confrontations with danger. They had a propensity for solidarity which supported their intractable negotiation positions with the state. Predictably, they conceptualized the state within a context of indigenous understandings of power and authority, self-esteem and "justice," a central feature being a reciprocal relationship of loyalty. Their history engages the creative tension, which Fred Cooper noted in E.P. Thompson's later work, between the industry's attempt to treat them as *abstract* labor power and their personal struggles to be recognized as *real* labor power.[5] They were important men in their villages and not simply an abstract category—"labor"—and their individual and collective values, priorities, and goals became the driving force of their history.

Behind these traditions of militance lay a curiously autonomous power which coal miners have in the workplace and is quite absent under the forms of supervision to which other industrial workers were subjected. The organization of work in dispersed underground sites makes managerial supervision difficult. And even with state control and corrupt underground supervisors, Enugu's miners created work cultures which expressed the degrees of workplace control that make coal miners so exceptional among industrial workers. Miners determined the frequency and intensity of their work, the length of the working day, and the organization of the labor process itself. Until World War II they created their own work groups and made critical decisions about the actual mining operations, decisions that constitute the intuitive skill that is so indispensable to survival underground.[6] Furthermore, most of the industry's workers integrated mine labor with farming, becoming permanent commuters and forcing the industry to accommodate its production schedules to the seasonality of the agricultural cycle.

Like coal miners elsewhere, the Enugu workers proved especially prone to industrial action and promoted ideologies of solidarity and democratic participation as prominent members of rural villages. This study recognizes and confronts the analytical tension between the specificity of their experiences as African men in a colonial industry and the universality of their responses arising from their working in an international industry—coal. Among the complex of factors underlining this similarity is the material reality of the workplace—the "pit"—and the shared experiences of men working under its uniquely grueling conditions of work. These conditions, common to all coal mines, have led David Frank, a Canadian labor scholar, to call the international world of coal mining a "country of coal" where "the people of this relatively unrecognized country have much history in common."[7]

These West African coal miners hold "citizenship" in this "country." They were called into being not by the Industrial Revolution, but by the imperialist partition and conquest of their continent. Colonialism reformulated the area's relationship to the world economy. It shifted from supplying human cargo for international slave trading, an anathema to the "free" market ideology of capitalism, to the export of tropical products to supply Europe's factories. The export economy required an infrastructure (i.e., railways and ports) and this infrastructure needed coal. Thus, the discovery of coal in Eastern Nigeria in the first decade of this century pulled thousands of Igbo-speaking men from the villages in southern Nigeria into the "country of coal."

The commonalties of the workplace in coal mining have made the literature of the industry in Europe and the Americas particularly salient for the study of Nigerian miners and have provided an opportunity to draw African labor history into the mainstream of Western labor historiography.[8] A number of themes and debates characterize this literature and are of mixed relevance for this study. I have found the ambigious role of the "independent collier,"[9] the relatively skilled miner whose control over the labor process is so strong that he often considers himself to be an artisan, to be of some relevance in understanding the proud and somewhat arrogant stance taken by the "pit men" in many of the industry's strikes. However, when one compares the control which Enugu miners exert over the labor process, it is far more compromised than that of European and American miners before mechanization. Most performed a distinct set of skills related only to the opening of the coal face, the cutting of the coal, and timbering the work space while other tasks, such as supporting the roof in roadways, pushing the tubs, etc., were performed by other workers.[10] But Enugu's mines were never significantly mechanized, partially because of unfavorable underground conditions, and partly because of state unwillingness to invest in expensive machinery. This created a workplace in which the miner's job was fragmented as if mechanization were about to occur but never does. Typically the literature portrays the miner as a labor aristocrat, ever insistent upon distinguishing his position from that of other less skilled—and less autonomous—underground workers and not always willing to join with others in solidarity against capital. This was one element of comparative importance between Enugu miners and their Scottish counterparts. Scottish miners, themselves only emancipated from serfdom in 1799, as noted in Alan Campbell and Fred Reid's "The Independent Collier in Scotland,"[11] held romantic attachments to the land and the personal validation it brings to assumptions of the autonomy of the patriarchal household. Even when the autonomy of these miners was eroded by the decline of the small collieries, they retained the ideology of their independence, transformed into a working class respectability which often made them reluctant to join in solidarity with less skilled workers against capital. This respectability was a core element in the consciousness of Enugu's miners but it did not lead them to reject solidarity. In fact, they played a vanguard role in cultivating the unity that informed the militant history of the miners through this period.

Secondly, I was particularly influenced by the literature that examines the connections between the ways that production was organized in the workplace—the labor process—and the impact that this had on both power relations and on the consciousness of particular groups of workers of the value of their skill. In this respect Keith Dix's *Work Relations in the Coal Industry: The Hand-Loading Era, 1880–1930*; Michael Burawoy's various studies, *The Politics of Production: Factory Regimes Under Capitalism and Socialism*; and Harry Braverman's *Labor and Monopoly Capital: The Degradation of Work in the Twentieth Century* were of major importance.

Worker consciousness is not just created nor expressed in the workplace alone. It is also cultivated or discouraged in the interactions between workers and the broader community. In this respect this study has benefited from the community studies of the mining industry. A central contradiction of coal miners' independence in the workplace before mechanization was the control that the company placed on the life outside the mines. Companies usually controlled housing, stores, regulated access to medical care, and ran the politics of the towns. Two excellent studies of the consequences of this power, Anthony F.C. Wallace's *St Clair: A Nineteenth-Century Coal Town's Experience With a Disaster-Prone Industry* and Mildred Allen Beik's *The Miners of Windber: The Struggles of New Immigrants for Unionization, 1890's–1930's*, presented models that contrasted with even the state-run labor camps in Enugu. Because of the miners' resilient connections with the rural villages, even an authoritarian state could not guarantee the types of economic and social control that made miners' communities such pinnacles of class conflict.

Finally, this study attempted to integrate gender and the organization of the labor process. In this respect several books were of major influence in strengthening this argument. One on the Chilean copper miners, Thomas Klubock's *Contested Communities: Class, Gender and Politics in Chile's El Teniente Copper Mine, 1904–1951*, has benefited from some of the newest research on masculinity and its correlation to jobs involving danger and manual labor. Similarly, Dunbar Moodie and Vivienne Ndatshe's *Going for Gold: Men, Mines and Migration*, a study of Southern African migrant workers, helped to situate a masculine work ethic into the workers' attempts to retain patriarchal control over their families even while spending years away as migrant workers.

This book also explores the connections between domestic and colonial labor policies as well as the less institutionalized contacts between these two groups of workers. The boundaries between metropolitan and colonial industry, British "working men" and "native" laborers, were more "imagined" than real. The context of work was often similar. Metropolitan production regimes were projected into the colonial workplace because of the imperatives of coal mining. Recruitment of management and their models of workplace discipline, decisions about extractive systems and production techniques, the procedures for dispute management and the standards of safety, accident compensation, workmen's compensation, all were transferred from the British coal fields. But they were modified to comply with colonial conditions and many accommodated British ideas about the deficient character of African labor. These ideas were often framed in the discourse of colonial racism. The power of this racial discourse in shaping the attitudes of British industrial officials and emphasizing African "difference" was especially remarkable because of the myriad ways that the Enugu miners' work culture and patterns of resistance resembled those of Britain's own colliers. The "African worker," the subject of colonial denigration, was an imperial fantasy which evolved as a social construction to rationalize the failure of colonial capital to transform work relations in the mines. Unblinded by colonial racism, management would have recognized the men's similarity with Britain's own miners.

But while the study seeks to establish the commonalties of Nigerian miners in the "country of coal" it does not imply that they did not bring unique characteristics to the workplace. In fact, Enugu miners operated under principles that emerged historically from the communities and villages in which they lived. These included gendered ideas of work and its rewards, forms of male association, standards of leadership, and their sense of "fairness" and "justice," all operating within the historical context of the period. They brought these ideologies with them into the workplace and used them to order their world. We can therefore define a work culture with two categories of elements: (1) those arising from the objective realities of coal mining as an industry and (2) others rooted in indigenous understandings of power and authority, work, leadership, self-esteem and improvement, and "justice."

Nigerian miners proved just as troublesome to the colonial state as did British miners to the metropolitan state which, during World War I, broached and initially rejected but later (in World War II), assumed state ownership of its own coal industry. While there is only anecdotal evidence that the state's experience with Enugu miners had any relevance to the reconfiguration of the British coal industry, at certain moments Colonial Office operatives were sharply conscious of the broader metropolitan implications of their policies towards the Enugu industry and its colonial workers. The specter of a state industry in the colonies, that promoted "free" labor for its educational value to the "native," violating the most basic principles of sound management and labor policy, was a condition that the Colonial Office sought to avoid. Thus it responded rapidly to each strike at Enugu which risked calling attention to the deplorable conditions of this "state socialist" industry. This was a special concern during the periods when state ownership of the British coal industry was being debated.

The commonalties of work and similarities in workers' protest strategies present an additional challenge to the conceptual barrier between European and colonial workers and encourage the scholar. Most literature on colonial workers emphasize their "difference" from metropolitan workers and ignore the ideological and social impact of the daily contacts between "native" worker and European "boss."[12] The authoritarian nature of colonial work cultures has led historians to force the personal relationship between European boss and African worker into a conflictual paradigm that masks a relationship that was far more complex. Evidence of joint participation by "native" foremen and British "bosses" in corrupt extortion schemes, and of the fraternal social relationships between others, indicate areas for further scholarly consideration.

A second factor that challenges a facile distinction between "metropolitan" and "colonial" labor was the similarity between British and Nigerian workers' patterns of participation in both the rural agricultural economy and in the coal pit. This encouraged me to look for other continuities in work and protest culture, organization of production, contributions of work to masculinity, et cetera, between "subject–worker" and British "boss." Most of the staff came from the northern coal fields of England, near Durham, and were familiar with a system of work organization that was most frequently used there. Management brought ideas to the workplace about the merits and skill requirements of particular types of work organization and the designation of tasks. Similarly, Enugu workers adopted a discourse of workers' protest culture, such as the use of the term *'ca' canny* for "go slow," a term from the Durham coal fields. These commonalties existed in juxtaposition to the separation of colonizer–colonized and challenge the underlying assumptions of much of the earlier African labor history that considers African workers to be so "different" from metropolitan. In this respect the concept of an imperial social formation proves most useful in describing a working class in which myriad exchanges occur across national boundaries that link workers.[13] An awareness of these continuities strikes African workers during the depression when their access to radios as well as contacts with European bosses—themselves members of the British working class—

planted the seed of membership to an international working class.[14] In the process I have tried to construct these African employees as colonial workers and as men in the multiple situations in which they live and work over time. I therefore reject an approach that constructs these men as exotic or primitive curiosities, as did both colonialist administrators and historians of the time.

## ENUGU MINERS IN THE HISTORIOGRAPHY OF AFRICAN LABOR

The research for this study began when African labor history was charting a long and often tortuous path away from the dominance of social scientific studies of African labor. Until the late 1960s African labor studies were dominated by political scientists, anthropologists, and sociologists who were preoccupied with the role of labor in nation building and assumed that trade unions were the highest expression of worker consciousness and class formation.[15] Most studies emphasized labor migration and used theories such as the "target worker" and "semi-proletarianized peasantry" to describe workers' resistance to industrial discipline.[16] This research agenda was shaped by a scholarly preoccupation with the mining complexes of southern and central Africa.[17] Similarly, African labor history strained under the shadow of more established (and more parochial) labor historiographies of the United States and Western Europe, and drew upon the traditions of the Marxist English social historians, such as E.P. Thompson, Gareth Stedman Jones, and Eric Hobsbawm.[18] By the mid-1970s Africanist scholars spoke of "new labor studies" which broke with the preoccupation with labor unions, strikes, and migrant labor and focused on a broader range of adversarial and subversive behavior through which, they argued, workers expressed their consciousness.[19] These studies moved beyond the workplace to examine laborers as social beings with positions in communities, families, and the broader society.

One area of particular concern was the formation of the working class in the early years of colonial economic transformation. In this respect the work of Keletso Atkins holds a special place.[20] She has written a redemptive project which challenged the pejorative characterization of the "lazy African" by reconceptualizing the behavior of early Zulu workers within the framework of an existing, and modifiably relevant, indigenous work culture. Atkins' work was of considerable significance for this study because it enabled me to understand the roots of the activism of those early Enugu workers, who were forced into an unfamiliar labor system—wage labor—and had to fashion their own ideological and associational weapons for survival. Until her study, few Africanist historians recognized an "African work culture" with its system of values attached to certain types of work, a moral economy of authority, and adaptation of rural forms of consultation to organize protests. This led me to investigate the connections between pre-industrial work systems and power hierarchies and the ways that Enugu workers experienced the capitalist workplace. From this perspective it was then possible to appreciate the complicated power relations that ensnarled workers in a labyrinth of old (rural) and

new (industrial) systems of power, authority, and control and to subsequently identify the points of contestation. These insights pushed the study ever deeper into the
workplace and to an examination of the labor process.

The recent work of Frederick Cooper was of similar value for the latter periods covered by this study. His *On the African Waterfront: Urban Disorder and
the Transformation of Work in Colonial Mombasa*, identified the benchmarks in
evolving policy debates among colonial administrators over the social dimension
of African labor. By noting the autonomy that casual workers had over dock work,
he illuminated the connections which policymakers made between such informal
labor systems and politically dangerous urban disorder. Colonial Office reform-
ers saw the nuclear family as central to creating a disciplined and "responsible"
workforce and post-war colonial governments embarked upon policies that took
them ever deeper into Africans' lives and ultimately into the African home.[21] In
Enugu, as elsewhere, while trade union experts reorganized workers' organizations, social workers and welfare experts monitored wives and children. They
could not conceive that a stable and moderate worker could come from an extended polygynous household, and the Nigerian government set about creating an
experiment in state welfare at the mines—a beautifully ordered labor estate replete with social services, schools, and recreational activities. The linkage between a stabilized and "responsible" workforce and urban order was a crucial
nexus for my study of the influence of perceptions of Enugu labor upon urban social policy and reform during the 1940s. And Cooper's subsequent study, *Decolonization and African Society*, helped me to contextualize state initiatives at the
colliery within the broader framework of imperial-level reform at the Colonial
Office. This permitted this study to identify the specific local conditions that challenged colonial policy as well as African workers' responses to various Colonial
Office interventions that occurred with increasing frequency during and after
World War II.

The study is therefore positioned within the debates, evolving theories, and historiographical traditions of labor history in general, and African labor history more
specifically. It has also drawn fruitfully upon the multidisciplinary contributions
of cultural studies and the new debates within race, class, and gender studies.[22]
Several proved to be of considerable salience in explaining the propensity of
Enugu's coal workers to engage in industrial action, in unlocking the mystery—
and preoccupation of a generation of African labor studies—of workers' political
awareness and the context and conditions in which the battery of norms and values that undergird their actions are cultivated.[23] Labor history, and indeed this study,
has profited greatly from the contributions of feminist studies, especially in their
problematizing masculinity as a subject of sustained examination.[24] Similarly, cultural studies have also encouraged me to examine the "worker" with an other than
economistic "lens." Together, feminist and cultural studies have challenged labor
historians to move from a crudely teleological materialism inherent in the proletarianization theory and forced scholars to engage the subjectivities that are an essential element of the "worker's" existence as a social being.

Of all the economistic explanations of worker activism the proletarianization thesis has proven especially inadequate for this study, because Enugu's workers' militance did not arise after their alienation from the land—this never, in fact, happened—nor did their protests follow the form of temporary, rural-based sojourners in the capitalist workplace. With the exception of a brief period in the early 1920s when recently recruited local men used desertion, in other words, a total withdrawal of labor, they employed orthodox forms of industrial protest to lodge their objections to conditions of work and pay. They met secretly to discuss grievances, sent delegations to meet with management, and, when this failed, hired Lagos lawyers to make representations before relevant government agencies.

The proletarianization thesis was also of limited value because of the varied residential patterns of the workers. Until World War II only a small number of "foreign" workers lived in Enugu's "native" quarters and labor camps, while the majority of the workers lived in local villages within a fifteen-mile radius of the mines. Most rurally based workers commuted daily to work or boarded weekly in labor camps or "native locations" of Enugu—returning to the village on weekends. This labor pattern is not easily accommodated in the models of labor systems employed by labor scholars. With one foot firmly in the village economy and the other in the mine, they constituted a category of workers distinctive from the "migrant"–fully "proletarianized" binary found in most African labor histories. They are not away from their homes for extended periods of time, nor did they have the wives and families with them in the towns and camps. However, their preferences to remain organically involved in their villages allowed the state to sharpen the distinction between proletarianization and stabilization. If we accept the conventional definition of proletarianization as the historical process through which the producer is pushed off the land—which in a rural economy is the primary means of production—and becomes dependent on the sale of labor-power for subsistence, then stabilization is the process through which a producer retains connections with the land but is periodically forced to perform wage labor on a consistent/permanent basis. Neither the state nor the workers wanted a fully proletarianized workforce. The political advantage to the colonial state of the latter over the former was recognized by colonial officials who were wary of the potential radicalization of a working class and the threat it could pose to social order.[25] Officials were far more comfortable believing that Africans were proverbial "men of the bush" whose mysterious proclivities to rebellion were rooted in their irrationality and were best countered by rather authoritarian powers vested in local colonial chiefs. Proletarianized Africans were "detribalized" Africans and there was no place for them within the mythologies of a peaceful colonial society. Nevertheless, the industry still needed access to an experienced rural male workforce at various points in its marketing cycle. Thus the men in the villages near Enugu became a pool of skilled labor employed and discharged as the industry required.

For their part, workers were loath to sever their connections with rural agricultural production and social life which played so prominent a role in their valorization as men. They were vested in the rural cultures and economies where they played the role of "independent and patriarchal proprietors over rural household production."[26] It was in this context of near seamless articulation of industrial and agricultural production that workers drew upon indigenous social forms to create new associations of worker consultation and activism.

The existence of this third type of "commuter" labor system suggests that African workers may have created far more varied versions of labor systems than is reflected in historical studies. It appears that despite the authoritarian nature of colonial work relations, African workers made more decisions about the conditions under which they will sell their labor power, the intensity of their work, and the organization of productive processes, than scholars normally recognize. While this should not exaggerate the power that workers have in production, especially given the despotic nature of the colonial workplace, it does challenge the idea that colonialists had hegemony in the labor process. In this respect this study emphasizes the contentious nature of colonial power relations at production sites even as African workers are subjected to authoritarian forms of managerial supervision.

## ALL THE "MEN" WERE WHITE
## AND ALL THE AFRICANS WERE "BOYS": RACE, CLASS,
## AND GENDER IN THE COLONIAL WORKPLACE

While in many respects this book is a social history of labor, I have exerted considerable effort to push the study deeply into the workplace.[27] To this end it carefully details the social context of work in the coal pit in which structures of power, Burawoy's "politics of production," influence the men's maintenance of employment, regulation of effort, and the possibilites for remuneration.[28] But the identities of the men who were "workers" were far more complex than a sterile category called "labor." They were husbands and aspirant husbands, fathers and sons, prominent members of rural and later urban communities, subordinates and "big" men. Thus, while the focus of this study is the workplace—the colliery—it assumes connections between a man's role at work and the role that these men played in their communities. In Enugu the miners played a prominent role as "modernizers" in their communities. The community expected that as "big men" the miners would dispense patronage, support community improvement, as well as fulfill more "traditional" norms of male prestige—having many wives, acquiring prestigious titles, and dispensing gifts. Thus the men's desire to fulfill these roles will be a constant factor acknowledged as an influence on their workplace behavior. These community-based expectations influenced many of the factors that impacted upon their work performance: their tolerance of difficult underground conditions, the frequency with which they withdrew their labor, and the forms of self-respect and humiliation which they attached to specific forms and conditions of work. In this respect the study differs from the type of overly materialist/economistic analysis, often characteristic of a particular form of Marxist analysis, which flattens and distorts labor, making these men into one-dimensional characters. This type of analysis fails to factor in those subjectivities that led working men to acquiesce to or challenge colonial work conditions. My own realizations of the fuller range of concerns held by African workers were emphasized repeatedly in my interviews with workers collected in research in Southeastern Nigeria. This is especially the case with the "pit men," the coal miners, who, labor historians have argued, tended to develop an artisan consciousness and were usually the vanguard of most confrontations with capital. The pride with which informants noted the successes of children educated by colliery wages, the number of wives they had, or the levels they'd attained in elite male associations all forced me to insert considerations of masculinity into my analysis of the causes of working class agitation. Thus I became attuned to these men's self-construction as influential community leaders and self-styled "progressives" who acted as protectors of their communities' democratic traditions. This importance of rural validation helped me to interpret managerial complaints about work performance and frequent absences as exasperated admissions of the failure of capitalist labor discipline on men intent to remain socially and politically active in village communities.

We conceptualize masculinity as both a set of cultural attributes and as a social status demonstrated in specific social contexts in which public affirmation is a central element.[29] The book's specific tasks around masculinity are, in the beginning chapters, to identify how gendered expressions of political power position some prominent local men to control the labor power of others and to deliver this, through forced labor, to colonial authorities. The second is to define how mine labor both reinforced and/or undermined older symbols of masculinity as well as created new symbols or expressions of masculine identity and power.

In Igboland, the process of "becoming a man" required a more public process than "becoming a woman."[30] While girls become women under the mother's tutelage, boys become men through a public competitive process in which they are tested by their peers and senior men. Manhood is "achieved" through various contests in which the boy/man proves himself. Coal mining incorporated many of these tests for manhood—a willingness to confront danger, the ability to lead others in a risky venture, the possession of an unusual skill that gave rewards. The book argues that a historically dynamic masculinity is an important component of subjective identity that related to the exercise of worker agency in the workplace, forms of collectivity through which the men identified and mobilized around their interests, and the roles that these men played within both their rural villages and the "native" areas of the colonial city of Enugu. Local rural communities had established processes through which this transformation occurred, as will be treated in the first chapter, but it was not a static process.

Although African labor history's investigations of industrial racism focus on southern Africa, racial inequalities were an endemic aspect of the colonial workplace.[31] The relations between working men are marked by a hierarchy of racialized power which pulls race, class, and gender into a synthesis whose character impacts upon the consciousness of African workers.[32] It is not productive to privilege one factor over the others but to recognize the intersectionality of these three aspects of identity. Nonetheless, analysis requires a fragmentation of this intersectionality although such distinctions seldom exist in lived experiences. Thus the book is about race and how an awareness of its existence becomes an important component of African workers' consciousness. My contention is that colonial racial superiority is not just expressed in the epithets or violent behavior of white bosses towards black workers but also in those split-second decisions they made. For example, testimony suggests that a series of racial assumptions lay behind the split-second decisions made by police commanders when they were confronted with militant miners in Iva Valley, November 1949. West African labor history has recently taken on the challenge of this intersectionality and has found a rich trove of insights into the factors leading African male workers to dig in their heels over conditions of work and of pay.[33]

However, the challenge to historical reconstruction is formidable: how to identify resources that allow an examination of the various ways in which "what it meant to be a man" changed over time. I have had to cobble together a tentative reconstruction of these changes by using oral testimony, fleeting observations of missionaries and military officials, and anecdotal references in published anthropological studies. These permit a hypothesis: in the opening decades of the industry conceptions of masculinity were especially influenced by the emergence of sharp status and power differentials among men rooted in the commercialization of the local economy during the several hundred years' participation in the slave trade. This established masculine norms—norms that reflected the ascent of a particular class, the wealthy merchant capitalist. The tension between these relatively new norms and the old will be explored in Chapter 1. The ascent of these wealthy men affected power relationships amongst groups of men—"native" and imperial, socially mature and immature—and between men and women. This is because these "Big Men" represented a "culturally exalted form of masculinity," which as a hegemonic model may only correspond to the actual experience of a small number of men.[34] Nonetheless, these men became a powerful model for male aspirations. Public demonstrations of masculinity—in polygynous marriage, in the membership in prestigious male associations, and in the workplace—became a central part of the experience of colliery men.

While it is useful to understand gender both as a "constitutive element of social relationships based on perceived differences between the sexes" and as a "primary way of signifying relationships of power,"[35] the hierarchies of power in colonial society require that we recognize "competing masculinities," which in colonial society reflect general racial hierarchies.[36] In Enugu's mines European bosses expressed a "hegemonic masculinity" which incorporated their position of power as enforced in the power relations within production. Constitutive elements of their power included knowledge of the organization of mining practices, the fact that they seldom performed hard manual work themselves, that they could be verbally and physically abusive to "native" workers, and that they used titles such as "boss" to enforce social space between them and the workers. The state endorsed their discretionary use of violence which constituted a culture of authoritarianism promoted to enforce industrial discipline. This brings in another dimension of the book's argument. I maintain that the workplace is far more than a site of production of use values. It is also a critical venue for the introduction, reproduction, and contestation of racialized colonial power relations. It is here that African "men" are transformed into the "native" through the racial organization of inequality as reinforced by brute force, and the white "boss" is established with the collaboration of the state. All African workers were subjected to brutal beatings and racial epithets which further denigrated their position as men. The humiliation of this process can still be heard in the impassioned recollections of informants who recount the demeaning treatment by white bosses. This pushed me to pay attention to race as it was constructed and performed in the workplace.[37] A brutally emasculating discourse demeaned the men and distinguished the white boss from the native laborer. This discourse used gendered terms to express subordination, which "is frequently associated with childlike immaturity."[38] All African job categories used the appellation "boy," denigrating all men to a permanent adolescence; "pick boys" were hewers, "tub boys" pushed tubs underground, etc. Even African supervisory staff were locked into these subordinate categories in a contradictory status of "boss boys."

This was the formative experience that made race real to Nigerian miners and established the meanings of "subject" and "ruler." In fact, the first body of legislation governing African labor in the colonies was a set of "masters and servants" acts. But there were a number of factors that challenged the efficacy of this emasculating lesson in colonial socialization. One came from the village and "native" township while the other came, ironically, from the same racist workplace. This important socialization "lesson" to colonial racial hierarchies proved easier to enforce in the workplace than in the general society. This was especially the case for the men who trekked to work daily from adjacent villages where white men seldom visited. Their wages purchased the symbols of modernity—bicycles, radios, and zinc roofs.

The occupational culture of coal mining, with its dangerous work conditions and exhaustive physical requirements, encouraged a solidarity among Igbo miners that reinforced Igbo norms of masculinity and enhanced their individual autonomy and power. This contradiction between the denigration of African men in the workplace and the affirmation of masculinity arising from the requisite physical strength, danger, and skill inherent in the work, laid a foundation for a masculine identity which was socially reinforced in the village and "native" areas of Enugu.

## THE STRUCTURE OF THE STUDY

Conceptually the book is divided into two sections. Chapters 1–4 are a social history of the source communities and discuss the formation of the labor force and its early confrontations with the state and the industry. Chapters 5–7 are a more orthodox labor study with discussions of the intricacies of disputes and the bureaucratic contexts in which post-war labor struggles were framed. This focus gives the second cluster of chapters a texture that is more specialized and challenging to non-specialists. A series of strikes which are broadly clustered in three key phases provide a central narrative of the text: (1) 1914–1920, the establishment of the industry; (2) 1920–1940, its consolidation; (3) 1940–1949, post-war period, its divestment, and decolonization.

The first two chapters of the book create the setting for the opening of the mines in 1915. Chapter 1 introduces the people of Udi district, an area in southeastern Nigeria where the mines are located, and explains the intersection of ecology, economy, and power with Igbo notions of masculinity. Its central task is to explain two apparently contradictory phenomena: (1) the historical processes that made the area a "labor reserve" with the consequent ease of recruitment of labor and (2) the ability of this labor to achieve a significant degree of control over the labor process, the supply of labor and to shape the culture of work itself. The chapter locates the workers' militance in rural gender and generational conflicts in which young and poor men struggled to establish households and to acquire the masculine symbols of prestige and status. It argues that the region's centuries'-long involvement in the slave trade fostered a class of merchant capitalists, prominent men called *Ogaranyan*, who created an "elite" masculinity that was represented in their polygynous families and membership in elite male associations, called title societies. As an elite model of masculinity, it was attainable by only a few men, but other men aspired to achieve indigenous norms of self-respect, personal achievement, and self-improvement.

The second chapter, covering the period of the conquest 1909–1914, focuses on the construction of the colonial state under the then current ideology of "indirect rule." It weaves together several threads, including the collective ideology of such state officials as Frederick Lugard, which shapes the models of social reconstruction that the state introduced with the conquest and the new structures of local political order that strengthened the power of wealthy men under the rubric of "customary law."[39] It situates the first recruitment efforts in the context of the violent construction of the colonial state which incorporated a group of wealthy former slave traders, the *Ogaranyan*, into local government. The imprint of their state-endorsed coercion gave the first stages of labor mobilization a military caste and elicited forms of resistance that swept through whole communities. Thus, as the Great War began, the Udi area erupted into a spate of convulsive uprisings that both interrupted the opening of the mine, and, in defeat, forced scores of men to the colliery.

In Chapter 3, which covers the Great War, the book goes into the coal pit to describe how British ideas about Igbo "otherness" evolved into racialized systems of "power in production." It argues that this colonial workplace reflected the principles of "indirect rule" through which rural life was reconstructed.[40] The chapter features an intricate discussion of the actual system of coal mining which set the material context in which underground workers developed a group consciousness. This chapter captures some of the fearsome and strenuous nature of this labor process which was such a determinative factor in the shaping of the workers' identity and in fostering forms of association that make them such a formidable industrial opponent to capital. As British managerial staff recognized, the evolving work culture of the Igbo miners would require adjustments in their organization of production and they complained that workers' resistance to industrial time and discipline was rooted in their "primitiveness." As the men remained involved in their villages they secured their positions as men but their participation in the industry was erratic. Ultimately the industry adjusted as it confronted the industrial implications of Igbo meanings of "manliness."

Colonial conditions are inevitably sites of competing masculinities, perhaps an ideological reflection of the contested nature of British hegemony in the early years of the colony.[41] Thus the "pick boys," "tub boys," and "rail boys" of the pit were influential, upwardly mobile, and prestigious men in their rural communities. They formed workers' organizations called *Nzuko Ifunanya* that became an industrial adaptation of the urban improvement associations, *Nzuko*, formed by the African elite to govern the transition to urban life. In the colliery these were mutual aid associations and negotiating bodies for the miners. In these myriad ways the miners gave their own definition to the category "worker."

The fourth chapter plunges into the chaotic industrial milieu of the post-war decade, when the colliery was racked by industrial disputes—six strikes between January 1919 and late 1921. It explores strikes themselves which were a product of many conflicting processes. They were led by "respectable" artisans and clerical workers, men from more distant and earlier "civilized" areas of Nigeria and the West African empire. Many were West Indians, Sierra Leoneans, as well as Yoruba from western Nigeria, who saw themselves as "civilized" men, and accepted a Victorian notion of manliness. For them wages were an indispensable component of their construction of meaning and status. By this time the city of Enugu had grown to over 10,000 inhabitants, encouraging an urban "manliness" among government clerks that was influenced by their self-perception as "loyal" employees of an imperial power they had supported during the Great War. This perception, of themselves as "subjects" of a civilizing power, fueled their protests which converged with the wave of post-war metropolitan unrest that resonated among the white civil servants in Nigeria. The prosecution of the clerical strikes shaped a culture of protest which introduced manual workers to sophisticated weapons of dissent. Thus colliery *Nzuko* commissioned professional letter writers to draft petitions that articulated their demands, while the less habituated rural-based workers withdrew their labor through desertion. By mid-decade, the sophistication of this protest culture was suggested when the miners coordinated their strike with a period of peak coal demand during the English General Strike of 1926. In 1922–1924, the repercussions of the "free" market in labor reverberated through a system of slavery in the countryside and slaves, locally called *Ohu*, forced to work in the mines, became unwilling to remain subordinate men. Their protest destabilized rural government in one of the adjacent areas and indicated how capitalist labor systems could erode pre-existing structures of labor mobilization and political/social subordination. However, it was not a "structure of power" that revolted but *Ohu* men pushed by coercion into "free laborers" and insistent that their status as "free men" be recognized within the idiom of their community.

The second section of the book, chapters 5–7, covers the period from 1920–1949, and has a more detailed explanatory texture than the previous section. Chapters 5 and 6 cover the period of policy elaboration concerning African labor and society. They have a distinctively different texture in that they detail a "regime" of power/knowledge characteristic of late colonialism. In a period in which colonialism was being challenged both by the colonized and by Britain's war allies, the state tried to demonstrate its legitimacy through the superiority of its knowledge. The state identified the institutions through which Africans could express their interests. Colonial society and workplaces were fraught with problems but the metropolitan state claimed to have the capacity to "delineate and bound the problem area and show that it knew how to set it right."[42] A battery of intellectuals and labor specialists was deployed throughout Britain's colonies to conduct social surveys, to collect statistical data on costs of living, and to delineate "legal" areas of conflict and spaces for legitimate contestation. They ignored African forms of knowledge and were loath to develop a meaningful understanding of the complexities of African life and the nuances of labor mobilization. They insisted that only British institutions of worker representation and disputes management were "modern" and "useful" and forced mine workers to abandon the *Nzuko* and use trade unions and joint consultative bodies. Moreover, these "experts" introduced a shared discourse through which all interactions between labor and capital were to be expressed. This discourse arose from European models of industrial relations and the welfare state. Thus the struggles of colonial industrial workers were plunged into a context of foreign procedures and institutions which these workers could not understand. In defense, the workers sought out leaders who could decipher the maze of legal instruments and mandatory procedures and employ the new discourse of industrial resolution. The colliery workers found such a man in Isaiah Ojiyi, a secondary school teacher with radical nationalist sympathies, only to have him reviled by the state as a manipulative demagogue.

Chapters 5 and 6 center on two major themes: (1) the changing nature of colonial labor policy forced by worker activism to accept responsibility for the reproduction of the colonial working class and (2) the state's simultaneous attempt to introduce more efficient systems of managerial control to regulate production and exert control over the social lives of miners in the villages and labor camps. The Nigerian state embarked upon a policy of labor force stabilization which pushed management into the workplace in ways that reduced hewers' autonomy, while the workers pushed ever more articulately to enhance and preserve the lives that they themselves had created. Management-sanctioned forms of representation were imposed with limited success in reducing activism because the leadership was seized by the old *Nzuko* leaders who now had more legitimacy through association with state-approved forms of worker representation.

Chapter 7 describes the events leading to the Iva Valley Massacre of November 1949 and locates the causes in the dissonance between African postwar expectations and the labor reforms introduced by a confident, yet arrogantly unaware, Colonial Office. The primary task of the chapter is to expand the customary treatment of the shooting beyond the interpretations of the official report, the Fitzgerald Commission Report. Both the Commission's hearings in December 1949 and the report itself require more penetrating analysis than can be accommodated in this monograph of the miners' entire history. However, I have used both to push the narrative beyond the Commission's analysis, most especially to challenge its scathing critique of trade union leadership at the colliery and in the national union movement. Disturbingly, with few exceptions the "official story" has entered the orthodoxy of the independence narrative.

Interestingly, the charge to the Commission refuted the Colonial Office's bounded concepts of "political" and "industrial" conflict. It was charged to examine the question at hand—the colliery's turbulent history and the immediate causes of the strike. But it was also instructed to rove freely and examine the state of the national trade union movement as well as evaluate the proposals for political reform as put forth by the Nigerian government. Again, the miners' struggle was subsumed under a national critique.

In examining this tragedy I have taken another avenue of investigation which includes both oral and documentary resources. However, continuing security restrictions over the archive deprived me of access to a crucial trove of materials, currently in the Foreign and Commonwealth Office, that are still not declassified despite the expiration of time restrictions. These included the Commissioners' notes, material submitted as evidence, and other memorabilia. Specifically, this encumbered my attempt to verify allegations made in testimony asserting the trade union organizer's role in misleading the miners to strike. However, I was able to use another series of Colonial Office files which detail decisions about the post-shooting disposition of the colliery manager, the police officer in charge, and the trade union leader, Ojiyi. These proved quite valuable. Secondly, I used the testimony published in the Commission proceedings. In many ways they read as "theatre" on whose stage played all the major actors in the industrial and political narrative of the industry and the birth of the independent Nigerian nation. These hearings also reproduced the same antagonisms between imperial officials and African subjects that had brought the industry to the brink in 1949. I found considerable divergences between the characterization of events and individual responsibilities as detailed in the Report and the testimonies of witnesses as in the hearings. A final source was oral evidence collected from eyewitnesses of the shooting. In this respect, my interviews have only scratched the surface. On each research trip I found additional informants who added new material and insights into the event and often reveal new problems and inconsistencies. However, a thorough analysis of these inconsistencies must await further study.

The Iva Valley sit-in strike, like many others during this period, was unwittingly sparked by the social reforms promulgated by the imperial state at home and in the colonies during and after World War II. While introduced to discourage disruptive work actions and to prevent social problems from feeding political radicalism they had the opposite effect.[43] Industrially the reforms reflected the emergence of industrial relations as a "scientific" field in the United Kingdom and its application to the colonies.[44] The joint consultation meetings, trade unions, labor dispute legislation, and compulsory arbitration failed to survive the deep antagonisms of late colonial society. These included the clash between post-war workers frustrated expectations, resentful white bosses resisting the dismantling of the colonial labor process and the shifting political landscape. Metropolitan colonial architects were also insufficiently aware of local industrial conditions, and the "men on the spot" who viewed all labor reforms with suspicion. Moreover, officials' persistent underestimation of the consciousness, tenacity, and sophistication of African workers led them to see most workers as naïve dupes easily manipulated by demagogic labor leaders more interested in politics than in industrial improvements. They were quite unprepared when the miners organized their own strike without the union leadership.

Additionally, both the colliery management and state officials resented the state's reform efforts which they saw as unwarranted concessions to an irresponsible nationalist and trade union movement.[45] The state's decision to use violence in November 1949 represented local political officials' opposition to the application of disputes management principles in the colonies and their emphasis on the political implications of this industrial action. In many respects this decision was an invalidation of a conventional fiction—that there was a distinct difference between an economic and a political dispute in the colonies.

The labor reforms created sharp tensions in the industry between labor and management. Similarly, state legislation enforcing bureaucratic systems of disputes management entangled the union leaders in consultations that undermined their standing with their workers. This encouraged the miners, the most militant sector of the workforce, to break away from the trade union and act to secure their fate. It was left to a single, nervous policeman—who approved the barrage of bullets that martyred the workers—to ignite this combustible mixture.

## SOURCES

The collection of evidence for this study was both challenging and rewarding. The destruction of scores of personal papers during the Nigerian Civil War forced me to collect fragments of material from a wide range of sources. This was partially compensated by the generosity of David Smock, P.E.H. Hair, and Agwu Akpala, who shared their research notes and documents which were conducted before the war. However, many record groups were permanently lost. For the opening years—the early twentieth century—both written and oral sources proved problematic. Although the study begins in the not too distant past—the early twentieth century—there is little written documentation of the early years. Few Europeans and literate Africans entered the area before the relatively late conquest, in 1909–1912. Moreover, the few available documentary sources—produced by colonial missionaries, state officials, and military commanders—filtered the complex and evolving reality of Igbo society through the static racialized vision of a conqueror as articulated in a discourse of the "civilizing mission." Thus these documents give only a dim glimpse of the concerns of this part of the study: indigenous labor systems and their transformation by the conquest, rural social relations of production, and men's status and generational conflicts.

The earliest missionary records from the Enugu area were a 1913–1914 series of Church Missionary Society minutes of exploratory trips by missionaries to consider the opening of mission stations and the mines and several diaries of technicians working on railway construction or on the opening of the mines. Both spoke only obliquely about the workers. There was some anecdotal material from the small group of westernized, literate Africans clustered around certain nodes of European contact—Lagos in the west and Calabar and Port Harcourt in the southeast. This evidentiary difficulty, which can only partially be compensated for through oral history, was an unavoidable difficulty in the first two chapters of the book. In some cases I have had to extrapolate from the accounts of travelers, missionaries, and political officials from 1914 to outline some possible scenarios of the periods before the conquest.

Oral sources have proven somewhat more useful in capturing some of the important transformations that occurred after the conquest. At the time of my first field work in Nigeria, in 1975, informants on the inaugural years of the industry were not difficult to locate. For most of the period of the study the industry recruited its manual workers from within a fifteen-mile radius and artisans and clerks from either two core areas in central (the town of Owerri) or riverian (Onitsha on the Niger River) Igboland. The pool of local informants was large and qualitatively diverse since few local men managed to become socially mature males or prominent without episodes of colliery work—whether to raise bride wealth to take a wife, to earn extra cash to bury a parent, sibling, or spouse, or to pay membership fees in prestigious male organizations. Virtually all the men in the adjacent villages wove waged colliery work into their individual economic strategies. Mining was such a central part of the economy of this area that it became a defining element in the regional identity of its inhabitants. It is with considerable pride that retired workers speak of their role in an industry with such illustrious credentials in Nigerian political history. It is still possible to visit adjacent villages and easily identify articulate men, many of whom were mentioned in government records, who are anxious to give their accounts of the labor history.

However, enthusiastic informants were often unable to remember important material from the more remote period. For example, I was especially interested in the forms of workers' organizations that predated trade unions, the *Nzuko Ifunanya*, and through which workers shaped and articulated grievances, organized work actions, and negotiated with management. This was an important concern because it gave important insights into indigenous work cultures and their adaptability to the industrial setting. Moreover, it indicated that these men were not just peasants "temporarily" engaged in wage labor (i.e., a semi-proletarianized peasantry) and unable or uninterested in creating viable organizations to structure grievances and protests. Most informants' recollections of early organizations elided with their proud memories of modern trade unions. Despite probing questions they insisted that they only had unions. This may have reflected their assessment that unions were "modern" organizations and their concern to present themselves to me, a foreigner, in the most progressive light.

A second limitation of oral sources is that they were still laced with the deep conflicts among various groups of workers, between "local" and "foreign" African workers, and between loyal union members and dissenters. Some of these divisions come from the "politics of production" and reflect conflicts arising from inscribed inequalities that were structured by the labor process. Still others reflect the complex transitions of labor systems as for example, the tensions between slave, *Ohu* men, and freeborn, *Amadi*, conscripted in the first labor force. The issue of slave descent is still of considerable importance today in the Enugu area and tensions arise over the selection of chiefs, admission into male societies, and marriage. As in most communities where affiliation is structured along lineage and kinship lines, it is generally known which families were descended from slaves and which from freeborn. Moreover, in the 1920s *Ohu* turned their exclusion into a basis for solidarity and secured state support to establish several autonomous villages and to change their name to *Awbia*. Thus today, most if not all people in certain villages or in designated wards of freeborn villages are known as *Awbia*.[46] These contemporary antagonisms are expressed in interviews. The accounts of freeborn reflect persistent prejudices towards descendents of slaves and interviews with slave descendants, which required special sensitivities, assumed a defensive posture.[47] Nonetheless, I was able to use these perspectives to capture the resilience of pre-colonial status divisions that suggest the depth of the impact of the Atlantic slave trade.

Archival holdings reflect a wealth of documentary material for the period, mostly from the post-1935 period, which arise from the industry's status as a parastal and the involvement of various multiple layers of state bureaucrats in its concerns. The official records of the colliery itself as well as the reports of the provincial residents, district officers, and urban authorities are in the Nigerian Archives, Enugu. Quite by luck I was able to locate a stack of files containing a series of monthly manager's reports in the Nigerian Ministry of Labor archives in Yaba, Lagos. At the time of my visit, these records were not catalogued but stacked on industrial shelves in a large abandoned warehouse. These began in the early 1930s and detailed weekly output, surveys of labor, accident rates, etc. I also found amongst the Colonial Records Project of Rhodes House, Oxford University, diaries of district officers and less prominent colonial officials as well as such notables as Major Granville St. George Orde Brown, the Colonial Office's first labor advisor, and Arthur Creech Jones, Labour Party leader. The British Trades Union Congress archives at the Modern Records Project at Warwick University, Coventry, gave important insight into the policies of the Congress towards the African labor movement and documented the experiences of the bevy of labor advisors who worked through the colonial service in fostering "responsible" trade unions.

Material on the colliery was found in a number of record groups in the Public Records Office, Kew Gardens. In addition to the official files of the Nigerian government, the series C.O. 508, there were wartime records of the Colonial Labor Advisory Committee and other coordinating bodies, such as the Social Services division within the Colonial Office. These were all useful as they indicated the official anxiety that surrounded nearly every incident of worker protest. This, in turn, encouraged me to determine the workers' understanding of this imperial concern. Both helped me to understand that this industry, although small in comparison with the mining complex in central and southern Africa, was quite pivotal both in respect to its role as the region's strategic fuel resource as well as a laboratory for British social policies affiliated with the welfare state and industrial paternalism. This point became especially salient in the correspondence after the Japanese victories in South Asia during World War II.

In creating this story I was especially concerned to find images that would often fill in voids in the verbal evidence. One of my most exciting finds came from the offices of the Crown Agents, the government's purchasing agent for goods and services for the entire Empire. This was a beautiful album of photographs from 1914–1915 taken during the construction of the Eastern Branch of the Nigerian Railway and the Udi Coal Fields. It is a remarkable collection of images that contain invaluable historical evidence of the massive organization of labor required for the construction of the railway. It included photos of chiefs, thousands of workers manually removing tons of earth, and several excellent photos of the Udi coal mine, the first colliery mine, as well as many groups of workers.[48] These images helped to confirm my assessment of ways work intersected with masculinity and the obstacles to managerial control over the labor process.

Finally, this study has benefited from the industrial ethos of Enugu which is surprisingly strong even though the industry is near dormant. A visitor today is struck by the way that the city proudly associates its identity with coal even though the industry has long since been eclipsed by the Nigerian petroleum boom. Throughout the city the words "Coal City" appear in the labeling of businesses, on banners, and, in the case of one area, "Coal Town," as a designation of a city area.

The city's industrial identity is most dramatically signified in two public statues. One, at the entrance of the airport, is an imposing statue of a proud, lone miner, with his pit helmet and his pick. The other, at the center of a major traffic circle, is a dramatic contemporary interpretation of the shooting. It is an excellent example of historical reinterpretation replete with heroic miners rescuing fallen comrades and standing firmly against guns. The accuracy of the statue as a depiction of what actually happened is not as important as the ways that Enugu residents incorporate the past in their current position within the modern Nigerian state. Having endured years of military rule, the people of Enugu proudly reflect upon the sacrifices that their brothers, sons, and fathers made for the birth of the Nigerian nation as if to reclaim their position with the contemporary state. As they recount the memory of their past industrial battles older men speak with pride about the ways that their labor supported the regional economy and the ways that mine work helped to develop their communities. It is the intent of this study to use these memories to inscribe these men in the industrial history of Africa.

## NOTES

1. For a discussion of the wave of post-war general strikes see Timothy Oberst, "Cost of Living and Strikes in British Africa, c. 1939–1948: Imperial Policy and the Impact of the Second World War" (Ph.D. dissertation, Columbia University, 1991).

2. See Agwu Akpala, "Background to the Enugu Colliery Shooting Incident in 1949," *Journal of the Historical Society of Nigeria* 3, 2 (1965): 335–64; and S.O. Jaja, "The Enugu Colliery Massacre in Retrospect: An Episode in British Administration of Nigeria," *Journal of the Historical Society of Nigeria* 2, 3–4 (1983): 86–106.

3. Agwu Akpala, *Managing Industrial Relations in Nigeria* (Case Study of Nigerian Coal Industry), Lagos, 1984; and David Smock, *Conflict and Control in an African Trade Union* (Stanford, 1969).

4. There are mines in South Africa (Natal) and Zimbabwe but there is only one monograph on these industries. Ian Phimister's *Wangi Kolia: Coal, Capital and Labour in Colonial Zimbabwe 1894–1954* (Harare, 1994).

5. Frederick Cooper, "Work, Class, and Empire: An African Historian's Retrospective on E.P. Thompson," *Social History* 20, 2 (1995): 239.

6. Royden Harrison, ed., *The Independent Collier: The Coal Miner as Archetypal Proletarian Reconsidered* (Sussex, 1978).

7. David Frank, "The Country of Coal," *Labour/Le Travail* 21 (Spring 1988): 234.

8. One particularly useful collection is a series of essays honoring the one hundredth anniversary of the United Mine Workers of America: John H.M. Laslett's *The United Mine Workers of America: A Model of Industrial Solidarity?* (University Park, PA 1996).

9. Royden Harrison, ed., *Independent Collier*.

10. This was a system called the Derbyshire system used in the Northern coalfields. While in many respects it represented the "deskilling" of the collier, Enugu miners nonetheless saw their job of cutting coal to be of crucial importance.

11. Ibid. 54–74.

12. One provocative study that pushes for these continuities is the discussion of gender/bending, race, and empire in the British coal industry of Anne McClintock's *Imperial Leather: Race, Gender, and Sexuality in the Colonial Contest*, (London, 1995).

13. See Mrinalini Sinha, *Colonial Masculinity: the Manly Englishman and the Effeminate Bengali in the Late 19th century* (Manchester, 1995).

14. For evidence of collaborations see Chapter 4.

15. The best review of the genesis of the field is Bill Freund's "The Historiography of African Labour" in *The African Worker* (London, 1988).

16. For a review of the literature in French and British Africa see Frederick Cooper's excellent study, *Decolonization and African Society: The Labor Question in French and British Africa* (Cambridge, 1996).

17. See Charles Van Onselen, *Chibaro: African Mine Labour in Southern Rhodesia*, (London, 1976); Charles Perrings, *Black Mineworkers in Central Africa* (London, 1979); Jane Parpart, *Capital and Labor on the African Copperbelt* (Philadelphia, 1983); Ruth First, *Black Gold: The Mozambican Miner, Proletarian and Peasant* (New York, 1983).

18. For an early review of the historiography of South Africa see Belinda Bozolli and Peter Delius, "History from South Africa," *Radical History Review*, 46/47 (Winter 1990).

19. See Robin Cohen's "Resistance and Hidden forms of Consciousness among African Workers," *Review of African Political Economy*, 19 (1980): 8–22.

20. Keletso Atkins, *The Moon Is Dead! Give Us Our Money!: The Cultural Origins of an African Work Ethic, Natal, South Africa, 1843–1900* (Portsmouth, 1993). Atkins was influenced by the work of E.P. Thompson in her article on the clashes between Zulu and European men over the temporal reckonings each was using to determine the wage period. These helped me to identify the role played by Igbo time systems in challenging the capitalist work week. See Keletso Atkins, "'Kaffir Time': Preindustrial Temporal Concepts and Labour Discipline in Nineteenth Century Colonial Natal." *Journal of African History* 29 (1988): 229–44.

21. Frederick Cooper, "From Free Labor to Family Allowances: Labor and African Society in Colonial Discourse," *American Ethnologist* 16, 4 (1989): 753.

22. One particularly useful contribution was Anne McClintock's *Imperial Leather*.

23. The discussion of the political role of African labor arose within the developmental paradigm which was a preoccupation of social science studies in the early 1960s. The classical articulation of the position that trade unions were of little political importance as a force of change in Africa is Elliot Berg and Jeffrey Butler, "Trade Unions," in James Coleman and Carl Rosberg, eds., *Political Parties and National Integration in Tropical Africa*, (Berkeley, 1964). Bill Freund points out that the year that this article was published, degrading the unions as instruments of nationalist transformation, Nigerian workers launched a successful general strike. Bill Freund, *The African Worker*.

24. There has been a veritable explosion of literature on masculinity. One particularly useful article is John Tosh's "What Should Historians Do With Masculinity?" *History Workshop Journal* 38 (1994): 185–202; see also R.W. Connell, *Masculinities* (Berkeley, 1995); David Gilmore, *Manhood in the Making: Cultural Concepts of Masculinity* (New Haven 1990); Harry Stecopoulos and Michael Uebel, eds. *Race and the Subject of Masculinities* (Durham, 1997).

25. For a discussion of this issue among British and French colonialists see Fred Cooper's *Decolonization and African Society*.

26. Dunbar Moodie and Vivienne Ndatshe. *Going for Gold: Men, Mines and Migration* (Los Angeles, 1994), 21.

27. I was influenced both by the work of Michael Burawoy and a series of essays in Andrew Zimbalist's *Case Studies on the Labor Process* (New York, 1979). See particularly Keith Dix, "Work Relations in the Coal Industry: The Handloading Ear, 1880–1930" and Michael Yarrow, "The Labor Process in Coal mining: Struggle for Control"; Michael Burawoy, *The Politics of Production: Factory Regimes Under Capitalism and Socialism* (London, 1985).

28. Michael Burawoy has critiqued much of labor studies for failing to really delve into the workplace and the labor process. He argues that only when scholars understand the power relationships created by the ways that production is organized can we understand the tensions among groups of workers and between workers and their erstwhile supervisors. See Burawoy, *The Politics of Production*.

29. John Tosh, 184.

30. One of the best recent studies of gender among Igbos is Ifi Amadiume's *Male Daughters, Female Husbands* (London 1987). Particularly see Chapter 5, "The Ideology of Gender."

31. This literature constitutes most of the studies on Southern African labor. For a now outdated review of South African labor history see Jon Lewis, "South African Labor History: A Historiographical Assessment" in Bozzoli and Delius eds., "History in South Africa," a Special issue of *Radical History Review*: 213–35.

32. For a collection on the intersection of race and class see Peter Alexander and Rick Halpern, *Racializing Class, Classifying Race: Labour and Difference in Britain, the USA and Africa* (New York, 2000).

33. Amongst one of the most interesting studies is Lisa Lindsay's work, which examines the Nigerian General Strike of 1945 in light of feminist theories of masculinity. See "Domesticity and Difference: Male Breadwinners, Working Women and Colonial Citizenship in the 1945 Nigerian General Strike," *American Historical Review* 104, 3 (June 1999): 783–812. The literature on masculinity and work is more developed in South African labor/history studies. See Dunbar Moodie and Vivienne Ndatshe's *Going for Gold* and Patrick Harries *Work, Culture, and Identity: Migrant Laborers in Mozambique and South Africa, 1860–1910* (Portsmouth, NH, 1994).

34. Andrea Cornwall and Nancy Lindsfarne, "Dislocating Masculinity: Gender, Power, and Anthropology," in Andrea Cornwall and Nancy Lindsfarne, eds., *Dislocating Masculinity: Comparative Ethnographies* (London, 1994), 19.

35. Joan Scott, "Gender: A Useful Category of Historical Analysis," in *Gender and the Politics of History* (New York 1988), 42.

36. Cornwall and Lindsfarne, *Dislocating Masculinity*, 18.

37. Thomas Noisike, Agbaja, Udi Division, Enugu, 7 June 1975.

38. Cornwall and Lindsfarne, *Dislocating Masculinity*, 18.

39. For a pioneering study of the "invention" of customary law see Martin Channock, *Law, Custom and Social Order: The Colonial Experience in Malawi and Zambia* (Cambridge, 1985).

40. The major study of indirect rule in southeastern Nigeria is A.E. Afigbo's *The Warrant Chiefs: Indirect Rule in Southeastern Nigeria, 1891–1929* (London, 1972).

41. Sinha, *Colonial Masculinity*, 7–9 and Conclusion; Cornwall and Lindisfarne, *Dislocating Masculinity*. For a provocative discussion of women in coal mining as a threat to British masculinity and dominance of the imperial hierarchy, see Anne McClintock, *Imperial Leather*, 112–118.

42. Cooper, *Decolonization and African Society*, 173.

43. The best description of the entire process is Frederick Cooper's *Decolonization and African Society*. In fact, this is perhaps the most superb book for non-Africanists to read on the major themes in labor historiography, the central contradictions in colonial labor policy, and the impact of African activism on policy formation.

44. Richard Hyman, *Industrial Relations: A Marxist Introduction* (London, 1975).

45. They were especially concerned with the Zikist movement, a fringe group of heterogeneous ideologists composed of young men disenchanted with the political wrangling of the more mainstream nationalist politicians. The only monograph on their history is Ehiedu E.G. Iweriebor, *Radical Politics in Nigeria, 1945–1950: The Significance of the Zikist Movement* (Zaria, 1996).

46. The word *Awbia*, means "stranger" in the village-groups that compose the Nkanu clan area. As a result of a civil war in 1922/23 between the slaves (*Ohu*) and the freeborn (*Amadi*), the slaves successfully got the colonial government to declare the term *ohu* to be illegal and to henceforth use the word *Awbia* to refer to them. Although this was clearly an attempt to

erase the stigma attached to the slave term it resulted in the slave connotation being attached to the new word—*Awbia*. This stigma continues today.

47. In one instance, when I was unsure how to broach the subject of slavery, I opened the interview by stating that I was, myself, a descendant of slaves. This relaxed the discussion and the group leader, Ephraim Ene, then stated that they were an *Awbia*, ex-slave, community. Interview with Ephraim Ene, Nnamani Onovo, Nwolie Nnamuchi, and Nnaaji Ogbodo Akegbe Ukwu, Enugu, 20 August 1986.

48. One such photograph was of a Chief of Uzuakoli, a prominent village in the Cross Rivers area of Igboland, and the men he supplied to the railway. The village was ecstatic when I gave them this picture while on a tour in the summer of 2000. They have since reproduced it and placed it in a prominent place in their local government house.

*PART I*

# THE CONTESTED BIRTH OF THE COLONIAL LABOR PROCESS: LABOR, COAL, AND THE STATE

# 1

# Udi District on the Eve of Conquest: Slavery, Power, and Resistance, circa 1909

> The development of the coal mines changed the villages in Udi division very much. It provided more jobs. It stopped much thieving and selling of people into slavery. Minimized hunger.
> —Thomas Noisike, former miner, Ezeama Owa, Udi[1]

This comment, by a former miner, expressed in contemporary terms the startling impact of the Atlantic slave trade on the area of southeastern Nigeria where the coal mines would open in 1914. The region had a history of intense involvement in the trans-Atlantic slave trade in which, as part of the Biafran hinterland, it contributed to the estimated 1.5 million Igbo slaves from the seventeenth through mid-nineteenth century. Recent statistical studies suggest that these exports reached a peak in the 1780s with a brief resurgence between 1820–1840 when palm oil and kernels replaced slaves as the region's contribution to the world market.[2] The palm trade continued the area's involvement in the world economy and further strengthened tendencies towards social stratification and accumulation which began during the slave trade period.

This long period of integration into a global mercantile economy shaped relations of production, valorized the accumulation of wealth in prestige goods and forms of currency, and strengthened the political influence of wealthy men. It also encouraged internal slavery and other forms of subordination which influenced masculine ideals and aspirations. This stratification affected the recruitment of Udi men into the coal industry, their ideas of just treatment and remuneration, and forms of leadership and self-organization that helped them to articulate and secure their interests in production.

Masculine status systems and the environmental constraints on their achievement made Udi into a surplus labor area and an auspicious site for the recruitment of labor for the mines. But the popularity of coal mining jobs and the area's role as a regional labor reserve did not make the men victims of management or the state control. It was virtually impossible to mold these men into a compliant and disciplined workforce. The extraordinary degree of control which the men had over the pace, intensity, and duration of mine work was the central paradox of the industry's labor history despite the mines' location in a labor surplus area. The causes of this paradox are examined below.

The chapter begins with the impact of the slave trade on the ecology and demography of the area, the pre-industrial systems of labor mobilization, and the emergence of incipient political hierarchies. The argument is organized around two points: (1) the constraints that the local environment placed on farming systems and the consequent ability of young men to raise the requisite wealth to marry and establish an independent household; (2) the ability of socially mature—married—men to gain access to the institutional hierarchies of prestige and status that created political power. Because of the diversity of land, labor, and settlement systems in Igboland, the discussion focuses on the villages adjacent to the coal mines in the Agbaja and the Nkanu regions of Udi.

Finally, the chapter establishes individual and collective perspectives on work and identifies a system of values attached to various forms of labor and their treatment that the men bring with them into the mine workplace. As Cooper has noted, colonial capitalism was not a hegemonic force ruthlessly grinding living workers into "abstract labor power."[3] Rather, as Atkins found in her study of nineteenth-century Zulu workers in South Africa, Africans in the workplace struggled to express their own definitions of useful work and just treatment. Colonial epithets to the contrary, workers found dignity through labor and "attached status, prestige, and self-respect to jobs and tasks assigned and performed."[4] By exploring pre-industrial labor systems and the values these workers attached to work, behavior, and initiatives, we can identify an "African work ethic." These men came from a pre-industrial work culture, in which status hierarchies, a variety of labor systems, gendered tasks, and expectations of compensation, shaped definitions of "work," time, responsibility, and self-respect. These Nigerian miners drew on this work culture to make their imprint on the organization and rhythms of colliery work. In so doing, they prevented capital from creating the "ideal worker."

The analysis of these labor systems is burdened by the problem of reconstructing the past with few written and oral sources. The area was not conquered until 1912 and missionary and traveler accounts only exist after 1914. Most oral sources were unable to give more than anecdotal evidence of labor systems, status structures, and masculine values, a limitation that makes it extremely difficult to historicize pre-industrial factors that influenced the behavior of workers in the early years of the colliery. It is especially challenging to get these sources to "speak" to the concerns of contemporary historical inquiry. These problems with sources have created a lively debate among historians of Igboland on the periodization of origins, the impact of the world market on domestic socioeconomic development, and the nature of political changes stimulated by the area's incorporation into the world market, a process of heightened intensity between 1600 and 1800.[5] Nonetheless it is possible to use fragmentary oral history, archaeological evidence, and the few early-twentieth-century written accounts to outline a tentative series of processes that *may have been* operative during the early years of the industry. These propositions are necessarily contingent upon the current state of historical reconstruction.

Given these restrictions it is difficult to historicize gender relations from fragmentary sources or to account for the extreme variation of customs and "traditions" that were considered "Igbo." However, coastal sources documenting the slave trade, most especially the new quantitative data, and local oral traditions, suggest an increased social stratification associated with the penetration of the world market and the circulation of prestige goods.[6] Many of these processes strengthened the gendered construction of political power and social status. The most extensive of early twentieth-century sources on Igbo society, a series of anthropological studies conducted in the 1930s, suggest a reconstruction of the values and norms of late nineteenth-century Igboland to reflect the mercantilist ethos.[7] Specifically, during the turn of the century, self-esteem, honor, prestige, and influence became important markers of male status giving gender a class-like dimension.[8]

## UDI AND THE ATLANTIC SLAVE TRADE: SOCIAL STRATIFICATION, ECOLOGICAL STRESS, AND ASCENDANT FORMS OF POLITICAL POWER AND MASCULINITIES

The Nigerian Government Colliery was located in Udi District, in the north central region of Igboland, an area in southeastern Nigeria. Virtually all colliery workers were Igbo-speaking men, the largest ethnic group in southeastern Nigeria, who occupy the area between the Niger and Cross Rivers and a narrow strip on the west bank of the Niger River. Today there are some 20 million Igbo-speaking peoples in the 15,800 square miles of their homeland. Some areas of Igboland have the highest population densities for rural Africa, and this appears to have been the case at the turn of the century. In the Udi area, densities of 400 to 1,000 per square mile were quite common.[9]

Igboland is in the Guinea coastal climatic area, a region of heavy rainfall on the West African coast.[10] However, within this broad region there are several micro-ecological zones with varying soil types, rainfall, and vegetation. The social impact of this diversity was manifest culturally and economically in strong regional identities. Although the Igbo shared dialects and other cultural traits before the conquest, they never perceived of themselves as a distinct "people" and operated within a strongly defined regionalism of uncertain origin.

Traditions of Igbo origin are inconclusive, but current research suggests that they originated in the savanna region of West Africa near the confluence of the Niger-Benue River.[11] During some still disputed period, they dispersed to the Awka-Orlu plateau and then to Owerri and the southeast. During the early Christian era one group, the Western Igbo, spilled over the Niger to inhabit the western shore of that river. Although the precise dates of these migrations are vague, archaeological excavations near Nsukka in the north found pottery 4,000–5,000 years old.[12] Historians believe that the heartland of Igboland was the triangulated area of Awka, Orlu, and Okigwi.[13]

People lived in village-groups or "towns," a cluster of villages founded by the offspring of a common ancestor, usually male but occasionally female. Individual villages were founded by descendants of this ancestor and their population belonged to related patrilineages. Villages were divided into wards or quarters inhabited by sub-lineages, called *ummuna*. Members of various *ummuna* lived in compounds, sometimes walled, other times simply a cluster of households near a central meeting place. The compounds were called *ezi* or *obi*.[14]

The *ummuna* was the smallest unit of political cohesion.[15] The status hierarchy of the *obi*, quarter, village, and village-group was gerontocratic and gave the oldest village in the village-group, the oldest quarter in the village, the oldest *ummuna* in the quarter, and the oldest man in the *obi*, a special social and spiritual place within the community. Although seniority by age was not necessarily transformed to political power, it did confer respect and prestige that could not always be secured by younger men of wealth.

In each village, growing rights to land were divided among the *ummuna* and subsequently, the extended family in the *obi*. All village land was of two types: farmland, *ala agu*, where people farmed but did not live, and household land, *ala ulo*, the site of the *obi*. Farming in the *obi* was restricted to women's gardens and permanent crops such as the oil palm and other trees.[16] The relative availability of farmland to household land reflected the stage of development of the town, which was driven by the requirements of male rural identity and status.

Land was more than a simple factor of production, and even during colonialism, urbanized men preserved their connections to the earth. It had spiritual significance, defined one's social status, and symbolized the solidarity of the community whether "town," village, or household.[17] It was the home of the ancestors who, while buried in the earth, were still considered present actors in everyday village life. The importance of land for village cohesion was expressed ritually in the prominence of the cult of Ani or Ala, the Earth Goddess. Ani was the custodian of the earth and guardian of human and public morality. Socially disruptive crimes like murder, the theft of yams, and child stealing offended her and the earth.[18] Every village, ward, and *obi* had her shrine which functioned like a town charter and validated a settlement's existence as a legitimate entity. Every myth of origin had the founding father or mother building, the *ihu ala*, a sacred area, in the village.[19]

A person's relationship to the land determined one's status as freeborn or slave. To be considered a freeborn person or *Amadi*, one had to be able to establish genealogical connections to the founding fathers of the village. In areas settled by successive waves of migrants fleeing slave raids, this "credential" often proved difficult to establish. Through an innovative spiritual process, the Ani cult established a common genealogy. People believed that when a person was buried, Ani supervised the transformation of the deceased into ancestors and his/her subsequent reincarnation in a newborn child. After several generational cycles of death and reincarnation, a spiritual genealogy was created through which formerly unrelated patrilineages became a common lineage.[20] This spiritual genealogy was a stabilizing force in both Agbaja and Nkanu villages.

The mines opened in an area called the Udi district, a region inhabited by two communities which the British called the Agbaja and the Nkanu "clans." Regionalism, migration, and village conflicts over land are recurrent themes in the history of the Udi district. These two groups lived in two ecologically distinct regions separated by a ridge, called the Udi escarpment, a "spine" of hills running north to south. The Agbaja lived in the area to the west of the ridge which had thin, sandy, eroded fields that offered no other attraction except as a redoubt. The prominence of migration in the legends of origin supports the hypothesis that the area was settled by successive waves of people fleeing slave raids and overpopulation in the palm belt to the south.[21]

Agbaja included eight village-groups:[22] Akpakwume, Atta, Egede, Abor, Udi, Ngwo, Eke, and Nze.[23] Before the conquest these villages had no permanent association save an occasional military alliance that often proved treacherous and unstable. The high population densities of Agbaja's villages, some reaching 1,000 people per square mile, and severe land shortages further support the thesis that the area was a refuge.

To the east of the escarpment is a fertile plateau, inhabited by the Nkanu "clan," of twelve village-groups: Akpugo, Agbani, Ihuokpara, Amagunze, Akegbe, Ozalla, Ugbawka, Nomeh, Nara, Amurri, Nkerefi, and Mburubu. Many of these village-groups are small but some, such as Akpugo, had 25,500 inhabitants in 1935.[24] Nkanu's demographic composition also appeared related to the various periods of Igboland's role in the world economy. In the nineteenth century Nkanu became the bread basket of the palm-belt villages to its immediate south.[25] Proximity to slave trading routes encouraged the incorporation of slave labor into local production systems as a supplement to the household. Consequently Nkanu farming communities included a number of prosperous farmer-traders and many villages with large populations of slaves. Many villages were highly stratified with "Big Men" who headed large compounds with scores of wives and many slaves. At the colliery both Agbaja and Nkanu were "locals" in contrast to "foreign" Igbo from more distant areas.[26]

The contrast between the ecology of the two communities—Agbaja and Nkanu—was reflected in their economic role in the region. The Agbaja were disparaged for either selling their children into slavery, or for themselves being enslaved. At the turn of the century people of Udi district lived in relatively small-scale communities, usually composed of patrilineal clans, devoted to regionally based agriculture and supplemented by craft production. In the vast majority of villages there were no chiefs and there was no precolonial state that united all of Igboland. Although the precolonial history of Udi is unevenly documented, oral evidence indicates that the supply of slaves and palm products for the world market profoundly shaped local conditions in ways that facilitated the recruitment of unskilled labor, and set the stage for violent conflict during the colonial period.

Migration features prominently in the tales of origin of most village-groups and the association of movement with self-improvement was an important part of Igbo culture.[27] This had significant implications for the labor patterns of the industry. This migration meant that the peoples of the area were in constant contact, and often confrontation, with their neighbors with whom they competed for land.[28] This struggle for resources may explain the strong Igbo ethos of individual and village competition and a persistent personal affiliation based on regionalism, which is projected into the industry as clan identity.

High population densities encouraged the development of a large group of skilled non-agricultural producers, traders, blacksmiths, and religious functionaries. They fostered a culture in which itinerancy became an adaptation to productive and ecological constraints. The migratory patterns of Udi's male farm laborers fit within this more general pattern found elsewhere in Igboland.

The origins of Igboland's involvement in the slave trade are obscure. However, there is some evidence that it preceded the New World sugar revolution of the mid-seventeenth century.[29] In the early seventeenth century a Spanish priest found significant numbers of Ibos among the slave population in Peru. By the eighteenth century, evidence of Igbo involvement is more substantiated. During the peak period of expansion of the Atlantic slave trade, between 1700 and 1800, Lovejoy estimates that 832,000 slaves, more likely one million, were exported from the Bight of Biafra, Igboland's coastal area.[30] Similarly, Manning notes that during the 1780s, most slaves destined to the New World came from this area and Angola.[31] Oral evidence confirms that the export of such a massive volume of slaves had a severe impact upon the political and social stability of Igboland's polities.[32]

The exact contribution of northern Igboland to the general slave population was difficult to determine. But anecdotal evidence and local traditions suggest that it was significant. Old Calabar and Bonny were the main ports of embarkation and both pulled slaves from the Igbo hinterland. In Sierra Leone, Sigmund W. Koelle, a nineteenth-century missionary, found several "Abadsha" (Agbaja) among the recaptured slaves he interviewed.[33] We also have the famous testimony of Ekwuno (Equiano), an eighteenth-century slave who became active in the British abolitionist movement.[34]

The involvement of Igboland in the slave trade is associated with the emergence of the Aro people as a powerful economic force in the mid-seventeenth century.[35] From their capital at Arochukwu, the Aro designed and operated an internal slave marketing system which organized the supply of slaves for the Atlantic slave trade in southeastern Nigeria from 1650 to the mid-nineteenth century and the domestic market thereafter.[36] They were custodians of a powerful oracle, *Chukwu Ibi-*

*nokpabi*, which served a crucial judicial function in disputes between villages. But their sacri-juridical role gave them economic power to organize and control an intricate trading network that spanned southeastern Nigeria.

The Aro were very active in Udi, which was the northern sector of their trading system and an important source area for slaves. It was their network that processed most Igbo slaves for export. Aro colonists operated from several settlements—in Eke, Ntegbe-Nese,[37] and Umuaga in Agbaja, and the Nike and Nara village-groups of Nkanu[38]—and from this vantage point near the commercial nerve center of the regional economy they gathered intelligence on prices, brought in imported goods, and purchased slaves.

All of the prominent merchant farmers, who would later work as labor recruiters for the colliery, were in some way associated with the Aro. At the time, the Aro still retained interest in impoverished Udi as a source of slaves both for use as labor for the domestic market and as sacrifices at funerals. Even as late as 1916, Ede Ani Chikiri, a wealthy merchant in Nara, South Nkanu, was caught supplying slave women to the Aro for sacrifice at funerals of prominent men throughout Igboland and the Delta.[39]

The socioeconomic impact of the trades became generalized throughout Igboland's intricate commercial networks which were rooted in ecologically diverse production systems. Social goods circulated through intricate commercial networks in which periodic markets,[40] usually held on one day of the four-day or eight-day Igbo week, were found in every village-group.[41] These markets framed the Igbo week and created a temporal context for the work rhythms of the coal industry. The market day was an indigenous day of rest that conflicted with the industrial week and "weekend."[42]

The social price of the system of slave supply was increased warfare, draconian legal procedures, social insecurity, and the violation of the restriction against enslaving one's own kinsmen.[43] In the Agbaja village of Umuaga, one elder recalled:

> People could be sold into slavery for certain offenses, ranging from stealing, adultery, inability to pay debts and contravening some sacred laws. But some people who were in great need of money could abduct one secretly, not minding if one was a relation or not, and sell him to slave agents.[44]

The export market growth created merchant capitalists, wealthy men called *Ogaranyan*, who by 1914 were well entrenched in the political economy and exemplified commercialized social markers of male status and prestige. All men were influenced by their consumptive habits which conspicuously incorporated imported goods.[45] They used slaves as both a labor force and as prestige "goods" to indicate socio-political status. This was the context in which village men constructed "masculinity."

The accumulation of wealth in Udi was more pronounced in Nkanu than in land-starved Agbaja. There merchant/farmers augmented their kinship units with large slaveholdings. Access to household and slave labor allowed wealthy men to be-

come successful farmers, or *diji*, growing the numbers of yams necessary to take
the prestigious yam title, *Eze ji*, or Yam King.[46] There were a number of such
wealthy men in the southernmost areas of Nkanu, and, to a lesser extent, in Agbaja. In Nara, an Nkanu village-group to the south, a junior but prosperous ward
of the village-group had become wealthy in people and influence. It was their pa-
triarch, Edeani Chikiri, who had over eighty wives and several hundred slaves. He
successfully convinced the British that he was the "traditional" leader and was appointed a colonial chief.[47] Similarly in Nomeh, a neighboring village-group, one
wealthy but junior patrilineage had seized judicial functions in their town using
their large number of slaves as enforcers, and exploiting commercial connections
with the Aro slave dealers to whom they sold offenders.[48] None of these new leaders nor their lineages would have had social rank under the old system that privileged age. Yet, as the reality of their economic power and consequent numerical
superiority made an impact on village politics, they were consolidating power.

After the conquest three such men became wealthy colonial chiefs by supplying conscripted labor for the railway and government colliery. Some were part of
a spiritual elite, men whose families controlled the performance of certain rituals
that shaped the political process in Igboland. The fact that all were tied into the
slave trade suggests the pervasive nature of the trade, its denigration of public
morality, and the importance of slaving for accumulation in the area. All had large
households of wives, slaves, and other dependents and were powerful in their own
right. The first mine workers in 1915 came from near Onitsha, through Eze Okolie,
an *Ogaranyan*, who was a wealthy *dibia*, or priest, and from Owerri through Chief
J.O. Njemanze.[49] While locally, Chukwuani Nwangwu of Ozalla, whose family
were Ani priests, and Onyeama Onwusi of Eke,[50] a prominent slave trader, supplied the mines and railway with men from their villages. The role of colliery recruitment in enhancing these chief's personal power will be treated in the next
chapter. Their ability to benefit from the colonial economy attests to the resilience
and adaptability of precolonial commercial elites.

In Udi, Nike became infamous as an important supplier of slaves to the Aro.[51]
Located on the northern fringe of Udi near the Igala people, they traded slaves from
the Igala, a non-Igbo group to the north, in exchange for horses.[52] They were allies of the Aro and located at the crossroads of two slave routes from the north.[53]
Similarly in Umuaga, Agbaja founded the largest market, Nkwo Agu, to supply
the slave trade. This market was surrounded in treachery. An elder recalled:

> one could not go to another town's sector of the market without being led by an
> armed elder. Any lapse in this protection might lead to [a] person's enslavement.[54]

A kidnapping by one village would surely evoke retaliatory war by the victim's
kinsmen. The special skills in warfare brought new families to power in the Nkanu
village-group of Agbani where a skilled warrior was elected leader and became
caretaker of the shrines associated with war and hunting.[55] With assistance of mer-
cenaries from the Ada and Ohaffia villages,[56] Nike waged war throughout Udi attacking Agbaja village-groups and selling prisoners to the Aro.[57] Nike retained

some whom they settled in satellite villages to protect from Igala attacks from the north.[58]

Concurrent with the ascent of merchant capitalists was the emergence of a military elite which defended communities against the kidnappings by slavers and war ravages of Aro allies[59]—the Abam, Ohaffia, and Ada Igbo—who cut broad swaths of terror across northern Igboland, attacking Nike, Agbaja, and several towns northwest of Onitsha in the 1890s.[60] In Udi the associated violence heightened the social insecurity of the period. Both Agbaja and Nkanu areas were shaken by this violence.

Communities in the southern parts of Nkanu were confronted with yet another threat. The Ezza, a militaristic Igbo group from the Cross River area, were expanding westward into Agbani's farmland. For them the turn of the century was a period of agricultural expansion stimulated by their unique farming techniques.[61] It was their pressure on Agbani, their neighbors to the west, that encouraged the ascent of military men as leaders. Among the Ezza, military values and mores were encouraged, and young men were schooled in the military arts throughout their youth.[62]

Wealth and proficiency in war were often related. Rich men purchased guns and ammunition, attracted dependents through lending money and other resources, and acquired a number of slaves through war.[63] This militarization influenced cultural life and was articulated in the valorization of military skills as a component of rural masculinity as well as the rise of "head hunting" as a symbol of virility. These were even expressed in the performance arts.[64]

The second phase of the area's integration into the world market came with the palm trade. With the decline of the slave trade in the mid-nineteenth century, Udi became the northern sector of a new regional economy focused around the supply of palm kernels and oil. This new economy built upon existing merchant elites, expanded family-based production to incorporate large numbers of slaves, and further commercialized the local social structure, gender hierarchies, economy, and political processes. In a type of ripple effect, while villages in the palm belt concentrated their productive capacities to the harvesting and processing of palm fruits and oils, communities to the north, especially the villages in adjacent South Nkanu, put new resources into the production of food to supply them. Men with labor resources and fertile or proximate fields were able to benefit from this new market. For Igboland's poor the "legitimate" trade did not end slavery but, by stimulating the internal market, actually increased it. The wealthy, on the other hand, profited considerably.

Socially this change was represented in the popularization of the "Big Compound" which became a powerful ideal of patriarchal aspiration. The "Big Compound" was the household of a prosperous or powerful man whose many wives, children, clients, and slaves gave him an inordinate degree of influence over village affairs, and enabled him to control vast amounts of labor-power. In addition to the appropriation of his family's labor-power, a man could purchase and work slaves. Slaveholding became an important characteristic of wealth. Because he had a large household, he was entitled to large farmland allotments and he could produce large surpluses.[65]

The slave household had to work for the owner at least one day of the four-day Igbo week. During the weeding and harvesting periods, the women and children of the slave household worked beside their freeborn counterparts. Masters also demanded a portion of the food crop produced by the slave household on the portion of their masters' farmland designated for their use.[66]

A second source of labor came from informal ties the "Big Man" developed with clients through the extension of favors, or lending of money or land. At the lower ranks of Udi society were the more numerous poor, *ndi ogbenye*, who were often forced by destitution to attach themselves to the powerful men in the village. Many became obligated to these men and were forced into relationships of dependency. This allowed these "Big Men" to extend their political influence among various families in the village, who could be called upon to work during periods of need.[67] Since the most intensive demands for labor were episodic, these could be fulfilled in the short term by such dependents.

The trade in palm kernels and oil placed extraordinary demands on family-based productive systems and, without a market in labor, slave labor was one of the major ways that merchants could augment household production. The processing of these fruits, for both oil and kernels, was exceedingly labor intensive. Both came from the same fruit: the mesocarp was used for oil and the palm nut for the kernel.[68] A thirty-six pound tin of exportable oil required three to five person/days. Northrup notes that at sixty-two tins per ton, it took 10,000,000 person/days to produce the over 20,000 tons of Nigeria's oil exported to Europe in 1863–1864.[69] By 1900, this amount had doubled. Thus the history of Udi supports Lovejoy's thesis that the ending of the trans-Atlantic slave trade actually stimulated internal slavery in Igboland.[70]

The palm trade continued the process of rural stratification in many Udi communities. This was reflected in a number of practices and associations that reaffirmed status and encouraged both men and, to a lesser extent, women to fulfill certain hierarchical norms.[71] Farming was such an important aspect of rural male status that no self-respecting man could afford to appear divorced from his farm, even when most of the labor was performed by slaves or hired help. His community would ridicule him were he not involved in producing his own sustenance. Thus, even men from areas with poor farming lands felt compelled by social conventions surrounding masculinity to "farm," no matter how little. Since each family performed its own farm work, only men who controlled large amounts of labor-power could grow the numbers of yams required to become *Eze ji*, or Yam King, a title which symbolized a man's expertise in farming. Therefore, many men aspired to head large households, the "Big Compound," with many wives, children, and slaves. This sociopolitical function of farming explains the miners' reluctance to sever their involvement in the economy of the village, a factor that thwarts managerial control over the duration of work in the coal industry.

## THE CHALLENGE OF THE SLAVE AND PALM TRADES: SOCIAL STRATIFICATION AND POLITICAL EXPERIMENTATION

The conditions of insecurity and the presence of these privileged groups challenged the very ideological underpinnings of village government. Oral evidence suggests that many village-groups were experimenting with new political forms. The ascent of the *Ogaranyan* forced a flexibility in the "traditional" governing system to accommodate their emergence as an important economic force. This mercantile elite was restricted from full political realization by the older Igbo political system in which social position, prestige, and influence were based on age. While village-wide decisions were made by all freeborn men and aged women meeting in council, the viewpoint of a wise elder was given more weight than that of a junior man. Despite the veneration of age as social status, Igbo society permitted enterprising men, regardless of their age, to validate their wealth and gain influence and political authority

The slave and palm trades created a complicated process in which traditions of broad-based political participation coexisted, with considerable difficulty, with sharp economic and social hierarchies. Igbo political systems observed certain customary governing traditions that together formed a body of socially recognized morals, practices, and forms of collectivity. These values which constituted a set of values that men attached to leadership, affiliation, and collective behavior may be called an "organizational culture." These traditions were not static and in the context of increased commercialization they were undergoing considerable change. Age, as a determinant of rank from the individual to the village-group level, was under assault within several Udi villages. The moral authority of elder men now required validation through an institution of wealth, the title society ranked associations which required fees. Additionally, in many village-groups the moral and spiritual position of the senior quarter of the village paled in comparison to the political influence that younger, but wealthier, village quarters could exercise.[72]

One Agbaja elder, Noo Udala, who in 1973 was 102, described the shifting patterns of authority in the late nineteenth century when men who belonged to expensive title societies contested the power of elders:

> As time went on, this gradation of authority right from the town to the family unit, depending on age as the criterion, gave way to the authority of the wealthy. ... In fact a rift developed, so that it became a common feature for some *ndi ishi ani* (elders) to be forced to take titles.[73]

Despite these challenges the prevailing principles of age rank and authority, enshrined in group practice and individual choice, were still embraced by most men and women. These principles shaped the men's responses to colonial governing structures that erroneously validated many *Ogaranyan* as "chiefs."

The prevailing ideology of Igbo politics emphasized a diffuse political process which venerated consensus and consultation at every level of social organization.

While aspects of this ideology may have accurately described some political processes, it was an oversimplification of the complex ways that political power and influence were exercised within villages on the eve of the conquest. Specifically, the ideology does not recognize the power inherent in a person's ability to influence the collective to adopt his point of view. In the precolonial period, with few exceptions,[74] there were no kings or even chiefs in most village-groups. The exercise of political power was shared by various corporate groupings and councils of men, and sometimes women at multiple levels. Executive powers were exercised by title associations, expensive ranked organizations composed of influential men such as the *Ozo*, as well as *Dibia* societies of local doctors and organizations of priests who administered oaths and maintained shrines.[75] Additionally, most village men belonged to secret societies which appeared masked and enforced social control.[76] Age-grades, or groups of men born during a three- to four-year period, brought together men from individual families and lineages to perform public duties, such as policing the village, insuring public morality, and monitoring their members' behavior.[77]

At the village level, all men met in a general assembly (*Amaka* or *Oha*) to decide on the control and regulation of economic affairs, war, peace, and defense, and to discuss judicial, administrative, and executive matters. There was little separation of powers as the *Amaka* made, interpreted, and executed laws. And it was in the *Amaka* that a man's prestige and influence could be politically exercised, and where his status could be transformed in political power.

This diffuse political structure valorized a man's ability to negotiate between various power centers that constituted a political skill. Men who become leaders in the *Amaka* were those who could reconcile different points of view and help the group reach compromise rather than dominate the group. Such a man would be selected for the *izuzu*, a select subcommittee of the *Amaka* formed to discuss a particularly difficult issue. Membership was restricted to men of prestige, wisdom, and balance. During deliberations the *izuzu* selected a spokesman, usually a man of strong oratory skills, a man who "has mouth" and who could present the decision to the general village in a persuasive way.[78] This presentation was important because only the *Amaka* could make the final decision and the collective judgment prevails.[79]

One crucial ingredient of Igbo organization culture which held implications for the mines' labor movement was the absence of the principle of representation. Although many levels of the polity selected representatives to confer in larger groups there were real limits on what a representative could exercise on behalf of his constituency. At the level of the village-group, political issues were discussed by delegates from the member villages, but they were not representatives and could not commit to a decision without a village consensus. All "town" decisions had to be by consensus of member villages. The only defined powers held by the "town" concerned the Earth Goddess, *Ani*, or common market sites.[80]

Although all decisions were through consensus of the freeborn, all men were not equally influential. Consequently, the opinion of all men was not given equal weight. As noted above, the international trade stimulated social hierarchies, all men did not control equal human and material resources, and all *Obi* were not of equal size, wealth, or influence. Thus, wealthy, successful men did attain political influence within these broadly participatory procedures.

## FARMING AND ECOLOGICAL CONSTRAINTS
## ON MASCULINE STATUS ACHIEVEMENT

As many men aspired to be *Ogaranyan* they stimulated a dynamic in which land tenure practices and farming systems propelled Udi into a pre-industrial labor reserve. When the area between Benin and Calabar focused on the production for export of the raffia palm, *elaeis quinensis*,[81] Udi's farming systems followed a rotating bush fallow system in which fields were worked only one season in a series of years.[82]

Farmers in both Nkanu and Agbaja focused on the cultivation of the yam, *Dioscorea cayanensis* and *D. tundata*. It was the most important crop in Igbo farming and required considerable ritual and technical expertise. This was especially the case in Udi where land fertility was fragile and unpredictable. It was considered a "prestige" crop and produced yields of from 1,500 to 4,000 pounds per acre.[83] In this respect it was a very efficient crop for areas with scarce farmland. The yam was a male crop, and legend says it sprang from the head of a male child ritually sacrificed in prehistoric times to create food for the community. Only men can perform the rituals that insure its growth.[84]

The fertility requirements of yam cultivation both shaped land tenure practices and influenced the spiritual life of the village. As a crop, the yam was suitable for land-deficient areas because it grew under large mounds that could be planted with other crops. However, the yam severely depleted the soil and forced the rigid system of rotational cultivation, which were interspersed with frequent ritual interventions by men to insure a good crop. Soil fertility was a severe problem because the tsetse fly prevented communities from having large animals whose manure could fertilize the fields.[85] These constraints created a preoccupation with fertility in northern Igboland, leading communities to rely on designated men to make ritual interventions that evoked sacred assistance to insure farm productivity. Additionally, communities used some variation of a rotating bush-fallow system in which fields were worked two or three seasons every four, six, or even fifteen years.[86] In a system called "block farming," the entire village designated a particular section of the land for farms that season.[87]

Under such conditions the qualitative nature of a family's farmland played a crucial role in its very survival. Individual growing rights came through the *ummuna*. A just distribution of farmland took into consideration differences in the quality of land—its fecundity, water, accessibility (distance from the household), all of which affected production. But an *ummuna*'s land allocation was determined by village councils in which merchant/farmers played a prominent role.

In Agbaja, where erosion and high population densities made farming precarious, men entered specialist non-agricultural occupations and monopolized ritual knowledge and craft specialization.[88] Women were associated with other varieties of yams, which, while having a lower status, were an indispensable source of food. This gender specialization deflected the society's dependence on the crops grown by women on compound gardens and between the yam mounds and reflected men's reluctance to permit women to convert their economic role into spiritual authority. In reality most households subsisted on the "female" coco yam, a tuber grown on smaller mounds, and cassava, an imported tuber that required less fertile soil, a shorter fallow period, and lower labor input.[89] Women's crops were augmented by a large number of vegetables (corn, okra, etc.) and small amounts of meat.[90] Thus labor devoted to food crop production was usually seasonal for men, but for women, largely constant.

The agricultural cycle imposed a rurally based rhythm which influenced the availability of male labor for the mines. During January and February both men and women cleared the fields for planting. Men felled trees, fired fields to produce ash, and gathered the sticks to train the yams. They also performed the skilled labor that produced seed yams for the next season. This involved cutting the yams that were then planted in the soil. Planting began with the first rains from late March to early April. Women and children scraped the ash into the hole and worked the topsoil around the hole until they created a small hill.[91] In some northern Igboland villages such as Ezza, a specialized group of men then built the huge mounds of soil (sometimes six feet or more) that protected the yam from the rains. While awaiting the yams, women planted their crops on the yam hills and in household gardens located near the compound which sustained the family during the long growing period of some 200 to 300 days. Men harvested the tubers from October through January and built the "yam barns," large wooden structures where yams were tied up until they were eaten.[92]

A man could exercise several options when he needed additional labor. He could either use slaves, employ itinerant labor, or call upon his age mates or work group. If he were the head of an *Obi*, or lineage group, he could appropriate the labor of all men and women one day in the eight-day Igbo week.[93] Or he could also trade labor among age grades, *ohe oru*, on a rotating basis, "paying" them with food or drink.[94] Thus prominent men were able to appropriate labor through clientilistic relationships with the poor.

The gender implications of Agbaja and Nkanu customary land inheritance practices deepened the stress on the agricultural system in the Udi area. Marriage was a prerequisite for male social maturity and an overwhelming preoccupation for young men. An adult man who is not married is called an *oke okporo* or "male woman," a disparaging term that any self-respecting man sought to avoid.[95]

Marriage established the basic unit of production, the household, and gave men access to the labor-power of women and children. Like many other pre-industrial peoples, the Igbo had a system of bridewealth that symbolized the transfer of the woman's potential reproductive (biological) and productive (labor-power) value from her father's home to her husband's home. The form of the bride price varied in the Agbaja and Nkanu areas of Igboland. In some village-groups it was a cash payment, while in others it took the form of labor service by the prospective groom to his future in-laws. In still other areas the bride price was only symbolic—constituting a "gift" of palm wine and/or a kola nut—and the significant expenditure came later in financing the series of rituals and ceremonies that authenticated the marriage.

A married son had rights to a section of the father's allocation of farmland and household land. In Agbaja the subdivision of land for successive generations created fields of less than the minimum acreage necessary to sustain the son's family. In this case men developed non-agricultural specializations, purchased food from elsewhere, or migrated to other areas where they farmed for hire or rented farmland to grow food for their households.[96] This receptivity to migration, a renowned characteristic of the Igbos in Nigeria, was an important influence on the colliery's labor supplies.

While we cannot determine with historical precision when this agricultural crisis began in Agbaja, it appears that by 1900 Udi's villages were overpopulated, land-starved agricultural communities, totally incapable of feeding themselves. Nonetheless, they were viable natal villages for the men who migrated seasonally in search of farmland and jobs. These men retained their familial rights to farmland, no matter how small.[97] The Enugu Government Colliery became an option to migration and supplemented farming. Thus, although household farms were too small to support a family totally dependent on farming, they were quite adequate as a supplement to a man's wages. Or, more precisely, farming became an important supplement to wage labor. The British thought that they had found large, controllable supplies of labor locked in an impoverished, land-starved "labor reserve." But Agbaja men saw the industry as an opportunity to synchronize mine work and agriculture. It was this dynamic that explains the paradox between the mine's inability to control the labor market and to establish industrial discipline in a labor-surplus area. By 1900 most of Udi's Agbaja village-groups were so overpopulated that they were areas of continuous settlement with small fragmented land holdings that were too small to sustain the family.[98]

## SYMBOLIC REPRESENTATIONS OF MASCULINE POWER: TITLE SOCIETIES AND PRESTIGE GOODS

Wealth alone did not confer political or ritual power. Authority and ritual sanction at the lineage level were integral parts of maleness.[99] Igbo differentiated between wealth (*ako, oba*), status position (*okwa*), and prestige (*odo*).[100] Even wealthy men had to strive to achieve prestige and influence through a cultural idiom that used both spiritual and material achievements as indicators of heightened status. To reach social maturity and influence, an Igbo man would engage in a number of processes that could enhance his status. This was signified by membership in prestigious societies or associations and possession of certain goods.

In pre-capitalist Igbo villages, wealth was attained through the control over labor-power or "wealth-in-people." It was the "continuous acquisition, creation, control, and appropriation of labour power" that was the "dynamic social principle" upon which most pre-capitalist societies in Africa were based.[101] Given the environmental restrictions on the productive base and the problems of storing wealth, prominent men and women could only symbolize *the potential* to generate it. These representations of wealth took symbolic forms and were converted into symbols of prestige and power.

"Wealth" was gendered and historically and culturally specific. Male wealth was represented in many symbolic forms: houses, many sons and wives and daughters, livestock, voluntary and involuntary titles, yam and cocoyam farms, a large yam store, *obaji*,[102] an extensive ancestral compound with surrounding land, *osisi uzo*, and food and cash-crop trees. On the other hand a woman's wealth was represented in ownership of livestock (fowls, dogs), rich garden and farm yields, many daughters whose marriage brought in-laws and presents, and many wealthy influential sons. In both respects "wealth" in "persons" was an important component of social status.[103] Women could take the *ogbuefi* title, the only voluntary title that both men and women could hold.[104] Some of these signifiers were actually congealed value (the yam store, and titles) while others, wives, and descendants, could *produce* value.

In Udi a series of products came to symbolize this form of conspicuous consumption: cases of imported gin, slaves, Dane guns, and yams.[105] Further, a wealthy man had large yam barns, côteries of slaves, and many wives and clients.[106] These were all symbols of his actual or potential control over the labor power of others. But the foundation of his wealth was his access to his wives' productive and reproductive capacity. A large number of wives signified the appropriation of a considerable amount of labor-power. As they produced children, their labor-power and hers became the main factor of production controlled by the household.[107] The constraints on reinvestment of wealth were not totally uniform in Udi, but were generally quite severe. In the Agbaja area, the thin sandy soils and large populations eliminated expanded agricultural production as an investment of wealth. In the Nkanu area where land was more fertile and well watered, some men did purchase slaves and used them to expand food production.

"Male" status was endorsed through spiritual and material achievement as indicated by membership in prestigious societies or associations. These associations validated personal achievement which the Igbo felt was demonstrated by success in the material world as permitted by the support of the ancestors, one's family, and neighbors. Membership in these associations conferred recognition of his role in furthering the interest of the *ummuna* as a whole (i.e., both ancestors, present members, and others yet to be born). In some respects these associations reflected the man's preoccupation with a conspicuous display of affluence. The display of wealth in symbolic form was an indication of the limited opportunities for reinvestment of the surplus in improved systems of production. Such wealth, often generated by trade and farming, was therefore "displayed" in ways that brought prestige to the man, his *obi*, and *ummuna*. Because material success indicated the sanction of the ancestors to one's neighbors it was an impressive display of potential or actual power.[108]

In northern Igboland, the rapid accumulation of wealth from international trade encouraged membership in exclusive title societies to become a compelling goal for many Igbo men and an important means of political expression for wealthy men.[109] Membership functioned as a way of testing political aspirants.[110] Titled men danced exclusive dances, sat on special chairs, wore dress that displayed symbols of status, and were buried in bigger funerals.[111] While there were numerous such societies, the most prestigious in most Agbaja village-groups was the *Ozo* title.[112] We have no record of the membership requirement before the conquest, but anthropologists reported in the 1920s that in Agbaja membership required a big feast, followed one year later by £20 cash, 100 fowls, another feast, and payment to an Nri[113] representative who performed facial scarification for £2 10s.[114] *Ozo* men were recognized as a sacred elite throughout Igboland because they were considered intermediaries between the dead members of the descent group, i.e., the ancestors, and the living. Their lives were restricted by taboos and scrupulously observed restriction. They were known by their *Itchi* marks and the regalia of office—a red cap, ankle cords, an ivory horn, and an iron staff. People were forbidden to harm an *Ozo* man, to remove his cap, or show any signs of disrespect. They held a protected status, and it was an abomination to kill them or members of their family. Because they represented the ancestors they were accorded powers to adjudicate disputes, especially over land, to stop fights, and to collect debts.[115] Their homes were a sanctuary and for a fee, one could borrow some of the insignia to use, when traveling, as a type of guarantee of safe passage. *Ozo* men were politically very influential in the village.

The distribution of goods and funds to society members was one mechanism, along with life-cycle ceremonies, for redistributing the social wealth generated by one household to others.[116] Some have even argued that this and similar redistributive systems prevented the development of a centralized Igbo state.[117]

The *Ozo* society was strongest in those towns incorporated in the Aro slave trading network. It was especially powerful in Umuaga, Agbaja,[118] where by 1900 it had usurped authority from lineage authorities.[119] An elder described this process of status reformulation and economic polarization that followed:

> In fact, much respect was given to these titled men, who because of their wealth were known as *ndi amadi*, as against *ndi ogbenye*, the poor. These *ndi amadi* then formed the governing council of the village or town. They took the initiative in calling meetings and soon, after some time, our elders were happy to be called to such meetings without any efforts to show the influence of their age at such meetings. During deliberations in the governing council of *ndi amadi*, the suggestion made by an *amadi* was more agreeable to those present than that of a poor elder, no matter if he was the eldest. I do not mean that we now have two separate governing councils. But what I am telling you is that even though the *ndi ishi ani* summoned meetings, the views of the rich titled men are more readily accepted. Both rich and poor still attended the council meetings.[120]

Wealthy merchants could sometimes assume the *Eze* title, perhaps the closest legitimate office to that of a "chief." It connoted leadership of a community and was "awarded to the man who, [had] good character ... the right lineage" and "could fete people and pay expensive fees to elders."[121] Found mainly in Onitsha Province the *Eze*, according to Jones, was a "convenient way for a self-made leader ... to consolidate his position as village group head by converting it into traditional office." In many areas only men descended from the original founder of the village could hold it.[122] But in Nkanu such positions of leadership "were reduced to a minimum" and political leadership was exercised through the senior grades, or the oldest man of specific, often senior, lineages.

But in South Nkanu areas, such as the village-group of Ihuokpara, the *Igojji*, or "Tying Cloths" title was the highest.[123] While most titles required higher fees to reach the upper more influential grades, not all titles were based on money. This was the case with the South Nkanu horse killer or *Obu Anyina* title, or headhunting societies, another reflection of the militarization of culture.[124]

One other type of title society had some relevance for the labor strategies of local men in the coal industry. This was the society of the yam kings, *Eze ji*, an association of the most successful farmers in the community. This title reflected the ritualization of agriculture,[125] a condition arising from the importance attached to the soil, as the resting place of the ancestors and domain of the spirit-force *Ani*. It emphasized the spiritual qualities of the "male" yam, *njoku* or *ihiejioku*, and the material role that yam played as the main sustenance for the Igbo. This ritual aura extended to farming itself, and, contrary to the colonial allegations of the "laziness" of Igbo men, farming was a respected profession.

A series of rituals dictated how the yam was grown, handled, and eaten.[126] A man became an *Eze ji* because of his agricultural knowledge, large labor supplies, and alleged support from the ancestors that enabled him to produce large surpluses of yams. To become a member he had to feed members of the society for a predetermined number of days and pay the required fees.[127] In 1920, entrance required a thousand "growing-sticks" of yams.[128] The prestige of this title was projected politically because these men could sanction political decisions with their religious authority. Their success, which signified the support of the ancestors, gave them considerable influence in village council meetings.

Masculinity was not just physical but also moral.[129] Many attributes of Igbo masculine power did not differ significantly from those of middle and working class men in Western societies: aggression, perseverance, stoicism, restraint but determination, achievement through hard-fought effort, bravery and courage, etc. Men were expected to help the less fortunate with resources from their household as well as sponsoring some development project in their village. Either practice, which redistributed resources within the community, earned one notoriety as a "big man" and benefactor. But such benevolence was not just male "generosity." Assisting others also established important ties of obligation and dependency that "bought" the support of the recipient in the many political conflicts and contests in village politics. These political benefits were not of small consequence in village politics during the colonial period. They were very pervasive qualities that were symbolized in art and ritual. Masquerades, in which men wearing masks acted out specific qualities, served to sanction certain social practices by suggesting divine intervention. Most masquerades were played by men, even those that were explicitly "female" and certain cults, such as *Odo*, and *Omobe*, had as their explicit function to discipline and subjugate women.[130]

One of the strongest signifiers of masculinity was *Ikenga*, a multidimensional concept that was a shrine, symbol, and an idea. The public form that *Ikenga* took was a mask, usually carved from a strong "male" wood. It depicted a virile man with horns, holding a long-bladed knife in one hand and a severed trophy head in the other. The mask symbolized a series of qualities that are valued as "manliness." The face was usually scarred with *ichi* marks, that symbolized the prestige of title taking, and the ability to endure the pain of the facial scarification. The knife symbolized action, willpower, and decisiveness, while the severed head meant hard-fought achievement. *Ikenga* masks usually had ram horns, but could have also been carved with two protruding eagle feathers. The rams exemplified a man's ability to stubbornly launch an attack on a difficult problem until it was resolved, and his ability to endure pain. But the ram's aggression was usually a last resort, and a good man would fight only when necessary, exercising restraint when confronted with a problem. The eagles were a "metaphor for forceful, heroic men of accomplishment."[131]

*Ikenga* were owned by male cults, individual men, and occasionally by women. The cult itself encouraged these traits among its members. Young men acquired an *Ikenga* at marriage and at subsequent periods in their life cycle when they accomplished an important feat.

The wealth generated by the slave and palm trades sharpened the contradiction between personal achievement and social responsibility. While the society valued individual success and achievement as a compelling norm, individual success came through human interdependence and reciprocity.[132] It was only possible if one had moral strength and the support of the ancestors and the community at large. Consequently, a man had to assume responsibility for helping the common good. One way of attaining prestige, respect, and fulfilling reciprocal obligations was by helping others to "get up," a recognition of the interdependence of human life. But the benefits of being a socially responsible and generous male, in the final instance, resulted in individual power, personal wealth, and prestige.

These contradictions in Igbo male values were further sharpened with the intervention of British rule. It was then possible for prominent men to accrue individual prestige and "ignore" their social responsibility to the group. These contradictions produced two tendencies: an extreme competition for personal achievement on the one hand, and a "concern" for the position of one's family, village, and village-group on the other. The political consequences of this tension will be discussed in the next chapter, when such prominent men became colonial "chiefs," inventing a tradition of governance at odds with the underlying principles of Igbo political organization.

The social repercussions of the slave and palm trades were felt throughout Udi's various village-groups. For men, it created new requirements for social maturity and the desired goals of social mobility. The stakes were especially high for the *ogbenye* (poor), who shared with wealthy men a compelling desire to enhance status. For Agbaja's young men, status attainment appeared difficult, if not impossible. Because of their poverty in land and resources they could not marry.

The acquisition of wealth, status position, and prestige were important factors behind worker agitation in the Enugu mines. These values were rooted in a pre-industrial rural ethic, but they were strengthened by participation in a capitalist industry. This process suggests that the proletarianization thesis may be an inadequate and limited concept to explain the behavior of colonial workers. Nonetheless, ultimately, their activism was motivated by goals that were not significantly different from those that encouraged coal miners' agitation in the Euro-American world: to support their families and themselves with dignity, respect, and honor.

Thus, at the time of the British arrival, Igboland was in the throes of violent socio-political change and economic transformation. These processes were far from peaceful, as development seldom is. Old political mores were being challenged by the realities of an insecure present. Adjustments in political structures and governing processes were being made to satisfy the insatiable needs of a mercantile elite rooted in both the past and present export economy of the region. These new elites, whose legitimacy was far from entrenched, were especially receptive to collaboration with the new colonial rulers as partners in the system of indirect rule. Many would become the first generation of "colonial chiefs" whose services would be indispensable for the recruitment and control of the coal industry's workers. Their involvement would introduce all these issues concerning masculinity and stratification into the mines.

## NOTES

1. Interview with Thomas Noisike, Agbaja, Udi Division, Enugu, 7 June 1975.

2. David Eltis, Stephen D. Behrendt, David Richardson, Herbert S. Klein, eds. *The Trans-Atlantic Slave Trade: A Database on CD-Rom* (Cambridge, 1999).

3. Frederick Cooper, "Work, Class, and Empire," 236.

4. Keletso Atkins, *The Moon Is Dead! Give Us Our Money!*, 6.

5. This debate is summarized in several of the essays in A.E. Afigbo's *Groundwork in Igbo History* (Lagos, 1992).

6. There is a rather extensive literature of slave ship captains' correspondence as well as missionary accounts. For a recent interpretation of these sources and a new analysis of the financial infrastructure of European-African trade relations see Paul E. Lovejoy and David Richardson, "Trust, Pawnship and Atlantic History: The Institutional Foundations of the Old Calabar Slave Trade," *American Historical Review*, 104 (2 April 1999): 333–55.

7. Several of the major ethnographic studies were based on research conducted in the late twenties and have been treated as contemporary accounts rather than as timeless doc-

uments. See P. Amaury Talbot, *The Peoples of Southern Nigeria*, 4 vols. (London, new edition, 1969); G.T. Basden, *Among the Ibos of Southern Nigeria* (London, 1921); Ibid., *Niger Ibos* (London, 1938); C.K. Meek, *Law and Authority in a Nigerian Tribe* (London, 1937). This latter study was conducted following the "Women's War" of 1929. The research was conducted during 1930–1931 and did not actually venture into northern Igboland, the location of the coal mines. However, Talbot's study, which specifically notes Agbaja and Nkanu, documents many similarities.

8. The *Ekwe* title is just one such symbol. The names of two such titled women appear in a recent history of Udi district: Akuenyi Nwofor (Oforama) and Uzodimma Ozobu. Innocent Uzeochi, "The Social and Political Impact of the Eastern Nigerian Railway on Udi Division, 1913–1945" (Ph.D. diss., Kent State University, 1985), 212.

9. National Archives, Enugu (hereafter NAE), OP/1070, Ondist 12/1/708, "Intelligence Report on the Village-Groups of Agbani-Akpugo," S.P.L. Beaumont, May 1935, 4.

10. W.B. Morgan and J.C. Pugh, *West Africa* (London, 1969), xxiv.

11. A.E. Afigbo, *Ropes of Sand: Studies in Igbo History and Culture* (Lagos, 1981).

12. Ibid., 4; Herbert M. Cole and Chike C. Aniakor, *Igbo Arts: Community and Cosmos* (Los Angeles, 1984), 1.

13. Cole and Aniakor, *Igbo Arts*, 1.

14. As with many aspects of Igbo culture, there is no agreement on the exact parameters of *ummuna*. In contrast with Afigbo, whose definition is used above, is Uchendu who says that the *ummuna* is a fluid term that "in its smallest sense means children of the same father but different mothers; in its widest referent is the patrilineal members, real or putative, whom one cannot marry." Victor Uchendu, *The Igbo of Southeast Nigeria* (New York, 1965), 39–40.

15. A.E. Afigbo, "Southeastern Nigeria in the 19th Century," in *History of West Africa*, vol. 2, 2d ed., ed. J.F.A. Ajayi and M. Crowder (New York, 1974), 535–36.

16. Ibid.

17. Aniakor, "Igbo Life, World View and Cosmology," *Genéve Afrique* 21, 1 (1988). 100.

18. Forde and Jones, *Ibibio-Speaking People*, 24–26.

19. Uchendu, *The Igbo of Southeast Nigeria*, 96.

20. This analysis is an interpretation of Horton's conclusions about the foundations of solidarity in slave villages in the Nike clan area of northern Nkanu. W.G.R. Horton, "God, Man and the Land in a Northern Ibo Village Group," *Africa* 26 (January 1956): 23–25.

21. Phillip A. Oguagha and Alex I. Ikpoko, *History and Ethnoarchaeology in Eastern Nigeria: A Study of Igbo-Igala Relations with Special Reference to the Anambra Valley*, Cambridge Monographs in African Archaeology 7 (Oxford, 1984), 239–40.

22. A village-group is a cluster of villages that claim to have been founded by the descendants of a common ancestor. Therefore the village-group of Ngwo, for example, will be composed of several villages, each with a legend of origin attributed to a son or daughter of the founder of Ngwo.

23. David Smock, *Conflict and Control in an African Trade Union: A Study of the Nigerian Coal Miners' Union* (Stanford, 1969), 18–19.

24. NAE, "Intelligence Report for Agbani-Akpugo," 1935, 4.

25. Robin Horton, "The *Ohu* System of Slavery in a Northern Igboland Village-Group," *Africa* 24 (1954): 311–36.

26. The latter, the first colliery workers, hailed from Owerri in central Igboland or Onitsha, the large commercial center on the Niger. Both areas had experienced earlier contact with European rule and integration into the world economy, and came to the colliery with

marketable skills honed in industrial missions and church schools. They saw themselves as more "civilized" than the locals whom they disparagingly called "*wawa*," or backward.

27. This is the case for many of the village-groups in Udi. See NAE, Onprof 8/1/4740, "Intelligence Report on the Nara Village Group, Nkanu Clan-Udi Division," 1934; Ondist 12/1/708, "Intelligence Report on the Village Groups of Agbani-Akpugo Group, Udi Division," S.P.L. Beaumont, 1935.

28. Cole and Aniakor, *Igbo Arts*, 2.

29. See Alonso de Sandoval, S.J. *De Instauranda Aeethopum Salute* (Bogota, 1956), a reissue of *Naturaleza ... de Totos Etiopes*, Sevilla, 1627, as cited in David Northrup, *Trade Without Rulers: Pre-Colonial Economic Development in South-Eastern Nigeria* (Oxford, 1978), 50–51. Although calculations of the numbers of slaves are actually estimates, Curtin and others estimate that between 1750 and 1810 slave exports from the Bight of Biafra rose from 4,500 to 14,000 per year.

30. Paul Lovejoy, *Transformations of Slavery* (Cambridge, 1983), 57.

31. Patrick Manning, *Slavery and African Life: Occidental, Oriental, and African Slave Trades* (Cambridge, 1990), 68.

32. The full extent of this impact, while not adequately recognized in Igbo historiography, is clearly evident in the interviews in a wide range of communities. See interview with Thomas Noisike, 7 June 1975.

I am currently directing a video/audio-tape oral history project, "Memory and the Atlantic Slave Trade: A Pilot Project in Southeastern Nigeria." The region's centuries of involvement in the slave trade and sheer magnitude of the victims (estimated 800,000 between the seventeenth and early nineteenth centuries) has seared indelible scars in the collective consciousness of these villages, reflected in the culture, current power struggles and lingering discriminatory practices against descendants of slaves. The key states of the project are Anambra, Abia, and Enugu. The project is jointly sponsored by the UNESCO/York University Canada Nigerian Hinterland Project, Office of the Executive Dean, Faculty of Arts and Sciences, Rutgers University, Rutgers Center for African Studies, Schomburg Center of Black Culture of the New York Public Library, and the Enugu Historical Documentation Center of Enugu, Nigeria. The tapes are available at the Schomburg Center, the Alexander Library of Rutgers University, York's Nigerian Hinterland Project, and the Enugu Historical Documentation Center.

33. Sigismund Wilhelm Koelle, *Polyglotta Africana* (London, 1854), 8.

34. Olaudah Equiano was captured in 1756. His *Equiano's Travels*, the story of his abduction and eventual liberation, was an important abolitionist treatise in the late eighteenth century. See Afigbo's attempt to locate Equiano's home in A.E. Afigbo, "Through a Glass Darkly," in A.E. Afigbo, *Ropes of Sand*.

35. Felicia Ekejiuba, "High Points of Igbo Civilization: Tha Arochukwu Period a Sociologist's View," in A.E. Afigbo, ed., *Groundwork of Igbo History* (Lagos, 1991), 315.

36. There are a number of studies of the Aro: K.O. Dike and Felicia I. Ekejiuba, "Change and Persistence in Aro Oral History," *Journal of African Studies* 3, 3(Fall 1976): 277–96; Felicia Ekijiuba, "The Aro System of Trade in the Nineteenth Century," pt. 1, *Ikenga* 1, 1 (January 1972); Ibid., pt. 2, *Ikenga* 1, 2 (July 1972); Ukwu I.T. Ukwu, "The Development of Trade and Marketing in Iboland," *Journal of the Historical Society of Nigeria* 3, 4 (1967): 647–62.

37. NAE, CSO 26/29601, "Intelligence Report on the Ntegbe-Nese Clan, Udi Division, Onitsha Province," S.P.L. Beaumont, 1933, 11, 35–36. Northrup, *Trade Without Rulers*, 136.

38. ONPROF 8/1/4740, "Nara Village Group."

39. Mrs. A.H. Richardson, "Account of the Pioneer Work in the Agbani Area of Nigeria undertaken by the Reverend Arthur Humphrey Richardson of the Primitive Methodist Missionary Society, 1916–1920," unpublished manuscript. London: Methodist Church Overseas Division (Methodist Missionary Society), 1976.

40. For a discussion of the Igbo market system, see Ukwu's sections of Barry W. Hodder and Ukwu I. Ukwu, *Markets in West Africa* (Ibadan, 1969) and Ukwu, "Trade and Marketing," 647–62.

41. The Igbo have two types of week: the little week, *Izu*, which is divided into four *Ubochi/Mbosi* or days—*Eke, Orie/Olie, Afo/Aho* and *Nkwo*—and the big week, *Izu Ukwu*, of eight days. In the big week the four days have the same name, and the second four days end in *ukwu* or "big." Hence the fifth day is *Orie Ukwu* (big Orie) and so on. Ukwu I.T. Ukwu, "The Development of Trade and Marketing in Iboland," and Meek, *Law and Authority in a Nigerian Tribe*, 36n.

42. The seminal discussion of this process in British labour history is E.P. Thompson's essay "Time, Work-Discipline and Industrial Capatalism" *Past and Present* 28(1967):56–97.

43. Some South Nkanu adapted "cleansing" rituals to enable them to sell relatives. See video interview "Memories of Pain and Loss Project" with Prince Harry Chukwuani, 8 December 1999, Ozalla, A/EN/NK/1. The Prince demonstrated a ritual involving a sacrifice to a sacred crocodile.

44. Paul Nwaba, oldest inhabitant of Umuaga, Agbaja as quoted in Isichei, *Igbo Worlds: An Anthology of Oral Histories and Historical Description* (Philadelphia, 1976), 76.

45. One of the most conspicuous examples of this culture is a series of decaying wooden Victorian mansions scattered throughout the palm belt. I saw some of these beautifully rambling mansions in the village of Mbieri, Owerri, in 1975. Most were two-story buildings with elaborate verandas and many bedrooms and wings. I understand that a number of them are still standing. [Communication from Dr. Austin Ahanotu, 14 July 2000, Enugu, Nigeria.]

46. A *diji* had to feed members of this society for a fixed number of days with yams from his barn, pay fees, and perform certain sacrifices to become a member. Afigbo, *Ropes of Sand*, 127–30. The symbols of this wealth were large "yam barns," wooden framed structures on which yams were tied to enable them to retain their freshness for long periods. For a fictionalized account of the significance of yams, see Chinua Achebe, *Things Fall Apart* (London, 1959).

47. Richardson, "Pioneer Work," 122.

48. NAE, OP/1070, "Intelligence Reports on Nomeh," Beaumont; "Village-Groups of Agbani-Akpugo," Beaumont.

49. On Eze Okoli, see Amadiume, *Male Daughters*, 137–40; for Onyeama, see Mabel Ifejika Okolo, "A History of Eke Community 1800–1993," (unpublished interviews, Owerri, 1979). On Njemanze, A.E. Afigbo, *The Warrant Chiefs: Indirect Rule in Southeastern Nigeria 1891–1929* (Longman, 1972), 64, 70, 72; and interview with J.K. Ohale in Amawom, Owerri, 9 August 1975. Ohale said that the chief supplied fifty to one hundred people in each group to the coal mines. Many would desert when they saw the conditions of work.

50. Onyeama's grandson, Dillibe Onyeama, wrote the biography, *Chief Onyeama: The Story of an African God* (Enugu, 1982). Although it is not an academic text, the book is nonetheless a valuable, synthesis of oral and archival information on the chief.

51. See R. Horton, "The *Ohu* System."

52. Oguagha and Ikpoko, *History and Ethnoarchaeology in Eastern Nigeria*, 239–40.

53. R. Horton, "The *Ohu* System," 311.

54. Interview with Paul Nwanba, 16 June 1973, in Isichei, *Igbo Worlds*, 76.

55. Oral tradition alleges that Eze Nwachi was the first man to call Agbani to arms when they were invaded by Awkananu, and was the first to secure a head. He was then elected leader and the oldest man of his lineage, and became the titular head of the town. His duties, however, were largely religious. In the past the descendants of Eze Nwachi were executive heads of the town, and heads of both *Ikoro* drums and shrines associated with war and hunting. See NAE, OP/1070, "Village-Groups of Agbani-Akpugo."

56. Phillip O. Nsugbe, *Ohaffia: A Matrilineal Ibo People* (Oxford, 1974), 25–32.

57. One Agbaja slave, Aneke (alias Thomas O'Connor) was kidnapped in 1819 and sold to the Aro who in turn dispatched him to the coast. Koelle, *Polyglotta Africana*, 8.

58. Ibid. These communities still exist and are today engaged in a struggle for political autonomy. They are still discriminated against. See Axel Harniet-Sievers, "Repercussions of Pre-Colonial Slavery in Contemporary Local Politics: The Case of Nike, Enugu State, Nigeria," unpublished paper presented at "Repercussions of the Atlantic Slave Trade: The Bight of Biafra and the African Diaspora," Enugu, Nigeria, 10–14 July 2000.

59. Elizabeth Isichei, *History of the Igbo People* (London, 1976), 82–87.

60. A.O. Arua, *A Short History of Ohafia* (Enugu, 1952). Also Isichei, *History of the Igbo People*, 81–87.

61. Ezza expansion was related to their ecology. Unlike most of Igboland, which had more rainfall, the Ezza's dry climate allowed them to leave mature yams in the ground until they were used. Thus their planting season extended through most of the dry season. Therefore each individual farmer could produce unusually large supplies of yams by planting seed yams in huge mounds of a cubic yard or more of soil. For this reason, Ezza cultivation was expansive, leading them to seize land from their neighbors. Because of this, military values permeated the culture. By the beginning of the nineteenth century, the Ezza were expanding to the west, pressuring the Nkanu village group of Amagunze. Isichei, Ibid., 88–89.

62. Ibid., 87–91.

63. R.F. Stevenson, *Population and Political Systems in Tropical Africa* (New York, 1968), 199 as cited in Amadiume, *Male Daughters*, 56.

64. Cole and Aniakor, *Igbo Arts*, 30.

65. Uchendu, *The Igbo of Southeast Nigeria*, 54.

66. See also Carolyn Brown, "Testing the Boundaries of Marginality: Twentieth-Century Slavery and Emancipation Struggles in Nkanu, Northern Igboland, 1920–1929," *Journal of African History* 37 (1996): 51–80.

67. Afigbo, *Ropes of Sand*, 129.

68. Processing involved "boiling or fermenting the fruit, depulping by pounding or mashing with the feet in a container and squeezing the depulped fiber by hand to obtain the oil." Palm nuts were then allowed to dry and later cracked to reveal the kernels. The production process was gendered. Men climbed the trees and cut down fruit while preparation for processing was usually done by women and children. There were two systems of oil production. In one, which produces "soft" edible oil, most labor was performed by women while in the other, for "hard" oil, most was done by men. Eno J. Usoro, *The Nigerian Oil Palm Industry* (Ibadan, 1974), 10.

69. Northrup, *Trade Without Rulers*, 186.

70. See Lovejoy, *Transformations of Slavery*, 153–58.

71. See Uzeochi, "The Social and Political Impact of the Eastern Nigerian Railway on Udi Division, 1913–1945," 212.

72. An additional example was Nomeh, where the most junior kinship group, Onoha Eze, became powerful because of its size, numerous slaves (over half their population), and wealth. While the senior quarter had ceremonial powers, the opinion of the more junior Onoha Eze patrilineage was valued in village decisions, and they were often called upon to settle disputes. They zealously used "their slaves as police to arrest and sell recalcitrant offenders." Onprof 8/1/4740, "Nara Village Group."

73. Interview with Noo Udala, Umuaga, Agbaja, 19 June 1973, cited in Elizabeth Isichei *Igbo Worlds: An Anthology of Oral Histories and Historical Description*, 73. For discussion of title societies see page 76.

74. These exceptions, in the precolonial period, included Onitsha where the *Oba*, or kingship came from Benin. See Richard N. Henderson, *The King in Every Man: Evolutionary Trends in Onitsha Society and Culture* (New Haven, 1972); Ikenna Nzimiro, *Studies in Ibo Political Systems: Chieftaincy and Politics in Four Niger States* (London, 1972).

75. See also continuing discussion on p. 43 of this book.

76. Elizabeth Isichei, *A History of the Igbo People*, 22.

77. Uchendu, *The Igbo of Southeast Nigeria*, 43.

78. Amadiume, *Male Daughters*, 14.

79. This description is based on Uchendu, *The Igbo of Southeast Nigeria*, 41–42.

80. Ibid., 44.

81. After the mid-nineteenth century, palm products gained commercial importance during World War I, when their glycerin content made them valuable in the manufacture of explosives. Previously the kernels became an important foodstuff for cattle, especially in Germany. The development of the hydrogenation process in the late nineteenth century led to its use in producing a cheap butter substitute, margarine, for the growing European working class. Anthony Hopkins, *An Economic History of West Africa* (New York, 1975), 129.

82. G.I. Jones, "Ibo Land Tenure," *Africa* 19 (1949), 313.

83. Amadiume, *Male Daughters*, 29.

84. Ibid.

85. Afigbo, "Southeastern Nigeria in the 19th Century," 451.

86. Jones, "Ibo Land Tenure," 311, fn. 1.

87. Uchendu, *The Igbo of Southeast Nigeria*, 24.

88. Ibid., 29.

89. The Portuguese brought cassava from America. It became an important food crop because of its drought resistance and high per-acre yield. Despite its utility cassava was considered an inferior crop associated with urban poverty. Ohadike discovered that it spread after labor shortages following the devastation of the Influenza Pandemic. D.C. Ohadike, "The Influenza Pandemic of 1918–1919 and the Spread of Cassava Cultivation on the Lower Niger: A Study in Historical Linkages," *Journal of African History* 22 (1981): 379–91.

90. Uchendu, *Igbo People*, 25.

91. Ibid., 24.

92. Afigbo, "Southeastern Nigeria in the 19th Century," 450–51. As with many aspects of Igbo culture, the farming practices varied with the village-group. This is a general description not intended to be definitive, but to give some sense of the division of tasks and interdependence of male and female agricultural labor.

93. Uchendu, *The Igbo of Southeast Nigeria*, 40.

94. Age grades were broad groups of men who were born within a certain period. For example, one group would include all the men born between 1920 and 1930. These men would remain in this particular group throughout their lives, moving from youth to intermediate

to elder. Each group had particular functions and prestige within the village. See Cole and Aniakor, *Igbo Arts*, 118.

95. Uchendu, *Igbo of Southeast Nigeria*, 86.

96. Jones, "Igbo Land Tenure," 315. The men of Agbaja were known for being blacksmiths.

97. This system of migrant labor, which predated colonialism, seems to support Hopkins' contention that an African labor market predated colonialism. Anthony Hopkins, *An Economic History of West Africa* (New York, 1975), 20.

98. Ibid., 96.

99. Uchendu, *The Igbo of Southeast Nigeria*, 92.

100. Ibid., 52.

101. For a complex discussion of "wealth in people" which creatively uses Marxist theory see Jeff Guy, "Analyzing Pre-Capitalist Societies," *Journal of Southern African Studies* 14, 1 (October 1987): 22; Beverly Grier, "Invisible Hand: The Political Economy of Child Labour in Colonial Africa." *Journal of Southern African Studies* 20, 1 (1994): 31.

102. This is a wooden house-like structure to which harvested yams are tied. This allows the yams to be stored until eaten without rotting, as they would if left in the ground.

103. For a discussion of this concept, see J.I. Guyer, "Wealth in People and Self-Realization in Equatorial Africa," *Man* (n.s.) 28 (1993): 243–65.

104. Amadiume, *Male Daughters*, 29.

105. Isichei, *The Ibo People and the Europeans: The Genesis of a Relationship to 1906* (New York, 1973), 33.

106. In most of Igboland yams would rot if left in the ground and therefore were removed during the dry season. As a system of storage they were tied to the walls of a wooden house, called a yam barn, where they remained dry and free from rot until eaten. The larger a man's yam barn the wealthier he was.

107. Jeff Guy, "Gender Oppression in Southern African Societies" in *Women and Gender in Southern Africa, to 1945*, ed. Cheryl Walker (Capetown, 1991), 33–47.

108. T. Uzodinma Nwala, *Igbo Philosophy* (Lagos, Nigeria, 1985), 191.

109. Afigbo, "Southeastern Nigeria in the 19th Century," 442.

110. G.I. Jones, *Report of the Position, Status and Influence of Chiefs and Natural Rulers in the Eastern Region of Nigeria* (Enugu, 1956).

111. Amadiume, *Male Daughters*, 31.

112. Talbot, *Peoples of Southern Nigeria*, vol. 3, 775.

113. The Nri were the sacred "kings" of Igboland. Historians feel that they were connected to the society unearthed in Thurston Shaw's Igbo Ukwu excavations. They were regarded throughout Igboland as a sacred elite and frequently performed particular ritualistic functions throughout the region. For further discussion of the Nri, see Afigbo, *Ropes of Sand*, 33ff.

114. Talbot, *Peoples of Southern Nigeria*, vol. 3: 775.

115. C.K. Meek, *Law and Authority*, 181–82.

116. Amadiume, *Male Daughters*, 29ff.

117. Cole and Aniakor, *Igbo Arts*, 5.

118. This village-group had the biggest market in Udi and it was completely generated by the slave trade. Isichei, *Igbo Worlds*, 76.

119. Interview with Paul Nwanba, Umuaga, Udi, 16 June 1973, as cited in Isichei, *Igbo Worlds*, 76.

120. *Ndi Ishi Ani* were the elderly men. Ibid., 73.

121. Jones, *Influence of Chiefs*, 16–17.

122. Ibid., 17.

123. Talbot, *The Peoples of Southern Nigeria*, 775, 778.

124. Ibid., 778.

125. Afigbo, *Ropes of Sand*, 126.

126. The women's crop was the cocoa yam which had its own ritual and proscriptions. These, however, lacked the prestige of the "male" yam. For a discussion of the gendered distinctions of these yams see Ibid., 127–28, and Amadiume, *Male Daughters*, 29.

127. Afigbo, *Ropes of Sand*, 127–28.

128. Yams are grown under huge mounds. Above the ground they grow long vines that are supported by sticks. Hence, a thousand "growing sticks" means a thousand yams, a considerable bounty. Talbot, *The Peoples of Southern Nigeria*, 778.

129. Dunbar Moodie makes this point. Moodie and Ndatshe, *Going for Gold*, 38.

130. For a discussion of these rites, see Cole and Aniakor, *Igbo Arts*, Chap. 4, especially 24–32.

131. This interpretation of *Ikenga* is based on my reading of Cole and Aniakor, *Igbo Arts*, 24–34.

132. Nwala, *Igbo Philosophy*, 194 and others. Uchendu, *Igbo of Southeast Nigeria*, Chap. 1; Cole and Aniakor, *Igbo Arts*, 24.

# 2

# "Chiefs," Slaves, Forced Labor, and Rural Resistance: Labor and the Contested Birth of the Colonial State, Udi 1909–1915

The disruptions of the turn of the century were insignificant when compared to the raw violence that introduced Udi to British rule. From 1904 to 1913 the colonial army cut a bloody swath throughout Igboland, forced, by the lack of an Igbo centralized state, to conquer the area piecemeal—village-group by village-group, village by village, quarter by quarter. The conquest proved ephemeral as villages conquered one month would rise up the next causing the army to retrace its steps over and over again.

But the most visceral and protracted violence of colonial rule was yet to come. It followed the institutionalization of the state on the local level. This was the "invention" of the so-called "Native Authorities," those colonial chiefs whose brief would be the daily and most intimate operations of the unlawful and brutal state. As noted earlier, in Udi there were many positioned to assume this role. For them wealth from the slave and palm trades had created prestige and considerable political power. But custom and political culture circumscribed their powers in deference to the diffuse governing process of Igboland. Now, the new state presented an opportunity for them to "reinvent" themselves, with more power, jurisdiction, and tyranny than could ever be exercised before. British military officers, who had been delegated as political officials, hardly knew where they were, much less anything about the people they had conquered. They were imbued with the power and arrogance of the machine gun, and identified "influential men" they assumed to be chiefs. After all, "all Africans had chiefs" and if they didn't in actuality, they *should have* in reality. Thus many *Ogaranyan* became "chiefs," finding in the embrace of colonialism the powers which their people refused to concede to them before the conquest.

The organizational philosophy that guided the political reconstruction of Igboland was "indirect rule," a concept that incorporated local "men of prominence" in the governing project. This was a partnership of despotism between an outlaw state and the local collaborators that it recognized. Further elaboration would follow in 1914 when the architect of "indirect rule," Frederick Lugard, came from northern Nigeria and fused the administrations of the north and south according to the political model of the centralized, Islamic north. But ruling southeastern Nigeria proved to be a "unique" experience fraught with pitfalls and embarrassing outbursts of local indignation. These outbursts threw into stark relief the weakness of the nascent colonial state. It was difficult to tread softly on local conventions and negotiate new contradictions.

At the center of the decision to incorporate local leaders into the colonial state was the intersection of labor and the land. Administrators feared that land alienation and sale to expatriate firms for mines and plantations would undermine the political authority of "chiefs" in their villages, whose power was allegedly based on their allocation of growing rights to families on communal land. Officials assumed that any policy that alienated and sold land undermined the "chiefs'" powers and reduced their effectiveness as partners in the preservation of the social order. This erroneous analysis of "traditional" power relations would not be abandoned until the government anthropological investigations following the "Women's War."[1] At that time women, who were often victimized by the "chiefs" and court messengers, revolted in disgust against the "chiefs" and taxation, and brought down the entire chief system with them.

In the initial and subsequent periods, much of the "chiefs'" power concerned the question of labor—supplying the thousands of workers needed by a state operating where no labor market existed. As "Native Authorities," the "chiefs" relished this new access to the labor-power of their erstwhile neighbors and often seized the moment to appropriate it for their individual projects.[2] In Nkanu, where Chukwuani Nwangwu secured an appointment, *Ohu* or slaves, fell victim to forced labor and the endless petty but disruptive abuses of a man made too powerful, too soon. While in Agbaja, a more calculating Onyeama coerced his people for state projects while seducing them with his patronage.[3] He carefully plotted his ascent to become powerful paramount chief.

For those so anointed, the tasks of governing were formidable and risky, for despite the military superiority of the state, Europeans were too few when one's villagers decided to end, once and for all, a "chief's" despotic rule. Thus, while "chiefs" used the colonial state to create far more than customary power, they could not earn prestige and authority in their villages unless they fulfilled Igbo notions of authority. The ability to mediate these two realities was based on the political sophistication of the chief, his access to important state functionaries, and the extent to which he could fulfill the goals and concerns of his people. The people of Udi, more Nkanu than Agbaja, made it very, very difficult for wealthy men called *Ogaranyan* to rule, and their resistance limited the nature of "indirect rule." To them the insatiable demand for labor was the most bitter violation of their freedom. They were required to supply it gratis, for long and unpredictable periods, often far away from their homes, and under the worst of conditions. And usually the same chiefs who seized them ran the labor camps where they lived as extensions of their "Native Courts," and served as paymasters. In violation of all conventions, labor systems, and local regulations, "chiefs" pulled men and women into the service of the state. The demand was almost immediate—even as the conquest was still in process. People were drafted to carry military equipment, clear roads and streams, and construct government rest houses. For those villages that fought the invasion, a stint of forced labor was most often their punishment. The work was hard and demanding. It was very difficult to see the difference between conscripted labor and the slavery whose destruction was promoted as the *raison d'être* of the conquest. Clearly the abolitionist impulse of the conquest was nominal, for consumption back home and ultimately not real, for state officials all recognized that the only way to get unskilled African labor was through force.

The people's reaction to these depredations was formidable and timely. During World War I when the British opened the Cameroonian front to the east in the fall of 1914, South Nkanu's people erupted in a vigorous but doomed outburst of retribution. For several months, a once cocky Lord Frederick, then Governor-General, Lugard had to concede to his superiors at the Colonial Office that he had no control over the area. The railway survey and mine construction had to await the conclusion of "this Udi business."[4] Chiefs were slain, courthouses burned, and Chief Chukwuani, who had ingratiated himself with the conquerors as a guide through his own villages, escaped, within an inch of his life. Onyeama, on the other hand, was more successful in fusing Igbo conceptions of authority with the despotic powers authorized by the colonial state. He was richly rewarded for preventing his people from joining the fray.

This is the context in which the Enugu coal mines began operations. Their working class was forged in the crucible of violence, social trauma, and imperial arrogance. Conscripts and prisoners made the first cuts into the earth. A regime of force, of "colonial despotism," permeated the labor process in the mines and was anchored in the coercive laws and militarism of early colonial rule. This production regime was a racialized system of industrial discipline in which "force prevails over consent" and "one racial group dominated through political, legal, and economic rights denied to the other."[5] The doctrine of "indirect rule" that pushed workers into the mines was duplicated within the mines as an industrial concept. It structured the daily deployment of labor, the labor process, systems of worker control, and industrial relations at the colliery. Specifically, management responsibilities were shared by a hierarchy of state functionaries, colonial chiefs, and European and "native" staff. Connections between the "native" staff and "chiefs" were sometimes personal and intimate, thereby insuring that industrial discipline grew roots as well in the rural villages, and rural systems of control found expression in the industry. Relations between the "native" staff and the workers were mutually hostile because the organization of power in production gave "native" bosses the same type of predatory autonomy in the workplace as the chiefs had in the village.

In one more important respect "indirect rule" made its imprint on the industry. In 1914 officials reorganized many chieftaincies and "Native Courts." The state arbitrarily grouped clusters of villages into administrative units under a paramount "chief." The groupings had more to do with administrative expediency and the limits on a district officer's ability to supervise numbers of villages than any pre-existing affiliation between village-groups. Without any scientific knowledge of the peoples of the area, the state introduced the category of "clan," which, in the European mind, suggested some intermediate social stage between the "tribe" and empire. In one fell, ill-informed swoop, colonial administrators transformed Udi regionalism, in which political alliances were fluid and temporary, into a fixed colonial category, "clan." A village's ability to negotiate temporary alliances, of a military or political nature, which was an adjustment to the uncertainties of the late-nineteenth century, now ended. As a new colonial category, the "clan" initially had little legitimacy, but industrial policy and this reorganization of "native" administration planted seeds of self-identity that were both strengthened and undermined by the exigencies of the working class in the mines.

The chapter begins in 1909 with the conquest and subsequent reconstruction of Udi. This sets the context for the supply, control, and activism of labor in the mines, which opened in 1915. It introduces the institutions of "indirect rule," the colonial "chiefs" and the Native Courts, and describes their role in recruiting and controlling labor. The political reconstruction of Igboland occurred in two phases, from 1909 to 1913 and from 1914 to 1930. Each phase had different implications for the concentration of wealth and political power in the rural areas, and the development of systems of labor mobilization, control, and resistance. The first phase featured the state's frantic attempts to stabilize rural society by appointing "chiefs" and using a series of coercive ordinances to force labor into early infrastructural projects. In Udi several prominent *Ogaranyan* embraced conquering armies and were rewarded with appointments that positioned them to accelerate their concentration of power, wealth, and influence in their villages. The ensuing corruption, extortion, and bribery sharpened the contradictions that were already visible in preconquest Udi. In outlining the second phase, from 1914 to 1930, the chapter focuses on the "early" period from 1914 to 1916 when Lugard's northern model of centralized rural power reduced state surveillance of the courts and permitted an elaboration and intensification of chiefs' abuses and corruption.

Britain's West African policy was still being shaped when the colonial armies entered Udi. Anne Phillips argues that until World War I, many in the Colonial Office still assumed that the development of the "tropical estates" could best occur through private British capital invested in mining and agriculture. The implications of this policy were the dissolution of communal land tenure, the development of a market in land, and the dispossession of village producers, who would become a landless laboring class. Officials also assumed that a similar process of proletarianization would follow the emancipation of the large slave populations found throughout Igboland, but especially clustered in the Niger Delta. But the possibility was gradually viewed with foreboding when it was realized that "African workers" would be beyond the authoritarian controls of the village chief and the other political and social institutions that ordered rural village life.[6] By 1912 some policymakers feared that proletarianization would generate such far-reaching social transformations that it would undermine the economic and social stability of the colony. Containing this process might have been beyond the capabilities of the nascent colonial state which, at any rate, could not exert the coercion implicit in the "wage relation."[7] The state had, therefore, to rely on the assistance of precolonial leaders in preserving social order. Since officials assumed that his political authority rested on his allocation of growing rights to families on communal land, any policy that alienated and sold land destroyed his power and hence usefulness as a partner in preserving social order.

While the specific policy towards communal land and the "chiefs" emanated out of Whitehall, it was encouraged by the "man on the spot," the field officer. It reflected less about the social realities of Igboland than a muddled British attempt to build and maintain a rural fantasy that existed only in their imagination. "Indirect rule" was rooted in the "invention of Africa," which incorporated Darwinist conceptions of social evolution interlaced with Catonist views of rural life, a life at home in England that was swept away by the harshness of industrial revolution. For the field officer, "colonial Africa" held all the personal ambiguities and contradictions about nature and civilization, distorted mythologies and racist constructions of early-twentieth-century Europe. This "imagined Africa" had no place for an African working class, a "detribalized" social strata, strategic and modern in its economic role, and progressive in its political impact on rural communities.

In the anxious years of the Great War, the opening of the Enugu Government Colliery industry was impatiently awaited by the expatriate commercial community and the Colonial Office as a local source of coal to feed the Nigerian railway and complete the infrastructure needed to effect the evacuation of Nigeria's agricultural and mineral exports. Thus, it was with great concern that the Colonial Office watched unfolding events in the industry, and evaluated the competencies of local managers and political officers in dealing with local labor. This was the only coal mine in West Africa and the Colonial Office did not permit local officials to jeopardize this important resource.

The chapter pulls together the threads of discontent and unrest that produce the uprising of 1913/14. The location of the uprising in the slaveholding regions of Nkanu, and not Agbaja, reveals the constraints that communities placed on the powers of colonial chiefs. In Nkanu, a large number of *Ogaranyan*, and the sharp class divisions between slave and free, prevented Chief Chukwuani from establishing effective control. But in Agbaja, an impoverished area with a few "Big Men," one man, Onyeama Onwusi, successfully prevented his people from rising up.

## "IMAGINING" IGBOLAND: BRITISH RACIAL IDEOLOGY AND THE POLITICAL RECONSTRUCTION OF UDI

The people here apparently before the advent of the Government were an unruly lot of marauders and their so-called Chiefs had little or no influence over them. Commanding Officer, West African Frontier Force, 9 November 1914.[8]

The image of Africa, in short, was largely created in Europe to suit European needs—sometimes material needs, more often intellectual needs. When these needs allowed, it might touch on reality; as it did in the empirical victory of tropical medicine. Otherwise the European Afrikaanschauung was part of a European weltanschauung, and it was warped as necessary to make it fit into the larger whole.[9]

The invasion of the Igbo hinterland did not actually commence until 1900. But it was merely the culmination of an encroaching colonialism spanning the second half of the nineteenth century. This intrusion was marked at one end by the establishment of the small British consulate to the west in Eko (Lagos) in 1851, and at the other by the termination of the charter of the Royal Niger Company in 1900. In the interim there was the economic recession of the 1870s and the scramble for Africa in the 1880s, when British merchants on the coast and the staff of the various "informal" imperial entities became a powerful lobby for imperial expansion. On the Niger River Sir George Goldie amalgamated the competing British trading firms into the Royal Niger Company and succeeded in 1886 in obtaining a charter that ceded both total political power and an economic monopoly in the lower Niger region.[10] Again the deprecations inflicted on the Igbo peoples on the Niger, in both their political and commercial dealings with Goldie's company, were rationalized by the ending of the slave trade and spreading civilization.[11]

To the east of the Niger, an earlier "informal" British presence was institutionalized in 1891 with the appointment of Major Claude Macdonald as commissioner and consul general over a new entity called the Oil Rivers Protectorate. While initially the protectorate status was defined rather narrowly to include only foreign control of external relations, by the mid-1890s British colonial officers were defining it to mean "unrestricted sovereignty."[12]

In the decade of the 1890s, the protectorate extended control farther inland by gradually destroying the sovereignty of all the major middleman trading states in the Delta.[13] The penetration of the interior followed two trajectories to the Cross and Imo Rivers, both important waterways into palm-producing regions.[14] Coastal British traders applauded the fall of first one, and then another, wealthy African merchant of the coastal trading kingdoms under the heels of "gunboat diplomacy."[15] Even when a ruler tried to submit peacefully, the British preferred total military subjugation to foreclose any semblance of residual civil rights, an important aspect of the establishment of the colonial state.[16] At the turn of the century, the Cross River area became an imperial preoccupation because it was considered the gateway to northeastern Igboland, and the citadel of the "notorious" Aro slaving empire.

This expansionism coincided with a new imperialist thrust promoted by Joseph Chamberlain, colonial secretary from 1895–1903.[17] Chamberlain's appointment to the Colonial Office symbolized a new imperial urgency in response to a growing German economic presence in West Africa.[18] Chamberlain initially envisioned developing the colonial "tropical estate" with infusions of private capital for plantation and mine development. The state's role would be to fund those crucial and expensive infrastructural projects such as the railways. Lurking behind his advocacy for state-owned railways was a concern that private capital was too ineffective to handle such pivotal ventures.[19] This skepticism would remain in the Colonial Office throughout World War I and would influence the ownership of the Enugu colliery.

In 1900, imperial expansionists confronted reluctance among important sectors of the British ruling class to support military annexation. Politicians and their supporters among the manufacturing and commercial classes launched a campaign to generate popular support for expansion. One part of this campaign involved creating a heinous foe whose removal was imperative to further the interests of British trade and the civilizing mission. The Aro, whose commercial and judicial role in the Igbo hinterland had been known to Europeans since the mid-nineteenth century, were suddenly maligned as an impenetrable barrier to British access to markets in the interior. They became a

> sinister "fetish" power, deeply involved with slave trading, indelibly opposed to European penetration and wielding very great influence over the politics of other states.[20]

The hundreds of village-groups who used the Aro oracle were characterized as poor, illiterate victims to an insidious, manipulative power. Not coincidentally, the Cross River area, their homeland, was the gateway to the rich palm markets of the interior and had to be opened to the "civilizing" influence of western commerce. Now this trading system, which for several centuries had brought European goods to the far reaches of Igboland, was an obstacle to "free trade." The Aro's role in resolving disputes among Igboland and Ibibioland's fragmented village-groups became a sinister manipulation of a "childlike," "gullible" people. As Isichei has argued, to the British they symbolized all that was wrong with Igboland and had to be eliminated.[21]

As elsewhere in Africa, abolition became the facade for imperial conquest giving the campaign a moral dimension. It was a crusade to abolish the slave trade as well as "the fetish . . . known as the 'Long Ju-ju,' which causes many evils."[22] With the Aro objectified as slave dealers, practitioners of human sacrifice, and "war lords" interfering with free trade, the state was free now to release unrestrained violence against their villages.[23] Predictably many of the Aro's undesirable characteristics were generalized to all of Igboland. In the discourse of both popular literature and official correspondence, the Igbo were the epitome of the "barbaric, uncivilized, immoral Africans" who needed colonial tutelage to protect them from themselves. It was the "white man's burden" to save these people and drag them, albeit "kicking and screaming," into the "civilized" world.

The punitive expedition against the Aro launched the first full-scale invasion of Igboland. It was authorized in late 1901 after intensive lobbying by Macdonald's successor, Sir Ralph Moor, consul of the Oil Rivers Protectorate from 1899, and the British merchant community in the Niger Delta. In preparation the protectorate had been transferred from the Foreign Office to the Colonial Office, and with the addition of the territories controlled by the Royal Niger Company, was renamed the Protectorate of Southern Nigeria.

The expedition, launched in November of 1901, was far from conclusive when it ended the following March.[24] The oracle was destroyed and several prominent Aro leaders executed, but the British only succeeded in forcing the oracle and slave market underground. The limited success of the expedition was an omen of the difficulties to come in the conquest of Igboland, but this was neither recognized nor heeded. Consequently, for the greater part of the first decade of the new century the West African Frontier Force (WAFF) was involved in the conquest of Igboland, conducting a village-by-village war to "open" the area to British commerce, administration, and "civilization." As Isichei notes, victory continued to be "curiously impermanent" because even after the razing of villages and uprooting of crops, the people "replanted their farms, rebuilt their houses, and failed to appreciate that they were a conquered people."[25]

The conquest of Igboland was rationalized on moral grounds in the racial paternalism so characteristic of this imperialistic period. British perceptions of the Igbo were shaped by a racial ideology rooted in the technological superiority of their society,[26] pseudo-scientific notions of racial evolution,[27] and idealized notions of a timeless yet capricious peasantry. Social Darwinist hierarchies, further mythologized by sensationalist speculation and reports of missionaries and abolitionists, were reinforced by travelers' reports of rampant slave trading, widespread slavery, human sacrifice, headhunting, and cannibalism.[28] These allegations were embellished by "observations" of pro-expansionist merchants, government officials, and missionaries. As this "primitive" image assumed moral decay, missionary societies found comfort in a coalition with commercial annexationists and military adventurers. Similarly, abolitionists played an important role in mobilizing broad popular support for the annexation of territory from Lagos to the Eastern Provinces, the area east of the Niger River.[29]

In the early years government policy was shaped by the "man on the spot," who came from the older, non-commercial middle classes of the church, armed forces, civil service, and learned professions.[30] They had a particular perspective on rural Africa that they considered static, timeless, and controlled by autocratic chiefs. These were the ideals embraced by the man who became the architect for "indirect rule" in Nigeria—Frederick Lugard. In 1897 Chamberlain chose Frederick

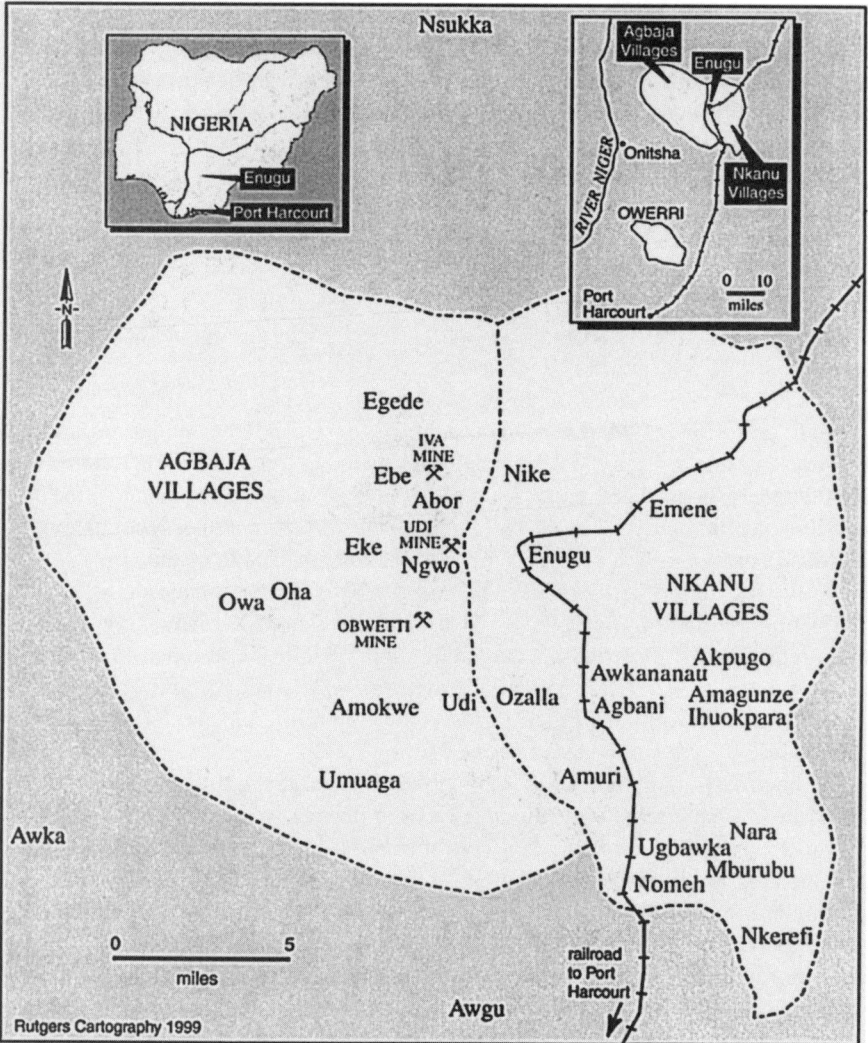

**Map 2.1** Udi District, circa 1917, showing villages mentioned in the chapter. (Rutgers University Cartography)

Lugard as commissioner for the Nigerian hinterland to implement his plans for the colony. As the chief government representative in southeastern Nigeria, Lugard played a special role in the evolution of labor policy and the opening of the colliery. In many respects, Lugard was quite typical of the military/political officer of the early colonial state, resembling in class origin, ethos, and training, the bulk of the colonial civil service. His father was both a priest and military officer in India where he grew up, and was typical of the type of man who entered the colonial service.[31] Lugard's ideas on governing expressed the ethos of this strata who saw themselves as impartial, above politics and guided by a sense of "fair play" and "justice" They understood administration as ameliorative and protective: it corrected the disruption and exploitation introduced by uncontrolled changes and the intrusion of individual selfishness. Their self-image was suffused with moral earnestness and self-righteousness, summed up in the imperial ideals of "trusteeship" and the "civilizing mission."[32]

After establishing and successfully commanding the West African Frontier Force, Lugard became high commissioner in northern Nigeria, a post he retained from 1900–1906. During this time he adapted the system of indirect rule to incorporate the political systems of the Sokoto Caliphate, the large imperial Muslim state established by the nineteenth-century Fulani jihads. He promoted the administration of state power through identified local government structures. There in the Muslim north's authoritarian and military hierarchy of the emirates, he found ideal structures to institutionalize his native administration. A clearly defined ruling class was willing to share power, thereby becoming the local level of the colonial state. Lugard's experiences in northern Nigeria influenced his response to the complexities of southern Nigeria. In 1912, he was charged to reconcile the disparate administrations of Northern and Southern Provinces during the amalgamation of the colony of Nigeria. The implications of his disdain for the south on the governmental model he imposed on Igboland will be explored below.

To colonial administrators, Igboland's political fragmentation, complex ambiguous political structure, and multiple levels of decision-making were political chaos. It indicated Igbo incapacity to rule. Lugard, like most of Nigeria's field officers, assumed that the African had an "essential incompetence in dealing with the evils of his own society," and therefore required the benevolent, though necessarily brutal, tutelage of British rule.[33] Thus, as Crawford Young has argued, "the new colonial regime, no matter how harsh and extractive, was axiomatically beneficial to the African subject."[34]

In the racialized discourse of the conquest, subordination was "frequently associated with childlike immaturity" and was represented as weakness or effeminacy.[35] As Dubow argued about racial discourse in early-twentieth-century South Africa, the intersection of imperial with racist thought merged in Lugard's "dual mandate," was rooted in scientific racist notions:

> Deeply embedded evolutionist assumptions together with the doctrine of "survival of the fittest" came to be applied to the human situation. . . . Racial thought . . . drew heavily on the metaphor of the family, an area where subordination was legitimized. Imagery derived from the biological sciences and the family gave rise to ubiquitous notions of the "dependent" or "child races."[36]

As "children," the Igbo were still "dangerous" and needed the tough, ruthless hand of the state or the "chief" to "force" them to mature. Colonial officers spoke of their "truculence," "savagery," et cetera. Given these ethno-historical perceptions of the colonial field officer and imperial scholars, it was little wonder that the

Igbo tumbled to the bottom rung of the human evolutionary ladder. They became the repulsive primitive "other" at its lowest level. The Igbo exemplified

> the discrepancy between "civilization" and "Christianity" on the one hand and "primitiveness" and "paganism" on the other, and the demands of "evolution" or "conversion" from the first stage to the second.[37]

These distinctions, so consonant with imperial economic designs, gained sustenance at the trough of scientific racism, and fascinated colonial officials as they comfortably settled on the upper rung of the evolutionary chain.[38]

The early proposals for political reconstruction emanated from this ethos and a series of ill-informed and inaccurate perceptions of the political organization of Igboland. The diffuse political structure was far less intelligible to colonial officials who craved order and clear lines of authority than the centralized systems of the Muslim north or the Yoruba states in the west. Further, coming from a culture of parliamentary monarchy, colonialist administrators looked for distinct institutional indicators of power and authority. Armed with their rural fantasies (and nightmares) and notions of "authentic" African "primitivism," they presumed that all African societies had indigenous chiefs who could appropriate communal labor and exercise necessary though tyrannical controls. Using these simplistic and erroneous assumptions, and blinded by imperial arrogance from recognizing their own ignorance, these early officials blundered their way through the first years of imperial reconstruction, creating "chiefs" along the way.

In theory "indirect rule" allowed the fragile new state to use indigenous governing classes to rule. It was a pragmatic philosophy because human and financial resources were wanting. Thus, the first local colonial government institutions in Udi were the "Native Courts," modeled after the coastal equity courts of the nineteenth century,[39] which adjudicated disputes between Europeans and the prominent local traders who led "houses."[40] The coastal pattern of state support for authoritarian local rulers was projected into the Igbo interior, where political power was diffuse and a political culture of popular participation prevailed. The imposition of this foreign political model would undermine, rather than foster, rural stability.

## THE CONQUEST OF UDI, 1904–1910

The first labor demands on Udi began with the conquest. While being bludgeoned into submission by the army, the people were forced, in defeat, to supply labor for a plethora of colonial projects. Under the law of conquest the military/political officer had total discretion over the intensity of state violence. There was "no semblance of rights in the hands of the subject community."[41] Since it had long been established that Africans were "barbarians," and any degree of state brutality was acceptable, villages were burned even when people surrendered. Looting and torture were not infrequent.[42] One man recalled that even the animals were shot.[43] But the trauma of this "war" did not translate into an easy victory. Annual expeditions against Udi villages continued from 1904 to 1908: (1) The Onitsha Hinterland Expedition of 1904 captured western Udi and Nsukka; (2) The Bende-Onitsha Hinterland Expedition of 1905 brought the eastern part of Udi under colonial control; (3) The expedition of 1906–1907 annexed central and southern Udi; and (4) in the final invasion of the Niger-Cross River and Northern Hinterland Expedition of 1908, the armies moved into the northern reaches of Udi and Nsukka and defeated the remaining village-groups in South Nkanu.[44] Guns ablaze, military officials identified "chiefs," gave them a "warrant" of office, and moved on to the next area. Although the first political officers were military officials, most village-groups were "barely" under imperial rule. The South Nkanu area, some distance from military headquarters in Udi, was especially problematic. The area's proximity to the Aro slaving networks led the *Ogaranyan* to be especially resistant to antislaving proclamations. Further, Nkanu's large slave populations began to exhibit signs of restiveness when "traditional" systems of their masters' control—coercion, extortion, and sale—were prohibited by the new state. The alchemy of these two developments made this a contentious area of state control.

For Udi these four years of conquest were an apocalypse.[45] The battles themselves were traumatic, aiming precision weapons and cannon against people with Dane guns and spears. Many times villages amassed to confront their enemy but were frightened off by the loud sounds of their weapons. Some, feeling they had no possibility of winning military confrontations, attempted to reach a peaceful accommodation. Others tragically confronted the West African Frontier Force. In desperation they fought with magic.[46] The trauma of this experience is engraved in the memory of old men who recall a particularly brutal officer in northern Nkanu as "The Destroyer."[47]

As the armies moved into the hinterland of southeastern Nigeria, military/political officials established Native Courts. These courts, headed by colonial appointed "chiefs," combined executive, judicial, and administrative functions, and violated the precolonial system. The court was promoted as a stabilizing force for conquered territories permitting the exercise of "customary" law.[48] But as Mamdani has emphasized in his recent study,[49] the content of "customary" law was far from settled by the turn of the century.[50] This was especially the case in Udi where the diffuse political system struggled to accommodate the concentration of wealth in the *Ogaranyan* social class. Village struggles between the *Ogaranyan* and the *isi ani* (elders) over the nature of the political system were ignored when a wealthy man was appointed colonial chief. To the British, "customary law" was whatever the "big men" claimed it to be. The *Ogaranyan* took the opportunity to claim as customary every right that would enhance their control over others, particularly those socially weak.[51]

By the conquest of Udi, the "Native Authority" system had evolved through a series of laws ranging from the Native Courts Proclamation of 1900 to the radical centralization of the courts by Lugard following the amalgamation of southern and northern Nigeria in 1914.[52] The courts of 1900 fell into two categories: minor courts of local chiefs whose members were appointed by the district commissioner but with a rotating presidency, and native councils, similarly composed of colonial "chiefs" but presided over by the district commissioner in his headquarters. The jurisdiction of both varied. Minor courts could only try minor civil and criminal cases, while the native council could consider major criminal cases, impose up to two years' imprisonment, and levy large fines. In 1903 the district commissioner became a member of all Native Courts in his district, a policy that aimed to increase the use of the courts as a vehicle for administration.[53] By 1906, following the amalgamation of the Southern Nigeria Protectorate and the Lagos Colony and Protectorate into the Colony and Protectorate of Southern Nigeria, the judicial functions of all warrant chiefs were subsumed under the Nigerian judicial system to reduce the abuses that were already visible. Thus the Supreme Court had the right to review any decision made by a Native Court, and the provincial commissioner and assistant district commissioner became *ex officio* members. The commissioner could become president, at his discretion, of any court in his area.[54]

These provisions did not prevent the courts from becoming fiefdoms controlled by the newly appointed "chiefs." The corruption of the courts was facilitated by their financial underpinnings, the "native treasury," whose court fees and fines paid the salaries and operating expenses for the court. The treasury was not covered by central auditing and was clearly subject to abuse.[55]

In addition to the "chiefs" whose appointments were legalized by a "warrant" or license to rule, there were the court clerks and messengers. In many cases the court clerk, the only literate member of the court, controlled the illiterate chief, and was often a "king maker" supporting the candidacy of prospective "chiefs." Litigants plied him with money and gifts since the outcome of a case could depend on whatever he recorded in the court books and on his "interpretation" of the "law."[56] Because the clerk received all written government communications demanding labor and various services, he kept all records of court proceedings, and collected fines. Many of these men were either from areas of Igboland with mission schools or from other parts of British West Africa.[57] The court messenger served summonses, guarded properties of the court, maintained order at sittings, guarded criminals, and carried messages from the court to village headmen, residents, and the district officer.[58] To the average inhabitant, messengers were a particularly heinous group. When they delivered government notices for forced labor, they terrorized communities, demanding bribes and "blind eye" gifts not to conscript villagers for government projects. Such a stint of forced labor would deprive the household of male labor, so crucial to the economy of the family and village.

Chieftaincy appointments in Udi usually endorsed *Ogaranyan*. The experience of Udi's two most powerful chiefs, Chukwuani Nwangwu and Onyeama Owusu, told below, shows the endless forms of corruption permitted under the "Native Court." The system held little resemblance to the preconquest legal process. The courts violated the most fundamental principles of the Igbo political system—the diffusion of power and broad-based political participation. Throughout Igboland the few strong "chiefs" had more ritual than political authority.[59] Although court appointments eventually rivaled title societies as symbols of prestige and vehicles of power, they lacked the ritual sanction that connected the indigenous system to the ancestors. Even though the principles of age as status were being challenged by "New Men" of wealth, older men were still respected for their age because they were close to the ancestors as well as an organic part of the community. While the oldest man of the senior lineage in most village-groups had certain ceremonial powers, his position "was not wholly or even mainly a political office, but signified the ritual status which its occupant enjoyed through his standing in the genealogical history of the group."[60] Even Big Men in many Udi villages, especially in the Nkanu area, whose wealth or military skill had earned for them some political power, nonetheless exercised their influence through recognized institutions and legitimate political processes, even as they were evolving. Certainly, *Ozo* title men and *Ogaranyan* in general had prestige and influence in village-based democracies, but their opinions could be ignored if considered unsound by the village council. The implications of imposing such an abrasive colonial political system on the people of Udi would be suggested by the period of unrest during the war. Before then, however, the people would be introduced to the "civilizing" influence of British rule through the brutality of the conquest.

## THE FIRST PHASE: *OGARANYAN* TO "WARRANT CHIEF," 1909–1914

Since the conquest was neither expeditious nor definitive, resistance did not end when initial hostilities concluded. While some villages used passive resistance, others, although defeated, remained truculent. Among the most difficult section to subdue was the South Nkanu area where powerful *Ogaranyan* headed households with large slave populations and many wives. Located to the east of the Udi escarpment, it was invaded in 1908. While some *Ogaranyan* threw in their lot with the colonialists, others continued to resist, especially those deeply involved in the domestic slave market. Two of the most remote Nkanu village groups, Nkerefi and Ihuokpara, both heavily committed to the slave trade, were actually beyond effective government control. These people, whose social structure was drastically transformed by the palm and slave trades, were extremely resilient. With considerable social stratification and a powerful merchant capitalist presence, these village-groups attempted to preserve the slave trade, their primary means of accumulation and an important source of labor for "Big Men." In some districts, the West African Frontier Force (WAFF) singled out slavers for special "treatment" and slave markets were destroyed.[61] The Amurri village-group, although visited several times in 1909, "refused to recognize the government in any way."[62] A similar fate befell Nkerefi, which was burned in June 1908 because it confronted the district commissioner and persisted in selling slaves at the Uburu market.[63]

The government set up headquarters in Udi on the escarpment that separated Agbaja from Nkanu. Many of the more remote villages correctly assessed the practical limitations on the ability of a single white man to closely monitor village affairs and awaited an opportunity to reassert their sovereignty. Overextended and limited by the absence of roads and clear waterways, the district officer could scarcely hope to visit all the areas in his district. Thus the most remote villages such as Nara, Nkerifi, and Ihuokpara were simply "left alone" unless they made some particularly obvious challenge to colonial rule.

With the conquest the echelons of the colonial state erupted like a rolling wave of terror. In 1907/08, in a frenzy of administrative energy, political officials established sixty to seventy courts in the Eastern Provinces alone. Political and administrative authority had to be established as quickly as possible because the army's control was very precarious and vulnerable to reversal in a general insurrection. Weakness, pragmatism, and expediency required the preservation of useful features of precolonial society and the "invention" of others. But the immediate need for unskilled labor required a systemic approach. Labor for the initial short term tasks could be generated by military force but more sustained supplies of unskilled labor, as was needed in railway construction and colliery work, required a more systematic solution. Assuming the presence of coastal political traditions, the military officials believed that they could use the "chiefs'" customary rights to communal labor to recruit workers. In reality such "customary" rights to labor did not exist. Nonetheless, the centralized political structures of the coast became the frame of reference for early labor legislation.

Slavery was at the center of colonial labor policy. It was the most important labor system, and its eradication was given as a reason for the invasion. In many areas it was the foundation for the coercive recruitment of the earliest workers. Several of the earliest laws tied the labor question to the brutality of conquest and gave the government the right to impose a labor punishment on any community found guilty of resisting colonial rule. The Collective Punishment, Unsettled Districts, and Peace Preservation Ordinances, which applied only to the Central and Eastern provinces, "legalized" punitive patrols against insubordinate villages. The Collective Punishments Ordinance (1912) tried to break village solidarity by punishing the whole community for refusing to identify a particular culprit.[64] The Roads and Creeks Proclamation of 1903 gave village "chiefs" the right to demand free labor for government projects. Most often, this became the occasion for work on the chiefs' fields as well.[65]

Although these laws were alleged to legalize "customary" labor practices, they actually introduced a far more authoritarian labor system than ever existed in Udi. This was partially due to the assumption that Udi's "chiefs" resembled the authoritarian Niger Delta "house" heads who ruled over women, slaves, and clients.[66] Slavery policy, emanating from the Delta, was ambivalent. While slavery was an anathema to the "free" labor ideology that colonial authorities used to justify the conquest, they feared that a public emancipation policy would be socially disruptive. Therefore, they merely banned slave trading and slave raids while leaving the institution itself intact. Lugard encouraged the hideous distinction between outlawing the "legal status" of slavery while not abolishing the "institution of domestic slavery."[67] He instructed his aides to "discourage the wholesale assertion of freedom."[68] This position was embodied in the Slave Dealing Proclamation of

1901.[69] But officials feared that even this moderate bill could accelerate the decline of the Delta's house system and passed the Masters and Servants Proclamation in 1901. Like masters and servants laws throughout the empire, this law "captured" labor by making it a breach of contract to desert.[70]

In 1901 they passed the Native House Rule Ordinance which reflected this anxiety about freed slaves.[71] The House Rule Ordinance should not have been applied in the Udi area, which had no "houses," but it became the "common sense" policy of political officers who were startled by the large slave populations in Nkanu. Both the Slave Dealing Proclamation and the House Rule Ordinance became law even though the social and political structure of Igboland was not as centralized as that of the Delta.[72] By using the House Rule Ordinance in concert with the Roads and Creeks Proclamation, the state fused a coercive form of capitalist wage labor and slavery. This wedded slavery to the recruitment of labor and endorsed the powers of slaveholders over their slaves.

In Udi the problem for colonial reconstruction was that no men in positions of leadership had the type of powers the state was prepared to authorize. Nonetheless, prominent men were either co-opted or brushed aside and replaced with collaborators. Officials even insisted that they could identify "house heads" who were in control of these villages. Often powerful *Ogaranyan* secured colonial appointments that further accelerated their acquisition of power.

In Onitsha Province three local men used the recruitment of labor for the colliery to enhance their power and prestige in the region. They sensed the benefits of collaboration early in the conquest and distinguished themselves by convincing their communities to welcome the invaders. While there were undoubtedly many others, these are the most thoroughly documented. Solomon Eze Okoli of Nnobi,[73] Chukwuani Nwangwu of Ozalla,[74] and Onyeama Owusi of Eke,[75] all *Ogaranyan*, were associated in some intimate way with the Aro slaving network. In Nara, a highly populated slaveholding area in South Nkanu, Edeani Chikiri, a renowned slaveholder, was appointed chief. Eze Okoli supplied the first coal workers who came with the new manager from Onitsha in the fall of 1914. Chiefs Onyeama and Chukwuani, both prosperous slaveowners and palm traders, supplied railway workers from the Agbaja and Nkanu areas of Udi. Although both claimed "customary" rights to conscript workers, no *Ogaranyan* could claim labor beyond his own household. Colonial field officers assumed that they were merely exercising the "customary" rights of a "house" head on the coast.

The careers of Chiefs Onyeama and Chukwuani demonstrate how opportunistic, wealthy men manipulated the state to attain far more power than was socially recognized, and attests to the extreme concentration of power encouraged by the Native Court system. Ironically their ascent fulfilled accepted Igbo norms of self-improvement and status development drastically deformed by the new colonial context. The consequences of their individual quests were the destruction of the very political system that promoted these ideals and values.[76] Both Udi chiefs were wealthy farmers and slaveholders before the conquest. Onyeama, whose father was a prosperous farmer and *Ozo* title holder, traded in slaves. He had an apprenticeship with the Aro with whom he had intimate commercial connections and who had a large settlement in Eke, his home town.[77] By the time of the conquest he had already diversified into trading in ivory, ornaments, and an assortment of European items. He used his itinerant trading activities and contacts with the Aro to acquire a considerable amount of wealth while still a young man, as indicated by his acquisition of the prestigious *Ozo* title. Like "New Men" throughout Igboland, the acquisition of a title transformed his wealth into political influence within the broad-based democratic traditions of Eke, his town.[78] However, because of the importance of seniority, intergenerational conflicts between him and the village elders blocked his political ascent. Before the conquest he still did not have the status, influence, and prestige of the older members of the society and was viewed as something of a brash upstart by village councillors.

Much of the information about Chukwuani is anecdotal. He was from the ritual elite; his family produced the important Ani priest of Ozalla, his home town. As a young man he lived for seven years in Arochukwu as a trader.[79] The connection between ritual power and wealth was intimate, and ritual leaders were often able to acquire goods in payment for services rendered. By converting these resources into slaves he produced surpluses that allowed him to purchase titles which conferred political power. Little is known about his other activities except that he owned many slaves and married many wives, further evidence of the material advantages held by the ritual elite. While many of these slaves were used in farm labor, others served as messengers and assistants in policing his area.[80] In Chukwuani's area, slaves, called *Ohu*, were in the majority of some village-groups. The political marginalization of such a large, subordinate community gave Nkanu village politics a heightened instability. The more enlightened members of the slave community quickly understood that without a recognizable legal status slavery was dead. But given the cautionary laws governing colonial slavery, it was incumbent on the slave to "declare" his own freedom. Masters, who often had Native Court appointments, tried to use the courts to crush this activism. The conflict between the two plagued Chukwuani's tenure as a warrant chief.

For both Chukwuani and Onyeama, the appearance of troops in their village was a defining moment, offering new opportunities which they immediately seized. Both assisted the military/political officers of the colonial administration. As chief priest of his town, Chukwuani "readily assumed a role of guiding the British around when they first came into the area."[81] Onyeama, having heard of the devastating power of the colonial army during his trading rounds, advised his village to welcome them rather than fight.[82] As a young titled man this advice must have rankled the authentic village leaders, the headmen, elders, and senior *Ozos*. However, his awareness of the devastating consequences of resistance, confirmed by the refugees running from burned villages and fields, allowed him to carry the village council with him. He then organized the village to welcome the invaders, supplying them with food, labor, and other amenities. Aware that they would appoint someone as local headman to assist in British rule, Onyeama manuevered to become an indispensable partner in enforcing law and order. Although he was obse-

**Photo 2.1** Chief Chukwuani, Nwangwu 1928 (Courtesy of Anayo Enechukwu)

quious in his attention to their needs, much to his consternation, his was not the first warrant appointment in Udi. The first appointment went to one Ozo-Nebechi Okachi,[83] another priest from Oghe village group, the first area occupied by the British.

Onyeama's ascent was tied to Agbaja's position as a labor reserve. Between 1908 and 1914 Onyeama plotted the course of his political ascent with the help of a court messenger, one Ibada of Awka. Idaba directed "important labor-recruitment messages through him and arresting[ed] dissidents in his chiefdom."[84] Even after Onyeama received his appointment in 1910 he continued to curry favor with the

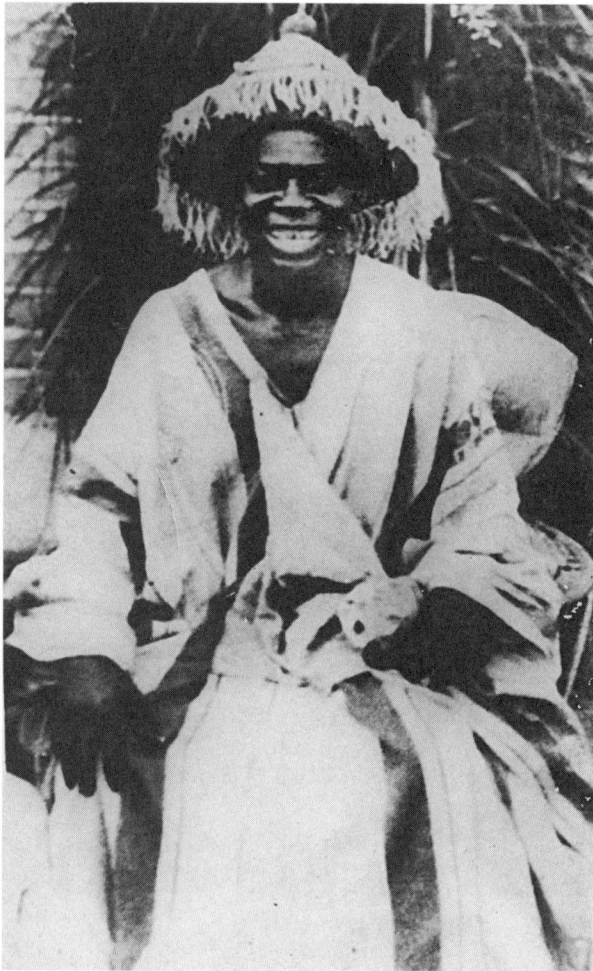

**Photo 2.2** Chief Onyeama Onwusi (Courtesy of Dillibe Onyeama)

political officials.[85] He positioned himself as a broker for both the Agbaja people and government agents:

> To the white man's stewards, he provided eggs and fowls; to other aspiring chiefs, he was the arranger of warrants and the channel of official messages; to traveling officials, he was the best in giving gifts and securing guides; to nearby communities, he offered early warning of offenses likely to anger the British authorities.[86]

Onyeama followed a two-pronged policy of cementing his relationship with specific district officers, and consolidated his power and influence in his and the adjacent villages. This latter process, which had led to his warrant, was facilitated by his position on the Native Court. He sensed that a key element in his relationship with political officials would be his ability to insure that his villages were firmly within the control of the government. To this end he created para-administrative and military bodies that deepened his control over the Agbaja area.[87] He had an intelligence system of spies that informed him of developments within his area, and a group of enforcers, the *Ogwumili*, that he used to collect tribute and terrorize his villages.[88]

**Photo 2.3** Chief Onyeama's Palace, built in 1914, 1977 (Courtesy of Dillibe Onyeama)

The powers Onyeama assumed within his territories were tacitly approved by political officers even though they overstepped the legal requirements of the Native Courts. Beleaguered political officers were all too willing to allow Onyeama to discipline his villages, as it reduced their burden to ensure observance of colonial law. Further, they allowed a bureaucracy to develop beneath the warrant chief because it facilitated the execution of their orders. Many chiefs divided their area into wards, each under an *Udumani*, headman or messenger, who implemented their orders.[89] The *Udumani* was responsible for recruiting forced labor under the Roads and Creeks Ordinance. The position of *Udumani* was often an entré into a warrant chieftainship upon the death of the warrant chief.[90] They also acquired wealth when litigants, wishing to influence court decisions, would curry their favor to reach the chief.[91]

The colonial state gave the "chiefs" power, but did not give them authority in the eyes of their people. Although colonial chiefs were "imperial creations," they were still a part of a village society that had its own criteria for power, status, and prestige. For this reason even the most authoritarian "chiefs" could not afford to ignore the cultural expressions of power within the Igbo polity. Chief Onyeama recognized this and paid obeisance to the old systems of acquiring authority even as he usurped the conventions and undermined them. One basic tenet of Igbo power and authority is reciprocity, and a powerful man became a "leader" by returning some of his wealth to his subordinates. Onyeama devoted considerable resources to fulfilling this ideal by cultivating clients through gifts of food and other prizes, and sponsoring festivals and contests. He operated his own soup kitchen and fed hundreds of the poor daily from his pig farms and yam barns. He was given the title *Oogbuzubosi*, "one who slaughters animals daily" in honor of this role. Like a monarch, he loved conspicuous displays of generosity and he often flung coins to the poor from the upper windows of his palace. Always acutely aware of the benefits of western education, he paid the school fees of all Eke children.[92] Even as a paramount chief, he entertained his subordinate chiefs lavishly, showering them with copious amounts of palm wine and food. In return he expected undying loyalty and compliance with his demands.

Thus between 1910 and 1914 the formal framework of the Native Court system of Udi took shape. It received its first test within months of the "chiefs'" appointments when it was used to perform its most important function: the mobilization of labor for state-sponsored railway construction to link the proposed colliery to the Delta coast.

## CREATING "FREE LABOR" WITH COERCION: FORCED LABOR AND RESISTANCE IN GOVERNMENT EMPLOYMENT 1913/1914

The British discovery of coal was accidental, but local people had used it for many years.[93] In 1909 early field officers used it to warm their post in Udi. Apparently a report of their findings to headquarters received little notice until the visit of the acting governor and his staff. Lt. Gerald Adams, a soldier in Udi, gave his account of the initial enthusiasm of the governor:

The Governor and the Commandant were quite excited, and all the evening the conversations ... ran on the advantages that would accrue to the district and to Southern Nigeria generally, if coal should be found in sufficient quantity to be a paying proposition. They discussed the ... building of a railway line to Udi, for the transport of the coal, that would run through the middle of some of the richest palm-oil country.[94]

The coal fields' location, some 150 miles north of the Bonny Estuary, necessitated a link with the Bonny coast from which coal could be transported to Lagos and points west. When a suitably deep channel was discovered at the Bonny Estuary, the rail route was finalized and a major port city, Port Harcourt, was founded. Named after the secretary of state for the colonies, Lewis V. Harcourt, the city became the southern terminus of the railway which was constructed between 1913 and 1915. While Enugu was connected with Onitsha by road, the principal mode of transport for the coal was the railway route.

The colliery was initially developed as an appendage of the Nigerian Railway system, which was to be the major consumer and the monopoly transporter of the mine's output. When the colliery opened in 1915, it was administratively a division of the railway. Its first fiscal allocation of £15,000 was debited from "Open Lines, Railways,"[95] and the annual reports for the colliery were included in those

**Photo 2.4** Ameke Railway construction, circa 1914 (Crown Agents)

of the Nigerian Railway. The first colliery manager submitted his accounts to the chief construction accountant, Port Harcourt. Administrative and financial matters related to the operation of the mines were under the administrative supervision of the appropriate official in the railway.[96]

The mines and railway were the two major capital works projects in the Eastern Provinces. When wartime cuts stopped other projects, the harbor works at Port Harcourt, the Eastern Railway, and the coal field received priority attention in the budget and from the colonial administration. Colonial Secretary L. Harcourt rejected the request for additional staff and funds for all other branches of the railway but that of Udi-Port Harcourt:

> In view of the present financial prospect I would sanction no more additional staff for railway construction at present, except so far as may be required for the Udi-Port Harcourt section and the Benue bridge. . . . The Udi-Pt. Harcourt section is the only one of any urgency and will be extremely useful by itself for carrying palm produce and coal to the sea.[97]

The construction of a railway from Port Harcourt to Enugu between 1913 and 1915 not only paved the way for the evacuation and distribution of coal, but sharpened the contradictions between the "chiefs" and their subjects. Between 1913, when rail construction began, and 1915 when colliery work started, Udi's people came under increased victimization by the Native Court officials. By the time William Leck, the new manager, arrived in Onitsha in late 1915, Udi was in open rebellion. Initially there was friction between the Igbo peoples and the authorities over the terms of the railway's existence, including the price to be paid for expropriated land, the terms of service as workers, and the role of the warrant chiefs as recruiting agents. At the outbreak of World War I, as preparations were being made in the area of the eastern branch of the railway, the survey parties encountered determined resistance from village-groups along the route between Udi Mine and the future site of Port Harcourt.[98] They were attacked and several surveyors killed.[99]

At the center of the problem was the recruitment of labor for the railway and road construction. Recruitment followed three systems: (1) bringing labor from a distance, which entailed certain costs but recruited small numbers of Hausa and Yoruba workers who, by this time, were accustomed to colonial labor policies and would work for lower wages than the easterners; (2) trading prisoners near the site to serve as a reliable labor force; and (3) a system called the "local method" or "political labor" in which warrant chiefs were engaged to recruit labor.

The "local method" was adopted under the assumption that requests through "native chiefs" would be accepted by their subjects who, it was alleged, were accustomed to serving their customary labor needs. Authorities assumed that these newly appointed government functionaries could generate labor during this delicate time. Most inhabitants of Udi had yet to be brought under British rule so the district officer ignored the methods used to obtain workers, becoming concerned only when a "chief" was unable to supply the specified numbers or when local villagers rose to resist these exactions.[100] The "chiefs," as newly appointed collaborators, were eager to assume these roles and felt secure in their actions with the military support of the new state.

The system usually worked as follows. The railway or colliery decided it needed a given number of workers. "Chiefs" in the local area were then told to recruit a given number of men and sometimes women. The "chief" dispatched court messengers to contact headmen in his villages to supply unskilled labor. Sometimes he would call up a specific age-grade, i.e., the "company of 1913." Other times a random selection of men would be made. When messengers were so dispatched they terrorized communities, demanding "blind eye" gifts to exempt a person from service, abducting women for ransom or as concubines, and seizing property.

Both Onyeama and Chukwuani used this system to provide unskilled workers for the construction of the railway from Port Harcourt to Udi. Under the Masters and Servants Act, they brought in workers, established courts in the labor camps, which they managed using their own paramilitary groups to keep order. Chief Onyeama used his *Ogwumili* force, as well as labor headmen who insured that workers, once in the camp, complied with regulations.[101] Onyeama had an elaborate labor recruitment system emanating from his Native Court. He contacted adjacent chiefs, instructing them to call up specific age-grades and ordered them to report to a series of transit camps where agents checked off their names against their villages.[102] He also used the court to enforce workplace discipline, all with the tacit approval of the political officers. Onyeama, as well as the other chiefs,

**Photo 2.5** Chief Eihukumere of Uzuakoli with railway workers, circa 1914 (Crown Agents)

were allowed to make deductions from their wages to cover feeding costs and other, less legal, expenses.

## THE SECOND PHASE: CREATING PARAMOUNT "CHIEFS," CREATING CLANS—AMALGAMATION, REFORMS, AND POLITICAL CRISIS, 1912–1915

The creation of "Agbaja" and "Nkanu" as clan categories arose from the reorganization of local government by Governor General Frederick Lugard when he amalgamated the Northern and Southern Provinces into the colony of Nigeria. The institutional structure for "clans" was embedded in the regional implementation of Lugard's reforms. Enamored with the system of local government that he created in the north, between 1912 and 1919, Lugard attempted to restructure the south's local government to resemble that Native Authority system. Between 1900 and 1906 he and his men refined the principles of "indirect rule" to accommodate the hierarchy of the Islamic state created by the nineteenth-century Fulani jihad. There the colonial state governed through the ruling class of the Sokoto Caliphate, the largest state in nineteenth-century West Africa. Exemplifying what Mamdani has called the privileging of an interpretation of "customary law" introduced by the nineteenth-century conquest states, the northern model used emirs, each professing loyalty to the *shakih* or head of the empire. After defeating the Caliphate in 1903, Lugard welcomed the ordered and regimented patterns of government as the framework for local government. In turn, the defeated emirs found that by cooperating with the colonial state, they could exert more power over their subjects than they could before the conquest. This partnership of Islamic and colonial state appealed to Lugard's preference for deeply ordered, authoritarian hierarchies in which each social strata performed its role and the ruling classes, who governed fairly but autocratically, insured order. Order was an obsession with the militaristic Lugard who ranked societies in a hierarchy determined by the degree of political centralization. To him, the "stateless" Igbo peoples, with their diffuse political processes, were deficient and "primitive." During the amalgamation he took on the challenge of "preparing" them for "indirect rule." In his treatise *The Dual Mandate* he used a teleological argument on the most expeditious way to encourage the development of "indirect rule." He proposed that government policy should

> hasten the transition from the patriarchal to the tribal stage, and induce those who accept no other authority than the head of the family to recognize a common chief. Where this stage has already been reached, the object is to group together small tribes, or sections of a tribe, so as to form a single administrative unit whose chiefs severally or in council ... may be constituted a Native Authority ... through whom the District Officer can work.[103]

To Lugard, the abuses and corruption of the Native Courts were not caused by too much power, but too little power in the hands of qualified "chiefs." His proposed reforms addressed these concerns and were driven by an overarching the-

ory that, given the right conditions, a strong "native" government could be cultivated in Igboland. He considered the corruption of the Native Courts to be the result of the collapse of "native society." He condemned the government in the
south—specifically the political officers and the Supreme Court, as well as the missionaries—for undermining the political leadership of local chiefs and preventing
the emergence of strong, responsible authorities who could be partners in colonial
rule. This ideology had deep contradictions. On the one hand he embraced the ideal
of a "pristine" rural Africa, stable under the authoritarian control of "chiefs." But
on the other hand, in cases where this authoritarian ideal had not yet emerged, he
felt it was the duty of the state to accelerate a "natural" evolutionary movement towards centralized power.[104]

His reforms were specific and myopic, arrogantly following abstract principles
rooted in his northern experience, and ignoring the warnings and experience of
southern political officials. Like a typical colonialist he distrusted specialists and
technicians and rejected the policy suggestions of the first government anthropologist, Northcote Thomas,[105] and argued that the best persons to understand the area
were the political officers who were "in daily contact with the natives."[106]

Lugard's official position was to protect "native" society from the disruptive European influences and to strengthen "native" institutions in preparation for eventual
self-rule. To cultivate responsibility and good government by "chiefs," he removed
the political officer from the presidency of the Native Court and created a position
of president, or Sole Native Authority. Concluding that there were so many "chiefs"
that it was difficult to identify those most qualified, he restricted the numbers of
chiefs to make appointments more competitive. Finally, in recognition of the excesses of court messengers he reduced the numbers attached to each court.[107]

In areas without paramount chiefs he instructed his officers to "encourage any
chief of influence and character to control a group of villages with a view to making him chief of a district later if he shows ability."[108] This policy gave Onyeama
and, to a lesser extent, Chukwuani, the opportunity to legitimize the elaborate personal bureaucracy and authoritarian powers they had carefully assumed since 1910.

Even before they were appointed paramount chiefs in 1917, they elaborated their
own legal structure and positioned themselves to accrue both wealth and power
with the Lugardian reforms. From 1 January 1914, when Lugard abolished all
courts, both chiefs lobbied to control the single court established per district. Lugard also allowed the courts to appoint unsalaried assistants and untitled men,
called "recruits," to assume the messengers' functions. This, in effect, legitimized
the chiefs' paramilitary groups. While Onyeama's *Ogwumili* became more powerful, Chukwuani created his own group, the *Umu Ojibo Chukwuani*, who were
equally abusive to his people.[109]

When Lugard created Sole Native Authorities and the paramount chiefs, the Resident, Onitsha, suggested Onyeama and Chukwuani as candidates. By then
Onyeama had become the most powerful chief over thirty-four village-groups, covering 686 square miles and including 137,500 people.[110] He had subordinate chiefs
whom he controlled through patronage, inclusion in the ritual of his court, and

sharing in the proceeds of his corruption. Similarly Chukwuani's position, though less secure than Onyeama's, was over the villages in the area called Nkanu. There were differences in the political economy of these two regions of Udi. Agbaja, with its overcrowded and infertile land, had evolved into a precolonial labor reserve with ancient traditions of male migration. Nkanu, on the other hand, had a strong agricultural base with rich fields in proximity to the palm belt. After 1915, the railway came through many of her villages. Nkanu men preferred farming to supply the villages of the palm belt, and later to provision the city of Enugu, which was founded as the headquarters of the mines. With these appointments "Agbaja" and "Nkanu" became official political entities of increasing relevance.

As the chiefs pressed unskilled labor from their restive populations, the fraudulence of their "customary" powers was exposed to, but not fully appreciated by, colonial agents. Confronting Lugard's plans was the reality of the limits of power that even Chief Onyeama could exercise. Forced labor assumed a stronger state and more control over land than was the case in southeastern Nigeria, and workers' protest took a characteristic form—desertion. Despite the degree of coercion in the camps and in the workplace, workers could still control when and with what intensity they worked. Increasingly, desertion was the protest of choice, and men demanded higher wages. By 1914 Lugard was frustrated by the realities of southern labor which defied his understanding of the "labor question" from the north, and indicated that the battery of laws that shaped colonial labor policy was ineffective. As construction of the Eastern Railway progressed in the first quarter of 1914, Lugard complained bitterly about the quality, cost, and discipline of the local labor.[111] Despite his theories on "native administration" he could not secure the type and volume of labor he needed. He was embarrassed by the railway's cost overruns from labor and the land disputes. In April 1914 he proposed in frustration that local labor be abandoned entirely.[112] While clearly impractical, the government did bring in contingents of workers from northern and western parts of Nigeria. He found these men more disciplined than the locals and in December he came ultimately to rely on prison labor. He complained:

> Increasing numbers of Hausas and Yorubas are being recruited. They do double the work and are not so difficult to feed since they eat rice and corn, whereas local men require yams which are difficult to procure and costly to transport. It was arranged also for the location of a large number of prisoners from Lagos and other jails at Port Harcourt, and this has been a most valuable addition to the labor supply.[113]

Despite the realities of forced labor and its moderate success, officially Lugard extolled the virtues of the free labor market and the popularity of wage labor with the "primitive" tribes. Ever sensitive to the critics of forced labor in England, he shrouded the recruitment methods in secrecy and lauded the power of the "free market" in labor which he knew did not exist in southeastern Nigeria. In May 1914 he insisted that wages had popularized railway work and was less than truthful in explaining the pay system:

I directed that every laborer have his wages paid into his own hands, in cash, and not through the intermediary of any "Chief" or other labor manager. These are the rules which I have always insisted upon, in spite of the extra trouble involved. The receipt of his wages by each individual without deductions by a middle man not only popularizes employment by the government but is the greatest incentive to free labor, and constitutes a most effective and practical blow to the system of forced labor and slavery which is so inherent in all African communities.[114]

Lugard knew that the "free market" did not work. Earlier that February 1914, 2,000 men left immediately after being paid for two weeks' service on the railway, leaving supervisors to lament that they were "just beginning to do good work and picking up the use of tools." The state was forced to raise wages from nine pence to one shilling per day to attract workers.[115] Although some casual workers were coming from the eastern interior area, the project was clearly quite reliant on penal labor and he waxed enthusiastic about their performance:

At Port Harcourt a large prison is now complete and is capable of housing 1,100 men. The prisoners perform good work at clearing, putting up buildings, etc., almost equal in fact to that of the laborer to whom is paid one shilling a day. Later on it is proposed to employ prisoners in off-loading ships. Arrangements will also be made to employ two thousand on the heavy banks and cuts in the Bende district.[116]

In January/February 1914 Lugard unsuccessfully petitioned the Colonial Office to tighten the loopholes in labor recruitment. He proposed an "ordinance to provide for the control of large bodies of laborers employed on government works" which specified fines of from one to two pounds for men who deserted an oral contract and for those who counseled them to desert from government projects. The proposed ordinance targeted his nemesis—the Lagosian elite, those educated African professionals and civil servants who attacked his brutal policies in the press. He detested educated Africans, whom he considered to be pretentious "charlatans." In Lugard's feudal-patriarchal mind, there was no place for "native" critics.[117] Opposition to forced labor was also among the many grievances championed by "native" lawyers in eastern towns. He proposed a £50 fine for anyone who "incites or counsels, or attempts to procure" any person who is working on government projects.[118] Harcourt objected and argued that the Masters and Servants Ordinance contained sufficient provisions to regulate the behavior of large groups of workers.[119] In fact, the Colonial Office knew that the chiefs themselves had methods of disciplining deserters and probably suspected that their methods might reek of coercion. An internal memo reviewed the punishment for deserters:

The ordinary system, I believe, is to ask the chief to furnish so many laborers, explaining the conditions of service. The chief furnishes them, and if they run away he provides some more. No doubt he deals with the men who run away. *But so long as he acts in accordance with the law*, that is a matter between the chief and the native labourers (emphasis mine).[120]

But this was precisely the problem. The law gave them such extraordinarily despotic powers that both Onyeama and Chukwuani operated with near impunity in their territories. In this case, Lugard was advised that the Colonial Office would "deprecate the enactment of the proposed ordinance."[121]

Lugard's instructions concerning the treatment of "native" labor formed the backbone of labor policy during this early period of colonial rule. However, in actual practice the treatment of Igbo labor reflected the rights of a conqueror to extract unpaid labor from the vanquished. Provisions of the Collective Punishment Ordinance of 1912 and the Roads and Creeks Ordinance gave chiefs the right to require free village labor for any project, was frequently evoked during the period of "pacification," and supplied sufficient workers for most infrastructural projects.[122]

Before the conquest there were no political rulers who could claim more than ritual authority over their villages.[123] Now there were men like Chukwuani and Onyeama, colonial "chiefs" with extraordinary powers. By late 1914 their coercive recruitment methods and authoritarian practices had the very effect colonialists attempted to avoid. The "chief's" despotic powers created such disorder that a second conquest was necessary at a period of extreme state vulnerability—during World War I. The consequences of the reconstruction of the local level of the colonial state for the recruitment and discipline of the colliery's first workers will be discussed below.

## "THIS UDI BUSINESS": LOCAL RESPONSE TO LUGARDIAN REFORMS AND FORCED LABOR

Within months of Lugard's reforms, and in the midst of the harsh labor demands of railway construction, the people of several Udi villages rose up. Government troops had been deployed to the east to meet the Germans on the Cameroonian front which opened in September 1914. The violence and terror surrounding labor recruitment only further accentuated the abuses of the paramount chiefs, Chukwuani and Onyeama, and their subordinates. There were earlier signs of trouble in late 1913 when survey parties were attacked on the route connecting Owerri and Onitsha.[124] Officials smarting under the criticism of anti-expansionist elite alleged that Lagos-based "ringleaders" were encouraging villagers to break with the government. Twenty-eight were killed and two wounded.[125] But in October Udi erupted in general insurrection against the warrant chiefs and forced labor.[126] The rebellion centered in the heavily slave-populated South Nkanu village-groups of Akegbe, Akpugo, and Amagunze along the Udi-Abakaliki road. In October 1914 the people of Akegbe killed sixteen Hausa traders, chased out their chiefs, fought both court messengers and the police,[127] and attacked several military encampments. In some areas people prepared for protracted war by building fortifications, "bush" camps, and setting booby traps.[128] In the village of Oye they killed a sub-chief for serving summons on a man in the village. Chief Yaro Onaga of Agbudu, Udi, an eyewitness to the revolts noted:

When our soldiers in Udi went out for Cameroons War then people at Akegbo [sic, Akeqbe] [thought] there's no soldier again and soldiers are never coming back to Udi. Then they have to state that they are coming to capture the very small number of soldiers at Udi.[129]

Lugard reported in November 1914 that "[t]he unrest in Udi district . . . has unfortunately interfered with prosecution of the railway survey and colliery work."[130]

Several companies of the West African Frontier Force were withdrawn from the Cameroonian front and dispatched to Udi. By November, six detachments of 200 men were operating in the Nkanu towns of Akebe, Akpugo, Amagunze, and Amuri.[131] Although the most visible targets of the rebellion were the warrant chiefs, the political officer at Udi recognized that the insurrection came from a deeper resistance to the entire colonial state.[132] Patrols were placed on the Udi-Abakaliki road where work for the railway was under way and preparations were being made in anticipation of the arrival of the new colliery manager.[133] The initial excavations of the Enugu Government Colliery would take place under armed guard amongst communities that had been bludgeoned into acceptance of the new colonial order. Some of their resistance infected the mines and hindered the new manager's efforts to recruit local labor.[134] At the conclusion of the revolt in April, the government estimated that about 250 men had been killed.[135] The uprising clearly indicated the reconstruction of Udi would not be easy. Just as such "chiefs" as Onyeama and Chukwuani seized every opportunity offered by the new political changes to cement their power, the people of Udi registered their rejection of these excesses.

When the colonial army crushed the rebellions of 1914, the Collective Punishments Ordinance again was used to require that the people supply laborers for either the road or railway construction. For the people in the vicinity of the new colliery, the labor punishment was even more onerous, for they were expected to supply workers both for the road to the Udi Colliery and for the initial stages of colliery construction. Villagers on the route between Onitsha and Udi had just completed one stint of road construction when they were called upon to prepare the road to the colliery. The railway engineer reported problems in Onitsha province in obtaining additional workers for the colliery road:

Sextant Onitsha reports difficulty in obtaining labour for road to Coalfields due to towns have been granted three months holiday. Do not understand. Can you kindly assist as most important that road be made for motor lorry in order to get Railway and Coalfields materials up.[136]

The government was not divided as to the propriety of using labor extracted as part of a peace settlement in constructing the railway. However, the lieutenant governor expressed his misgivings over the use of unpaid labor in completion of this project:

I am doubtful, however, as to the wisdom of insisting on free labor for the Railway, but there is no objection to this being one of the conditions of their surrender, although in all probability it will be found better, after matters have settled down, to pay for the labour so employed.[137]

For the government, however, the construction of the railway presented problems as the recalcitrant Igbo workers resisted the new capitalist wage system. The turmoil in the rural areas was the context in which the coal mines opened and the city of Enugu-Ngwo (Enugu) was founded. For the men of Udi in the environs of the mine, the period would bring a rapid transformation that would make them into "new men." It would also place them at the center of West Africa's export economy because, as producers of coal, the premier fuel of the region's railways, they would become a pivotal sector of the area's small working class.

## NOTES

1. See Judith van Allen, "'Sitting on a Man': Colonialism and the Lost Political Institutions of Igbo Women," *Canadian Journal of African Studies*, 62 (1972): 165–181.

2. Mahmood Mamdani, *Citizen and Subject; Contemporary Africa and the Legacy of Late Colonialism* (Princeton, 1996), 56.

3. Onyeama was an extraordinary example of a man who could create an empire within colonial rule. He was careful, however, to observe the principle of reciprocity in Igbo politics and developed a vast social welfare system even as he extorted and oppressed his people. He was known for feeding hundreds of poor daily, and paid the school tuition of all the children in his village of Eke, Agbaja. Onyeama, *Onyeama*, p. 59.

4. Isichei, *History of the Igbo People*, 133–36.

5. Michael Burawoy, *The Politics of Production*, 226.

6. Anne Phillips, *The Enigma of Colonialism: British Policy in West Africa* (London, 1989), 29.

7. Ibid., 11.

8. ONPROF 1/15/3, Captain Massey to Acting Lt. Governor, Onitsha. 9 November 1914.

9. Phillip Curtin, *The Image of Africa: British Ideas and Action, 1780–1850*, Vol. 2 (Madison, 1973), 480.

10. John E. Flint, *Sir George Goldie and the Making of Nigeria* (London, 1960), 9.

11. Elizabeth Isichei, *The Ibo and the Europeans: The Genesis of a Relationship to 1906* (New York, 1973); E.J. Alagoa, *The Small Brave City-State: A History of Nembe-Brass in the Niger Delta* (Ibadan, 1964).

12. Crawford Young, *The African Colonial State in Comparative Perspective* (New Haven, 1994), 92.

13. Obaro Ikime, *Niger Delta Rivalry: Itsekiri-Urhobo Relations and the European Presence 1884–1936* (New York, 1969); Alagoa, *The Small Brave City-State*.

14. S.N. Nwabara, *Iboland: A Century of Contact with Britain, 1860–1960* (Atlantic Highlands, NJ, 1978), Chap. 5.

15. Afigbo, "Southeastern Nigeria in the 19th Century," 482–83.

16. Young, *The African Colonial State in Comparative Perspective*, 92.

17. Margery Perham, *The Native Economies of Nigeria, vol. 1., The Economics of a Tropical Dependency*, ed., by Daryll Forde and Richenda Scott (London, 1946), 6–7.

18. Phillips, *The Enigma of Colonialism*, 27.

19. Ibid.

20. Elizabeth Isichei, *A History of Nigeria* (New York, 1983), 367.

21. Isichei, *The Ibo and the Europeans*, 131. She cites A.G. Leonard, "Notes of a Journey to Bende," *Journal of the Manchester Geographical Society* 14, (1898): 190–207.

22. Public Record Office, Colonial Office (hereafter PRO, CO) 520/10, Memorandum of instructions with regard to the Aro Expedition, 12 November 1901 as cited in Nwabara, *Iboland*, 100.

23. Young, *The African Colonial State in Comparative Perspective*, 93.

24. Isichei, *A History of the Igbo*, 130.

25. Ibid., 367–68.

26. Michael Adas, *Machines as Measure of Men: Science, Technology and Ideologies of Western Dominance* (Ithaca, 1989).

27. Curtin, *The Image of Africa*; Saul Dubow, "Race, Civilization and Culture: The Elaboration of Segregationist Discourse in the Inter-War Years," in *The Politics of Race, Class and Ethnicity in 20th Century South Africa*, ed., Shula Marks and Stanley Trapido (New York, 1987), 19.

28. Nigerian National Archives Ibadan (hereafter NNAI), CSO 1/21/5. Enclosure 1, O.C. Commanding Nkerefi Patrol to O.C. Southern Nigerian Regiment, 4 November 1909 as quoted in Innocent Uzeochi, "The Social and Political Impact of the Eastern Nigerian Railway on Udi Division" (Ph.D. diss., Kent State University, 1985), 91.

29. Cotton interests were especially anxious to replace American supplies with imperial cotton. Churchill noted that the protectorate of Nigeria would not be economically beneficial for England unless its commercial development could be enhanced. The possibilities of opening areas to cotton growing was contingent upon railway development. T.N. Tamuno, "The Genesis of the Nigerian Railway," *Nigeria Magazine*, 84 (1965):31–43; W.I. Ofonogoro, "The Opening Up of Southern Nigeria to British Trade and Its Consequences," (Ph.D. diss., Columbia University, 1971), 247–50.

30. As cited in Bruce Berman, "Bureaucracy and Incumbent Violence: Colonial Administration and the Origins of the 'Mau Mau' Emergency," in *The Unhappy Valley: Conflict in Kenya and Africa*, vol. 2, *Violence and Ethnicity*, Bruce Berman and John Lonsdale, eds. (London/Ohio, 1992), 234; see Margery Perham, introduction to *Yesterday's Rulers: The Making of the British Colonial Service*, Robert Heussler (New York, 1963), xx; Rupert Wilkenson, *The Prefects: British Leadership and the Public School Tradition* (London, 1965), 4.

31. See Margery Perham and Mary Bull, eds., *The Diaries of Lord Lugard*, vol. 4 (Evanston, 1963), 18.

32. Berman, "Bureaucracy and Incumbent Violence," 235.

33. Berman argues: "The characteristic beliefs of colonial administrators in paternalism and social hierarchy, their emphasis on reciprocal obligations of ruler and ruled, and their preoccupation with order and control reflected a traditional concept of authority and society. There was an archaic, even atavistic quality to colonial administration, as if it represented the last place where the old prerogatives and power of a ruling elite could be exercised." Berman, "Bureaucracy and Incumbent Violence," 237.

34. Young, *The African Colonial State in Comparative Perspective*, 98.

35. Andrea Cornwall and Nancy Lindsfarne, "Dislocating Masculinity: Gender, Power and Anthropology," 18, 19.

36. Dubow, "Race, Civilization and Culture," 72.

37. V.Y. Mudimbe, *The Invention of Africa: Gnosis, Philosophy and the Order of Knowledge* (Bloomington and Indianapolis, 1988), 20.

38. In the ideological context of the conquest of southeastern Nigeria, in this period it was not generally recognized that serious study of subject peoples could actually assist administration. A.E. Afigbo, "Anthropology and Colonial Administration in South-Eastern Nigeria, 1891–1939," *Journal of the Historical Society of Nigeria* 8, 1 (December 1975): 21. With the exception of two studies by field officers, no scholarly studies were made of the Igbo until the appointment of the first government anthropologist, N.W. Thomas, in 1909. Despite his extensive investigation, no one in the field seriously considered his work relevant for policy development. Thomas published five volumes on the Igbo-speaking peoples before Lugard rejected his reappointment in 1913. Northcott W. Thomas, *Anthropological Report on the Igbo-Speaking Peoples of Nigeria*, part 1, *Law and Custom of the Ibo on the Awka Neighborhood* (London, 1913), and part 1, *Law and Custom of the Asaba District* (London, 1914).

39. The institutional form of "indirect rule" evolved through trial and error from the Niger Delta Courts of Equity. In 1891 the first courts had been established to govern the Oil Rivers (Niger Coast) Protectorate. It was promoted as a way to avoid the emnity of the "chiefs" and give "stability and permanence to what had been achieved by force of arms." Omoniyi Adewoye, *The Judicial System in Southern Nigeria, 1854–1954* (Atlantic Highlands, NJ, 1977), 41.

40. The "house" was a kin-based commercial and political unit that was ruled by a merchant who had life or death powers over his household. The "head" was a middleman between European traders and inland palm-producing villages. The "house" included his family, which was considered something of an aristocracy, many freeborn subordinates who were his employees, and usually a large number of slaves. Slaves engaged in trade and war, an interminable by-product of shifting trading relations and disputes. Trusted slaves, who could represent the "head" in negotiations with supplier villages and with European supercargoes, could retain a portion of the earnings. There is evidence that it evolved from kin-based villages in the Delta area. See T.N. Tamuno, *The Evolution of the Nigerian State* (New York, 1972), 325; K.O. Dike. *Trade and Politics in the Niger Delta 1830–1885: An Introduction to the Economic and Political History of Nigeria* (Oxford, 1956), 34–37. Alagoa, *Small Brave City-State*.

41. Young, *The African Colonial State*, 93.

42. For the best description of the conquest in Udi, see Uzeochi, "Eastern Nigerian Railway."

43. Ibid.

44. Tamuno, *The Evolution of the Nigerian State*, 44; Uzeochi, "Eastern Nigerian Railway," Chap. 2.

45. For the most thorough summary of the invasion of Udi, which made extensive use of oral testimony and colonial records, see Uzoechi, "Eastern Nigerian Railway," Chap. 2, 35–64.

46. Isichei, *History of the Igbo People*, 123.

47. NNAI, CSO 26/211, "Report on Nkanu (North) Villages of Udi Division, fo. 5, Clark; NNAI, CSO 26/19, "Report on Adaba, Nkume, Okpata, and Umulokpa Villages of Onitsha Division," no. 7, Stone and Milne; NNAI, CSO 26/211, "Intelligence Report on Nkanu (North) Villages of Udi Division," 1933, p. 5, as cited in Isichei, *Ibo People and the Europeans*, 142.

48. For a discussion of the "invention" of the "customary," see Terence Ranger, "The Invention of Tradition in Africa," in *The Invention of Tradition*, eds., Eric Hobsbawm and Terence Ranger (Cambridge, 1983), 221–62.

49. Mamdani, *Citizen and Subject*, 117–23.

50. The most authoritative study on the "invention" of customary law is Martin Chanock's *Law, Custom and Social Order: The Colonial Experience in Malawi and Zambia* (Cambridge, 1985).

51. Mamdani, *Citizen and Subject*, 122. For a reference to the conflict between elders and the "Big Men" see Chapter 1. In some village-groups the *Ogaranyan* were called *Amadi*.

52. For a discussion of the evolution, see Adewoye, *The Judicial System*, Chap. 6.

53. Ibid., 43.

54. A.E. Afigbo's *The Warrant Chiefs*, 101.

55. Ibid., 127.

56. Adewoye, *The Judicial System*, 180.

57. Several were from the Gold Coast Colony or Sierra Leone. See Afigbo, *The Warrant Chiefs*.

58. Ibid. 174.

59. G.I. Jones, "Chieftaincy in the Former Eastern Region of Nigeria," in *West African Chiefs: Their Changing Status Under Colonial Rule and Independence*, ed., Michael Crowder and Obaro Ikime (Ile-Ife, Nigeria, 1970), 312.

60. Afigbo, *The Warrant Chiefs*, 35.

61. W.A. Beverly, *Military Report on Southern Nigeria, 1908*, 2 vols. (London, 1908); NNAI, CS 1/21, 5 Encl., no. 1, O.C. Commanding Nkerefi Patrol to O.C. Southern Nigerian Regiment, 4 October 1909. Both as cited in Uzeochi, "Eastern Nigerian Railway," 56.

62. NNAI, CSO 1/21, 5 Encl., no. 2, (Conf) in Egerton to Secretary of State, 27 November 1909, as cited in Uzochie, "Eastern Nigerian Railway," 57.

63. NNAI CSO 1/21, 5 Encl., no. 1, O.C. Commanding Nkerefi Patrol to O.C. Southern Nigerian Regiment, 4 November 1909, as cited in Uzeochi, "Eastern Nigerian Railway," p. 56.

64. During this period, a group of Lagos "native" lawyers fanned out into the southeastern provinces from the cities of Onitsha, Warri, and Calabar. Canvassing the area just behind the "pacification" armies, they showed villagers how to challenge the government in court. They also drove up the cost of land much higher than it had been in the northern area of the country, when the Kano railway was built. See PRO, CO 583/14, Harcourt Memorandum, 19 May 1916; Lugard to Harcourt, "Eastern Line First Progress Report," 22 May 1914. They were often successful in the Nigerian Supreme Court where they clashed with the district officer. In 1911, the court ruled against one district officer who imprisoned one of these lawyers because he refused to remove his hat. The district officer was taken to court and fined £20 and court costs. Justice William H. Stoker stated, in an interesting ruling, that there was "no such thing as a political officers' privilege and there were a lot of 'honorables' around who had no right to the title." But the Supreme Court Ordinance of 1911 limited the court's jurisdiction to the more settled and developed areas of the east and central provinces, and ended these lawyers' official presence. Adewoye, *The Judicial System*. See Chap. 4, especially 117–26.

65. Tamuno, *The Evolution of the Nigerian State*, 318–19.

66. By the end of the century, the "house" system was showing signs of distress. Some "houses" were actually headed by slaves. Jaja of Opobo is one luminary example. Many heads had lost control over their slave members who both refused to work for the head or to pay customary fees. Dike, *Trade and Politics*.

67. F.D. Lugard, *The Political Memorandum: Revision of Instructions of Political Officers on Subjects Chiefly Political and Administrative, 1913–1918*, 3d ed. (London, 1970), 218.

68. Ibid., 224.

69. This model, first used by the East India Company government in 1843, outlawed slave dealing and removed slavery from its legal status. It did not inform the slaves of this development, but had they left their owners, the courts could not have been used to reclaim them as property. In West Africa it was seen as an ideal method of outlawing slavery without creating social and economic disruption. Suzanne Miers and Richard Roberts, *The End of Slavery in Africa* (Madison, 1988), 12–13.

70. "House" heads could contract young "apprentice" workers (up to age sixteen) for periods of up to five years. Following a barrage of criticism by metropolitan abolitionists, the proclamation was amended to include a quarterly review of the impact of the law by the British commissioner. But later, in 1902, the law was tightened and the period of apprenticeship was extended to twelve years. Tamuno, *The Evolution of the Nigerian State*, 324.

71. It fined disobedient or vagrant "house" members and authorized the "head" to claim a percentage of their profits and/or earnings when employed outside the "house." Further, it imprisoned any person hiring "house" members without the consent of the "head." Despite humanitarian opposition, the ordinance remained in force until 1914.

72. PRO, CO 588/1, No. 15 of 1903, clause 5(a) as cited in Tamuno, *The Evolution of the Nigerian State*, 319. J.C. Anene, *Southern Nigeria in Transition: 1885–1906* (Cambridge, 1966), 308.

73. The most extensive discussion is in Amadiume's *Male Daughters*, 137–40.

74. There are no studies of Chief Chukwuani. The most extensive treatment is in a local study by a non-historian, Anayo Enechukwu, *History of Nkanu* (Enugu, 1993). See Chap. 12.

75. Despite his prominence, Onyeama has not received serious study. With the exception of anecdotal references to him in Afigbo's *Warrant Chiefs*, there are only two studies: Onyeama, *Chief Onyeama*; Felix C. Mgboh, "Biography of Chief Onyeama," (Research paper of History-Civics, Alvan Ikoku College of Education, Owerri, Nigeria, June 1980). There was a fourth chief in the Owerri area, Chief Njemanze, who brought in large numbers of Owerri men. However, he has not been studied to the extent of the other three.

76. Anayo Enechukwu, *History of Nkanu*, See especially Chap. 12.

77. Onyeama, *Chief Onyeama*, 21.

78. Ibid., 24.

79. Interview with Chief Nwafor Chukwuani, Enugu, Nigeria, 15 June 1975 and Prince Harry Chukwuani, Ozalla, 18 July 1999. See several pages in Enechukwu, *History of Nkanu*, Chap. 12.

80. Enechukwu, *History of Nkanu*, Chap. 12.

81. Interview with Nwafor Chukwuani.

82. Onyeama, *Chief Onyeama*, 26.

83. Ibid., 28.

84. Interview with Chief Edwueme II, Egede, 19 February 1972, as cited in Uzeochi, "Eastern Nigerian Railway," 122.

85. Onyeama, *Chief Onyeama*, 28.

86. Uzeochi, "Eastern Nigerian Railway," 122.

87. Robert L. Tignor, "Colonial Chiefs in Chiefless Societies," *Journal of Modern African Studies* 9, 3 (1971): 350.

88. Onyeama, *Chief Onyeama*, 40.

89. Afigbo, *The Warrant Chiefs*, 104.

90. The regalia of colonial power, which included a "cap and staff," were introduced as a way of decorating these men and creating a "tradition" of warrant chiefs and satisfactory headmen. Afigbo, *The Warrant Chiefs*, 105, see photo on p. 81.

91. Ibid., 104.

92. Onyeama, *Chief Onyeama*, 67.

93. The special commissioner in West Africa of *West Africa* magazine alleges that a Captain Mitten "discovered" the coal deposits after noting "the habit of certain natives of burning in their homes coal chipped from the hillside," *West Africa*, 24 February 1917, 76.

94. Rhodes House Library, Mss. Afr. s. 375 (1), "Miner and Executioner," contained in "Five Nigerian Tales," Lt. Gerald Adams, n.d.

95. PRO, CO 683/26, Director Nigeria Railway to Under Secretary of State for the Colonies, 23 September 1914.

96. PRO, CO 583/26, M.E. Bland, General Manager Railway to Commissioner Onitsha, 18 December 1914.

97. PRO, CO 583/26, Harcourt Minute, 1 September 1914; PRO, CO 583/26, Lewis V. Harcourt Minute, 1 September 1914; PRO, CO 583/44, "Address of the Governor-General," Proceedings of the Second Meeting of the Nigerian Council, 29 December 1915, 8–9.

98. PRO, CO 583/14. Harcourt Memorandum, 19 May 1916.

99. Ibid.

100. Afigbo, *The Warrant Chiefs*, 176–77; PRO, CO 583/9, Baynes Minute, 18 February 1914.

101. Only anecdotal information is available about this group. Dillibe Onyeama, who relied on oral testimony, notes that Onyeama selected members from Ngwo, Nsude, and Eke who participated in wrestling and boxing matches he staged at Eke. Tignor and Mgboh suggest that they terrorized Onyeama's villages as a paramilitary force. They were not paid cash but "in kind and lived primarily on loot and plunder," and even seized other men's wives. Onyeama was very big on "inventing" regalia so they wore a distinctive uniform—long red caps and matching uniform. Tignor alleges that "the *Agwumili* (sic) ... literally terrorized local communities committing all kinds of crimes, including a number of murders, with impunity." And, he asserts that the impending government prosecution of Onyeama for complicity in several murders they committed was the reason behind Onyeama's suicide in 1934. Onyeama, *Chief Onyeama*, 40; Tignor, "Colonial Chiefs," 350; Mgboh, "The Biography of Chief Onyeama," 12.

102. Interview with C.O. Ude, Amokwe, Udi, February 23, 1972; interview with Chief J. Nwankwo, Eke, Udi, March 7, 1972 as cited in Uzeochi, "Eastern Nigerian Railway," 125.

103. F.D. Lugard, *The Dual Mandate in British Tropical Africa* (Hamden, CT, 1965), 217–18.

104. For a discussion of Lugard's policies, see Afigbo, *The Warrant Chiefs*, Chap. 4.

105. Thomas, *Anthropological Report*, vol. 1–4.

106. Afigbo, *The Warrant Chiefs*, 158.

107. Ibid., 126, 162 for summary.

108. Ibid., 137.

109. Enechukwu, *History of Nkanu*, 288.

110. Onyeama, *Chief Onyeama*, 43.

111. PRO, CO 584/15, "Report on the Cost of Construction of Eastern Railway," Lugard to Harcourt, 12 June 1914.

112. Ibid., "Nigerian Eastern Railway Construction Estimate—First Revise," 22 April 1914, enclosure in Confidential dispatch, Lugard to Harcourt, 12 June 1914.

113. Ibid., Lugard to Harcourt, "Eastern Line First Progress Report," 22 May 1914.

114. Ibid.

115. PRO, CO 583/21, Lugard to Harcourt, 18 December 1914.

116. Ibid., "Eastern Railway Progress Report," 18 December 1914, enclosure in Lugard to Harcourt, 6 January 1914.

117. Ranger, "Invention of Tradition in Africa," 220.

118. PRO, CO 583/9, "An Ordinance to Provide for the Control of Large Bodies of Labourers Employed on Government Works," 24 January 1914.

119. Ibid, Harcourt Draft Despatch, 20 February 1914.

120. PRO, CO 583/9, Baynes Minute, 18 February 1914.

121. Harcourt Draft Despatch, 20 February 1914.

122. Tamuno, *The Evolution of the Nigerian State*, 45.

123. Jones, "Chieftaincy in Southeastern Nigeria."

124. NNAE, Onprof 1/15/3, Lt. Governor's Office Onitsha to H.E. Governor-General Lagos, 16 November 1914.

125. PRO, CO 583/12, Despatch from Lugard, April 15, 1914.

126. Ibid.

127. PRO, CO 583/32, Despatch from Lugard to Harcourt, 29 April 1915.

128. PRO, CO 583/20, Lugard to Harcourt 19 November 1914.

129. Interview with Chief Yaro Onaga, cited in Isichei, *A History of the Igbo People*.

130. PRO, CO 583/19, Lugard to Harcourt, 10 November 1914.

131. Interview with Chief Yaro Onaga, Isichei, *A History of the Igbo People*. PRO, CO 583/32, T. W. Dann, DO Udi, "Final Report Upon Operations of the Udi Patrol," 18 February 1915, enclosure in Lugard to Harcourt, 29 April 1915.

132. PRO, CO 583/32, T.W. Dann, DO Udi.

133. Ibid., Lugard to Harcourt, 29 April 1915.

134. Documentation of the Udi Revolt is included in two records series, NNAE, ONPROF 1/15/28 and PRO, CO 583 files /12, /14, /19, /20, /23, /32; Akinjide Osuntokun, "Disaffection and Revolts in Nigeria During the First World War, 1914–1918," *Canadian Journal of African Studies* 5, 2 (1971): 180.

135. PRO, CO583/31, Despatches February-April 1915.

136. NNAE, Onprof 1/15/28, Engineer Warri to Commissioner Onitsha, 16 March 1915.

137. Ibid., District Officer Udi to Commissioner Onitsha, 31 March 1915.

# 3

# CREATING THE COLONIAL WORKPLACE AND THE COLONIAL CITY: ENUGU AND THE COAL FIELDS DURING WORLD WAR I

With the Udi uprising defeated, the state concentrated on establishing the coal industry and the city of Enugu. Enugu was a new type of settlement—a colonial city—and the colliery a new system of production—the capitalist mine. Both emerged under the watchful eye of Frederick Lugard, then governor-general of Nigeria. Lugard's personal interest in the city and the industry arose from his belief that while wage labor was of educative value for African labor, Africans should remain socially rooted in their rural communities away from the "dangerous" temptations of urban life. But neither the city nor the workplace was shaped only by colonial officials. African men and a small number of women from both local and more distant areas entered Enugu and the colliery and shaped them according to their life strategies, values, concerns, and cultures. With the oppression of the chiefs in the countryside, Enugu became a refuge for men and women seeking "freedom" and it would never be the ordered, racially segregated colonial city that Lugard hoped to create. In a similar manner workers in the mines, both voluntary and coerced, conditioned the industry to accommodate the rural rhythms that pulled them away from their jobs to farm or to fulfill village social obligations. They too forced management to acknowledge a limited control over the supply of labor and the labor process itself.

For the slave and freeborn men of Udi, most especially the young, unmarried men, the conquest presented new possibilities and challenges. On the one hand, they had to develop strategies to avoid the disruptive impact of the chief's exactions on their lives. On the other, they tried to position themselves to benefit from any new opportunities that emerged under the nascent state and new market economy. Subordinate men—the young, slaves, and the indigent—became adept at evading the exploitation of their superiors (i.e., senior men, *Ogaranyan*, slave-owners) in the village. The Udi uprising during the war had proven that direct confrontation with the colonialialists was futile and it was prudent to make a judicious accommodation to the new conditions. The problem was how to manipulate this new system of authority while avoiding a conflict with the state, most notably the chiefs. Both the city and the industry offered new possibilities.

This chapter examines the war years as a formative period in the history of the industry and the city of Enugu. It investigates the many ways that local men maneuvered against authoritarian chiefly control, forced labor, and workplace exploitation by "native" and expatriate staff. Despite the context of extreme state oppression, workers secured some measure of control over the terms under which they sold their labor-power, the organization of work in the mines, the intensity with which they were prepared to work, and the frequency with which they presented themselves at the colliery. They molded the workplace according to their culture, beliefs about work, and their strategies to improve their positions as men in the village. In so doing they exemplified the creative strategies that early African workers developed to insure that they benefited from the colonial experience. Their work culture and the priorities they attached to village life enabled them to negotiate areas of control within the labor process at the mines and to humanize and define urban life in Enugu.

During this period colliery men established patterns of resistance that crystallized in a wave of disruptive strikes in the wake of World War I, the subject of Chapter 4. Some of these wartime protests reflected the problems posed by rapid urbanization for the region's food system, as well as the difficulties of monetizing new currencies. Others were related to colony-wide grievances of both African and European civil servants after the Great War. The connections between this unrest and the agitation of civil servants and workers in England, demonstrated that some African workers saw themselves as part of a larger community of British civil servants with legitimate expectations of improvement while working for the state.

Although some coal employees saw themselves as workers or loyal staff, racism prevented colonial authorities and the industry's managers from recognizing the similarities between Nigeria's miners and their British counterparts. In the mid-nineteenth century, British miners were fiercely independent, reserving the right to work when they pleased in the mines and, alternatively, to farm on their own fields. They shared "the common traditions of the peasantry" and considered themselves to be "rural tradesmen and not proletarians." In many important respects their values clashed with the needs of the coal companies of the mid-nineteenth century:

> They believed that certain crucial decisions concerning the mining of coal, such as the length of time they should spend underground and how much coal they should put out, lay within the prerogative of the coal getter and not of the capitalist or manager. . . . These values clashed at every point with the rationale of the new companies, with their emphasis on work discipline and company paternalism."[1]

Enugu's miners shared these values, but, unlike British miners, were able to preserve them throughout the industry's history because as a state enterprise, the colliery was never solely driven by the imperatives of the capitalist market. Because Enugu miners used farming to temper their reliance on the coal industry, their consciousness reflected elements of the peasantry and of independent rural craftsmen contracting to work on mutually agreeable terms.

They absented themselves from the mines to participate in the planting and harvesting seasons in their villages, and to fulfill social obligations (i.e., funerals, marriages, festivals, etc.) to their families and communities. And to the dismay of management they sold their labor-power in small and irregular units. The British interpreted this spirit of rural-based independence as confirmation of their racist assumptions about the irrationality, laziness, and inherent moral inferiority of African workers. Their interpretation of the workers' behavior said more about the "imagined" Africa in their heads than the reality of the society they had conquered. The reality was that these men had developed strategies to elude the "market." A closer examination of rural life, and an acknowledgment of the integrity of Igbo society, would have revealed a competing economic strategy with its own rationality and validity. Since Africans would not respond to the market in ways that satisfied employers and the state, the salient characteristic of the "African worker" became his "Africanness" and as Cooper has noted the two words seemed to express two incompatible concepts.[2]

Self-improvement and commitment to uplift the village, two dynamic norms of Igbo masculinity, also influenced the men's behavior in the industry and the role that mine workers played in village politics. They were a progressive force, challenging the autocratic policies of the chiefs while operating from a position of considerable prestige. The progressive role they played in the village also drew upon an urban political culture in Enugu where men from more distant regions of Igboland and all regions of Nigeria created new institutions of association, urban socialization, and power.

In the city, skilled laborers and clerical workers in the railway and the colliery formed organizations, called *Nzuko*, to give shape and order to urban life. They created networks that acculturated newcomers to city life, established judicial procedures for settling disputes, transferred resources to the rural village, and functioned as labor bureaus for men seeking jobs. And because they incorporated artisans and clerks, the literate, Christian elite, as well as laborers, they became an important context for disseminating the nationalist ideas emanating from the westernized elite in Lagos. War propaganda that emphasized the rights to self-determination, democracy, and equality resonated with the grievances that the Nigerian elite held against the Europeanization of the colonial service at the turn of the century.[3]

**Photo 3.1** Workers digging first boreholes, circa 1913 (MS.AFR.s. 384 b No. 71–Bodleian Library, Oxford)

The city offered protection and "freedom" to subordinate men who used Enugu to challenge the exercise of chiefly authority in the villages. "Coal men" emerged as a contentious social group, the inevitable consequence of the industry's existence and in sharpening contradiction with colonial rural policy. The rural-based miners transferred and adapted these liberal ideas to the villages where they became an ideological counterpoint to the despotism of the chief. As a group the elite and the coal workers opposed the state policy that favored "traditional" chiefs and consciously campaigned against both Onyeama and Chukwuani. By the war, the city had become a center of anti-chief agitation, further popularizing it as a refuge for rural dissidents.

Current historiography of coal miners suggests that the workplace—the coal pit—plays a far more important role in shaping the consciousness of coal miners than does the factory for other industrial workers. It is therefore important to launch this study with a rather detailed technical discussion of the mining of coal and the relations of power in the workplace. Specific extractive techniques influence the miners' workplace autonomy and self-identity. Work relations at Enugu evolved under a limited managerial style that mirrored the "indirect rule" practices being used to stabilize rural villages. Both the state and the industry used men whom they designated as local "leaders" to control their populations. The connection between the village and the industry was made quite intimate through the use of the "Na-

**Photo 3.2** Early coal miner in his village (MS.AFR.s. 1507 Fol. 3–Bodleian Library, Oxford)

tive Courts" to recruit workers, and the "chiefs'" appointment of representatives to supervise them in the mines.

The exercise of workplace power was far more complex than the simple relations in production, and it involved myriad problems for management. It was relatively easy to get men to the mines, but could they be made to produce? If so, for how long and with what degree of exertion? As Burawoy and Cooper have argued, colonial production regimes require special forms of political support in the legal and political system.[4] In this respect the "Native Court" system proved useful. Chiefs willingly used them to try men for infractions of industrial discipline. The connections between the chiefs and their industrial representatives gave management new ways to supervise the men inside the mines as well as outside in the villages and camps. As noted in the previous chapter, local chiefs ran the labor camps using their own paramilitary groups.[5] But these levels of coercion were more difficult to enforce in the city where the state was forced into an uneasy alliance with the new urban associations organized and largely controlled by the African elite.

## FROM LABOR CAMP TO CITY:
## ENUGU AND EARLY URBAN CULTURE, 1914–1919

When mining operations commenced, just as Europe entered World War I, economies were affected elsewhere in state projects in Nigeria to support the war effort. But the opening of the colliery was considered a priority and went forward as scheduled.[6] Supplies of Welsh coal, the primary fuel source of the railway, were erratic because of industrial unrest there and the danger posed by German U-boats. Government moved quickly to exploit the coal fields. The first mine, Udi Mine, opened in 1915 and a second, at Iva Valley, in 1917. Shortly after, Obwetti Mine was opened. All three functioned until 1936 when the old Udi Mine was closed. For the period of this study the Iva and Obwetti mines were the principal workplaces.[7]

Enugu coal was sub-bituminous, and while it compared unfavorably with the Welsh steaming coal that it replaced at the railway and Scottish bituminous coal, it was superior to both in ease of ignition and combustion. It was, therefore, a good steam coal for locomotive boilers.[8] But its chemical and physical qualities were a disincentive to extending the market beyond the regional area. As a "soft" coal it broke easily, disintegrating with each handling into ever smaller—and less usable—chunks. A considerable proportion of undersized coal was useless in steam furnaces. Moreover, under tropical conditions its high carbon content made it prone to spontaneous combustion. Thus, most purchasers intentionally held small reserves, a practice that made the market especially vulnerable to work stoppages which workers often scheduled during periods of coal scarcity.[9] Enugu workers were acutely aware of the constraints on reserves and planned their protests accordingly.

The railway was the industry's major transporter and consumer, and was originally the chief administrative unit over the industry. Both were assigned to the

Nigerian Transport Directorate with the colliery being an appendage of the Nigerian Railway system. The first skilled surface workers and clerks were also seconded from the railway.[10] They came from Britain's black colonies throughout the Atlantic World—Sierra Leone, British West Indies, as well as more colonized areas of Nigeria—Western Nigeria, and Onitsha, on the Niger River. All administrative and financial matters related to the operation of the mines were under the administrative supervision of the appropriate official in the railway.[11]

The railway was the key factor in the coal market and had its seasonal vagaries. This caused an irregularity of work, characteristic of most coal industries. While in temperate countries fluctuations in the availability of mine work reflected seasonal temperature change, Nigerian coal miners found their work interrupted by the export calendar for the colony's agricultural goods. From October to December the trains transported ground nuts, leaving few cars to evacuate coal from the colliery. Then mining operations were reduced, shifts cut, and workers dismissed, only to be re-engaged when wagons were once again available. In Scotland this type of mining seasonality led miners to value a certain autonomy by maintaining their fields and livestock as insurance against the off season. Similarly, in Enugu workers negotiated mine work with the gendered farm cycle in their villages. Men's farming chores increased during three specific periods: from January to February, March to April, and parts of October. At that time the men absented themselves from the mines to work their fields. As luck would have it, the railway and farming cycles did not always coincide. Thus management was forced to discharge and re-engage workers on the one hand, and futilely seek workers on the other.

The railway schedule reduced the workers' ability to integrate colliery jobs with agricultural labor because they were not always able to get work when they wanted it. Although the industry's irregular labor needs frustrated those workers who wanted full employment, it discouraged the development of an African proletariat, a social class that the state had anticipated with dread.[12] These conflicting policies and priorities made it very difficult to stabilize the colliery's industrial relations.

When the mines began production in 1915 the workforce was an eclectic collection of forced and voluntary unskilled labor, prisoners, unskilled contract workers, and voluntary clerical workers and artisans. This heterogeneous mixture of men with differing skills and commitments to wage labor under different systems of labor control, and familiarity with the capitalist workplace, created eclectic patterns of protest and work culture in the industry. In the initial period, it was the artisans and clerical workers of the railway, who organized the first protests. Although they looked down on the manual workers underground, their forms of protest nonetheless became a model for subsequent wage bargaining by the more "local" underground laborers. Because the railway and coal industries were functionally linked, their respective workers also had close ties. During the war the influence of militant railway workers on the less seasoned colliery workers was noticable. The connection was especially close because unrest in one industry affected the other since it interrupted either the coal market or the supply. As the older of the two, the railway workers were the vanguard for the wave of protest during and immediately after World War I, which incited the first wave of unrest in the colliery. Even in this early period both groups understood their strategic importance to West Africa's colonial economy, and they protested in individual and coordinated ways against the organization and conditions of work, the quality of their life, and their pay.

Work relations in the Enugu mines demonstrated many of the characteristics of the colonial capitalist workplace. An overt and explicit system of racial authority was deliberately crafted in the early mines and the city. Colonial "whiteness," a new, socially constructed category, had to be concretized and empowered if it were to become a signifier of authority and a crucial element in social control. This is not to imply that Africans could not see the physical difference between themselves and the "white" authorities, but difference did not mean superiority nor hegemony. That had to be created and legitimized. Certainly, after the brutality of the conquest, Africans could see the destructive power of a colonial army, but this army was not "white" but black soldiers under white command. Thus the conquest alone did not imbibe "whiteness" with power. Furthermore, the people did not necessarily believe that Udi's subordination to British rule was the result of their "inherent, biological inferiority," an assumption made by Lugard who supported scientific racist notions. The people of Udi were overpowered, but this was a subordinate status contingent upon the state's ability to create "enduring forms of dominance."[13] Such forms were not well established in the first half-decade of colonial rule. Thus the racial dimension of colonial power had to be deliberately encouraged in myriad structural and ideological ways. Self-representation played an important part in this process, and officials were intent on emphasizing their cultural and racial superiority over their Nigerian subjects.

In the first three years of the war, the city of Enugu did not formally exist. There was only a military outpost at Udi (see photos 3.3 and 3.4) and a cluster of labor camps near the mine entrance and at the site of the railway station. During the war there were three camp sites: "Coal Camp" in Enugu proper and two "unofficial" camps, Ugwu Alfred (Alfred's Hill) and Ugwu Aaron (Aaron's Hill), which were administered by "native" labor contractors.[14] African workers lived in "bush" camps in the valley near the Udi escarpment, and Europeans lived in temporary housing high on a ridge overlooking the future site of Enugu. During this period, when conditions were so rudimentary, political authorities like Lugard attempted to institutionalize the racialized system of authority implicit in colonialism. For race to become an important expression/signifier of power in a recently conquered area, colonial "whiteness" had to be given meaning and authority. This was especially important when there was so little difference in the material conditions and living arrangements of both colonizer and colonized. Both lived in "bush" houses, with thatched roofs and dirt floors.[15] Until the town was formally designed with boundaries between "European colonizer" and "African subject," Africans had to interpret the political meaning of European settlement high on the Udi escarpment. In case the significance was missed, there were the "hammock boys." The Euro-

**Photo 3.3** Udi military outpost, circa 1913 (MS.AFR.s. 384 b 99–Bodleian Library, Oxford)

pean underground manager, overmen, mechanics, and electricians lived on the escarpment. From this period until after World War II, men carried them in hammocks to the mines daily.[16] The impact of this ritual of racial power and privilege on the men's consciousness was so dramatic that thirty years later, nearly every miner cited this practice as an example of racism in the mines.[17]

The land for the town and the mines was acquired from Udi "chiefs" in a process of dubious legality through which the Ngwo village-group lost almost all its arable land.[18] From 1914 to 1917, even before the settlement was legally recognized as a township, hundreds of men were drawn to the site by the unrest in the countryside and in anticipation of the arrival of the railway and mining operations. In 1917 when the Iva Valley mine was opened, over 400 "bush" houses were built for the camp.[19] Most of the artisans and clerical workers had been trained in Church Missionary Society schools in Onitsha, Owerri, and to the west in Lagos.[20] They, and those unskilled laborers who were dragooned by chiefs Onyeama and Chukwuani, were the first settlers in Enugu. The clerks and artisans formed a cosmopolitan community with links to the Lagos elite that had mobilized so vigorously against the conquest and protested discrimination in government employment. Furthermore, they had declared war on Lugard, whom they attacked in their press as the archetypically arrogant imperialist.[21] In August 1916 the Enugu group wrote

**Photo 3.4** Mining conscripts in Udi (MS.AFR.s. 384–Bodleian Library, Oxford)

the Church Missionary Society's Niger Mission on behalf of 100 rail, colliery, and prison workers, offering to construct a church and requesting a minister.[22] Many were Yoruba converts who held their own weekly church services, while others were Igbo clerical workers both from Owerri province, about 100 miles south and from Onitsha town. They made Enugu an Igbo city of "stranger" Igbo from the more developed and earlier colonized areas of Igboland. Even before the town was formally laid out you could see the contours of an African urban culture. In the midst of a bush camp, these men created an urban African life that challenged Lugard's assertions that Africans were essentially rural beings.

By late 1915 there were 400 workers at the colliery of varying origin.[23] The formal layout of the town was made by a senior health officer with frequent interventions by Lugard. (See Map 3.1.) Lugard's ideas about urban design were representative of early-twentieth-century British theories about urban planning. In reaction to the nineteenth-century industrial city, early-twentieth-century planning emphasized "health, light, and air," in a type of "environmental determinism" which sought to resolve "social pathologies" by the manipulation of physical space.[24] Segregation, largely but not exclusively racial, was an important colonial modification of these general principles.[25] Lugard clearly understood the importance of creating the Manichean worlds of the colonizer and colonized.[26] The order of the European Reservation was a metaphor for the cultural superiority and order

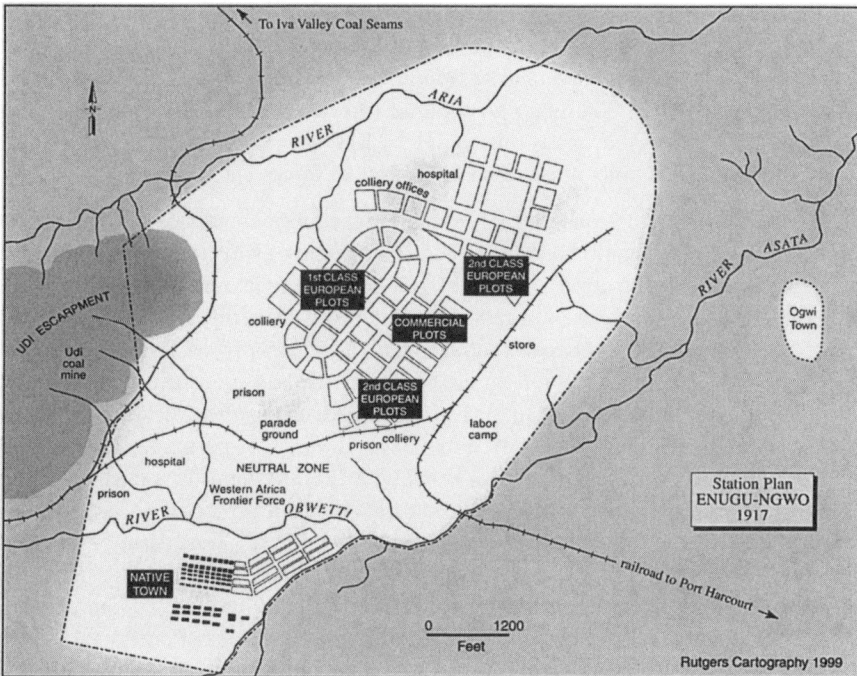

**Map 3.1** Enugu, 1917. Drawn from PRO, C0583/67(4) Station Plan No. 107, Government Station, Enugu-Ngwo. (Rutgers University Cartography)

of British society. It is contrasted with the disorder, dirt, and chaos of the African area, the "Native Town." His most elaborate musings on the spatial requirements of this racialized authority are expressed in intricate and obsessive detail in Lugard's memorandum on "Townships." Here he explained the racial protocol of colonial Nigeria to his political officers.[27] The design of Enugu was an important aspect of the new authoritarian structure because it gave physical form to the racial and class stratification that constituted colonial order. Residential segregation was also important because it symbolized cultural, racial, and class boundaries in a space (the city) shared by European/African, colonizer/subject, black/white. Such boundaries were especially important in spaces where Africans and Europeans were in daily contact—the city and the colonial workplace. In these spaces such "markers" had political significance. Lugard translated racial segregation into principles of urban design and "native" control in the layout of Enugu, which he initiated during a visit in February 1915. His ideas exemplified a second characteristic of British colonial design—the obsession with health or "the sanitation syndrome."[28] He detailed a mile-wide *cordon sanitaire* between the "nearest European dwelling" and the "native area"—a separation that he wrote of in his *Political Memorandum*. In an exemplary statement of this racialization of early health problems, he expressed his racism in the discourse of public health and social hygiene:

The first objective of the non-residential area is to segregate Europeans, so that they shall not be exposed to the attacks of mosquitoes *which have become infected with the germs of malaria or yellow fever*, by preying on Natives, and especially on Native children, whose blood so often contains these germs. . . . Finally, it removes the inconvenience felt by Europeans, whose rest is disturbed by drumming and other noises dear to the Native [emphasis mine].[29]

The meticulous attention that Lugard paid to the more mundane aspects of urban planning (i.e., specifications of the yards of frontage to surround each compound in the European Reservation, the height at which tree branches should be clipped) was far more than an aesthetic preoccupation.[30] It was an obsessive acknowledgment of the relationship between spatial organization and power. Urban design was a part of "native" control and in an area so recently, and precariously, conquered it was hence *politically* important.[31] To Lugard, Africans, after all, were not urban people, and no one in a position of authority in Enugu was particularly concerned with encouraging urban African life. But Lugard found that it was much easier to design the layout for the town and to pontificate about urban order and "native" control than it was to create the type of colonial city he desired. Men poured into Enugu, fleeing oppressive conditions in the countryside, looking for new opportunities, and women came seeking to escape unwanted marriages.[32] They settled where they could, taking advantage of the inevitable chaos of early settlement.

Enugu also became a refuge for runaway slaves fleeing masters who were exploring new ways to use their labor more systematically.[33] In the South Nkanu area, slave-owning *Ogaranyan* were contracting with the government to supply workers for construction of the railway, which passed their area en route to Enugu. Many slaves, *Ohu*, were drafted into this workforce. Quite often they did not understand the concept of "paid labor." They assumed that their work for the government was the same as the "unpaid" labor they supplied to their owner. But the wage experience was enlightening and transformative. One elder, an ex-slave from the Nkanu village-group of Ugbawka recalls his gradual awareness of the new forms of freedom which the labor systems of colonialism brought:

I and Edenwede Ogbu of Isigwe were pace setters sort of, to the *Ihus* or *Obias*. We were the first set of people to enlist personally to the Europeans without the consent of the chief for their personal betterment. . . . I was among those sent by the chief to work in the construction of the railway line from Otakpa, now in Imo State. Otakpa was where the Nkanu people under Chief Chukwuani of Ozalla joined in the railway construction. . . . All payment for those that were sent out by the chief whether on the coal mine or railway construction was directed to the chief. We were left with nothing but at a later date the chief started giving us small amount of what each of us realized. This was after we had realized from the Europeans that we were paid for the job we had been doing for long. Because of the chief's action we deemed it unnecessary not to be obligatory to the chief. In the circumstance, we started looking for our own greener pastures for personally paid jobs and the most possible area to look for jobs was in Enugu.[34]

Lugard found that it was very difficult to prevent a permanent urban-based working class from developing.[35] Despite his efforts these immigrants began to form associations with an urban cultural autonomy distinct from the rural culture and warrant chiefs preferred by colonial authorities. The first form of association created by the working class and urban *salariat* helped to cope with the problems of urban life in the disorganized environment of the nascent colonial city.

During the war Enugu's African elite began to hold "family" meetings,[36] called *Nzuko*, in which the "sons abroad" from large patrilineages of specific villages in Owerri, discussed "home" and common urban problems.[37] As the largest contingent of urban workers, colliery men played an important role in these associations, which gave urban life shape and structure. Each *Nzuko* had its own officers—a president and a secretary. The first meetings occurred during the war and included the skilled and educated wage earners who were excluded from village politics because of the state preference for indirect rule by "traditional" rulers. When the "family" groupings proved too small in scale, they amalgamated to form district-wide unions. The first union in Enugu, the Owerri Union, was founded in 1917 by a colliery clerk when Enugu was still the "bush."[38] The functional relationship between the *Nzuko* and the district meetings was similar to that of the individual villages to the council of the village-group. Each *Nzuko* sent two representatives to the "union." The autonomy of the constituent unit was scrupulously respected, decisions were made by consensus after extensive consultations in which all participated.

Because colonial urban policy assumed little responsibility for the social reproduction of the urban working class, these unions stepped into the breech. They created networks for jobs, extended loans for business ventures, taught new values, and assisted with funerals of members. Although authorities deeply distrusted them, they had a strong civic consciousness, informed by Christian education. They worked as partners with the state in preserving urban order by "checking and eliminating the number of undesirables" in town,[39] adjudicating disputes among members, teaching social discipline, and inculcating new values that habituated the men to the capitalist workplace.[40] They encouraged new notions of time and idleness through an almost obsessive insistence on promptness, enforced through fines at their meetings.[41] Although the state tolerated them and welcomed their assistance in controlling the city's population, officials suspected, quite correctly, that they were a training ground for political leadership that inevitably would challenge colonialism. They were a "forum for political expression and a structure within which new groups could assert their leadership."[42]

Because *Nzukos* included both the literate and illiterate men, they were an excellent forum for the political ideas being debated in the Nigerian press after the war. An environment of heightened expectation swept through wartime Nigeria.[43] This led artisans and clerical workers to be optimistic that the government would be responsive to their complaints. Additionally, they assumed that postwar political reforms would give them some role in the state, a hope that proved illusionary. Moreover, inflation made it difficult for these skilled and clerical workers to live in a style commensurate with their self-identities as "respectable" men. To make matters worse, many of them were being retrenched under new discriminatory policies. The war popularized ideas that resonated with the anti-imperialist agitation of Nigeria's most radical newspaper editors, most notably Thomas Horatio Jackson, editor of the *Lagos Weekly Record*.[44] Jackson launched attack after attack in his press against Lugard, leading the governor in 1917 to propose a censorship bill that was subsequently rejected by the Colonial Office.[45] The propaganda about democracy and Woodrow Wilson's calls for "self-determination" shifted the international discourse around colonialism and led to a reformulation of the rationale for the colonial state. Authorities argued that the new task of colonialism was to guide the ascent of the uncivilized peoples of Africa through "mandates," "trusteeship," and "native paramountcy."[46] This new paternalistic packaging was virulently attacked by the educated elite who were particularly disgruntled by the renewed commitment to "traditional" rulers.[47] But they also positioned themselves to manipulate the inherent contradictions in this ideology. They too were British servants, and the Crown, as arbitrator of superior British law, could not ignore their claims as loyal British subjects.[48]

The seditious political content of elite discourse was disseminated to the village and broad sectors of the urban African community through the membership base of the unions. They included a cross section of all "respectable" sectors of urban society, thereby making the group a conduit for radical ideas to the illiterate working class.[49] Politically, these unions rallied opposition to the rural chiefs, and their ideas filtered into the village through the coal miners who daily went between mine and village.[50] As self-anointed agents of modernization, civilization, and progress, members assumed the task of marshalling resources to develop the village. In addition to raising funds for village improvement, they also served as advocates for rural communities with the authorities and sent delegations to meet with responsible government officials.[51] They presented a dilemma for the rural "chiefs." Their resources were important for village development but their hostility to the institution of "customary" colonial chieftaincy ultimately undermined the powers of rural "chiefs."

While the role of urban "unions" in nationalist political mobilization has been recognized, their relationship to working class agitation has not been explored.[52] However, in cities like Enugu, these "union" members were in the forefront of the early labor struggles in the city. This particular strata was most aware of the forms of protest that were within the rights of subjects of the British Crown.[53] The prominent role played by colliery employees in the "unions" created a structural connection between this new type of association and the industry's workers. There is documentary evidence that the "unions" and the cultures of protest that they fostered were adapted to industrial protest. While the precise dates of the foundation of colliery-based *Nzuko* are not known, the rash of strikes that spanned the latter years of the war and the twenties indicates the existence of worker organizations that planned and coordinated protests and selected deputations to negotiate with management. The structure of these worker organizations and their role in the first series of colliery protests will be examined next.

These associations established a syncretic organizational culture with elements of indigenous leadership patterns, consultative forms, and western organizational techniques. In the urban *Nzuko*, men learned the technical skills of running organizations, structuring and presenting grievances, and mobilizing support. In so doing, they presented an organized challenge to the state's ability to make the colonial city and workplace. The workers were not the only inhabitants of the city. Many of the others were less concerned with presenting such "respectable" opposition to the state. They were the men who seized "illegal space" to forge new types of households with several men, usually single, and one or two boy-servants. Their presence gave Enugu a definite male working class "flavor."

As authorities designed the physical space for Enugu, the new manager organized work and created structures of power and authority to instill industrial order. But he did not work in a vacuum. The Igbo men in the industry defined the limits of managerial control and carved out areas of freedom and autonomy. The relations of power in the early workplace were the context in which the miners developed their notion of moral economy. As they measured their experiences against the moral and social framework that shaped their approach to work, they created new patterns of resistance. The Enugu workplace was a new and unpleasant experience, fraught with danger. It required that they become a different type of man—a colonial worker. This workplace operated under different rules, conventions, and regulations than the rural economy with which they were most familiar. A harsh system of authority and regimented work rhythms were enforced through racial discrimination and violence.[54] While as a capitalist workplace it required their habituation, mining was work and the men had well-formed ideas about work.[55] It was these ideas that they adapted and applied to their experiences at the colliery. These constituted a work ethic.[56]

## MINING OPERATIONS BEGIN: THE PHYSICAL CONTEXT OF AN EVOLVING WORK CULTURE

On 23 June 1914, William J. Leck was selected as manager of the future Udi Mine by Professor John Cadman of the University of Birmingham, the Colonial Office's technical adviser, and J. Eaglesome, director of the Nigerian Railway and Works. He was only twenty-five years old but had seven years' managerial experience at Whithaven and Mill Hill Colleries following his training as a mining engineer in the Northumberland area, Britain's largest coal fields.[57] Leck sailed for Nigeria in September 1914, reaching Onitsha several weeks later and finally arriving at Udi in February 1915, only a few weeks after the insurrection was crushed.[58] Leck's departure from Northumberland was well-timed. The war plunged those coal fields into a deep recession with the loss of the German, Belgium, and Baltic (Russian) markets that imported 80 percent of the area's output.[59] Nigeria was a fortuitous move that would prove decisive for him. It launched a career in the colonial civil service. He would remain in Enugu for the next thirty years.

The mines proceeded at a remarkable pace given the insurrection, inexperienced labor force, and war-induced shortages in the desired tools and equipment. The railway reports of 1915 and 1916 expressed the general manager's anxiety as his reserves of imported coal dwindled. The first shortages appeared in March 1915 when railway officials estimated their supply could only last twenty days.[60] The reserve of Natal (South African) coal was used up and the hostilities in Europe made further supplies of Welsh coal doubtful. By May the locomotive superintendent reported that he had only two weeks' reserve and had resorted to burning firewood, which was less efficient and also dangerous, especially during the *hamartan* or dry season. By the beginning of June, with all coal stock depleted, most trains were being operated with wood as fuel and in 1916, the railway lost twenty-six wagons burned by sparks from the wood.[61] Thus, the British commercial community in Nigeria was ecstatic about the new Enugu coal fields. In February 1917 reports from the "field" in their key journal, *West Africa*, noted with enthusiasm "it is certain that Udi is one of the world's great coal fields."[62]

Coal extracted in the course of the initial excavations could not immediately meet the shortages caused by the war, but by the end of 1915, 8,000 tons were stacked at pit head awaiting the railway (see Photo 3.13). The railway arrived in May 1916. The year 1917 marked the refinement of the coal transport system and more capital works at the colliery, manifest in the increase in coal output to 85,405 tons. The new Iva Valley Mine delivered at a rate of 130 to 150 tons per day. By September 1917, Lugard felt confident enough of the mine's output to announce

**Photo 3.5** Construction of railway to the Udi Mine, circa 1915 (Crown Agents)

that supplies were available for sale to the commercial and shipping community in Nigeria and other West African colonies.[63]

The government usually recruited workers from villages near such major projects under a system called the "local method." But because of the unsettled nature of the district it was considered more prudent to bring workers from Onitsha and Owerri. Political conditions also required that clear institutions of authority and colonial control be established at the colliery, where a handful of Europeans tried to transform men, who had just been defeated at the battlefield, into industrial workers. The warrant chiefs and their associates were brought into the enterprise as recruiters, managers of the labor camps, and as "native" staff in the mines. The chiefs' main representatives were the "boss boys," who brought in their crews and were in charge of particular underground districts. It was expected that they would handle all grievances their teams had, just as the warrant chief did in the village.

Lugard also took a personal interest in the colliery and the railway and regarded both projects as a type of experiment in social engineering. His dispatches to the Colonial Office were decidedly enthusiastic, as if he felt his massive project was truly bearing fruit. He visited the area soon after Leck's arrival in February 1915, and again in April.[64] At that time, he reported that mining operations were well underway. The miners were:

**Photo 3.6** Port Harcourt—Arrival of first coal train alongside the S.S. Sir Hugh (Crown Agents)

engaged in driving an adit tunnel in the opposite hill across a ravine, where he expects to strike the same seam at 1073 foot level. From thence a short colliery line will convey the coal to the main line.[65]

In December 1915 he boasted to the Nigerian Council that "free" labor had already convinced the "savages" of the value of wage labor, a claim that fell quite wide of the truth.

> Prompt and fair payment, combined with kindly treatment have resulted, I am told, in an actual competition for employment, and those wild tribes who year by year, and indeed only a few months ago, had to be coerced by armed forces, with loss of life, are already learning confidence and acquiring wealth by honest labor.[66]

Despite Lugard's proclamations, very little of a "free market" in labor was in evidence at the colliery site. On the contrary, an atmosphere of militarism and coercion hung over the labor camps, with the warrant chiefs sending in their conscripts under the watchful eye of their paramilitary police or a trusted "boss boy." The indomitable Chief Onyeama was especially adept at creating an elaborate system of labor control that extended into the labor camps themselves. According to local sources he developed his own surveillance system with spies and court messengers who ran his transit camps, which were located along the route of railway construction from Port Harcourt. He was alleged to have had his own "labor agents who checked off laborers against their communities." At the Iva camp, his largest camp, he deployed workers to the various projects, including the colliery.[67]

Leck brought his own workers from Onitsha who had been drafted by Eze Okolie, a warrant chief. His brother marched them to Udi under the guard of the hated court messengers.[68] Among this group was a contractor, Alfred Inoma, who has been immortalized by Ugwu Alfred (Alfred's Hill), a small settlement of mud houses perched on a spur near the Udi escarpment. Alfred's Onitsha men preferred to segregate themselves from the local Udi people whose dialect was unfamiliar, and whom they considered too uncivilized and backward. Gabriel Mbamelu, one of the first miners in Alfred's team, tells of his harsh experience in being pushed into the mines:

> We were forced to carry barrels of cement from Onitsha to Udi where they were building Udi Customary Court. A barrel of cement will be carried by four persons from Onitsha to Udi, though they will be changed by another four men when they're tired. That is they will be eight. When we reached Udi we were forced to continue the construction of the present Miliken Hill [a road]. When we reached Enugu, we were forced to start working in the mine. Oh! We Suffered! We cannot go back for we were under the guard of court messengers. We at long last discovered that working in the mines is beneficial for we are being paid and we were no more being harassed by the chief.[69]

Mbamelu's gradual accommodation to the mines was fairly typical for young men who were usually the targets of the corrupt chiefs. Even with Onyeama's elaborate system of camp control, young men could still escape persecution by disappearing into the mass of humanity clustered around the mines. Leck's control over these men was precarious. In 1916, when the mines employed 700 men, he was helpless to prevent 150 from leaving when he reduced wages from nine pence to six pence per day.[70] During this period Leck could not convince the local people to go underground. They greeted with a certain skepticism Leck's claim that they would carve mines out of the hills.[71]

By international standards the Enugu mines were not extremely hazardous because they had negligible amounts of black damp and fire damp, the explosive gasses that make coal mining so dangerous.[72] There was also a little coal dust, which was also explosive and caused silicosis or "black lung." Without the danger of gaseous explosions, management became less diligent about ventilation in its general engineering scheme.[73] It was also assumed that, as tropical people, Africans would be quickly acclimatized to harsh underground conditions. Nevertheless the mines were bad enough to frighten away many locals who were brought there by their chiefs. They resembled a dark, steamy, muddy hole, with a precarious roof. Lighting and ventilation were inadequate and most men worked in near total darkness.

Mining operations in May 1915 engaged a crew of 106 laborers and a skeleton staff of one or two European supervisors. Leck introduced an engineering design that dominated production at Enugu throughout this study: the *pillar and stall* system. This was the extractive system used in his home, Britain's north coal fields. He considered it to be most suitable for the natural conditions (i.e., condition of roof, size of seam) and "native labour available." In the year before the railway reached Udi, in May 1916, Leck directed these new workers in the basic construction of the mines, driving main roadways to the limits of coal deposits. The initial process of driving main roadways and side entries, which constructed the mine, was performed by teams of men called "special labor gangs," a broad work category that included a number of underground and surface workers whose jobs were essential to mining operations, but were not considered skilled.[74] These gangs included railmen, timber drawers, and a series of men who *rip* or heighten the roof of the roadways. The timbermen set timber to support the roadways, and railmen lay rails for the tubs used to carry coal from the work face to the surface. However, in the year before the railway reached Udi, coal was carried in head baskets either by young boys or by prisoners.

The special labor gangs built the main road, or *adit*, into coal outcroppings on the side of the hill. Branching off from the *adit* at specific intervals like ribs from the spine, were secondary roads or *side entries*. The *side entries* were mutually parallel and extended some distance into the seam. The area between two *side entries* was called a *panel*, and was managed as a distinct unit of the mine. The actual mining operations were launched from these entries into the coal. Each group of miners opened a coal face at regular intervals along the *side entry*, working from the entry back into the coal. (See Figure 3.1.)

The heading is the miner's workplace, the coal face where he excavates the coal. The dimensions of the space depend on how wide he makes the coal face, and the

**Photo 3.7** Boys with baskets of coal (Crown Agents)

height of the seam. During this period, seams varied from three to six feet thick. When working a thin seam the men spent their shift kneeling or prone in the damp darkness; with the four-foot seam, they stood spread-eagle with their backs touching the roof of the room. The average coal seam in Udi Mine was four feet, thus permitting the driving of "roads" of sufficient height.[75] The driving of the headings was called *development*, and divided the district into pillars fifty feet by eighty

**Figure 3.1** Pillar and Stall Mining Diagram
Bird's-eye view of a typical Enugu mine district that is being worked in "development." Coal is extracted in the process of dividing up the site. Pillars are left to support the roof. The extraction of the pillars is called "robbery." As the pillars are mined, the area is temporaroily supported by timber which, when withdrawn, allows the roof to collapse.

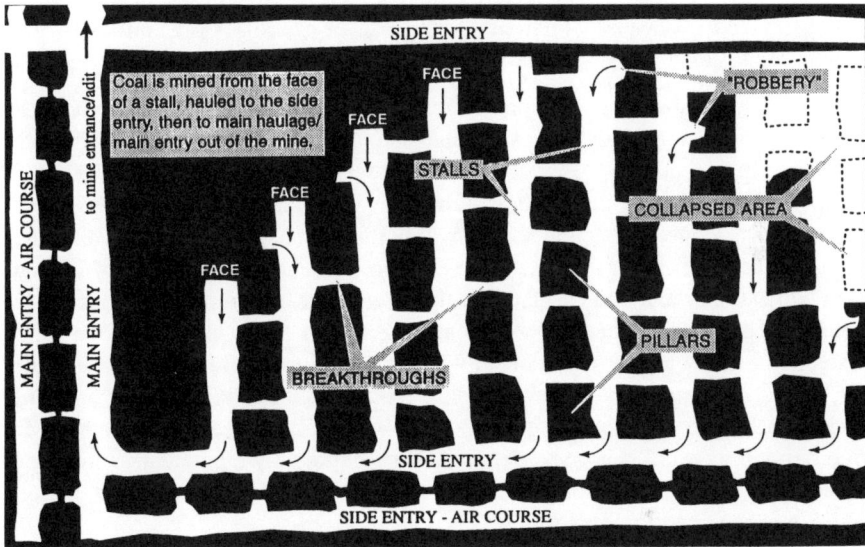

feet for future extraction. Coal was produced during this process, but it was considered more exhausting and therefore usually paid higher piece rates. When the extraction was complete and the whole area had been *developed*, the pillars were removed in a process called *robbery. Development* and *robbery* could occur at right angles with the coal cleavage, *on board*, or parallel with the cleavage, *on end*.[76] Working on a coal face that was *on end* was easier because the coal came off in sheets with the line of main cleavage. If the entire coal-bearing area was divided into pillars before any extraction occurred, it was called *whole working*, and after the pillars of coal were subsequently removed, the area was called *in the broken*.[77]

The working of coal whether in a heading, in *development*, or a coal face in *robbery*, involved several operations which were usually performed by skilled hewers: setting the timber for roof support, laying the track from the roadway to the coal face, undercutting the coal, bringing the coal down by shot firing or wedges at the roof, shoveling the coal into the tubs, and pushing the tubs to the main road. Conventionally, in Europe these operations were performed by a single miner before the introduction of machine production in the late nineteenth century. The skill inherent in mining was complex and involved the miner's being sensitive to threatening work conditions, such as the fall of the roof or presence of gas, making correct judgments about the depth of the undercut, and having the manual skill to bring down coal in large marketable chunks. They all involved manual skill, bodily dexterity, and mental alertness.[78] But the broader society did not recognize the specialized nature of these skills. It has been argued that coal mining exhibited many of the characteristics of a craft:

> the essence of a craft is its dependence on a precarious combination of manipulative skill embodying a physical training and a judgment requiring both experience and intelligence. The resulting almost unanalyzable pieces of expertise constituted the "knacks" of a trade and the essence of a knack is its difficulty of communication.[79]

As male manual workers, the possession of these skills and "the aggressive celebration of physical strength" were key contributing factors to the masculine ethos that developed in coal mining.[80] Hewers, called "pit men,"[81] had a self-identity of skilled workers and were proud, independent, self-improving, and resentful of supervision.[82] These values defined a social hierarchy within mining communities in Britain. They would similarly emerge as important bases of a proud identity among hewers in Enugu.

In Northumberland and Durham, Leck's home area, all preliminary tasks to the actual coal getting were performed by specialized workers.[83] Under the "Derbyshire system," hewers only hew the coal and put it in the tubs.[84] Other workers set timber, lay the rails, and remove stone to make roadways of sufficient height, and build packing walls. To Leck this fractionalized division of labor seemed appropriate for "the African worker," whom he deprecated with typically ethnocentric arrogance for being incapable of handling more than a single task.[85] This was the system upon which he organized Enugu's mines.

At the coal face the miners' first action was to *shear* the seam with two parallel vertical cuts, one to the right, the other to the left. This defined the coal face to be worked. Then, lying prone on the wet floor, the hewer *kirved* or undercut the coal, and made a cavity by *holing* or *bottoming* out the coal about two feet from the floor.[86] The cut would be three to five feet into the seam. This was the most dangerous and demanding phase of extraction. A miner would spend several days or weeks, on his side, *holing* the coal with a good part of the operation being performed lying *under* this shelf of coal with wedges of wood supporting the overhang. His second task varied with the quality of the coal. In some cases the coal was dislodged by driving wedges or pneumatic picks between the coal face and the roof, bringing the whole section down.[87] In Enugu, however, it was brought down by explosives, called *shot firing*. A European shot firer drilled holes at appropriate angles into the coal face and set the explosives. When detonated, the coal fell on the floor. In the third phase of the operation, the miner loaded the dislodged coal into tubs, which were supplied by "tubboys" from the main roadways, and to which he attached his tally disk with his employee number, so that he was credited with the output. The tubboys then pushed the tubs to the main roadways where haulage men transported them to the surface. When the hewer performed all these tasks he was said to have been within the "single place tradition." In Enugu the typical work group was one railman, eight tubmen, eight hewers, and two timbermen.[88] Each miner had a number emblazoned on a token which he attached to the tub of coal that he produced. This allowed mine clerks to assess the amount of coal he produced and hence his pay.

Poor ventilation and lighting, flooded work areas, and high temperatures with near saturation point humidity cut the hewers' productivity and created respiratory illnesses. Moreover, the entire operation was performed in near total darkness. Most lighting at the coal face was by candles or a makeshift lamp, which filled the air with smoke. The reflections of one miner who began in this period, Thomas Noisike, on how lighting reflected industrial power relations:

> In these days we use a lamp with an empty perforated can and an engine oil is poured into it and cotton inside. This automatically becomes a lamp. One disadvantage is that it was always smoky in the mine. Carbide caps was used for some time. Then candle was introduced later for the pick men and tub men. Carbide lamps is for the headmen and the timber boy and the rail boy. Because candles were very cheap it has to be supplied to the poor labourers. Carbide is costly that's why is for the headmen.[89]

Although candles were an improvement over the makeshift lamps, they were easily extinguished, leaving the workers in pitch darkness. Another informant recalled:

> Candles were being used then as a light inside the mine. Whenever the candle light goes off one has to find another pickman or tubman nearest to his location to light it up again. Because the mine is very, very dark, that you cannot see without light you have to find your way by feeling blindly along the walls or along the rail line to next person's position to light up your candle. Whenever there was much heat inside the mines the candle light goes as soon as it is lighted.[90]

It was not the heat that extinguished the candles but the low levels of oxygen. In mining engineering history, the development of ventilation was related to attempts to remove noxious and explosive gases from the mines. But since the Enugu mines had little gas or dust, management took a rather relaxed position on ventilation. The deeper the mines plunged into the hills, the more problematic ventilation became. Consequently the mines had humidity levels approaching 100 percent saturation and average temperatures above 85 degrees Fahrenheit. Oxygen deficiency worsened as one moved from the main roads to the work sites. The oxygen level above ground was 20 percent, but in new roadways it was a dangerous 13.4 percent.[91] Initially the ventilation problem was controlled by drafts from two furnaces, but as mine workings spread out, this method proved ineffective.

By the end of 1917 a Sirroco fan, capable of replacing 40,000 square feet of air, was installed. But this was also of limited effect in the scattered workings.[92] The pillar and stall, with its large numbers of roadways and isolated work faces, was a very difficult area to ventilate.[93] Hewers adjusted their effort to compensate for these poor conditions. European managers noted that most hewers were unable to work vigorously for a full shift. They worked for a few minutes before returning to the roadways to cool down and rest. It became customary for hewers to work in pairs quite like the *marra* of the Durham coal fields,[94] with one hewer working while the other recovered.[95] The Enugu hewers worked barefoot, wearing only a loincloth, with small fans protruding from the back.[96]

Water was always a problem and became even more so when the Iva Mine was opened in 1917. As the workings extended, many seams encountered water subsidence, especially in those districts located under river beds. Water seepage from surface streams flooded the coal face and caused frequent cave-ins.[97] It was evident even in 1915/16 that roof timbering would be a far larger cost than had been anticipated.[98] The sheer difficulty of working under these conditions was described by an early miner, James Alo, who began in 1916.[99]

> In some sections of the mine water reaches one as far as the chest. Special labourers it is their duty to draw the water inside the mines to outside. Hewers stay inside the water and do their job. When they came out from the mine their body would look like that of a lizard.[100]

Mine work was so unlike any work local people had experienced that despite state attempts to use local luminaries as recruiters, the local Enugu people were at first reluctant to enter the mines.[101] The exhaustive nature of these operations, and the uncomfortable positions in which they were performed, led the men to develop workplace traditions that adjusted their expenditure of effort to these conditions. The roadways usually had a brisk air flow, but at the coal face, because it was a dead end, there was little if any air flow and oxygen levels were dangerously low.[102]

Despite these intolerable and substandard conditions, management assumed that Africans could be induced to work in them. When they saw that the workers couldn't, they said it was because of some inherent deficiency in Igbo work culture or a physiological problem with their bodies. Management accused the men of "slacking" or alleged that the local diet had such poor nutritionional value that the men could not sustain consistent effort.[103] It was never acknowledged that 100 percent saturation rates, oxygen deficiency, and high temperature would be a disincentive for productive labor.

The first miners were given no protective equipment, nor training in safe mining practices. Although fully aware of metropolitan standards, management was not particularly concerned about the safety of their workers. African workers were cheap, plentiful, and expendable. Leck did little to bring the colliery up to recognized mining standards until forced to do so by the workers themselves, in a series of strikes in the late thirties. At that time the workers used conditions in English and American mines as the standard for their demands. Leck assumed that African workers could be made to perform under far more severe conditions than British miners. This was most obvious in the substandard conditions that he allowed to exist. A source gave this description of a hewer coming to work in the thirties: "wearing only a loincloth, carrying his pick and shovel on his head, a water gourd in one hand and a candle pan in the other."[104]

What little safety equipment they had was usually improvised by the men themselves. There were no helmets to protect them from roof collapse, and the men worked barefoot where the damp, fine coal cut into the feet. Injuries to the feet or

**Photo 3.8** Hewers with leg wraps, circa 1915 at Udi mine. Note the improvised shin protectors and baskets used to carry coal on the head. (Crown Agents)

hands from coal tubs, and from roof collapse, were the largest percentage of accidents in the mines. Early photographs show that even in 1916 the men had makeshift wrappings on their legs to protect the shins from injury while kneeling at work.

The assumptions that Leck made about the standards of workplace safety for African workers were rooted in the particular way that race, class, and gender (masculinity) intersected in the discourse on coal mining. Coal mining had already been associated with the concept of "race" before the British even discovered the mines. McKlintock noted that since the 1840s, race and gender were conflated during the attempts to bring British coal miners under factory-like discipline. In public discourse the fierce independence and protest culture of the coal miners were considered evidence that they were a "'race' apart, 'outcasts,' historically abandoned, isolated and primitive."[105] Although celebrated by labor historians today, symbols of a fiercely independent working class masculinity, their militancy during this time was seen as a badge of their backwardness.[106] For men like Leck, this association between race and coal mining must have been especially salient in Enugu, where the miners were truly a distinguishably different race. The fact that the British had well-formed ideas about this race—the black race—and where it was situated in the evolutionary hierarchy, facilitated all types of racialized assumptions about the physiological impact of these working conditions on African labor. This was reflected in the general conditions under which Enugu's miners were forced to work. British miners' conditions were the most arduous and dangerous of any other industrial workers, and their agitations had led to improvements in safety regulations and working conditions by World War I.[107] But despite advances in metropolitan standards of protective clothing, underground atmospheric standards, lighting, et cetera, management reproduced conditions in Africa that were a hundred years behind those of England. Even as late as 1940, a Colonial Office labor adviser visiting Enugu commented that he doubted that anyone but Africans could be induced to work under these conditions.[108] Managers also accepted as "normal" high accident levels, maimings, and serious injuries that they attributed to the "primitiveness" of the men.

Nonetheless, when Gabriel Mbalemu entered the Enugu mines, he joined an ancient brotherhood of the "country of coal."[109] He entered an "occupational lifeworld characterized by both fear and pride, leading to warm but a rough male camaraderie on and off the job, and high levels of personal tension resulting in high absenteeism and frequent work stoppages."[110] He developed the intuitive skill that allowed him to survive the danger, psychological strain, and exhaustive work regime. He constructed a proud self-identity as a "coal person" which gave him prestige in his village. Granted, as a colonial worker, there were particularities to his experience that set him apart from his "brothers" in the United Kingdom: the racial hierarchy in the mine, a managerial contempt for recognized protective standards, the frequent use of physical violence as discipline, and an overarching managerial attitude that Africans could be *made* to work under conditions that were unsuitable for Englishmen. A double standard evolved, giving British staff limited exposure to the severe underground conditions while perpetuating them for Africans. This convention persisted despite the clear signs that underground conditions reduced African productivity and interfered with their willingness to sell their labor-power on a consistent and predictable basis. Thus, while Mbalemu and other early miners may not have been aware of how different their conditions were from their metropolitan "brothers," they nonetheless had their own ideas about work. In the final analysis, it was the industry that had to accommodate to their priorities.

## NEGOTIATING THE WORKPLACE:
## RELATIONS IN PRODUCTION AND STRUGGLES
## OVER CONTROL AT THE COAL FACE

The management structure and system of industrial relations at Enugu resembled an industrial application of "indirect rule." It shaped the recruitment and daily deployment of labor, the systems of labor control, and the entire structure of industrial relations at the colliery. It was a colonial policy and concept, based on a series of erroneous assumptions about the nature of African political systems, and it therefore permitted abuses that would be intolerable in British mines. While there are many accounts of the disastrous consequences of "indirect rule" policies for rural Igbo society, historians have not examined the impact of this philosophy on the workplace.[111] As was the case with the "warrant chiefs," in the mines African intermediaries were given many managerial and supervisory functions, with little European supervision. The chiefs' "boss boys" and various other "native" supervisors handled daily colliery operations. With the general manager insulated from the daily supervision of the men, a culture of predation emerged in which both African and European bosses used corruption, extortion, and physical violence to push the workers to produce.

As men like Gabriel Mbalemu entered the pit each became entangled in a maze of exploitation that extended from the corrupt chiefs in the village to the "native" and European supervisors in mines. His experiences were shrouded in the darkness of the mine, invisible to a disinterested general management and hidden from political authorities. The coercion which surrounded him was not gratuitous but a "solution" to a seemingly intractable problem that confronted the management daily. Getting the worker into the mine was only one part of a complex process. The second part was converting his labor-power into labor, in other words, getting the men to work with sufficient energy for the time that they were being paid. There were several ways of achieving this. One was to organize production around self-regulating groups who were paid piece-rates. The second was to use a "system of coercion."[112] Both were used in Enugu. Only in the colonies could this "system of coercion" be used. In metropolitan Britain the pay system was structured around the problem of getting the men to produce. For this reason, coal mining had perhaps the most complex wage system of any other industry, incorporating various bonuses to compensate for unanticipated geological problems, the unique skill demands, the severity of working conditions, and the inherent danger of the workplace. The fundamental distinction was between piece-rate wages (tonnage rates) and day rates.[113] In Enugu the miners (hewers, pit boys) were the only workers on piece-rates, the rationale being that the main producers needed financial incentives to work.

The basic managerial structure of the colliery included a general manager, the highest ranking official over all the mines, his deputy, and underground managers

**Photo 3.9** Proud miners at mine entrance; such work required skill and ability to use tools. The pride of work is seen in the faces and comportment of these men, circa 1915. (Crown Agents)

who supervised all underground operations. At the mine level there were technical supervisors, European overmen, whose ranks by the 1920s included West Indians and some Yoruba from western Nigeria.[114] They supervised groups of work districts with assistance from Igbo foremen or headmen, who ran a particular work district. Within these districts teams of miners or other classes of labor worked under their respective "boss boy." Of all the supervisory staff, the men complained most bitterly about the exploitation of the "boss boys." From the position of the worker, the "boss boy" was the most powerful "native" supervisor in the mine. He decided who worked and where he would work. He was responsible for discipline which he often executed beyond the workplace in the villages with the help of the chief and Native Courts. He used physical violence, extortion, and fines to force the men to produce. His power over individual men was ominous and arbitrary.

The "boss boy" had control over the hewers' wage-earning capacity. He could place the hewer on a difficult coal face which reduced his shift output. Hewers could be assigned to work on three types of faces: development *on board*, development *on end*, and *robbery*. All development work was more strenuous than robbery and it paid higher piece rates. However, certain development sites were more difficult than others. Work *on board* was harder than *on end* because the coal face was at right angles to the natural cleavage of the coal and required more skill and geological knowledge. The men gave an Igbo name to this coal, *ukpaka*, a hard oil bean tree. Work *on end* was parallel with the cleavage and the coal peeled off with the cleavage. Thus working on such soft coal or *akwukwa*, produced higher yields and required less skill.[115]

There were also geological variations in the work sites. At some faces the coal seam was split with rock, or it might have a fault, a break in the seam that was filled with dirt, sand, or stone. Some faces required the removal of stone, called dead work, before coal could be extracted. Since the hewer was only paid for the amount of coal he mined, time spent working the stone was money lost. In England's northern coal fields, the vagaries of the geology of the mines were accommodated by the men themselves. They developed a system of equalizing the risks of difficult coal faces by drawing lots every few months, a process called *cavilling*.[116] In Enugu, however, such democratic traditions had not evolved, and placement was in the hands of the "boss boys," thus becoming another instrument used to dominate workers. Allegations of these abuses by the "boss boys" were recurrent themes in the interviews with miners, suggesting that they were rather widespread. One miner recalled: "What happened was that if you were in logger head with the boss, he will always send you to the most difficult side of the mine until you are able to give a tip or bribe him."[117]

The "boss boys" and headmen selected their work crews daily from the men in the labor camps.[118] Consequently, they alone knew who was in their crew. In some cases they received the wages for their entire work crew.[119] The consequences were predictable:

> The Colliery was paying its workers by the month. The boss-boys and headmen exploited this and often arranged to dismiss labourers a few days before pay day and take on other men. The headmen then drew the pay for the whole month and kept it for themselves that of the dismissed men. The paying officer could not check this because he did not know the labourers individually.[120]

The second most hated group were the interpreters whose power came from their intermediate position between colonizer and the colonized. All underground European supervisors relied on them to translate instructions.[121] Interpreters extorted money from the men by threatening to falsify management commands and mistranslate instructions.[122] One Agbaja tub man complained:

> Interpreters caused the sudden dismissal of many workers. They really were very wicked to workers. When they find one resting in the working place and if such a one refuses to bribe him he would accuse such a one [of] sleeping on duty or accuse him of one serious offense which will le[a]d to his dismissal. They always report them to the Europeans who dismissed such a one.[123]

As would be expected for men in such intimate contact with Europeans, they became trusted confidants whose opinion was often solicited about particular workers. They often functioned as surrogate "Europeans" and were permitted to beat the miners.

> Interpreters were taking bribes. They would flog the African if he wouldn't do it. He would offer a bribe so he won't get punishment. Sometimes he did this for a promotion. The interpreter would recommend him as a hard workers if you give him a bribe. Promotions weren't regulated. You can be sacked without reference.[124]

In their defense, one former interpreter reflected on these accusations:

> The Africans have no Senior Service men in the coal mine. So each of the Europeans has interpreter. If the workers were demanding [a] wage increase and they haven't got it, they thought that it was the interpreters who told the European not to give the wage increase.

When asked about the accusation that they took bribes, he noted, "Everybody wants a wage increase. It is not only the labourers."[125]

Because of their intermediary role in production, they were some of the few Africans allowed to live in the European Reservation area. Their proximity to European residences privileged them to observe the nuances of British culture, which they used to their advantage. By using these cultural insights they made themselves indispensable to the production regime and in at least one instance, were caught collaborating with a European supervisor in extorting the workers.

For the workers 1917 was a year of discontent. The war had caused inflation that was reflected in high food prices. This was exacerbated by shortages in metal coinage, which was replaced by paper currency. The new economy was not sufficiently entrenched to monetize such a worthless commodity as "paper," and traders as well as workers refused to accept it as legal tender. Further, the sudden growth of the coal labor camps and the city of Enugu created a considerable urban population without a rational system of food supply. Rural communities could have been induced to supply some of this population's needs, but the existence of so permanent an urban market had not been fully appreciated. Many work stoppages occurred simply because workers had to return home to get food from their own farms.

A lightning strike on 28 March 1917 highlighted these transitional problems and protested one form of corruption in the mines.[126] The underground workers

**Photo 3.10** European underground manager and tubmen. A European underground manager, circa 1915. Notice the lamps and his protective clothing, including pith helmet and boots. The workers used candles to light their work, had no protective clothing and worked barefoot. The tub is filled with coal. (Crown Agents)

"downed tools" to demand increased wages. Inflationary pressures were severe and few of the urban-based workers could actually live on their wages. They also protested token cheating which deprived hewers of the income coming from their production. Little is known about the leaders or organization of the industry's first strike, but it appears that some rudimentary workers' organization was evolving.

The informal network of coercion and corruption, using the industry's supervisory staff and the Native Courts, was not sufficiently entrenched nor coherent to suppress all worker initiative. Resistance took many forms; direct and indirect, individual and collective, physical and cultural. In the early years most laborers' resistance was unpredictable and informal, usually consisting of the withdrawal of their labor from the workplace. For example, several hundred men brought from Bende, in central Igboland, deserted to a man when they saw the nature of underground conditions. Agbaja miners, who had unskilled underground jobs, refused to work more than two weeks in the month, returning home for a fortnight allegedly to supervise their farms.[127] Soon after the strike the industry was hit by seasonal labor shortages during the farming period from May to July. While technically the men were "farming," these men were also insuring their presence in the political and cultural life of the village. In the early years men escaped the controls of the

**Photo 3.11** Young men with head baskets at mine entrance (Crown Agents)

court messengers and absconded from Enugu, returning to their villages. Even there the chiefs weren't always strong enough to force them to return to the mines. Management also had difficulty insuring that men, once appearing at the job, would, in fact, remain throughout a full shift, or pursue their tasks with requisite effort. The arrangement of the mine with its multiple entrances facilitated unauthorized departure because these were "*adit*" mines and the men could stroll out when they wished. Even as late as 1947 European managers complained that men often left the coal face without notice, not to return for several days.[128]

**Photo 3.12** Miners with tallies around their necks. A group of hewers, circa 1915. A tally, like the ones worn around the necks of two men in this photo, is attached to the worker's tub to identify his output. (Crown Agents)

Enugu's managers were confronted with a generalized problem affecting colonial capital in Africa—how to get Africans to "adapt to the work rhythms of industrial capitalism: to the idea that work should be steady, and regular and carefully controlled."[129] These struggles over the duration and frequency of work were struggles over time—its use and calibration. The management, running a state capitalist en-

**Photo 3.13** Udi Colliery Adit, coal stacked at the mine entrance (Crown Agents)

terprise, structured the industry's production rhythms according to industrial time. Shifts were eight hours, three eight-hour shifts constituted a full day, and five and a half days constituted a week. The working month varied with the number of weeks.

As a preindustrial people the Igbo had a notion of "task time," and while they worked vigorously to accomplish a particular task, work ended when the task was completed.[130] Additionally, they had their own system of time-reckoning, that of a four-day week and an eight-day week, and it did not coincide with that of the industry or the state. From the standpoint of the industry the key aspect of this system was that both included a day of rest. The exact day varied with the villages in a village-group. For example, one Ngwo village may observe one day while another village would observe a different day. The rest day was an important cultural institution, scrupulously observed as a socially important practice that helped village-group cohesion and economic life. It is a day when people refrain from farm work, attend the market, and do household chores, hobbies, and entertainment. Village festivals also occur.[131] Since villages have different rest days, observance of the rest day would not be reflected in high absenteeism on a particular day. But if work patterns coincided with what early missionaries noted about church attendance, when it was virtually impossible to get new converts to attend church on a rest day, one would expect that many men would be absent on their village's rest day.[132]

Ironically, the Igbo week resolved one problem usually confronting African colonial capitalists: the separation of work time from leisure time, but it did so to the disadvantage of the capitalist. While the rest day insured this separation, it was the worker and not the employer who determined when the rest day occurred. Even when employers could be said to have succeeded in instilling new labor habits, eliminating irregular work rhythms, and teaching an awareness of the calibration of time and its frugal use, they still had to make concessions to the seasonal rhythms of the countryside "with its festivals [and] religious holidays."[133] This was the case in Enugu during the early years. Some men moved in and out of the mines, weaving wage labor into a rurally based pattern of economic survival. Mining jobs helped finance preindustrial social rituals that were important for village cohesion and personal status. For one miner, these obligations were his incentive for entering the mines.

> I joined the mine when I felt like. In those days what normally happened was that whenever the villages wanted to celebrate certain feasts, people will rush to the mine to get money. (That is to work for sometime) and get money for their feast. When you must been you retire home to celebrate the feast with the money you got from mining work. When the money finished you go back again to another money. Payments in those days was every two weeks. This was the method I joined the mining work. Nobody forced me.[134]

Other work habits accommodated the general severity of working conditions underground. In England it was assumed that miners would have high absentee rates because this was not an occupation in which intense efforts could be continuously expended.[135] Predictably, hewers and haulage workers had the highest absentee rates.[136] In Enugu when conditions became unbearable the men simply left the mine, returned to their villages, and remained there until they wished to return.

Additionally, as noted above, workers also curtailed their effort when underground ventilation problems were onerous. They took long rest periods in the main roadways and sometimes left as well. Rather than improve conditions, the industry simply hired additional workers, getting the work from two or three men that they should have received from one. Because of absenteeism and overproduction it became a workplace tradition to use twice the number of men needed to work a full shift. Thus redundancies of 100 percent were a common feature of labor deployment in the mines. This managerial accommodation to African work patterns, and the men's adjustments to poor working conditions, were possible because the Agbaja area functioned as a labor reserve.

At some point during the war, the men formed associations to discuss their grievances and conditions at work. Although the manager assumed that the "boss boys" and "native headmen" would handle grievances, often they *were* the grievance and the men had little confidence in them.[137] The exact origins of these organizations, called *Nzuko ifunanya*,[138] or "meetings," are not clear, however, they appear to be related to the urban unions. Anecdotal references to "unions" organizing a 1920 strike suggests that they began during the latter years of the war. The *Nzuko* fulfilled many of the functions of a trade union and mutual aid society.[139] They met to discuss such grievances as "food shortages, token cheating, bribery and corruption in the obtaining and retaining of jobs and in the allocation of work on hard or soft coal faces."[140]

They were structured by job category and included both "foreign" and "local" men. The basic structure followed the job classifications at the mines. Each of the major labor classes, such as "Special Labour," in other words, machine workers, timber drawers, railmen and timbermen, held their own meeting under a president and secretary known as the "Head Committee" which would represent their men in a "Special Labor Meeting." Similar structures were formed for each category of work. Their meetings were held either in the mines or in remote areas. The meetings were very secretive because the men were aware that both European management and "native" supervisors tried to suppress them. Since they were plagued by spies, usually "boss boys" and interpreters, the men tried to use oaths to enforce secrecy.

Although the colliery *Nzuko* may have had roots in the urban "tribal" unions, they differed in significant respects. They were working class organizations that represented all workers. Secondly, they were not organized by clan, but incorporated all groups of workers, regardless of their home village. This universal aspect confused the village "chiefs," especially from among the Agbaja, who could not understand how their countrymen would follow the "foreigners" who held many of the leadership positions. The types of men who were elected to head these various *Nzuko* had many of the same qualities that, noted earlier, were prized in village leadership. R.H. Croasdale, a rather unsympathetic district officer, suggested that men of "energy, personality and slight extra knowledge of affairs," were selected by the "ordinary unsophisticated local men," allegedly because they could produce concrete gains.[141] The *Nzuko* were important institutions for consultations as well as political education. They provided an institutional structure for discussion and interchange between foreign "sophisticates" and local "primitives." The impact of this connection could be seen both in the villages and in the mines.

## THE MINE "BOY" AND THE VILLAGE "MAN": MINING AND IGBO CONCEPTIONS OF MANLINESS DURING WORLD WAR I

The horrors of underground mining and the "manliness" that coal mining encouraged was supported by many Igbo notions of masculinity. As noted before in Chapter 1, the strongest masculine qualities were represented symbolically in the *Ikenga* sculpture and cult. Manhood was defined morally rather than biologically, and included staying power, bravery when confronted with danger, and strength, both physical and moral.[142] All of these qualities were tested by the exhaustive, dangerous, and oppressive conditions in the mines.

The miners' position in the workplace also affected their social role in the village. They were agents of "progress" in Agbaja villages where they earned considerable esteem. With piece-rates they could earn a higher wage than the other classes of underground labor. Their wages financed many improvement projects in the impoverished communities of Agbaja. These projects—schools, roads, zinc roofs, bicycles—all symbolized modernization in their community. They also used these wages to attain status within the cultural idiom of their village. They joined the higher ranks of title societies, institutionalizing their prestige within the sacripolitical structures. But their ideas about manliness were being reformulated because of the new opportunities and ideologies created under colonialism. One Agbaja worker, Samuel Onoh, used his income in both "traditional" and "modern" ways. He invested in his children's future by funding their education, married six wives, and bought membership in the Ozo society:

> The development of [the] coal industry did a lot to my village. But for coal industry civilization would have not reached us as early as it had reached us. The coal industry initiated me into Ozo title. Now I am Ozo Samuel N. Onoh. I was able to train up my children, build good houses. We contributed money and build schools and churches.[143]

With six wives he had attained the *Big Compound* ideal that had captivated so many men at the turn of the century.

This economic foundation allowed the men to participate as influential members of village life. As industrial workers they symbolized the new opportunities offered by the colonial economy. But, despite the state policy to discourage proletarianization and the "dangerously" disruptive behavior it produced, these men rapidly became adversaries of the chiefs, even when their primary residence was in the village. One Agbaja miner commented on the political role that miners saw themselves playing as a force against corrupt chiefs:

> The miners were most modern and power[ful]. Because they were always after democracy. And they don't allow the chief by opposing him to harass his people. And [they] always succeeded in opposing him.[144]

As early as 1919 a political official complained about the problems "colliery boys" caused for the chiefs in the village-groups, or towns, most heavily involved in the industry:

> This system of boys [in Enugu-Ngwo, Abor, and surrounding towns] living in their town and working at the mines is not one I prefer. The trouble is that the colliery boys living in the towns will not obey the chiefs who complain to the Political Officer that these boys are loafing in the towns and will not obey them.[145]

Too disruptive to live in the rural towns and too threatening to the tenuous urban order to live in the city, the mine worker challenged all imperial fantasies about the nature of African rural society. Their very existence contradicted the patterns of authoritarian rule that officials tried to insinuate into village politics. Their insistence on "democracy" challenged what colonial authorities assumed was an endemic authoritarianism rooted in African society.

As against this prestige was the racist culture of the colonial workplace, in which managerial control was represented in job titles that infantilized men who were regarded with such prestige in their own communities and villages. Thus *pick "boys"* (hewers) undercut coal and loaded the tubs. *Tub "boys"* hooked the tubs to the central haulage system in the main roads. Tracks were laid by the *rail "boys,"* and *timber "boys"* reinforced the roof with timber. Such infantalized racial titles were offensive to the men but they had no recourse until they had developed a stronger labor movement.

As the Great War came to a close, labor problems and transport difficulties reduced the mines' output. Four mines were worked that year—Udi and Obwetti, the oldest mines, were in *robbery* while two sections of Iva, Little Iva, a temporary production site, and Iva Main, the future major site, were less advanced. In July roads had been driven throughout Little Iva, pillars had been demarcated and *robbery* commenced at eight sites. At Iva Main, the newest mine, miners were concentrated on *development*, a process that was proceeding at the slow rate of thirty-six yards per month partially because of the lack of power-driven drills. In April a new *adit*, Palm Valley, was opened to the Iva reserves. By the end of the year, 130 yards had been reached and a second road to connect it with Udi Mine reached twenty yards. Work at the coal face employed over 2,000 workers.[146]

But just as the manager reported on the encouraging labor situation, a crisis in labor supply struck the mines. In November 1918 the Influenza Pandemic hit Udi district, causing widespread devastation and discouraging local people from coming to the mines. There were 39,510 deaths in Onitsha Province's estimated population of 1,970,000. As is often the case with natural disasters, the people of Udi sought respite in their traditional medicinal and spiritual practices, resorting to some rituals which they themselves had come to consider repugnant.

> In the town of Agbaja nine out of ten people seemed to be down. The roads were deserted. Here and there across them could be seen clumps of feathers and ashes—the sacrifices of *dibias* to keep away the spirits that bring the disease.[147]

The epidemic had such an impact on the villagers that even today it is used as a reference point for birth dates and other significant events. For three weeks all production at the mines stopped just as the mines' production dramatically increased from 409 tons per day in January 1918 to 805 tons per day in July 1918.[148]

## NOTES

1. Allan Campbell and Fred Reid, "The Independent Collier in Scotland," in *The Independent Collier: The Coal Miner as Archetypal Proletarian Reconsidered*, ed., Royden Harrison (London, 1978), 56.

2. Frederick Cooper, *Decolonization and African Society*, 56.

3. The story of this grievance weaves a thread through all histories of the elite at the turn of the century. For a discussion, see Kristin Mann, *Marrying Well: Marriage, Status, and Social Change Among the Educated Elite in Colonial Lagos* (Cambridge, 1985).

4. See Michael Burawoy, *Politics of Production*; Cooper, *Decolonization and African Society*.

5. Uzeochi, "Eastern Nigerian Railway," 119–20.

6. PRO, CO 583/26, Lewis V. Harcourt, Minute, 1 September 1914; CO 583/33, "Address of the Governor-General," Proceedings of the Second Meeting of the Nigerian Council, 29 December 1915, 8–9.

7. Agwu Akpala, "Background to the Enugu Colliery Shooting Incident in 1949," *Journal of the Historical Society of Nigeria* 3, 2 (1965): 337.

8. Powell Duffryn, Technical Services, "First Report to the Undersecretary of State for the Colonies, Colonial Office, Dover House, Whitehall, S.W. 1 on the Government Colliery, Enugu, The Characteristics of the Coal Produced and the Investigation into the Other Coal," G–17.

9. Ibid., Section G, "Chemical and Physical Examination of Enugu Coal."

10. NNAE, P.E.H. Hair, "Enugu: An Industrial West African City," (mimeograph, 1954), 1.

11. PRO, CO 583/26, M.E. Bland, General Manager, Railway to Commissioner, Onitsha, 18 December 1914.

12. For much of the early twentieth century, colonial authorities spoke of the disruptive impact of "detribalized" Africans. Lugard, for example, argued: "It is, as I have said, very desirable that Natives should as far as possible live in their own towns, under their own Chiefs and Native Courts." Frederick Lugard, *The Political Memorandum: Revision of Instructions of Political Officers on Subjects Chiefly Political and Administrative, 1913–1918*, 3d ed. (London, 1970). The more orthodox definition of proletarianization assumes that workers are totally separated from the means of subsistence. However, Dunbar Moodie has argued that in the case of migrant labor cultures in Africa, movement back and forth between rural farms and the mines may, in fact, not be so significant. "Once workable land became scarce or migrant remittances were so fully used for basic subsistence that the land lay fallow, then proletarianization was complete, even if people continued to migrate and families remained in the rural areas." Moodie and Ndatshe, *Going for Gold*, 22.

13. Young, *African Colonial State*, 95.

14. Alfred's Camp was established by an Onitsha contractor, Alfred Inoma, who refused to live with the "locals" from Udi. He returned home in the twenties, and subsequently Awka men flocked to the camp from the village of Nneni. By the late thirties it was an Nneni colony. See Hair, "Enugu," 129. Interview with Gabriel Mbalemlu, Michael Nwakuache, and Clement Egbogimba, Ugwu Alfred, 5 July 1975.

Aaron's camp was founded by Aaron Elo, a native of Owa, an Agbaja village. He was recruited by Leck and fled Owa because of the incessant demands of Chief Onyeama. NIGCOAL 2/1/138, Local Authority, "Census of Enugu"; interview with Mokoro Osakwe, 8 July 1975 and Clement Ude, 9 July 1975, Ugwu Aaron, Enugu.

15. Nonetheless, British culture was transferred to the "bush." The missionary/anthropologist Rev. G.T. Basden noted on a visit to Ngwo village-group Udi in 1916 that it was "the custom in Ngwo to sit at the fire as in England." Church Missionary Society Archives (hereafter CMSA), University of Birmingham, G3A/0 1913–1916, Rev. Basden, "Report on Visit to the Udi District."

16. This continued until 1947. Duffryn, "Characteristics of the Coal," D–138.

17. See interview with Eze Ozogwu, Amankwo, Udi, 2 June 1975.

18. This initial grant was augmented several years later by another "gift" to the state. The people of Ngwo knew nothing about their "chiefs'" deed, but eventually, as they realized the reduction in their farmlands, they demanded preferential hiring in mining posts.

19. C.H. Croasdale, "Report on the Enugu Colliery," 1938. The original report was lost from the National Archives, Enugu, during the Biafran War. I thank Dr. P.E.H. Hair, formerly of the University of Liverpool, for lending me his personal copy. The title sheet and several pages are missing.

20. CMSA GBA 3/0 1913, "Visit to the Udi District," Rev. G.T. Basden.

21. Fred I.A. Omu, *Press and Politics in Nigeria 1880–1937* (Atlantic Highlands, NJ, 1978), 50–55.

22. CMSA, G3.A 3/0, 1913–1916, "Niger Mission," Eso Nzeche and eleven others, Ibo Christians at Coalmines to Bishop Tugwell, 24 August 1916.

23. Ekene Michael Gbanite, "Third World Urbanisation: Enugu, Nigeria," (Ph.D. diss., The New School for Social Research, New York, 1978), 83.

24. Anthony D. King, *Urbanism, Colonialism and the World Economy: Cultural and Spatial Foundations of the World Urban System* (London, 1990), 53–54.

25. Within the first plans for Enugu's design were two areas for European settlement: one, for "first class" Europeans, the other for "second class Europeans," a transposition of metropolitan class structure to the colony. However, both were within the European reservation. PRO, MPGG/129, Station Plan No. 107, Government Station, Enugu Ngwo, 12 March 1919.

26. Frantz Fanon, *The Wretched of the Earth* (New York, 1963).

27. Lugard, *The Political Memorandum*, 405–422.

28. Maynard W. Swanson, "The Sanitation Syndrome: Bubonic Plague and Urban Native Policy in the Cape Colony, 1900–1909," *Journal of African History* 18, 3 (1977): 387–410. For a discussion of the intersection of medical knowledge (or ignorance), urban planning, racism, and segregation, see Phillip Curtin, "Medical Knowledge and Urban Planning in Tropical Africa" *American Historical Review* 90 (1985): 594–613.

29. These erroneous views of the ways malaria was transmitted reflected early twentieth-century assumptions about contagion. Lugard, *Political Memorandum*, 416.

30. Ibid., 416.

31. Ibid., 417.

32. Uzeochi, "Eastern Nigerian Railway," 217.

33. Horton, "*Ohu*," 334, and C. Brown, "Testing the Boundaries."

34. Interview with Mazi Anyionovo Nwodo, Uhuona, Ugbawka, 18 August 1988.

35. Frederick Cooper, "Urban Space, Industrial Time, and Wage Labor in Africa," in *The Struggle for the City*, ed., Frederick Cooper (Beverly Hills, 1983), 7–50.

36. Much of this discussion is based on the Croasdale report which was researched in the late thirties. He is the primary source for the information on the colliery's *Nzuko*.

37. *Nzuko* is a rather generic Igbo term meaning any type of "meeting." Therefore the urban "tribal" unions were also called *Nzuko*.

38. Croasdale, "Report on the Enugu Colliery," 19.

39. E.P. Oyeaka Offodile, "Growth and Influence of Tribal Unions," *West African Review* (August 1947): 939.

40. Ibid. Offodile, himself a member, says men learn "simple social discipline and courtesy."

41. David Smock gives a more contemporary example of how these societies foster clock awareness. In speaking of one such association, the Peace Union of Okwe Village in Ngwo Uno, an organization of colliery employees, he notes the obsessive consciousness of time. They had a ten minute break for refreshments, which was rigidly enforced, and an increasing scale of fines for being five, ten, and fifteen minutes late. David Smock, "From Village to Trade Union in Africa," (Ph.D. diss., Cornell University, 1964), 70.

42. James C. Coleman, *Nigeria: Background to Nationalism* (Los Angeles and Berkeley, 1958), 215.

43. See Omu, *Press and Politics in Nigeria*, Chap. 7.

44. For a brief biography of Jackson, see Omu, *Press and Politics in Nigeria*, 50–55. See also Chap. 7 for the struggle between government and the *Record* during and after World War I.

45. Omu, *Press and Politics in Nigeria*, 192–94.

46. Akinjide Osuntokun, *Nigeria in the First World War* (Atlantic Highlands, NJ, 1979), 314.

47. Upon Lugard's retirement in 1920, the *Lagos Weekly Record* sarcastically attacked him as being "the victim of exaggerated personality induced by the autocratic power conferred upon him through the discretion of Lewis Harcourt," Osuntokun, *Nigeria in the First World War*, 90. Throughout his administration Lugard carried on a running battle with the Lagosian elite and attempted to muzzle their newspapers. See Omu, *Press and Politics in Nigeria*, 88–103.

48. This Anglophile ideology, which was quite prominent among this sector of the African people, has recently been examined for both South African and Nigerian examples. See Brian Willian, "An African in Kimberley: Sol T. Plaatje, 1894–1898," in *Industrialization and Social Change in South Africa*, ed. Richard Rathbone and Shula Marks (London, 1982), 238–58; Brian Willian, *Sol Plaatje: South African Nationalist, 1876–1932* (Berkeley, 1984), and Kristin Mann, *Marrying Well*.

49. The concept of "respectability," a theme in British history, has also been treated in African labor historiography. Cooper has examined it in terms of the shift in colonial labor policy in the 1930s towards grooming a "respectable" working class that was distinct from the undisciplined, erratic, casual laborer. See Frederick Cooper, *On the African Waterfront: Urban Disorder and the Transformation of Work in Colonial Mombasa* (New Haven, 1987).

50. Lugard noted in his *Political Memorandum* that: "It is ... very desirable that Natives should as far as possible live in their own towns, under their own Chiefs, and Native Courts. Only Aliens ... who reside for purposes of trade and access to a railway siding, or Natives who are employees of Europeans, or artisans, and those who administer to the requirements of the community, should as a general rule be allowed to live in the actual precincts of a township." Lord Lugard, *Political Memoranda*, 417.

51. Offodile, "Growth and Influence of Tribal Unions," 941.

52. See Hair, "Enugu," 284–317; Immanuel Wallerstein, "Voluntary Associations" in *Political Parties and National Integration in Tropical Africa*, ed., James S. Coleman and Carl Rosberg (Berkeley, 1964), 318–39; Offodile, "Growth and Influence of Tribal Unions," 937–41; Coleman, *Nigeria*, 213–15.

53. This is the subject of Kristin Mann's *Marrying Well*. For a discussion of the South African variant, see Willian, "An African in Kimberley," and Willian, *Sol Plaatje*.

54. Michael Burawoy argues that management must secure consent from the worker for the terms of exploitation in the capitalist workplace. See *The Politics of Production*, 226.

55. For a discussion of the concept of "habituation" in reference to African workers, see Robin Cohen, "Resistance and Hidden Forms of Consciousness Among African Workers," *Review of African Political Economy* 19 (1980): 8–22.

56. The pioneering study that raises the issue of an African work ethic is Atkins' *The Moon Is Dead!*.

57. PRO, CO 583/15, William J. Leck to Colonial Office, 25 May 1914.

58. ONPROF 1/15/28, DO Udi to Commissioner Onitsha, 19 January 1915.

59. Barry Supple, *The History of the British Coal Industry, Vol. 4, 1913–1946: The Political Economy of Decline* (Oxford, 1987). This was especially disastrous for the miners in

the northern coal fields because their union had agreed to accept a "sliding wage scale" which pegged their earnings to the price of coal. When this plunged, it threw thousands of miners into utter destitution.

60. These shortages were partially due to dislocations in the wartime coal market, and partly to labor unrest in the Welsh coal fields. In 1913 the two major coal fields for export were South Wales and northeast England. South Wales had superior deposits of anthracite, dry steam, and coking steam coal, and the northern coal field districts of Northumberland and Durham were the major source of prime coking fuel and gas-making coal. The early months of the war (fall 1914) immediately disrupted the export-oriented fields of the British coal industry. By 1915 workers throughout England protested the rapidly rising inflation. The miners joined in late February with a demand for a 20 percent wage increase based on national and not district variations. The biggest crisis, however, was in South Wales where militant miners and recalcitrant owners brought the war effort to a standstill in mid-July 1915. Supple, *British Coal Industry*, 49, 62, 64–69.

61. PRO, CO 741/1, Nigerian Railways, "Minutes of the Board," 1916.

62. *West Africa*, 24 February 1917, 76.

63. PRO, CO 583/46, Lugard to Secretary of State for the Colonies, 3 September 1917.

64. Croasdale, "Report on the Enugu Colliery," 9.

65. PRO, CO 583/31, Lugard to Harcourt, 9 April 1915.

66. PRO, CO 583/44, Address of the Governor General, Proceedings of the Second Meeting of the Nigerian Council, 29 December 1915.

67. As cited in Uzeochi, "Eastern Nigerian Railway," 125–26.

68. Interview with Gabriel Mbamelu, 5 July 1975.

69. Ibid.

70. Hair, "Enugu," 125.

71. Ibid. Leck wrote later in an article that when they were told "that it was the government's intention to drive roads into the hills, they were very skeptical and would not entertain the idea." Hair quotes an article written by Leck in 1932. He does not give a full citation.

72. Black damp is air in which oxygen has been displaced by carbon dioxide. Fire damp is the very dangerous methane gas. It is highly explosive in even small quantities and prone to spontaneous combustion. Dave Douglass, "Pit Talk in County Durham," in *Miners, Quarrymen, and Salt Workers*, History Workshop Series, ed., Raphael Samuel (London, 1977).

73. Powell Duffryn found that ventilation air reached 94 percent saturation the first 1,100 feet from the entrance and increased rapidly as one approached the working face. Levels of 100 percent were detected. Duffryn, "Characteristics of the Coal," D–70.

74. The issue of which jobs were designated "skilled" and "unskilled" would become a point of contention between labor and management during a strike in 1937. See Chap. 4.

75. PRO, CO 657/2, Nigerian Railway Administrative Report (hereafter NRAR), 1916. In August 1916 the seam was over six feet tall. From the main shaft the men opened headings right and left every twenty-five yards. There were fifteen such headings. Basden, "Visit to the Udi District."

76. I.C.F. Stracham, *Coal Mining Practice*, vol. 1 (New York, 1958), 265.

77. H.F. Bulman and R.A.S. Redmayne, *Colliery Working and Management*, (London, 1896), 324.

78. Campbell and Reid, "The Independent Collier in Scotland," 59.

79. J.R. Harris, "Skills, Coal and British Industry in the Eighteenth Century," *History* 61, 202 (June 1976): 182, as quoted in Harrison, *The Independent Collier*.

80. John Tosh, "What Should Historians Do With Masculinity?: Reflections on Nineteenth-Century Britain," *History Workshop Journal* 38 (1994): 186.

81. Colls takes great pains to explain the distinction between a "pit man" and a "collier." "The word 'pit man' with its gendered connotation carried with it meanings of social bearing; other men were 'colliers' compared to 'pit men,' and others again were labourers compared to colliers." Robert Colls, *The Pitmen of the Northern Coalfield: Work, Culture, and Protest, 1790–1850* (Manchester, 1987), 12.

82. Ibid.

83. For a good discussion of the system of work in these fields, see M.J. Daunton, "Down the Pit: Work in the Great Northern and South Wales Coal Fields, 1870–1914," *Economic History Review* (2d ser.), 34, 4 (November 1981): 582.

84. Ibid., 585.

85. Powell Duffryn noted in 1947 that this tradition may have been justified when the industry first opened, but had since become an uneconomic practice. Duffryn, "Characteristics of Coal," D–164–65.

86. Campbell and Reid, *Independent Collier*, 58.

87. Supple, *British Coal Industry*, 30.

88. Duffryn, "Characteristics of Coal," D–19.

89. Interview with Thomas Noisike, Ezeama Owa, Udi, 7 July 1975.

90. Interview with B.U. Anyasado, Owerri Town, 23 July 1975.

91. This calculation was made in 1947 by the Powell Duffryn company. Oxygen levels relied on natural air currents. When the mines were only a few hundred feet from the entrance, they were not severe. However, as the workings branched off the main roads into the seam, one could assume that the levels would drop. Duffryn, "Characteristics of Coal," D–70.

92. PRO, CO 657/4, NRAR, 1917.

93. Duffryn, "Characteristics of Coal," D–82–83.

94. *Marras* are two men who work the same coal face either together or on opposite shifts. The system developed in the north coal fields. They are partners in more than an industrial sense, and have a powerful bond that extends to their families as well. For a discussion, see Douglass, "Pit Talk in County Durham," 227.

95. NIGCOAL 1/1/10, "Research on Hot Climate Physiology: Experimental Subjects," Dr. W.S.S. Ladell, 12 December 1946.

96. See Hair, "Enugu," 194.

97. PRO, CO 657/4, NRAR, 1918.

98. Ibid.

99. "During that time you could stay outside and sight somebody working in the mine." Interview with James Alo, former worker, 6 July 1975.

100. Interview with James Alo. Another informant mentioned that the water in the mines also served as a toilet, for human waste floated throughout the mine workings. Interview with J.K. Onale, Amawom, Owerri, 9 August 1975.

101. NNAE, ONPROF 1/15/28, Commissioner Onitsha to Engineer-in-Chief, Port Harcourt, 13 March 1915.

102. Experiments in the 1940s found that some areas had dangerously low oxygen levels of 13.4 percent. One could safely assume that conditions were at least as bad, if not worse, in the opening decades. Duffryn, "Characteristics of Coal," D–82.

103. As we shall see later, in the thirties this analysis of African culture would become an important rationale for the developmentalist thrust of colonial policy. For a discussion

see Cooper, *Decolonization and African Society*, Chap. 4. Also see Orde Browne's ideas. PRO, CO 554/125, Granville St. George Orde Browne to O.G.R. Willians, 15 February 1946; Granville St. George Orde Browne, *Labour Conditions in West Africa*, Cmd. 6277 (London, 1941), 61.

104. Hair, "Enugu," 194.

105. Anne McClintock, *Imperial Leather*, 115.

106. McClintock notes that authorities considered that one indicator of backwardness of coal miners, an indicator that cast aspersions on the "manliness" of the profession, was the inclusion of women, who were being "unsexed" by work in the mines. Ibid., 116.

107. See Supple, *The History of the British Coal Industry*, 99–111.

108. PRO, CO 554/125, Orde Browne to OGR Willian, 15 February 1940.

109. This is the title of a review essay on several coal mining texts. It is a very apt description of the universalizing characteristics of coal mining. David Frank, "The County of Coal."

110. Moodie, *Going for Gold*, 18.

111. The classical critique of indirect rule in eastern Nigeria is Afigbo's *The Warrant Chiefs*.

112. Burawoy, *The Politics of Production*, 236.

113. The logic of selecting pay systems was based on the manner in which specific jobs fit into the labor process. Piece-rates were paid where "intensity of effort was necessary to maintain production, continuous supervision was impossible and incentives were judged to be necessary." Usually hewers, tubmen, timbermen, and roadmen would be in this group. Day-rates were paid to men "whose work was irregular, unskilled, routine, or dependent on production of others or problems outside their control." However, at Enugu, only one category of worker, the hewer, was on piece-rate pay, an indicator of managerial ineptitude. Supple, *The History of the British Coal Industry*, 36, 37.

114. Nigerian Railways and Udi Colliery Administrative Report (hereafter NRUCAR), 1924/25. On Yoruba workmen, see interview with Anieke Chiegwu, Umuagba, Owa Imezi, 6 July 1975.

115. Interview with Onoh Ozoani, a former tubman and pick man, Ameke, Ngwo, 18 November 1991.

116. There is an entire culture surrounding the *cavil*. It was usually held every three months, and meant a day off, as well, which the men usually spent in the public house drinking. No work could be performed because the equipment would have to be moved from the previous period's work site to the new site. Douglas, "Pit Talk in County Durham," 239.

117. Interview with James Ogbodo, a retired "tubboy" and "pick boy" in Obuofia Akagbe, 2 June 1975.

118. Croasdale, "Report on the Enugu Colliery," 25.

119. OP 45/1921, Railway Construction: Recruitment of Labour and Arrangements for Control Thereof, cited in Akpala, "Enugu Colliery Shooting Incident," 341.

120. Interview with Chief Thomas Ozobu, Imezi, Owa, Udi, 21 June 1975.

121. Interview with B.U. Anyasado, Owerri Town, 23 July 1975 as cited in Carolyn Brown, "History of the Development of Workers' Consciousness of the Coal Miners at Enugu Government colliery, Nigeria, 1914–1950" (Ph.D. diss., Columbia University, 1985), 98.

122. Ibid., 140–46.

123. Interview with Anieke Chiegwu, Umuagba, Owa, Imezi, 7 July 1975.

124. Interview with J.K. Ohale, Amawom, Owerri, 9 August 1975. Ohale himself was an interpreter in the late twenties.

125. Interview with Augustine Ude, Umuaga, Udi, 5 August 1975.

126. Croasdale, "Report on the Enugu Colliery," 62.

127. For a fascinatingly complex discussion of gender in Igbo villages, see Amadiume, *Male Daughters and Female Husbands: Gender and Sex in an African Society* (London, 1987).

128. Duffryn, "Characteristics of Coal," D–185.

129. See Frederick Cooper, "Colonizing Time: Work Rhythms and Labor Conflict in Colonial Mombasa," in *Colonialism and Culture*, ed., Nicholas B. Dirks (Ann Arbor, 1992), 209.

130. Thompson has traced the problems of imposing clock awareness that preoccupied British industrialists for several centuries, as they transformed English country people into a proletarianized workforce. In his discussion, Thompson assumed a historical accommodation of wage labor to industrial time. However, in the British coal industry, conflicts over the calibration and use of time characterized workplace struggles until the mechanization and nationalization of the industry after World War II. E.P. Thompson, "Time, Work, Discipline and Industrial Capitalism," *Past and Present* 38 (1967): 56–97. Keletso Atkins has traced a similar process of struggles over time as a pivot of resistance by Zulu day workers in nineteenth-century Natal, South Africa. Keletso Atkins, "'Kaffir Time': Preindustrial Temporal Concepts and Labour Discipline in Nineteenth Century Colonial Natal," *Journal of African History* 29 (1988): 229–44.

131. Ukwu, "Trade and Marketing," 128.

132. See Richardson, "Rev. Arthur Humphrey Richardson."

133. Thompson, "Time, Work," 397.

134. Interview with James Alo, Okwojongwo, 6 June 1975.

135. Supple, *The History of the British Coal Industry*, 58.

136. In the Durham mines when workers encountered conditions that interfered with their production, they stopped and renegotiated their piece-rate to reduce the burden of such conditions on the worker. Douglass, "The Durham Pitman," in *Miners, Quarrymen and Saltworkers History Workshop Series*, ed. Raphael Samuel (London, 1977) 205–95 227–28, 239.

137. Duffryn, "Characteristics of Coal," D–183.

138. *Ifunanya* is difficult to translate, but its closest English meaning would be "self-help" or "mutual aid."

139. Most evidence of *Nzuko* comes from the intelligence report written by C.H. Croasdale, the local authority and the colliery's first labor officer. He was appointed in 1937 following a strike that forced a thorough investigation and reorganization of the colliery's managerial structure. See Croasdale, "Report on the Enugu Colliery," 28–30.

140. Ibid., 29.

141. Croasdale, "Report on the Enugu Colliery," 29–30.

142. Moodie and Ndatshe, *Going for Gold*, 38.

143. Interview with Samuel N. Onoh, Ngwo-Etiti, Nigeria, 9 August 1975. Onoh began work in 1915 as a tubman and worked up through the ranks until he became an underground foreman after World War II.

144. Interview with Augustine Ude. Ude began work at the colliery in 1919 when only ten years old as a messenger. In 1922 he became an interpreter and was the subject of many complaints by miners. His name was raised many times in my interviews as a perpetrator of extortion and bribery.

145. PRO, CO 657/4, Nigerian Railways and Udi Coal Mines Administrative Report (hereafter called NRUCMAR), 1919, E.M. Bland, General Manager, 96, as cited in Uzoechi, "Eastern Nigerian Railway," 208. Here he means rural settlements/towns, not Enugu.

146. NRUCAR, 1919.

147. PRO, CO 583/77, "The Influenza Epidemic of 1918 in the Southern Provinces of Nigeria," J. Beringer, Sr. Sanitation Officer, 5 September 1919, as cited in D.C. Ohadike, "The Influenza Pandemic of 1918–1919 and the Spread of Cassava Cultivation on the Lower Niger: A Study in Historical Linkages," *Journal of African History* 22 (1981): 384.

148. Ohadike, 384; PRO, CO 657/2, Report on the Nigerian Railways and Udi Coal Mines, 1918.

# 4

# THE POSTWAR CONJUNCTURE: AGITATION, URBANIZATION, AND THE EMERGENCE OF A CULTURE OF PROTEST, 1920–1929

As I look back on these early days ... I think I must come to the conclusion that the 1920's were critical for us. It was during this period that the Nigerian workers began to understand what it meant to be an inferior; to be subject to the "busts" and "booms" of Western capitalist manipulations. While the suffering of our workers was great, they learned to stand on their own feet. They expressed themselves by means of strikes and unrest which the British did not appreciate. More important than the strikes were the expressions of fraternal interest in workers elsewhere. We did not have an effective trade union organization in the 1920's, but we had a lot of Nigerian workers who thought and acted like trade unionists.
—Michael A. Imodou, founder of the Nigerian Railway Workers Union.[1]

The signing of the armistice escalated the industrial and political unrest that emerged during the war in both Nigeria and England. At the colliery, workers exhibited increased sophistication in the timing, organization, and strategy of their industrial protests. There were some six strikes from January 1919 to early 1921, followed by a second wave in 1924–1925, and a final crisis in 1929. The protests by clerks, artisans and "pick boys" in 1917, 1918, and 1919 had been successful in securing pay increases to meet wartime inflation. But industrial protest in the twenties was more tenacious and widespread, engulfing categories of labor heretofore uninvolved, and drawing in the "backward" Agbaja and Nkanu workers who usually protested by deserting. The recurrent character of these industrial actions, the use of accepted forms of worker protest, the assumptions that workers made about the social responsibilities of the state, and their manipulation of the policy dissonance among state actors, indicates a qualitative change in the consciousness of the workers. They operated from a position that, as workers, they deserved to live and work under certain conditions, and they wanted the state to secure these conditions on their behalf. Most importantly, even the "locals" were becoming industrial workers with the same fierce independence as the coal miners of England, and more especially Scotland.[2] These miners continued to be committed to their rural communities and economies. It became increasingly clear that behavior that appeared transitory in the first years of the industry was in fact a permanent feature of the colliery's work culture. The men molded waged work around the seasonal rhythms of farming and their rural social obligations. Participation in festivals, rituals, and celebrations established their existence as socially mature men and were not abandoned. These types of linkages between agriculture and mining were fairly typical of late eighteenth- and early nineteenth-century Scotland where garden plots and a few animals were important survival strategies for coal's off-season. In Enugu miners bargained, quite successfully, for time to tend their farms, or absented themselves from the pit to seek food from home. This behavior encouraged some from among the policy staff to argue the advantages of state-supported housing with neat garden plots. But a government consensus on the degree of freedom miners would be allowed to have regarding their social reproduction proved to be elusive.

Poised against the evidence of an emerging worker consciousness was a colonialist construction—the "African worker." He was a "lazy slacker" and "irresponsible juvenile" rooted in backward "traditions," "undisciplined," and unable to comprehend the vagaries of the market. He lived in the imagination of European colliery staff and state officials, and reflected ethnocentric assumptions about African abilities, racism, and a nostalgic view of an ordered, and repressive, rural life.[3] While vilifying African men as being too "backward" to become disciplined workers, colonial officials somewhat envied their lives in the bucolic, yet seductively primitive, rural village.

This colonialist prism prevented the manager, Leck, from seeing these Enugu men as miners. Despite his awareness of the deeply rooted traditions of independence, resistance, and absenteeism of the Northumberland miners (English), all he could see in the Enugu miners was "difference." They were "boys" and not industrial "men" and their elusiveness from the labor market was interpreted as an indication of their "laziness" and "primitive" character. However, in reality a diverse colliery working class was defining itself in the township, labor camps, and villages. It was shaping an identity that challenged systems of production control in the workplace as well as those icons of "indirect rule," the colonial chiefs in the village. In somewhat superficial respects this endeared them to the nationalists as a symbol of militant anti-colonial resistance.

This chapter explores the causes, organization, and ideologies behind this postwar activism and traces the contours of an emerging culture of protest drawing upon indigenous ideas of leadership and driven by personal economic strategies. This culture was expressed in a new instituion of collective action, *Nzuko Ifunanya*, that preceded trade unions. Nzuko syncretized Western voluntary associational forms with Igbo principles of corporate affiliation. The postwar agitations expressed personal and collective definitions of "just" and "unjust" compensation and treatment for employees and an evolving set of expectations from the colonial state. Protest forms reflected differential employment patterns, residential options, and variations in the regional significance of wage labor. These ideas were first expressed by urbanized "foreign" clerical, artisan, and skilled underground workers, but by mid-decade this protest culture was rapidly embraced by local men even as they fought assiduously to maintain their connections with their village. This labor model that synthesizes industrial and farm labor was an important dimension of the response of African workers to colonial capitalism.

This chapter outlines the complex strategies that workers used to mediate the capitalist workplace. As Fredrick Cooper argued in his tribute to E.P. Thompson, we must capture the ways that African working people shaped the capitalist workplace and reject the homogenizing tendency of industrial capital to transform them into abstract "labor power."[4] Labor militancy is not always an index of proletarianization. The only workers who wholeheartedly embraced urban residence were the "foreign" workers from Onitsha and Owerri whose homes were too distant to allow daily commuting. The local Agbaja and Nkanu who drifted into the workforce either lived in the village and commuted daily to work, boarded in Enugu during the work week, and returned home on weekends or, in a very few cases, established residence in the city. In the postwar period at Enugu a strategy emerged that enhanced the workers' role as political and economic participants in their villages. Increased wages became a commonality for fully proletarianized workers, the "foreign" urbanized workers, and their rural-based "local" counterparts. Both felt an enduring commitment to remit resources for the development of the home village. But while the "foreigners'" involvement in village politics was more remote, the philosophical orientation was still against the city, which they considered "made and owned by the white man."

For "local" weekly or daily commuters the connection was more intimate and they were active and respected participants in the social and political life of the village. Steady and adequate wages from government work allowed them to preserve and enhance their role as men in the village, and gave them enough bargaining power to shape a pattern of work that maintained this involvement. Although this pattern contradicted the capitalists' conception of work discipline, punctuality, and fidelity, it nonetheless indicated the permanent place of mine work in their social reproduction. They were committed to work at the colliery but on their terms.[5] Their high rates of absenteeism, equally characteristic of their British counterparts, were also related to the danger and unpleasantness of their work site. They were social beings and not just a social category, and their priorities, complaints, and goals had to be examined in light of their overarching concerns.[6] The industry accommodated itself to this pattern.

After the war Enugu workers recognized their increased power in a nascent labor market that was further weakened by the influenza epidemic, new demands for unskilled labor from the extension of the Eastern railway to Kaduna, and the construction of the Southern Protectorate headquarters in Enugu. These conditions pulled even harder at the fragile fabric of the labor system. Even when export markets collapsed during the recession of 1921, the labor market was too weak to attract workers, and management experiments with various systems of recruitment had limited success.

This chapter makes several arguments. First, it contends that the postwar period was a critical conjuncture for the development of a *culture of protest* with an evolving ideology of reciprocal rights and responsibilities of employers, employees, and the state. In this new culture, workers used delegations, strikes, petitions by professional letter-writers, and pre-trade union organizations to place their grievances before the industry. Even inexperienced, unskilled workers came to the workplace with goals, expectations, and approaches to work that shaped their responses to the material conditions of the mines and their relationships with fellow workers, supervisors, and European staff. These formed a moral world against which they measured their experiences in the mines. As workers for a state industry they had specific expectations of treatment that reflected the cultural dimensions of political authority. Their ideas about political authority reflected Igbo notions of the responsibilities of leaders in which reciprocity was an underlying principle. They accepted the ideology of "progress" and "personal improvement," which they were told were the reasons for imperialist conquest. However, the exact nature of this "progress" was not just a reproduction of the ideologies of colonialist architects. It was filtered through the cultural idiom of their communities and incorporated gender ideologies that reflected the deep social transformations of the early twentieth century. Igbo men were committed to their families and villages, and utilized mine work in creative ways to fulfill old and new masculine norms.

Second, the chapter explores the connections between the men's position in the hierarchy of production and the self-identity and consciousness that this encouraged. As the men entered the various sectors of the underground workforce and learned the tasks that constituted their jobs, they developed an acute awareness of the power relations in production. One part of this awareness empowered them to organize collective action at favorable moments with good effect. Another part of this awareness led them to challenge colonial forms of industrial discipline that victimized them daily. The unfavorable conditions at work and the harassment and brutalization by various "native" and European staff encouraged the workers to experiment with new organizational forms to mobilize around their interests. The organizational patterns that they developed reflected Igbo sensitivities, political structures, and processes, but were filtered through the new challenges of the industrial workplace, the city, and the political institutions introduced by the colonial state.

Thirdly, the chapter argues that the organization of work, and the ways in which workers relate in the process of producing coal, shapes the struggles that occur in the mines. By identifying the lines of authority within the various systems of extraction, one can outline the conflicts, autonomy, and interdependence of various categories of work.[7] This sociology of production, aptly analyzed by Michael Burawoy, and noted in the previous chapter, allows us to identify the points of friction and potential for collaboration between workers, and to understand the forces that encouraged and encumbered collective action.

It is therefore argued that as African workers interacted with each other and with European staff, they both experienced and reproduced "particular social relations" and the "political and ideological notions that regulate production."[8] These notions, that included the assumptions about white and African labor, constituted an "apparatus of production" which was reinforced by the legal and "customary" parameters of colonial labor policy. In Enugu the centrality of "indirect rule" in both the workplace and general society was an important aspect of this apparatus. The "Native Court" and its officials were charged to supply and discipline labor from the villages. And the mines reproduced the corruption, extortion, and graft which they sponsored in the villages outside.[9] The ability of workers to defend themselves against these industrial abuses was initially circumscribed by their vulnerability to strong rural chiefs and the weakness of their movement. But by the end of the decade, they had begun to chip away at the hegemony of "boss boys" in the disciplinary structure of the mines.

In the workplace, points of friction between various categories of workers and the African and European supervisory staff created a dynamic that affected the operation of the mine. These contradictions in the workplace were the cause of much of the unrest in this and subsequent decades, and reflected Burawoy's "politics of production," that is, the exercise of power and authority within the production process.[10] By identifying how individual men and categories of men affected the pay pocket of a worker, the dynamics and contradictions between men in the workplace can be traced.

The chapter will establish the connections between the organization of work and the miners' involvement in village life, which brings the villages in Nkanu and Agbaja into our analysis. While a full social history of rural life requires more sustained research, anecdotal references in the archives and corroborating interviews suggest that the socioeconomic ascent of colliery men in their villages was watched with foreboding by political officials and "chiefs" alike. They became vectors of new, and often insurrectionary ideas in the countryside and championed new definitions of "freedom" that challenged the "imagined" authoritarian order that colonialists created in the rural areas. The interplay of these men, asserting their position as social beings, and the management's perception of them as mere "units of labor," makes this a particularly rich period in the history of labor at the colliery.

## THE CITY OF ENUGU: A CRUCIBLE OF POLITICAL AND INDUSTRIAL FERMENT

By the end of the war Enugu had many of the trappings of a full-fledged colonial town. The layout was complete and it now had a "native" and European area, expatriate trading firms, and several schools run by the Church Missionary Society and the Roman Catholic Church.[11] In addition to the colliery labor camps at Coal Camp, Iva Valley 1 and 2, and Riverside Camp, there were several for railway, the Public Works Department, the police, prisons, and other government agencies.[12] The housing stock was still rather rustic with over 500 "bush houses," but the opening of the industry and railway attracted the major expatriate trading firms and the Christian missionary societies. The competition for "souls" between the Protestant (Church Missionary Society and Primitive Methodists) and the Catholics (Holy Ghost Fathers) was already in full swing, and by the twenties both had churches and schools in the city.[13]

The city grew rapidly during World War I and became increasingly cosmopolitan. It was a bustling working-class town in which most wage laborers worked for the state. Fully 7,000 of its 10,000 inhabitants were employed by various government departments in 1927.[14] Of this total there were 200 African staff and some 786 skilled workers and artisans (colliery skilled workers, carpenters, bricklayers, fitters, etc.) with incomes of £40 a year.[15] The varieties of jobs in government employment gave Enugu's African population a class complexity uncommon in most Nigerian cities. The railway always had a significant number of artisans, men who worked as electricians, mechanics, fitters, et cetera. Many were seconded to the colliery, where they constituted the most conscious sector of the mines' working class. All had had some prior training, often in mission schools, and considered themselves in a class apart from the "common" laborers.

Spanning all categories of government employment were a crucial group of clerks, all literate, Christian men, most often from areas considered more "civilized" than Enugu. Some were also employed as civil servants when the administrative capital was moved to Enugu in 1929. These men played a prominent role in establishing and running the many urban improvement ("tribal") unions that created some order in the city and became important sites for networking and the practicing of valuable organizational skills.

The steady wages of government employees stimulated a small but significant African business class in transport, real estate, and commerce. Predictably, Udi's own Chief Onyeama was among the most prominent, having invested his recruitment and trading income and proceeds from extortion in land. There was also one trader and lorry owner named Brodrick, from Benin, who owned Enugu's first hotel and cinema.[16] The large working class also attracted a service sector of tailors, "native doctors," goldsmiths, and the ubiquitous letter writers whose services were so critical to the pattern of protest at the colliery. These men, often semiliterate and familiar with the law, framed working class grievances and complaints in the petitions to the government. James Jaja of Oha, an ex-slave of King Jaja of Opobo, was a railway worker and petition writer[17] who became famous throughout Onitsha Province until his death in the late fifties.[18]

Although in many respects Enugu was a typical colonial city (i.e., the predominance of single men, overcrowded housing, poor sanitation, and a *cordon sanitaire* between the "Native" and European areas), it differed in many significant ways from colonial towns in settler colonies. For example, urbanization did cause adjustments in gender roles, but working class men did not delegate domestic tasks to prostitutes, as White has described in Nairobi.[19] Neither did they perform "female" tasks which, as socially mature men, they considered to be beneath them. They used young boys, usually relatives, to cook and clean for them. In Igbo society mature men did not cook, and they did not trust non-relatives to cook for them.[20] The boys also returned home with the men on weekends and brought back yams and food on Sunday. It was not uncommon for several men to share one "boy servant." This use of junior men to perform women's tasks suggests that one critical social differentiation for males in Igbo society was between men and boys.[21] The boys also assumed tasks that symbolized the man's position in the workforce. In a ritual of workplace status they carried the "pick boys'" tools to work daily.[22] This preservation of socially mature male privilege created problems for urban officials who were confronted with overcrowding in the labor camps.[23] "Small boy" servants outnumbered women and children in the colliery's labor camps.[24] But state officials never reached a consensus on the organization of space in Enugu, unlike more strictly controlled settler towns like Johannesburg, Nairobi, and Lusaka.

While the working class elaborated an urban culture, colliery employees transformed the countryside as well. In the twenties only a third of the colliery's 2,000 employees lived permanently in the city, and were usually "foreign" skilled or clerical Igbo and others. Another third of "local men" lived in the various labor camps and commuted home to the village on weekends. The final third lived in the villages within a fifteen-mile radius of Enugu and commuted daily to work.[25] These differential commitments to urban life did not prevent the enlightenment and modernity of the city from influencing the countryside. On the contrary, both daily and weekly commuters thought of themselves as, and were perceived by others to be, a progressive force in their villages. District officers often mocked their self-confidence and prestigious position in the village. For these men steady wages from colliery work brought enhanced status in the village as patriarchs.

After the war the discontent of the elite found institutional expression in the founding in 1920 of the National Congress of British West Africa. While this early nationalist organization did not successfully galvanize the support in Lagos that it had in Britain's other West African colonies, Sierra Leone and the Gold Coast, it nonetheless systematically articulated the grievances and demands of the educated elite.[26] During this period the elite became aware of the commonality of their issues with their counterparts in the African diaspora. While Africans were underrepresented in the Pan African Congress movement organized by W.E.B. Du Bois, Nigerian newspaper coverage fostered a sense of the international dimension of the struggle for the rights of the black man. Even stronger racial awareness emerged with the Garvey Movement, whose development between 1920 and 1925 was followed with enthusiasm in West Africa.[27]

These new ideological formulations around the central pivot of race and colonialism encouraged challenges to the colonial state. They crystallized in a national mobilization that engulfed both European and African civil servants. These movements pulled in the colliery workers who had their own specific difficulties.

## THE POSTWAR CONJUNCTURE: RADICALISM, SEDITION, AND RECALCITRANT WORKERS

World War I had as much of an impact on Nigerian coal miners as it had on their British "brothers." Both Welsh and Nigerian miners felt that the state treated them unfairly after they had given so much to the war effort, and both had been forced by conditions to strike during the war. After the armistice they continued to press their dissatisfaction with economic conditions. For Nigerian government workers, the severity of the wartime economy was exacerbated by imperial economic policy. Bulk purchasing agreements, import shortages, and price ceilings offered by British expatriate firms reduced the income for the thousands of farmers selling palm products. The economic impact deepened with trade dislocations following the banning of popular German merchants, who had purchased over £4,000,000 in Nigerian agro-exports before the war. Wartime inflation was exacerbated by shortages of silver specie which the United Kingdom used to finance the war. The hoarding of coins by trading companies and individuals pushed prices higher.[28] The introduction of paper currency, widely unpopular and often rejected by traders, increased prices exponentially.[29]

Some of the economic conditions that sparked Nigerian unrest were common to both Britain and Nigeria, and encouraged an atmosphere of political discontent and labor unrest that erupted after the war. In early 1919 English miners struck for a 30 percent wage increase, a six-hour day, and nationalization of the industry.[30] The political environment was so unstable that in January and February, British soldiers rioted demanding demobilization. Additionally there were disturbances in Glasgow and Belfast, and threatened strikes in public transport in London.[31] This unrest encouraged government to pay attention to colonial protests.

The first series of colliery strikes were connected to the postwar unrest of African and European civil servants. The reverberations of metropolitan unrest rippled through the European and African civil service in Nigeria. Africans in the Nigerian Civil Service Union petitioned for salary increases and protested discriminatory treatment in 1918 to no avail.[32] But officials could not ignore European colonial servants who in early 1919 formed the Association of European Civil Servants in Nigeria. They launched an escalating campaign for wage increases and improved conditions of service. In the vanguard were the European rail workers whose strike threat led to wide-ranging concessions on salaries and pensions. African workers also succeeded in securing a 30 percent wage increase.[33] The degree of militancy of the European civil servants shocked Lord Milner, Secretary of State for the Colonies, who considered them to be very close to seditious.[34] For African civil servants, this conflict produced a crack in the facade of imperial cohesion and racially based control. Emboldened, they began to agitate to emphasize their grievances.

While in most respects these men were a westernized elite, the dissonance between their cultural affinity with England and their political critique of the racism of British rule created an ambiguity that was expressed in both cultural and political ways. While they fought against racism in the government service they viewed laborers with disdain, and resented having to live so close to their "social inferiors" in the "native" areas of town. Thus to them, low wages and squalid living conditions were both cultural and economic issues and they joined their counterparts in Lagos and Port Harcourt in a postwar general strike for higher wages and against the color bar.

Among the most compelling demands of the Nigerian staff was the call for an end to job discrimination. From the late nineteenth century, the African westernized elite had increasingly lost prestige as the state replaced them with British civil servants at the turn of the century. The color line became an important indicator of colonialism's racial system of authority, and restrictions on the upward mobility of African staff were onerous, especially for men who considered themselves to be the epitome of the civilized Victorian gentleman.[35] Since the turn of the century racial issues had long been grist for the mill of the Nigerian press, whose lively agitation attracted the attention of literate and illiterate Nigerians alike. Now, after a war fought against injustice and for democracy and self-determination, these protests continued with renewed vigor.

The political and labor unrest in England, and the agitation of expatriate civil servants and the Nigerian educated elite, created a discourse about the responsibilities of the state to those workers who had sacrificed for the prosecution of the war. The Nigerian elite felt their loyalty to the British state was not being repaid, as the state was supposed to bring progress, advancement, and "civilization" to the colony. Instead, the government's treatment of its African civil servants made it difficult for them to progress or to live as civilized men. Their meagre wages made it impossible for them to support their dependence on prohibitively expensive imported clothes, furniture, and the like. To them the conditions in which they were forced to live were humiliating. In Great Britain the theme of the social responsibility of the state was thrown into public debate in February and March 1919 by national hearings convened by the Sankey Commission that investigated strikes in the coal industry. In dramatic presentations before the commission, the Miners Federation of Great Britain detailed the harsh realities of their lives.[36] These testimonies captured public sympathy with their brilliant use of the occasion to describe the severe conditions of work, and the poverty suffered by their families, which they contrasted with the lush, prosperous life of company owners. By framing their argument around the concept of social responsibility and the expectations of better treatment by the state, the British miners provided a discursive framework with broad resonance for the Enugu miners. In early 1920 this would become a reference point for the first series of strikes.

While the activism of the colliery workers was contextualized in national and metropolitan political and labor unrest, it was activated by the specific conditions and concerns of their own reality. In addition to the hardship from general inflationary pressures, they faced food shortages resulting from the rapid growth of Enugu. Colonial officials had failed to create a food system to feed the burgeoning urban population in the city and in the labor camps. Rural agricultural systems of the area were unable to adjust to this sudden demand, and food shortages stopped coal production many times as miners returned home for food.

## THE COLLIERY RESPONDS TO THE GENERAL STRIKE: DECEMBER 1919–FEBRUARY 1920

The strikes following the influenza epidemic of 1918 were related to the economic dislocations after the war and the socioeconomic consequences of rapid urbanization. The city of Enugu Ngwo (later Enugu) grew so quickly it strained rural food systems.[37] The shortages were exacerbated by a drought in the Udi area. Attempts to organize the local chiefs for supplies of yams faltered over the issue of payment in paper currency. The crisis was articulated in protests at Enugu in late 1919 and early 1920.

The initial unrest began in mid-1919 when merchants' rejection of paper money sent the price of yams, the food staple of Igbo communities, on an inflationary spiral. Unpopular £1.00 notes were exchanging for 11 shillings in cash.[38] Both European and African colliery staff joined the workers in registering the unpopularity of paper currency.

> The question of immediate importance to assist the Railway and Colliery to secure a measure of success in its general working is, to ensure an adequate supply of metal coinage without delay, in replacement of the present currency notes which are universally unpopular and have raised local costs in every way.[39]

These initial labor problems also arose from a contradiction in labor policy. Fearing the presence of unpredictable, "detribalized" African workers, the state did not want to make the city into a magnet for ambitious or dissident villagers. But the mines needed a stabilized labor force. If the state wanted to keep production running, it had to provide sustenance for at least this segment of the workforce. The necessity for this social infrastructure was demonstrated when work stopped in April and later in August while men returned to their villages for food.

From December 1919 until February 1920 colliery artisans initiated a series of strikes that coincided with a general strike led by railway workers. The strike culminated in an escalating series of protests by African government employees that included complaints about racial discrimination in wages, job titles, and racist treatment by expatriate staff. A racial incident sparked an action in the railway when a British employee ridiculed African members of the African Civil Servants Union in Lagos.[40] While the nerve center was Lagos, Port Harcourt, the terminus of the eastern branch of the Nigerian Railway, became the command center for the strike in the eastern provinces. The first series of postwar Enugu strikes were inspired by this national dispute, but had specific grievances related to the problems in both the industry and in the city.

There is little documentation on the first strike in December 1919, but three events occurred that would characterize worker activism in the colliery. First, the men contacted the general manager of the railway in Lagos rather than negotiate with Leck the colliery manager or local state officials, showing their understanding of the administrative structure of the colliery as an appendage of the Nigerian Railway. Secondly, they compared their condition to that of the English miners. And thirdly, they threatened to burn down the houses in the camps.[41]

The following February workers organized intermittent strikes around the food shortages, which may actually have been just the men returning to their villages to get food. The railway strike in Port Harcourt prevented the resolution of the Enugu dispute because it hindered the transport of yams to Enugu from Agbani, a key Nkanu farming village where the yams had been collected. On the ninth, artisans struck against the currency situation and food shortages in the markets. In addition, a smallpox epidemic raged through Udi, further complicating the labor shortages in the mines.[42]

On the night of February 17, when it appeared that the strike was subsiding, all the Agbaja miners left Iva Mine.[43] While possibly influenced by the artisan strike on the tenth, it appears that the major cause was the brutally harsh treatment of men from Agbaja supplied by Paramount Chief Onyeama. The assistant surveyor reported that after working the required half-day on Saturday, the fourteenth, these men were forced to carry palm oil from Eke to Enugu Ngwo all that night and again on Sunday, the fifteenth.[44]

The strike exposed the weaknesses in the labor market and the contradictions inherent in the state's labor policy. The district officer gave his opinion of its causes:

> The whole strike was only brought in the Colliery Manager's opinion and mine by the dilatory action in not sending silver here after many applications from him and the Resident and the District Officer. This shortage had been reported many times and it was left for the laborers to force the hand of the Government by a determined strike to produce the silver, which must have been there, as is proved by the General Manager's (Railway) wire of which I have a copy guaranteeing three quarters of the Colliery pay in silver.[45]

Despite the general thrust of colonial policy that ignored the reproduction of the urban labor force, the state was forced to organize a system that controlled the price and supply of food if it wanted colliery operations to continue. The strike had temporarily stopped on February 10th[46] when the district office promised to obtain yams and sell them for paper currency below the market rate.[47] Officials tapped

the Native Court system to secure yam supplies for Enugu, thus opening new opportunities for the chiefs' personal enrichment at the expense of the population,
but farmers were reluctant to comply. The hated court messengers were dispatched
to villages to collect yam supplies. In the rich Nkanu area this request added to a
litany of offenses committed by Paramount Chief Chukwuani and the other *Oga-*
*ranyan*, contributing to a climate of unrest that would be manifest in dramatic detail, with a massive slave revolt in 1922.

This was at best a temporary solution to the complex dislocations caused by the
rapid urbanization of Enugu. During February the resident and district officer of
Udi canvassed the adjacent divisions requesting thousands of tons of yams, but
their transport to Enugu was initially complicated by the rail strike and later by the
underdevelopment of the road system. Throughout February and March solicita-
tions of yam supplies met with the same problem that generated the Udi strike—
the shortage of hard coinage to pay chiefs.[48] The chiefs preferred "I.O.U.'s"
redeemable in silver currency when supplies arrived. Later in March when the Acting Lieutenant Governor H.C. Moorhouse met with the chiefs at Awka to negotiate yam supplies, he found that their reluctance to accept paper currency led them
to hold up yam supplies:

> It is clear that a certain number of the Chiefs were holding back supplies of yams
> which they had ready for sale because they were paid in currency notes. I had
> just previously explained to them that possibly three or four months must elapse
> before the new token coinage was available, but I put forward the suggestion that
> ... they would be given I.O.U.'s by the D.O. which would be ... redeemed by
> the new token coinage. The suggestion was very favorably received.[49]

While the temporary arrangements would pacify the colliery strikers in February,
a long-term solution required considerable planning and an elaboration of market
relations in labor and food. This would not occur until well into the decade.

In the February strike, the workers behaved like a seasoned working class. While
the district officer reported on the seventeenth that the strike appeared settled, several days later it resumed under the influence of the railway workers. The district
officer reported:

> Agitators arrived from Port Harcourt last night and got all colliery on strike today
> as well as local department. Have thought it necessary ask troops send 20 men
> here as preventive measure. Am seeing colliery people this afternoon. Will in-
> form that their promise to work is broken. Propose therefore distribute collected
> yams to local staff unless they return work.[50]

On the twentieth the whole colliery went out on strike and despite the district
officer's attempts to restrict access to yams, it was not until February 23 that all
mines were in full operation. The strike was led by artisans formed in a rudimentary workers' organization, possibly the *Nzuko*, which negotiated with the management. The administration also noted that the strikers were in contact with Port
Harcourt. The assistant district officer reported that he was visited by representa-

tives of a "Union" (*Nzuko?*) who put forth their demands for food and payment in silver. The state responded by dismissing the leaders.[51]

The strikers used normal forms of industrial protest, demonstrating their growing maturity as a workforce. They picketed workers who didn't support the strike, forcing the assistant district officer to request troops for protection. They tried to shut the mines through sabotage, by smashing a condenser and pump used for removing water from the mines. The February 19 settlement crumbled on the twenty-first, when the strikers left work in solidarity with the thirty artisans who were dismissed for leading the strike. Ignoring subsequent instructions from the railway workers in Port Harcourt to return to work, the walkout demonstrated the relative independence of the Enugu strikers. On February 23 the Iva Valley strikers visited Udi Mine to generate support among other workers.[52]

Both the state and management tried to restrict the strikers' access to the food market but, given the relaxed managerial style of industrial "indirect rule," it was difficult to identify cooperative workers.[53] Even when the food market was moved to the executive compound to facilitate the screening of buyers, such restriction was impossible because there was no labor registry of workers, and the district officer remarked in exasperation: "When selling yams to the Colliery Staff the timekeepers even did not know their own men."[54]

These first strikes introduced a pattern of protest that indicated a keen awareness of political hierarchies. Despite the managerial structure of the industry, the men considered political authorities to be the "Big Men" of the district. They solicited the assistant district officer (ADO) to mediate between themselves and the manager. They explained that "the Political Officer owned the division."[55] Despite his formal refusal to intervene—"it was not my business to correct their complaints"—he nonetheless crushed the strike. The district officer evoked his powers to underscore the state's refusal to extend trade union rights to African workers. He reported:

> They then went off to see Mr. Leck who refused to re-admit the dismissed artisans, and the "Union" definitely asserted to me that they would picket. So I gave them a very clear and solemn warning as to likely consequences and definitely stated that I should take every means possible to secure free egress from the camp to the Mine for the non-strikers, and after a somewhat lengthy consultation they collapsed.[56]

Confronted with this ultimatum the men shifted their negotiating position and agreed to return to work if the dismissed artisans could remain in camp until pay day. When this was granted the strike was over at Udi and Iva.

Although the artisan leadership was fired, the strikes succeeded in securing significant raises of 10 percent for salaried local staff, a 30 percent raise over 1918 wages. Higher paid staff received graduated increases. The burden of these wages fell heavily on a contracting market for coal. Both the marine department and private shipping companies reduced their purchases because the war had ended. When output dropped from 145,407 tons in 1918 to 137,844 tons in 1919, labor's percentage of the colliery's cost of production rose steadily from 29.51 percent (1918) to 36.41 percent (1919), and to an astronomical 49.91 percent in 1920.[57] Despite this onerous burden, the state could ill afford to risk further work stoppages.

The gains of the colliery's staff encouraged skilled workers to protest, and a second wave of strikes hit the colliery in March. These were led by a new but most critical group—the miners themselves. On March 10 the hewers or "pick boys" struck for an additional war bonus and they brought out all classes of labor with them on March 12. This second interruption of production, occurring amidst the problems of the small pox epidemic, led the state to revise the recruitment system run by the chiefs.

The tumult of the early year continued from May until the end of 1920. From May through August the "pick boys" agitated for additional war bonuses and a 2 shilling increase in their piece-rates. By the end of the year it was clear that the colliery needed to develop a better system of obtaining labor, and once securing it, deploying it in production.

The role played by artisans, and the key producers in the colliery, the "pick boys," gives insight into the priorities, intolerances, and expectations of these workers. It is not coincidental that they should be in the vanguard of this period of unrest. Both were foreigners and members of the urban ethnic unions which, by now, had cultivated a style of protest adapted for the mines. In sending deputations and using petitions, they used a rather standard form of citizen protest.

The artisan class, like the clerical workers, saw themselves as part of an enlightened group with a skill—writing—that was valuable, if not indispensable, for the smooth operation of the industry. As "foreigners" they assumed an awareness of colonial society that came from their earlier exposure to mission education and colonial administration. They were loyal members of the colonial civil service and they emulated the radicalism of their European counterparts. They were enemies of "traditionalism," and most especially of the rural chiefs, and contributed to a general environment of resistance and protest characteristic of urban life. They were what officials feared—"detribalized" Africans beyond the moderating influence and control of their chiefs. But in their urban associations they were an important pillar of urban order for a beleaguered colonial administration, reliant on "native" allies both rural and urban

Their politics was anti-"traditionalist" and they led the urban opposition to the chiefs. Complaints by the chiefs of the insurrectionary influence of these urban "sophisticates" became more frequent after World War I, and most officials shared their concern about this autonomous urban population. Missionaries also became alarmed at the flight of young men to the city. In 1928 they remarked that large numbers of young men of the church were leaving the villages for Enugu town.[58] It was quite easy for young men, disenchanted with the depredations of the rural chiefs, to "flee" to Enugu and join other discontented men and women in the city's several "shanty" towns, areas of African autonomy.

The "pick boys," on the other hand, had a consciousness arising from their role in production, and the status these jobs gave them in the camps and home villages.

This consciousness was not specific to men working in Enugu. It often emerged wherever coal mining occurred. The hewers were at the pinnacle of the hierarchy of production. All jobs in the industry—including the more "respectable" clerks and artisans—were dependent on their work. The viability of the colliery as an enterprise rested upon their effort, skill, and bravery. They were the only workers on piece-wages, thus making their earnings contingent upon their skill and effort. This reinforced their awareness of the importance of their skill because their ability to use tools and interpret the geology and other conditions affected their output, and hence, their wages.[59] In this period, the hewers were largely from Owerri, while the local men were in "special labor" gangs or haulage.[60] Until this period, most strikes were led by artisans, but in the twenties the miners "came into their own" and expressed a self-confidence and pride characteristic of coal miners everywhere. Like their counterparts in England, the United States, and elsewhere, they now had a keen awareness of their indispensability and were in an excellent position within the labor process to do something about their wages.

Toward the end of 1919 there were signs of an economic crisis. The prices of palm products began to drop. The return to "normalcy" by March 1920 did not mean that the labor problems of the colliery were over. Labor supplies were still short because the labor market had not recovered from the influenza pandemic. Moreover, the smallpox epidemic, the labor demands of other government departments, and the paper currency crisis still made recruitment difficult. The district officer called for the expansion of the catchment area for recruitment.[61] The Enugu district officer proposed a rational recruitment system that deployed labor masters to check off names of village companies.

Cognizant of the labor shortage, the hewers requested that they be permitted to take on assistant hewers and "tubboys" in an arrangement that resembled the *butty* system of the Yorkshire coal fields.[62] The "tubboys," who were also paid by the hewers, in turn took their own "helper" "tubboys." The master hewer was paid a tonnage (piece) rate and he in turn paid his "helpers." The "helper" hewer paid his corresponding "helper" "tubboy." The "helpers" did not appear on the official roster of men actively employed at work on a particular day. By some accounts, the hewer, tubmen, and their respective assistants functioned as a team with interchangeable work functions.[63] Given the pride the hewer had for his skill it is very doubtful that such an egalitarian distribution of tasks actually existed. However, the principal hewer was clearly the leader and the recognized worker who was paid the wages by the management, and he then paid the helpers.[64]

The hewer contractor system continued until 1937 when a strike settlement brought it to an end. The contractor system had several implications for the development of the workers' movement and the productivity levels at the mines. First, it provided an opportunity for the super-exploitation of the "helpers" and "tubboys," because their payment was at the discretion of the principal hewer. Secondly, it distorted the productivity figures for hewers from 1919 until 1937 when it ended. It was virtually impossible for management to accurately assess the real output and the development of skills of the workforce. In fact, the radical increase in output per man shift mentioned above in 1921/22 and 1922/23 could be attributed to the beginning of the system.[65]

Finally, the hewer-contractor system was an important factor in the consolidation of hewers' consciousness. Coal miners usually had artisan aspirations and felt that their skill, bravery, and geological intelligence were undervalued by the general society in England. Part of the reason for this was the manual nature of their work, which appeared indistinguishable from the tasks performed by less skilled men, in other words, "company" men, and partly because their product was expendable. It was difficult for the general public to see the difference between coal produced by a "skilled" hewer versus an "unskilled" hewer.[66] However, in becoming a contractor, the Enugu hewer added one more element to the spectrum of characteristics that fostered artisan consciousness. He owned his own tools, hired his own assistant who was paid from their tonnage, conceptualized the work, and determined the hours of work.[67] He could, and did, walk out of the mines when he so desired.

It was therefore no coincidence that from the twenties, when this new system of work and recruitment developed, the coal miners and the hewers became more assertive within the generalized militancy of the colliery's workers.

## BECOMING A MINER: THE TANGLED WEB
## OF RECRUITERS, 1919–1922

Despite the economic pressures of the postwar economy on Udi's farmers, the colliery's labor supplies remained tenuous. The demographic impact of the pandemic, the demand for labor to construct a railway extension to the north, and the construction of government buildings for the relocation of the southern secretariat to Enugu pulled at the fragile labor market. Market forces and the old coercive systems required some modification. The state wanted sufficient supplies of "free labor," but only without wrenching the "native worker" from the moderating influence and autocratic controls of village rulers. This was a contradiction that plagued the state for most of the colonial period. The labor crisis led authorities to explore two radical proposals to stabilize labor supplies. One, offered by the district officer of Enugu, called for the appointment of a labor officer who would develop a census of all eligible men in each village, keep records of labor needed, and select men from specific villages to fulfill requests. Governor Hugh Clifford found this to be unacceptable because it implied coercion.[68] The other, offered by the railway manager, suggested stabilizing labor by establishing housing estates modeled on domesticity myths and rural fantasies mythologized in English and Welsh mining villages.

> Would it be of any use if we constructed a good type of hut giving each labourer a certain quantity of ground and inducing him to bring his wife and family with him and make their permanent set of employees who might also produce colliers in time as is the case in England and Wales.[69]

But that was precisely what the state feared—militant mining villages like those of Wales and Britain.

The two proposals, one which linked the state directly with forced labor, and the other, that risked creating militant mining villages were rejected by the central government. The state preferred to work through the "native" "chiefs." The "chiefs" were still considered indispensable to civil peace and were reinforced when their people rose up in protest. Their role was assured, at least until the Igbo women went to "war" in 1929 and destroyed the fraudulent "warrant chief" system.

In addition to the contractors, the state used the Native Court chiefs to supply labor. This was forced labor which increased the discontent in the countryside. In some cases, men coerced to work in the mines were able to protest once there by deserting, which was common among men from the Agbaja and Nkanu areas. But many men had difficulty avoiding repeated conscription.

Among the most critical functions of the Native Court system was the mobilization of African labor for those projects that preceded the existence of a "labor market." As persistent shortages demonstrated, despite its abuses, this arrangement was still ineffective. It became more so after a strike in the winter of 1920.

The entrapment of reluctant villagers in the court's labor recruitment net led to complaints that went largely unheeded. Despite his abuses it was impossible for Chief Chukwuani to pull his men away from commercial agriculture. One of his subordinate chiefs claimed innocence to accusations of extortion in a petition in 1919. In his denial of extortion, he implicated the Paramount Chief Chukwuani, who used his "customary" rights to labor as a village priest to trick his men into going to Iva Valley but explained how villagers resisted:

> I heard the townspeople say that they had to turn up with hoes to Chukwuani's house (Paramount Chief under D.O.). They left their hoes there and went to Iva Valley. They were at Iva 21 days when they came back to his house, they said they would work no more. And [if] they did not work for a month they would get no pay nor would the chief. The people refused to go back to work and demanded their hoes. I said they did not want money. They ran back and did not finish this work and got no pay nor did I when I ordered people to work. I did not take any money.[70]

Even with this extortion and oppression, labor was still not forthcoming. A frustrated district officer painted this exaggerated picture of the freedom of villagers pushed into the mines. He advocated a more "rational" recruitment scheme.

> A man is detailed by his chief to do a month's work. He starts off and on the way his wish persuades him that the Chief must have meant a fortnight. He arrives and goes to camp. So far as I know he can do what he likes. There are no rules. Even if there are, he can break them all with impunity. The only form of control is his pay, the amount of which depends upon his punctuality. If he is such a nuisance that he is sent away it is probably the very thing he wants. In any case when he feels inclined and his respect for the order of the Chief and the Government

has dwindled sufficiently he packs up and goes home. There are no binding agreements for duration of work, no by laws, nothing.[71]

Descriptions of the earliest labor camps (noted in Chapter 2) attest to far more coercion than the district officer cared to acknowledge. What frustrated some officials was their inability to operate a sufficiently coercive labor system to obtain numbers of required workers, or to insure that once at the mines, they would remain. This reached to the heart of the "West African labor problem." A colonial economy built on peasant production could not risk weakening that peasantry in the interest of supplying labor for an industry that was, after all, auxiliary to the peasant economy.

Further, as Phillips has argued for the West African colonies, the state was too weak to exert the coercion required to enforce wage labor, a coercion that took several centuries to dispossess the peasantry in Britain where the state was on more solid ground. But as the Enugu case demonstrated, the colonial state was so weak it could only be "sustained ... through a complex of shifting alliances with local rulers" which, as seen in Enugu, "dictated the terms on which colonialism operated." At the crux of Enugu's labor problem was free access to land. As long as a man could return to his land or migrate elsewhere to farm, he would not be a dependable "worker." There could be no landless proletariat. Colonial authorities believed that the preservation of rural stability and economy required that the state support the chiefs to insure that relations of communal land tenure remained. This being the case, the state was forced to rely on the "chiefs" to supply labor, and at least in the early decades, was quite dependent on their whims, which in the case of Chiefs Chukwuani and Onyeama were considerable, and whatever degree of coercion they exerted.[72] It was this situation in which local rulers micromanaged their populations, victimizing them in petty ways, that generated resistance in the Nkanu areas of Udi during World War I. The weakened colonial state failed to win legitimacy in the eyes of the people because of its close association with the abusive chiefs. In many ways, as Phillips has argued, "the state ... was incomplete and undeveloped ... in many ways a mere facsimile of a state."[73]

Despite their schemes to extort and coerce their people, neither Chukwuani nor Onyeama could prevent the massive desertions when their men returned to their farms or absconded to the city. Both understood this weakness and seized the moment to conscript labor for their own economic activities. Onyeama was more successful than Chukwuani, often jeopardizing supplies of unskilled labor in the industry. In the case of Agbaja men, mine labor did not exempt them from the chief's own activities. In January 1920 Leck complained that his men were being forced, after work, to carry Onyeama's palm oil to market throughout the night. An Udi field officer described such a caravan:

> Last month when I was coming on here to see the Resident ... I saw on the road many hundreds of men and women, carrying oil into Enugu Ngwo, when I reached there I asked them from whom they came and the answer was "From Onyeama" the total number of people must have been well over 700.[74]

This abuse interfered with the colliery's functioning. Colliery overmen complained:

> When used for carrying oil after their Colliery day's work is finished they usually return for work at 7 or 7:30 (very tired) instead of at 6 AM quite fresh. Hence a proper day's work cannot be got out of them.[75]

Onyeama's efforts appeared self-defeating because he could not prevent his men from deserting when forced to work all night. Often men deployed for a month only lasted two or three weeks before they became ill or simply left.[76] If he had anticipated this, Onyeama would probably have measured his earnings from trading activities against income from mine recruitment and deferred to the former. In February 1920 the district officer and colliery officials, concerned because of the acute labor shortages, complained of Onyeama's recalcitrance and insubordination alleging that:

> He takes on contracts glibly without the slightest idea of what a contract is, and will try and wrigle [*sic*] out when the question is put up to him."[77]

There is no evidence that the lieutenant governor ever responded to the complaints of local officials.[78] The "chief's" abuses were considered a "traditional" exercise of his rights to his people's labor. Officials were too dependent on Onyeama to discipline him. Rather than censure him in March 1920, Lieutenant Governor Moorhouse increased recruitment incentives with a fee schedule. Chiefs were given £10 per shift per 100 surface workers and £15 for underground. The differential reflected two things: the importance of underground labor for the colliery's operation, and secondly, recognition that getting men underground may, in fact, require extra coercion. The revision was agreed to in a private meeting between the chiefs and Moorhouse after a mass recruitment meeting at Eke, Onyeama's home town.[79]

The district officer convened a meeting in Eke to attract men previously employed by the colliery. He offered to pay any man who returned to work for two months the old rate plus a 20 percent war bonus. At the end of two months this pay would be retroactive to 1 January 1917.[80]

But ensuing months showed that neither chief met his quota of workers to the mines. Onyeama was well on his way to becoming a "modern" businessman, eager to identify opportunities in urban real estate and he did not entertain the illusionary models of colonial control that the field administrators held. He knew he was powerful and he was pursuing his own model of development. But he was also aware of the threats that urban leaders posed. He knew he could not supply all those workers he was contracted to recruit. In April he supplied only 220 of the promised 600–900 Agbaja laborers. At the end of May, 700 workers left Iva Valley mine before replacements arrived. The real limits of even Onyeama's powers were underscored in June when he was unable to force some 200 new workers to work underground, requiring that recruitment be extended into Bende in Owerri Province.[81]

The 1920 crash fostered changes in recruitment alliances and gave the state a chance to renegotiate its new recruitment arrangements with the chiefs. Modifications reflected a slackening coal market and the fact that a considerable part of the workforce was coming to the mines independent of the chief's efforts. Despite the crisis of 1918, mine jobs and other employment in Enugu had gained popularity for many reasons. Young men from Agbaja and slaves from South Nkanu began to see wage labor as an important way to resist the interminable demands of abusive warrant chiefs, *Ogaranyan*, and slaveowners. Secondly, for Agbaja workers, it replaced their migration to less-populated areas as farm laborers, and allowed them to become influential men by establishing households.[82]

Under the new arrangements Chukwuani and the Nkanu chiefs found it especially difficult to prevent voluntary labor, and became more abusive as they struggled, in vain, to contain the flow of labor to the colliery and Enugu. Their actions generated another protest from their communities. In Chukwuani's area, these grievances became ensnared in the agitations of *Ohu* pressuring to be treated as equals. Throughout South Nkanu the unrest destabilized the Native Court system and led to his dethroning.

It was difficult for the "chiefs" to prevent men from voluntarily signing up for mine work.[83] Their men could always run away to one of the squatter areas of Enugu. The city became a safe haven for exploited men seeking relief, and with personal initiative, trying to earn a living. For Agbaja's young men, casual labor in Enugu offered an opportunity to reach male majority, that is, they could raise the money to marry and acquire those prestige goods so necessary for cementing alliances and becoming powerful.

The first signs of trouble in the slave-holding area of Nkanu came in 1920 when the owners and the entire freeborn community attempted to prevent the *Ohu* from using their new wages to improve their status in mixed villages by joining title societies. As we have noted before, Nkanu villages were the breadbasket of the region, employing slave families in the cultivation of large yam surpluses. With the settlement of Enugu, there were new incentives for the *Ohu* to push for more autonomy from their masters. Commercial agriculture offered them new options for accumulating wealth. For those who were conscripted into railway and colliery work, the problem came when their owners tried to seize their wages in compensation for services lost.

For Nkanu's slaves, or *Ohu*, residence and jobs in Enugu were used to renegotiate their social position within the village. The situation appeared more disastrous for Chief Chukwuani than for Agbaja's Onyeama. He could not guarantee control over the restive slave population who were empowered by the freedom of wage labor. Many had been drafted to work on the construction of the Port Harcourt-to-Enugu branch of the railway. Others had been conscripted to work in the mines. They challenged degrading and brutal customs such as the sale of their women for sacrifice at funerals and demanded the right to perform prestigious rituals consummate with their position as working men with income. They also demanded the same rights to land as freeborn men, arguing that this should be in compensation for their years of working gratis for their owners. They had learned the meaning of "unpaid labor," a concept from the capitalist workplace, and in applying it to justify their claims to land, they challenged the very foundation of slavery.[84]

The crisis bode unfavorably for Chief Chukwuani. In February 1921 he lost his appointment to the Native Court, his paramountcy was dissolved, and some of his villages were redefined as entirely outside Udi District.[85] By January 1922 he was only a minor chief over the Ozalla village-group.[86] In August 1922 his role as surface labor supplier was revoked because voluntary surface labor was abundant. The political eclipse of Chukwuani had been some time in coming, and this withdrawal of official recognition can be said to be as much a matter of political consequence as a reduction of cost overhead justified by labor supply.

An unsympathetic district officer linked the unrest to the rising expectations of *Ohu* workers.

> Serfs ... who worked at the Colliery and on Construction of the line, enjoyed good pay and complete temporary independence, on their return home did not relish a reversion to discipline. They started an agitation which led to bitterness which is only now subsiding and in some towns to blood-shed.[87]

Unlike Agbaja where Onyeama was a "big fish in a little pond," the "pond" in South Nkanu was quite crowded. Agricultural wealth had generated complex hierarchies of wealthy men, slaves, and non-slave poor. Chukwuani was just one of the many *Ogaranyan* in the region's village-groups. While Onyeama was unrivaled in wealth and power in Agbaja's poor villages, in Nkanu, Chukwuani was challenged by such "big men" as Edeani Chikiri of Nara,[88] and Nweke Obodo of Akpugo. Chukwuani's problems of labor supply came from his political weakness, and the state recognized the worthlessness of this alliance. But South Nkanu posed an even greater problem for the colonial state. Its *Ogaranyan* persisted in holding slaves and these slaves were becoming restive.

While Chukwuani's arrangement was terminated, the terms of Chief Onyeama's contract for underground labor were only modified. As early as March 1921, only twelve months after the original agreement, the Resident of Onitsha proposed a reform of the chief recruiter system by ending the bringing-in fees and introducing annual stipends to Chiefs Onyeama and Chukwuani. As paramounts, they were henceforth to receive £500 and £400 respectively.[89] Payment to lesser chiefs was to come from this lump sum.

This salary reflected revised expectations that the chiefs were not recruiting new labor, but maintaining a specific number of underground and surface workers. It was important to "keep them sweet" for, while they might not have been able to *produce* workers for the colliery, they might actually have been able to *prevent* men from reaching them. Onyeama's payment was contingent upon a daily underground work force of 1,500 men. If the workforce dropped below this, Onyeama lost £50 per quarter, and if it went below 1,000 the agreement was to be renegotiated. In the case of Chukwuani, the labor force on the surface was to be 900, and when it dropped to a minimum of 600, he forfeited £30 per quarter. A decline below 600 would result in renegotiation.

The scheme was approved by the lieutenant governor and went into operation on a trial basis for one year—June 1921 to 1 June 1922. In February 1922, the manager reported that the agreement was "quite successful" in maintaining the requisite laborers at the mines.[90] The management at this time preferred political recruiting, remaining to some extent hostage to the chiefs' power, and to the vagaries and competition of the open market for labor. In 1921 the railway itself had been recruiting in the Udi district and the manager feared that if their subsidies ended, the chiefs would simply direct labor to the railway which was offering a capitalization fee of four pence per day for each man recruited and fed by the chief.[91] While Chukwuani was dismissed and demoted, Chief Onyeama of the Agbaja, as supplier of the more critical underground labor, required comparatively subtle treatment. By July Agbaja workers had 100 percent redundancies; only 454 of the 900 were needed daily.[92] There were two ways to cut labor costs, either reducing wages or the salary of the broker. In 1922, the hewers' piece-rate was reduced by almost 30 percent from six pence to four pence per tub.[93] It was inexpedient to do away with the power of Chief Onyeama in the face of this lower wage, complain as the management did at the high price of £41.13.4 per month that they were obliged to pay him.[94]

In August 1922 R.C. Wilson, then acting manager, proposed a sliding scale that gave the government more flexibility and considerably reduced the financial burden of the chief's payments. Onyeama received a minimum quarterly payment of £100 and maximum of £150 according to demand for labor.[95] Onyeama tried to protect his recruiting fees, arguing that he was not responsible for the recession. The £500 subsidy (which he was obliged to share with his subchiefs) was unacceptable. He argued that he should not be blamed because the coal market contracted:

> Remember that a trader does every year but some years should be misery and others unmisery, therefore the misery of this year did not refer to our side as we are in readiness to supply labourers for our work whenever they are wanted.[96]

Wilson proposed this table of retaining and recruitment fees in August 1922:

**Table 4.1** Chief Recruiting Fees, 1922

| Up to a daily average of | Retaining fee |
| --- | --- |
| 500 | £20 plus recruitment fee of £20/ quarter |
| 500 to 1000 | £20 plus recruitment fee of £20/ quarter |
| 1000 to 2000 | £30 plus recruitment fee of £45/ quarter |
| 2000 to 3000 | £40 plus recruitment fee of £45/ quarter |
| over 3000 | £50 plus recruitment fee of £75/ quarter[97] |

Chief Onyeama warned:

> Therefore, if you are still claiming the reduction of the fee during this period of misery, we also have to claim that our money should be increase when the good time might prevail for it.[98]

Onyeama's recruiting income had steadily deteriorated since the spring of 1921. It had gone from £15 per 100 men per month and £10 per 500 in 1921 to £500 per year which he then distributed to his subordinate chiefs. Now, with the 1922 revision of the agreement, which was effective January 1923, he was placed on a £200 "political subsidy" with no specific fee for recruitment. The lieutenant governor specified that this subsidy was not to come from colliery funds. The revisions clearly showed that the chief's days as a labor recruiter were numbered. Ironically, having helped to create the working class, often using force and corrupt practices, the chiefs found that they now had become redundant. Despite his attempts to bargain with the administration and the management, he was forced in the end to accept their offer.[99] He made it clear, however, that should a shortage in underground labor result in the future, the colliery would have to pay dearly for his services.

> I have granted my own consent to the Agreement but as it is now written, I therefore hope that it is well confirmed and will not be terminated as per year. In fact, we have to say this before the period that is if you require more labourers for your work, that of Abaja, we must ask for more increment.[100]

The drive for productivity seemed to be brilliantly successful. In one week in September 1922, a record quantity of coal was extracted. It is evident that several factors combined to make this possible, among them being the emphasis on *robbery* rather than *development*, which meant that tubs were easier to produce and hewers' wages in aggregate would not decline.[101] Management was not oblivious to the necessity of keeping its master hewers satisfied, and indeed was entering into a new relationship with hewers which could only be called collusion in the way it led to the exploitation of unrecognized "helpers."

Coming out of the 1921/23 recession, the colliery's management had proven its ability to trim production and costs as need be. The costs of production per ton had been reduced, single shifts were mandated, and half the recognized labor force was retrenched by 1922/23. The uneconomic Obwetti Mine was abandoned in July 1923. But certain costs could not be shirked. Mine districts that were temporarily abandoned still required some labor and capital inputs to prevent permanent deterioration. The roof supports that rot every few months required replacement to prevent a roof collapse. Water that seeped into most of the Iva and Udi work faces had to be removed or serious flooding would damage the mine.[102]

Expansion of the workings after 1923 entailed investment in more machinery and plant. Management distinguished between extraction and "capital work" in the annual reports. The official figures of output during the mid- and late 1920s are given in Table 4.2.

**Table 4.2** Output per Worker, 1923/24–1929/30 in CWT[103]

| Output per shift | 1923/24 | 1924/25 | 1925/26 | 1926/27 | 1927/28 | 1928/29 | 1929/30 |
|---|---|---|---|---|---|---|---|
| Per "boy" on coal surface & underground | 13.4 | 13.8 | 11.9 | 13.88 | 13.692 | 14.77 | 16.12 |
| Per "boy" incl. capital work | 10.7 | 11.4 | 11.7 | 12.73 | 12.40 | 12.99 | 14.28 |
| Per hewer/shift | 3.5 | 3.7 | 3.55 | 3.45 | 3.48 | 3.69 | 4.02 |

*Source:* Nigerian Railway and Udi Coal Mines Report for the years 1923/24 to 1929/30.

By 1923 the mines had temporarily weathered the period of acute labor short-age and had begun to attract a sufficient flow of voluntary labor. However, Chief Onyeama continued to receive his "political subsidy," which insured his coopera-tion in not interrupting the flow of workers to the mines. The management was therefore able to concentrate on developing the mines and embarking on major capital works. The mine plant changed from being a group of semipermanent "bush" houses and sheds to a group of concrete structures illuminated by electric lights. Underground, many roadways were reinforced with concrete and steel beams and an electric haulage system was completed, thus reducing the cost of head porterage to the mine surface. Electrification also assisted in improving con-ditions of ventilation and flooding as fans and pumps were installed. However, both failed to solve these problems and miners on most work faces labored in high tem-peratures and often in several feet of water. The improvement of the mine plant in-creased the percentage of the cost of production owing to electrification and maintenance of machinery. However, increased annual output as well as output per shift per hewer ("pick boy") facilitated the expansion of production.[104]

Higher volume and lower production costs permitted the management to lower the price of coal at Lagos from 49 shillings per ton to 42.2 shillings per ton in an attempt to expand the market. Anticipating an upswing in trade, the management embarked upon a fairly ambitious program of capital development. The amount of £17,414 was allocated for culverts, drains, and retaining walls at Iva Mines, and earthworks, tracks, surface drains, and small station buildings on the surface.[105]

In 1923/24 the mines were opened only 225 1/2 days (in 1922/23 they worked 241), but the total output increased by 62,317 tons. When there was a slight resur-gence in demand from the Nigerian and Gold Coast Railways, the workforce was again increased to its previous level—1,435 Africans and 27 Europeans. The hewers produced 3.5 cwt per shift in continuation of an upward trend. While *development* at Udi Mine was halted until electric power was available, four districts at Iva were worked in *development*. The railway transported its largest coal cargo to date—87,376 tons since the slump in agro-exports released more wagons.[106]

Near the end of 1924 the Enugu Electrical Plant had sufficient power to electrify the Udi Mine. By February 1924 a record 23,286 tons was produced in twenty-two days. These production surges were possible despite a month-long strike from December 1924 to January 1925 and a reduction to 220 working days.[107]

The largest productivity increases were exhibited by the hewers or "pick boys," whose annual output rose from 585 tons in 1921/22 to 1,003 tons in 1922/23. This increase was partly due to the emphasis on *robbery*, but also of course, because of the increased presence of the unrecognized workers on coal. In one week in September, 7,031 tons were produced—a record for the mines.[108]

Management's strategy for mine development anticipated a world recovery and expanded demand by the Nigerian Railways. In 1924, however, the government was not at all confident of the wider marketability of Enugu coal. Among the reasons that Governor Hugh Clifford gave for rejecting the case for privately capitalized coal mining in the Enugu coal field by Sir Alfred Jones of the Elder Dempster Lines, was the fact that Nigerian coal was not competitive with South African coal.

> Up to the present time, the demand for our surplus coal, as has already been pointed out, has fallen short of potential production: and an invitation to this Government to share this already inadequate demand with other producers, for the present at any rate, lacks any allurement.[109]

The governor went on to justify a defensive attitude towards the government's labor supply, suggesting that it would not tolerate the piracy of its slowly developed labor force because of the strategic importance of coal for the railways. The government monopoly was thus confirmed.[110]

In 1924/25 the mine's workforce was 1,336 African laborers and 25 African and West Indian staff. For the first time the administrative report mentioned the size of the artisan group in the workforce—104. An unspecified but increasing number of artisans were West Indians, a reflection of the employment crisis in the Caribbean and a further manifestation of the management's attempt to find highly skilled labor at a cost below European wages.[111]

Despite the cost of electrification of surface shops, offices, and inclines, the cost of power and machinery per ton dropped from 9s. 8.1d in 1922/23 to 4s. 11.5d in 1929/30. This drop in the cost of production was relatively constant throughout the decade.[112]

## THE JANUARY 1925 STRIKE: RUMBLINGS OF A PROLETARIAT REFINEMENT

By 1925 the majority of the workforce had been attracted to the mines voluntarily. A substantial nucleus of a modern proletariat committed to wage labor for its subsistence existed. Approximately one-third of the workforce lived in Enugu, and the other two-thirds came from the villages clustered around Enugu within a ten- to fifteen-mile radius.[113] But many of those "local" men boarded in the town and camps during the week. The strike was organized by the "pick boys," the miners themselves. Although it was of considerable duration, there is little documentation concerning the event in the archives.

The strike closed the mines for three weeks. The hewers were calling for a return to the 6d. per tub rate. The wage cut made during the recession 1920–1923 had not been authorized by the colonial administration, but neither had it overruled the colliery manager. The "pick boys" or hewers demanded a 50 percent increase in piece-rates retroactive to 1920, the time of their negotiations with the Resident. The management rejected the demands and dismissed the protesting miners, allowing them to be chased into the woods by the station magistrate and four policemen.[114]

Very little is recorded about the organization, size, and leadership of the strike; however, it is likely that it was led by the men's *Nzuko*.[115] One of the leaders singled out by management, European staff, and African headmen was Edward Okafor of Umouji, Onitsha division. He was dismissed for insubordination when he and his group refused to work on a hard coal face in March. Edward petitioned the manager, claiming "victimization" by the European underground foreman and the African foreman, and receiving no satisfaction, went as high as the Resident who subsequently ruled against him. The management apparently notified other government departments to refuse him employment, and he reported being blacklisted by both the railway and the Public Works Department.[116]

Following the dismissal the other hewers were "restless" and threatened a strike, prompting a meeting with the Resident in April in which demands were made. There is no record of the demands, but the incident, coming on the heels of the previous 1920 strike in which "foreign" hewers played a key role, encouraged the management to be receptive to overtures by Agbaja clans seeking a monopoly on mine employment.

In 1924, record outputs occurred in the period from April to August, but shrinking demand led to a drop to only 10,579 tons in December when the strike occurred. Although the strike closed the mines for three weeks in January, output still rose to 242,582 tons in 1925/26. There is no evidence that dismissal of the striking hewers reduced productivity. Likewise, there is no indication in the cost per ton which dropped from 6s 2.2d to 5s 4.5d. Plainly, the aggrieved hewers were not numerically significant and their interests as individual workers were not aligned with those of the Agbaja hewers and their "helpers."[117]

Following the strike the administration attempted to improvise grievance machinery. In recognition that the center of the militancy was with the urbanized "foreign" skilled workers, the railway stationmaster was instructed to make monthly visits to the labor camps to solicit complaints from the workers. The manager reported that no complaints were made to the stationmaster in 1925.[118]

On the heels of the abortive strike, the management was approached by representatives of the Agbaja clan group, who argued that insofar as the land on which the mines were located came from them, they should have exclusive rights to the jobs in the mine. Management knew that the Agbaja's were not sufficiently skilled to perform the higher-level jobs at the colliery. But thinking that the "backward" Udi-based miners would be malleable workers, it decided to comply whenever possible with the request. Another factor tempered the management's inclination to comply with their request for all the mine jobs. The Ngwo, as a village-group, also argued that since the colliery was located on their lands, they alone should enjoy the proposed monopoly of mine jobs, thus undermining the pan-Agbaja claim. The management opted to follow a pattern of preferential hiring, again using Chief Onyeama and elected to train Agbajas for all categories of labor in the mines. Within five years the Agbajas were more than a majority of the underground workforce. "Foreigners" became largely confined to clerical and administrative positions.[119]

The short work stoppage between December 1924 and January 1925 did not really disrupt production. The Iva Mine was the mine of future exploitation and thus received considerable capital expenditure during 1925/26. A new tippler chute, retaining walls, and drainage ducts were built during the period. However, insufficient electrification made it difficult to control water seepage which had reached an unmanageable level. The mines had used hand methods of removal prior to electrification, and some districts were abandoned during the year pending installation of electrified pumps. At Udi mine, however, where water was less of a problem, *development* work proceeded throughout the period. Main headings were extended and over fifty pillars of coal were mined. The management expected a resurgence of demand and laid a solid foundation for expanded mining operations.[120]

But the cavalier attitude management assumed with the conditions of work had severe consequences. The human costs of intensified production included a major jump in the number of accidents. In 1923/24 seventy minor accidents and one death were recorded. But the following year, 519 minor and two fatal accidents are noted.[121] The cause of the accidents was never specified but the two fatalities were both from "falls of roof" while timbering roadways. If the pattern of accidents followed those of subsequent years which were detailed in the reports, the large majority were related to haulage. The potential for haulage-related injuries must have been great since most miners used only candles until the late 1930s.[122] Mine electrification involved only main roadways and not the actual coal face.

## THE COLLIERY RESPONDS TO THE ENGLISH GENERAL STRIKE OF 1926: THE JULY 1926 COLLIERY STRIKE

Despite the comparative inferiority of Enugu coal on the world market, the colliery was an important imperial asset during the prolonged coal strike in Great Britain, May to November 1926. As Britain's first state-owned coal mines, Enugu colliery was especially important, given the unpredictable nature of the metropolitan coal industry. The relationship between the two industries—one colonial, the other metropolitan—suggests that the boundaries between "native" labor and the British working class were more permeable than is usually assumed. In mid-May the colliery was asked to expand its operations to supplement supplies of coal in England. The mines quickly prepared to meet the new demand for coal. The colliery manager summoned the district officers of Udi and Awka to assist him in rehiring former miners from their districts. He needed 220 hewers, tubmen, timbermen, and railmen for Udi Mine, and 280 of the same categories for Iva Mine. The mines decided to resume the second shift, terminated earlier because of the trade slump, and hired new workers using the warrant chiefs. The labor shortage continued into the new year. The district officer of Enugu, however, cautioned that it would be useless to try to obtain gangs as "they generally refuse to go into the mine." He suggested instead that some of the "more reliable" men be sent to their villages to assure the men that the work was not so dangerous.[123]

Recruiting extra labor became difficult because of labor demands by other government departments in the Enugu area. The Southern Secretariat was moved to Enugu, creating a strong demand for labor, and railroad construction in the northern section of the Eastern Railway Line attracted workers who might otherwise have come into the mine workforce. Nonetheless, by the end of 1926 the mines hired 400 additional workers, extended its working days to 282, an increase of 58 days over the previous year, producing a record output of 353,274 tons. The increased output, 90,000 tons, was roughly equivalent to the 95,823 tons purchased by the Elder Dempster and Company shipping lines.[124]

In July of 1926, in the midst of this tight coal market, the predominantly Agbaja day laborers, tub, rail, and timber, walked off their jobs demanding a one-penny increase which would raise their wages to 1s 3d per day. Agbaja men held that series of underground support jobs, often called "dead work," that facilitated the "pit boys'" jobs. They were all on daily wages rather than tonnage rates, as were the hewers, and could therefore not increase their income by working harder. The payment of day wages to such a broad spectrum of the underground workforce encouraged solidarity and collective action. With day rates, increased effort had no impact on income. Thus, securing higher wage rates was crucially important for this group of men. The strike was short, lasting from July 12 through 14. In this case the "locals," whom management assumed to be much less militant than the "foreign" workers, acted on their own. They realized that, given their position in the labor process, they could bring the industry to a standstill even though they were considered "unskilled" workers. By timing their action in a period of a tight coal market, they had clearly learned an important strategy for industrial action. Coal supplies were desperately needed for bunkering ships during the British mineworkers' strike, and given the shortage of unskilled workers in Enugu, they had little to fear from replacement by "scabs." Timing a strike at such a period, when the Nigerian government had been asked to help the metropole in time of need, must have embarrassed the government. It moved quickly to resolve the issue.

Demonstrating that they too understood the administrative hierarchy of the state, the Agbaja daily paid workers refused to meet with the local railway magistrate, who functioned as the judicial authority in Enugu. They insisted on seeing the higher officials. The Resident of Onitsha province was despatched immediately to negotiate personally with the miners. Because of the urgency of the situation, the colliery manager conceded to the miners' demand and granted the one-penny wage increase.[125] The miners who resumed work on July 14, however, were clearly continuing the foreign skilled workers' tradition of timing their collective action to exploit conditions of high coal demand. They also understood that local officials were the lower and less powerful echelons of the administrative structure concerned with their behavior. This aspect of the strike, ignoring local political officials and management, would be repeated time and time again in the mines and in most cases would meet with success.

The strike also revealed another important change in the workers which the management did not fully appreciate. Having assumed that preferential hiring of Agbajas would prevent future strikes, the management faced a strike by the most "backward" sector of their workforce. In contrast to the 1925 strike in which the "foreigners" from Onitsha, Awka, and Owerri played a leading role, this one was led by the "locals." The workplace experience of the "unskilled" Agbaja special labor gangs had encouraged them to use conventional forms of worker protest, rather than leave the worksite as they had done in the past. They understood that by downing tools they could restrict production. Without their tubs, the hewers could not produce. Without their timber, no new work faces could be opened, nor roadways reinforced. The relationship between this consciousness and position in the workforce would be demonstrated in the next decade, when these same "unskilled" workers eloquently explained why their wage demands were reasonable.

In 1926/27 it appeared that the long-awaited economic recovery was close at hand. While the general strike in the United Kingdom created a sudden demand for Udi coal, the tin companies on the Jos plateau increased their demand over 300 percent to 6,093 tons when the Eastern Railway reached Bukuru. The colliery hired 400 additional workers and attempted to meet the expanded market. Iva Mine was still problematic, however, even though parts of the working districts were electrified. Most Iva work was in *development*, in anticipation that the demand would continue its upward swing. *Robbery* was hindered by flooding until the complete electrification of the working faces.[126]

As the colliery continued preparations for expansion, the market suddenly collapsed with the settlement of the English strike. The market for 90,000 tons of coal used to bunker ships suddenly reverted to Welsh sources. The market contraction was so significant that even though the tin mines' demand increased to 29,000 tons in 1927/28, it was insufficient to maintain the production levels of the previous year.[127] The mines were never able to recover their record low levels of cost. The overhead of the plant was expanding as mechanization and electrification projects were completed. Electricity expenditure increased by over £2,000 in 1928/29 and maintenance for building and machinery by nearly £1,000. The operating cost per ton rose slightly from 63.62s in 1927/28 to 64.06s in 1928/29. The workforce decreased from 2,169 to 2,101.

The accident rate, however, remained very high—956 minor accidents.[128] Nonetheless, the management still saw no reason to either provide protective equipment for the haulage workers and tubboys, the groups that sustained the bulk of these injuries, nor to train the men in safety procedures. There were no first aid workers on call and no one in charge of instructing the men in safe mining practices. At this point, the workers did not realize that the mining standards that governed their workplace were significantly inferior to those in the metropole. Although their earlier strikes, in 1920, were associated with their awareness of the connection between themselves and their metropolitan brothers, not until the next decade would they have a comprehensive conception of the types of conditions that should exist within their workplace.

## ATTACKING THE "CULTURE OF PREDATION": WORKERS CONFRONT "BOSS BOY" CORRUPTION, THE STRIKE OF 1929

At the close of the decade underground workers had gathered considerable experience in structuring grievances, identifying foes, and mobilizing, relatively successfully, to protect their interests. Emboldened by the successes of other strikes, they bravely attacked the supervisory strata to whom they were most vulnerable. In 1929 the workers struck not against the manager, but against the types of exploitation he allowed to develop in the mines. In September 1929 the hewers walked out because of illegal deductions by "boss boys" from their pay. The colliery management responded by prosecuting several "boss boys" and nine were convicted for extortion and corruption in the magistrate's court. The administration felt that it had successfully solved the dispute and concluded in the Onitsha Province Annual Report of 1929: "There is reason to believe that strikes arising from a similar case are unlikely to occur for some considerable period."[129]

Again, the administration and management demonstrated their self-imposed ignorance of the entire network of "native" supervision and discipline in the mines. The system of industrial relations at the mines was characterized by spontaneity, lack of planning, and ineptitude. Management understood the network of extortion and corruption in the mines, but as long as this secured industrial discipline they paid little attention to the costs that the workers had to pay. In fact, the system of labor recruitment and control at the colliery was a microcosm of the problems inherent in the indirect rule system at large. It gave ample opportunity for individuals chosen as warrant chiefs and their assistants to enrich themselves at the expense of the population they were supposed to be governing. At the mines this role was played by the "boss boys." Individually, the miners were powerless to reject the demands for bribes by the "boss boys." If a miner refused to pay a bribe, the "boss boy" retaliated by placing him on a difficult work face where he was unable to win large amounts of coal. Alternatively, he could arrange with the European overman to have the miner fired. Management neglect was not coincidental but expressed a generalized assumption that the "boss boys," as men from the village, should be given carte blanche in the mines. Extortion, illegal seizure of wages, and physical violence meted out by the "boss boys" was of little concern to management.[130]

The similarity in complaints against corrupt "boss boys" and interpreters indicated that both functioned as informers and collaborators on the mines. They attended workers' meetings and informed the administration on the ringleaders who were subsequently dismissed. The men attempted to use "traditional" methods of securing solidarity and began using oath-taking at their secret meetings.[131] As the working class became more conscious and organized, curtailment of these practices was considered a priority.

When the decade opened, increased state investment in chiefly recruiting systems increased rural abuses and caused unrest both in the village and in the industry. With colonial chiefs, "boss boys," and "native foremen" involved in securing labor, monitoring the labor camps, and resolving worker grievances, the degree of abuse was formidable. All echelons of the colonial state chose to ignore the exact processes that chiefs and "boss boys" used to produce and control workers at the mine. Despite the role of forced labor in stimulating the uprisings during the war, government still held to the belief that the autocratic chiefs were only exercising the normal prerogatives of "traditional" rulers, and the government simply tightened the link between chiefs and labor recruitment following the war. Again they were surprised when rural discontent reached a dramatic pitch in 1922/23 among an especially vulnerable sector. In Nkanu slaves (*Ohu*) rose up against conscription for colliery and rail work, the owners' seizure of their wages, and escalating violence against their families. In their rage they crushed local structures of state power, the "Native Courts," and forced the state to negotiate a new social space for them in rural communities. The protest was a revolutionary attack upon old, pre-colonial social hierarchies. It quickly became violent leading to the murder and eviction of dozens of slaves and, in retaliation, their attacks upon the freeborn, *Amadi*. The state was forced to constitute a punitive patrol and canvass the village-groups in the south Nkanu area for several months. I have argued elsewhere[132] that this constituted a crucial period of protest for the *Ohu* because through these struggles they forged a new identity demanding that henceforth they be called *Awbia*, a word meaning stranger. Unfortunately discrimination proved more tenacious than names and the new term came to be understood as but a euphemism for *Ohu*, slave.

For the state the price of expedience and alliances with the oppressive ruling class should have been recognized as the survival of the state itself. Similarly in the industry, worker protest against the chiefs took the form of desertion, voluntary enlistment into waged jobs, and strikes. But both systems would be reinforced until the colony faced the imminence of yet another world war and a dangerous eruption of colonial working class activism.

## NOTES

1. Personal communication to Peter Gutkind, 24 June 1964, as quoted in Peter C.W. Gutkind, "The Emergent African Proletariat," Centre for Developing-Area Studies, Occasional Paper Series, no. 8 (McGill University, Montreal, Canada, 1974), 7.

2. In the eighteenth and early nineteenth centuries, when coal mining was still practiced like a craft, colliers, as independent men, felt that a responsible miner should have "enough land to provide himself and his family with basic subsistence when the coal trade was slack." As garden space was crowded out by mining expansion, a nostalgia for this agriculturally based independence pulled Scottish miners to the American coal fields at the end of the century. Many mined on the east coast but purchased land in the midwest to reproduce the economic independence they had long lost in Scotland. Campbell and Reid, "The Independent Collier in Scotland," 65–67.

3. Barrington Moore, *Social Origns of Dictatorship and Democracy: Lord and Peasant in the Making of the Modern World* (Boston, 1966), 491–97, ff. These characteristics have been called "Catonism" by Moore, who argues that it emerges when "commercial relationships have begun to undermine a peasant economy" and conservatives, often landholders, adopt repressive methods of control. The ruling classes spoke of the need for the "moral regeneration" that characterized the "good old days." Bruce Berman has used this construction to describe the typical Kenyan field service officer and his autocratic reign in the countryside. In terms of Enugu, however, the romantic rural past informs the support for and ultimate complete fabrication of, a rural political structure—the colonial chiefs and their courts—not with authenticity in the area, but with considerable intellectual and emotional appeal to the individual civil servant or high official in the colonial service. See Berman, "Bureaucracy and Incumbent Violence," 230–37.

4. Frederick Cooper, "Work, Class and Empire," 235–41.

5. Their elusiveness from the control of capital is a variant of the forms of transitional "worker" behavior that characterized early U.S. and British workers. Herbert Gutman, *Work, Culture and Society in Industrializing America* (New York, 1977), 3–5; E.P. Thompson, *The Making of the English Working Class* (New York, 1963); Thompson, "Time, Work, Discipline." Thompson also found that early British industry had to accommodate to rural rhythms.

6. Cooper, "Work, Class and Empire," 239.

7. For an intensely interesting comparative treatment of the Northumberland and Welsh coal fields, and the impact of work systems on unionization and social life in the coal villages, see Daunton, "Down the Pit."

8. Burawoy, *The Politics of Production*, 7–8.

9. For the major study on indirect rule, see Afigbo, *The Warrant Chiefs*.

10. Burawoy, *The Politics of Production*, 122.

11. NNAE, P.E.H. Hair, "Enugu," mimeograph, National Archives, Enugu 1954, 162–63.

12. NNAE, NIGCOAL2/1/138, "Census of Enugu," n.d.; Hair, "Enugu," 159.

13. See Felix Ekechi, *Missionary Enterprise and Rivalry in Igboland 1857–1914* (London, 1971), especially Chap. 4.

14. Hair, "Enugu," 76.

15. Calculations based on J.G. Lawton's Assessment Report, Enugu Township, Enugu Division 1927. See Table 6, Uzoechi, "Eastern Nigerian Railway," 166.

16. Hair mentions Brodrick but little more is known of this enigmatic man. He mentions that Brodrick invested his income in "traditional" ways by marrying many women. Hair,

"Enugu," 93. An interview with one of Brodrick's sons in Enugu indicated that he was a prosperous and sophisticated businessman who owned a number of commercial enterprises (bakery, stores, laundry, carpentry shop, printing press, mechanics shops, etc.) as well as sponsored cultural institutions (football team, a brass band, social club, etc.). In fact, he claims his father employed a number of Europeans to manage his businesses. Brodrick appeared to straddle values of the "new" capitalist economy and the "old" pre-colonial forms of status indicators. He validated his wealth in "traditional" ways—58 wives and 42 children—cementing through kinship ties linkages with important political and economic families. It was said that he was from the family of the *Oba*, or King, of Benin, the area of Nigeria renowned for its beautiful bronze sculptures. The son argues that when he died the wives and children were manipulated by unscrupulous lawyers and the "fortune" quickly dissipated.

Interview with Thomas Osanogoze Brodrick, Enugu, 16 July 1999. Such "indigenous" entrepreneurs are still an understudied group within African social history. This strata has been researched in Lagos by Kristin Mann, but there are no similar studies of Enugu. See Kristin Mann, "The Rise of Taiwo Olowo: Law, Accumulation and Mobility in Early Colonial Lagos," in *Law in Colonial Africa*, ed., Richard Roberts and Kristin Mann (Portsmouth, NH, 1991).

17. These men were sometimes called "bush lawyers" because they were a paralegal group assisting in petitioning the courts, drafting contracts, and debt collecting. Despite government attempts to remove them, they continued to serve a function for both urban and rural litigants through the 1930s. Although they were significant to the social history of Nigerian cities, to my knowledge, there is no systematic study of their history. For a good introduction to their role within the judicial system, see Adewoye, *The Judicial System*, 188–97.

18. For an extensive discussion of the rise of King Jaja and his significance as an indicator of rapid change in the Delta, see Dike, *Trade and Politics*.

19. The one study on prostitution focuses on the Cross Rivers area where the town, Akunakuna, became the Igbo name for prostitute. See Benedict Naneen, "Itinerant Gold Mines: Prostitution in the Cross River Basin of Nigeria, 1930–1950," *African Studies Review* 34, 2 (September 1991): 57–79. On Nairobi see Luise White, *All the Comforts of Home*, (Chicago, 1990).

20. For an interesting treatment of these themes with the miners' "brother" industry, the Nigerian Railway, see Lisa A. Lindsay, "Shunting Among Masculine Ideals: The Nigerian Railway Men in the Colonial Era" (paper presented at the annual meeting of the African Studies Association, Orlando, Florida, 1995).

21. Tosh, "Masculinity," 183.

22. Croasdale, "Report on the Enugu Colliery," 23.

23. Ibid.

24. In 1938, there were 4,300 camp residents and over 700 were servants, who outnumbered women (685) or children (584). Ibid., 7.

25. Hair, "Enugu," 71.

26. Coleman, *Nigeria: Background to Nationalism*, 191–96.

27. The first conference in Paris, 1918–1919, was held to influence the Peace Conference. Subsequent conferences continued throughout the twenties. Coleman, *Nigeria: Background to Nationalism*, 188. For the most recent and eloquent discussion of the conflicts on Africa by the early twentieth century's two major African-American leaders see "Du Bois and Garvey: Two 'Pan-Africas'" in David Levering Lewis' Pulitzer-prize winning, *W.E.B.*

*Du Bois: The Fight For Equality and the American Century, 1919–1963*, (New York, 200). For Garvey see Robert Hill's *Marcus Garvey and the Universal Negro Improvement Association Papers* (Berkeley, 1983–200), 9 vols.

28. W. Ibekwe Ofonogoro, *The Currency Revolution in Southern Nigeria 1880–1948*, Occasional Paper No. 14 (African Studies Center, University of California, Los Angeles, July 1966); Osuntokun, *Nigeria During the First World War*, 292.

29. Ofonogoro, *The Currency Revolution*.

30. Supple, *History of the British Coal Industry*, 123.

31. Ibid., 122.

32. There were a whole series of discriminatory practices that elicited African protest. Africans had not received a wage increase since 1906 and there was a ceiling of £300 per year on African employees, regardless of qualification and job. Africans weren't qualified for pension until thirty-seven years of service. Most usually died before they could receive it. They also complained that the use of the word "native" when referring to African medical officers was derogatory. Osuntokun, *Nigeria During the First World War*, 296–297; M.A. Tokunboh, *Labour Movement in Nigeria: Past and Present* (Lagos, 1985), 22.

33. Wogu Ananaba, *The Trade Union Movement in Nigeria* (New York, 1969), 11; Osuntokun, *Nigeria in the First World War*, 296–297.

34. Osuntokun, *Nigeria in the First World War*, 295.

35. The best social history of these Victorian Nigerians is Kristin Mann's *Marrying Well*. For a synthesis of their political role see Robert July, *The Origins of Modern African Thought* (New York, 1967).

36. In his presentation to the Sankey Commission, the president of their miners' union noted that miners were "really claiming, because of their usefulness to the State, because of the dangerous nature of their employment, that they are entitled to a higher standard of life." *Sankey Evidence*, I QQ 4353, 6893 as cited in Supple, *History of the British Coal Industry*, 128.

37. Enugu Ngwo was actually the village-group that lost much of its farmland to the colliery. As the town became known as Enugu, Enugu Ngwo continued to be the name of the village-group.

38. Ofonogoro, *Currency Revolution*, 21.

39. NRUCMAR, 1919.

40. Tokunboh, *Labour Movement*, 23–24.

41. Croasdale, "Report on the Enugu Colliery," 62–63.

42. ONDIST 12/1/1562, Exec. Udi to Res. Onitsha, 17 February 1920; Exec. Enugu to Res. Onitsha, 19 February 1920.

43. Ibid., Exec. Udi to Res. Onitsha, 17 February 1920.

44. Ibid., CM to DO, 17 February 1920, enclosure in Acting DO to Resident Onitsha.

45. Ibid., CM to Res. Onitsha, 15 February 1920.

46. The district officer noted that "It appeared on February the 13th that the strikers were coming into hand but apparently the 'Union' got word from Port Harcourt and came out again on the 17th. It became necessary to transfer extra police from Udi." Ondist 12/1/1562, Asst. DO to Res. Onitsha, 3 March 1920.

47. Ibid.

48. The DO noted, "I can it is true make the chiefs to send in yams but the supply is easily exhausted and one cannot starve the local native upon whom we rely for native food-stuffs. A further point is that though the chiefs are supposed to be more intelligent than their people, they do not understand paper any more." Ibid., Assistant DO to Res. Onitsha, 3 March 1920.

49. Ibid., Moorhouse to Res. Onitsha, 24 March 1920.

50. Ibid., Exec. Udi to Res. Onitsha, 21 February 1920.

51. Ibid., Exec. Udi to Res. Onitsha, 24 February 1920. It is unclear if only artisans were on strike. Croasdale, in his report on the colliery, claimed that all surface workers were on strike 21–23 February. Croasdale, "Report on Enugu Colliery," 65.

52. ONDIST 12/1/1562, Assistant DO to Res. Onitsha, 3 March 1920.

53. Ibid., Exec. Udi to Res. Onitsha, 23 February 1920.

54. Ibid., Assistant DO to Res. Onitsha, 3 March 1920.

55. ONDIST 12/1/1565, Asst. DO to Res., 3 March 1920.

56. Ibid.

57. NRUCMAR, 1919.

58. CMSA, G3A3/0, 18 July 1928.

59. Harrison, *The Independent Collier*, 57.

60. This is a generic term that refers to men who, in United States coal-mining history, were called "company men." These were men who drove the coal roads, laid tracks, timbered the main roads and coal face and, in Enugu, operated the pumps. They were in a rather broad job category that management considered to be unskilled. In the thirties they contested this designation when they agitated for wages and explicitly articulated the skills implicit in their work. See Chapter 5.

61. ONDIST 12/1/1562, DO and CM to Res. Onitsha, 14 February 1920.

62. The *butty* was a contractor who arranged with the owner to work a specific seam of coal at a set rate. He then brought in his own workers whom he paid from the group wages he was given. The system is considered very exploitative in British coal mining. Douglass noted: "it would be he who collected the money and paid it out (if you were lucky). Most men were robbed blind. I have heard older Yorkshire miners say that after working a full week, bloody hard ... they would have to fight the butty man in the pit yard to get their money" (Douglass, "Pit Talk in County Durham," 228). In Enugu there was only anecdotal evidence of conflict between the men. In 1943 a new manager tried to introduce a system of group work and group pay. The men protested that it was "like a contractor." See Chapter 6.

63. See Akpala, "African Labour Productivity—A Reappraisal." *African Quarterly*, 12, 3 (1972): 233–51.

64. Ibid., 236–37; Reports on the Colliery Department, 1938, Sessional Paper, No. 11 of 1939.

65. It is difficult, however, to determine if all hewers used the system, or at what point it actually ceased to exist, because management took over the direct manipulation of a surplus labor force through the system of "rostering," keeping large numbers of workers on the books who were recognized but employed only at the discretion of the colliery. From this point the manager, not the hewer, determined the composition of the productive unit.

66. See Campbell and Reid, "The Independent Collier in Scotland," and Harrison, introduction in *The Independent Collier*, 4–5.

67. Prisilla Long, *Where the Sun Never Shines: A History of America's Bloody Coal Industry*, (New York, 1991), 59–61.

68. ONDIST 12/1/1562, Hugh Clifford, "Copy of Minutes by His Excellency and His Honour the Acting Lieutenant-Governor," 30 July 1920.

69. ONDIST 12/1/1562, J.M. Bland, 15 July 1920, enclosure in "Letter with enclosed reports," 4 August 1920.

70. NNAE, C.S.E. 1/218/14, "Petition Against Conduct of Chief Eze Okoli and Chief Onyeama," 16 February 1919.

71. ONDIST 12/1/1562, DO Enugu to D.O. Udi, 7 June 1920, enclosure in Acting DO to Resident, Onitsha 11 June 1920.

72. Phillips, *Enigma of Colonialism*, 10–11.

73. Ibid., 11.

74. ONDIST 12/1/1562, Acting DO to Res. Onitsha 17 February 1920.

75. Ibid, CM to DO 17 February 1920, enclosure in Acting DO to Res. Onitsha, 17 February 1920.

76. Ibid., D.J. Murphy, Assistant Surveyor to C.M. 17 February 1920.

77. It is very unlikely that a shrewd businessman like Onyeama was ignorant of contract law. He was, quite probably, hiding behind ignorance and pursuing his priorities. Ondist 12/1/1562, Acting DO to Res. Onitsha 17 February 1920.

78. Correspondence to this effect is in the file Ondist 12/1/1562.

79. Ibid, H.C. Moorhouse to DO Lyons, 9 March 1920.

80. ONDIST 12/1/1562.

81. ONDIST 12/1/1562, Moorhouse Minute, 21 March 1920; CM to Res., 6 April 1920; Exec. Udi to Res. Onitsha, 31 May 1920; Acting DO to Res. Onitsha, 11 June 1920.

82. This raises a question about the complexity of precapitalist forms of labor mobilization. In this case men had historically left the home village to work while retaining land claims in the village. This contrasts with another option, which would be to leave the home village to seek fertile areas for colonization. G.I. Jones, "Igbo Land Tenure."

83. Interview with Mazi Anyionovo Nwodo, Uhuona, Ugbawka, 18 August 1988. See quotation in Chapter 3.

84. For a discussion of the role of waged work in stimulating the Nkanu slave uprising in the twenties, see Brown, "Testing the Boundaries of Marginality."

85. ONDIST 12/1/1562, DO Enugu to Resident, Onitsha, 11 August 1922; Resident to Executive, Enugu, 17 August 1922.

86. Ibid., DO Enugu to Resident Onitsha, 11 August 1922; Resident Onitsha to Executive Enugu, 17 August 1922.

87. NNAE, OP 268/1921, A.G.C. Owen, "Memorandum," 2 September 1923.

88. When visited by Rev. Humphrey Richardson, Edeani had over eighty wives and untold numbers of slaves. See Richardson, "Pioneer Work." I thank Mrs. M.J. Fox, archivist, Methodist Church Overseas Division (Missionary Society), for locating this valuable manuscript.

89. NRUCAR, for the Year Ending March 1922.

90. ONDIST 12/1/1562, Resident Onitsha to Secretary, Southern Provinces, Lagos, 5 May 1921; Ibid., 20 February 1922.

91. Ibid., Resident Onitsha to Executive Awka, 7 May 1921.

92. ONDIST 12/1/1562, "Confidential Memorandum," CM to DO Enugu, 2 August 1922.

93. NRUCAR, 1924/25.

94. ONDIST 12/1/1562, CM to DO Enugu, "Recruiting Fees-Chief Onyeama," 2 August 1922.

95. Ibid., DO Enugu to Res. Onitsha, 3 August 1922; DO Enugu to Res. Onitsha, 11 August 1922; Res. Onitsha to Exec. Enugu, 17 August 1922.

96. Ibid, Chief Onyeama to CM, 21 August 1922.

97. ONDIST 12/1/1562, CM to DO Enugu, "Confidential Memorandum," 2 August 1922.

98. Ibid., Chief Onyeama to CM, 21 August 1922.

99. Ibid, Resident to CM, Memorandum, 4 September 1922, enclosure in DO to Res., 4 November, 1922.

100. Ibid, Onyeama to CM, 21 August 1922.

101. NRUCAR, 1921/22, 1922/23.

102. Ibid.

103. A CWT is a hundredweight. In England this is 112 pounds.

104. NRUCAR, 1921/22, 1922/23.

105. Ibid.

106. Ibid.

107. NRUCAR, 1924/25.

108. Ibid., 1922/23.

109. Nigerian Legislative Council, Sir Hugh Clifford, G.C.M.C., Address of the Governor (Lagos, 1924), 50.

110. Ibid.

111. NRUCAR, 1924/25.

112. NRUCAR, 1922/23 to 1929/30.

113. See P.E.H. Hair, "Enugu: An Industrial Urban Community in Nigeria, 1914–53," in *Proceedings of the Second Annual Conference (Sociology Section) of West African Institute of Social and Economic Research* (Ibadan, 1953), 156.

114. NRUCAR 1924/25; Agwu Akpala, "Background to the Enugu Colliery Shooting," 347.

115. Few of the petitions to the management remain and only tangentially relevant documents exist in colonial records. We only know that skilled underground workers or hewers from Awka, Owerri, and Onitsha town participated in the strike. It was rumored that Onyeama may have encouraged the strike. However, most of the participants were actually "foreign" men over which he had little influence. For a discussion of the strike see Nigerian National Archives, Ibadan (hereafter, NNAI) CSO26/1 "Onyeama-Recognition as Paramount Chief of Abaja Tribe (2), Subsidy of." Confidential Memorandum from the Secretary, Southern Provinces, Lagos to the Chief Secretary, No. c.1/1925 of 14 February 1925.

116. Ibid.; Ondist 12/1/1562, Res. to CM, 11 March 1925; CM to Res., 12 March 1925.

117. NRUCAR, 1924/25.

118. ONPROF 1/26/99, "Onitsha Province Annual Report for the Year 1925."

119. Ibid., Res. to Exec. Enugu, 28 March 1925; File no. PA 260, "Labour Force Colliery Department, Towns of Origin," (destroyed) as cited in Akpala, "Colliery Shooting," 339.

120. NRUCAR, 1925/26.

121. Ibid., 1923/24, 1924/25.

122. See Chapter 3.

123. NIGCOAL 1/24/29, Manager to DO Enugu, 11 May 1926; Manager to DO Awka, 18 May 1926; DO Enugu to Manager, 14 January 1927.

124. NRUCAR, 1927.

125. Ibid., Ondist 12/1/1562, Res. Onitsha to CM, 12 July 1926; Magistrate Enugu to Res. Onitsha, 12 July 1926.

126. NRUCAR, 1926/27.

127. Ibid., 1927/28.

128. Ibid.

129. ONPROF 1/28/203, Onitsha Province Annual Report, 1929.

130. Interview with Chief Thomas Ozobu, Imezi Owa, Udi, 21 June 1975.

131. Interview with B.U. Anyasado, Mbieri, Owerri, 23 July 1975.

132. Brown, "Testing the Boundaries of Marginality."

# PART II

---

# THE ECLIPSE OF COLONIAL PRODUCTION RELATIONS: WORKERS' VICTORIES AND DEFEAT

# 5

# THE COLLIERY ON THE EVE OF WAR: STATE INTERVENTION IN THE HOME AND THE WORKPLACE

The stock market crash sent ripples through the Nigerian coal industry. Having weathered the recession of 1922 the workers were again forced to adjust to economic crises over which they had little control. The coal market contracted as the tin mining companies withdrew entirely and the railway cut back staff, reduced trips, and Africanized its salaried workforce to reduce costs.[1] The colliery's management used typical strategies to accommodate the depression but there were no strikes during this period. The men were somewhat restive in 1931 when jobs were withdrawn, shifts reduced, and wages cut. But there were few alternatives to these jobs, and they were restricted. In such a bloated labor market, those hewers who had work became even more important in the village and urban areas as a means to the few mining jobs available. Opportunities to earn cash through agriculture also declined as the price of palm products reached an all-time low in Onitsha, the major market.[2] Farmers producing for Enugu were hurt by the reduction in government wages and employment. The colliery workers' wages were reduced in July 1931. Daily paid workers (i.e., tub, rail, and haulage men, etc.) suffered a cut of 1d in 1 shilling while the hewers' piece-rates were cut from 4d to 3d per tub. The old Udi mine was closed in 1933, reopened briefly in 1934, and abandoned permanently in 1936. Colliery men apparently returned home, and in 1934 the mines found it virtually impossible to get labor from Udi.

That third of the colliery's workers who lived either in the camps or the "native" locations were most drastically affected by the collapse. Conditions in the colliery's camps, which were substandard during the best of economic times, deteriorated further. The colliery still felt no social responsibility for its labor force and clung to the myth that their connections with the countryside cushioned the blows of economic crisis. The men were disgruntled but in this crisis it was difficult to organize collective action. Though signs of economic recovery were visible in 1935, by 1936 their frustrations reached a boiling point that pushed the industry into another wave of worker agitation. Coming after the unrest of the twenties, the workers drew upon the experience of "foreign" and "local" leaders of the *Nzuko* and the strategies they had used quite successfully to extract concessions in that period. This period became the most tumultuous phase in colliery labor history and was actually the initial phase of the protracted struggle between labor and (state) capital that continued, with increasing intensity, through World War II. These disputes incorporated the seeds of the subsequent postwar struggles that culminated in the tragic shooting of 22 miners at the Iva Valley mine in November 1949.

As Britain approached World War II, the political environment in Enugu changed. Nnamdi Azikiwe, the most prominent nationalist leader, had returned to Nigeria in 1937 and started the first of his "Zik Group" of papers, the *West African Pilot*.[3] The *Pilot* was read avidly by Enugu's clerical workers whose presence gave the city Nigeria's highest literacy rate with 40 percent of its 13,000 inhabitants able to read. The March 1937 strike stimulated unrest among other groups of government workers, and government agencies struggled to meet the demands for restoration of depression cuts.[4] The political ferment in the city attracted the support of both the rural- and urban-based miners. The rural men took back the radical ideas to the village. Such ideas heightened the generational conflict between the "angry" young men who generally opposed "traditional" leadership.[5]

Metropolitan officials became less patient with the bungling of governments such as Nigeria or of colonial managers, like William Leck. This was especially the case after the uprisings in the West Indies and on the Northern Rhodesian Copper Belt.[6] In both cases a labor dispute quickly moved beyond the workplace and swept discontented colonial subjects into a convulsion of violent protest. Shaken by the threat that these posed for the colonial state, and by implication, the empire itself, the Colonial Office attempted to prevent the political ramifications of chaotic labor policies. Under attack, the metropolitan state sought to rationalize colonialism and secure social peace by advocating economic development. Development required increased production and, given the resistance of African workers to colonial industrial regimes, governments had to become more concerned with the ways that African laborers lived and worked. The Colonial Office had a model of social policy that it tried to implement from the late thirties: order society around a disciplined, working class, intervene in the workplace to make that class more productive, and in the homes to make it more disciplined.

Indigenous initiatives in utilizing income, forming associations, and tapping into a generalized nationalist discourse of the period demonstrated African conceptions of development. Nigerian workers shaped their workplace and family life and reformulated their ideas about work, personal dignity, and masculinity in numerous creative ways. These contrasted with colonial assumptions about the static, "primitive" state of their societies. Fortunately for historians they have left a richly documented record of their ideas in a series of petitions and letters written by professional letter writers, and in their voices that came through in the minutes of consultative sessions with management. In these documents they expressed their ideas about the conditions under which they lived and worked and their visions for the future. Their words also revealed an awareness of their economic importance and a pride in their arduous work, all sentiments characteristic of coal miners throughout the world. Through these sources the "primitive" coal "boy" emerges as an honorable coal miner.

This chapter covers a period from March 1937, when the "pick boys" strike occurred, to August 1939 when the system called "rostering," or sharing work, began. It describes the escalating context of class struggle between workers on the one hand, and the industry's management and the political authorities on the other. Building on previous discussions of the nature of work in the industry, it moves beyond the workplace and describes those more general social factors that stimulated worker unrest. As such, the chapter argues that it is precisely because the men are full social beings that they fought most vigorously to force their industry, a state industry, to treat them as industrial men, with families, goals, and conceptions of personal and community improvement. Further, I argue that contrary to racialized characterizations of colonial supervisors, they were, in many respects, quite similar to the independent, truculent, and proud coal miners that expatriates left at home in the United Kingdom.

This unrest occurred in an imperial context of increased Colonial Office attention to the state of labor relations within the colonies. In the beginning of the decade, the International Labor Organization (ILO) moved towards establishing international standards in the areas of employment, penal sanctions, wage-fixing machinery, and protective legislation. While most colonial powers assiduously deceived the League in its reports, in England there were some stirrings of reform as early as 1930. Secretary of State Sydney Webb sent a circular dispatch to all colonial governors urging them to introduce trade union legislation. Nigeria was slow to respond to these overtures. It was left to a conservative government in 1935 to carry through a policy of labor reform. In 1937 events pushed the local administration to action, for they were faced with a plethora of strikes, to which the Enugu workers contributed.

Also in 1930, the Colonial Office established a coordinating body for the purpose of developing the broad outlines of imperial labor policy. The Colonial Labour Committee drew upon representatives from a series of government ministries, but few of its members could be considered "expert" in the field. As a policy coordinating body the committee stumbled along, struggling to conceptualize colonial "subjects" as colonial "workers."

In Enugu changes in social and labor policy began in 1937, following a strike by the "pick boys" that March. They called for conformity to metropolitan industrial standards regarding the treatment of workers in the workplace and their places of residence. The demands called for improved conditions for their families, for monetary compensation for injuries and death, for financial rewards for long-term service, and for government intervention into the workplace to insure that the conditions under which they worked were comparable to metropolitan standards.

Although the positive results were imperceptible in London, administrative changes at the colliery had begun almost immediately following the 1937 strike. By early 1938 the major pillars of a coherent reorganization were in place. The Colonial Office attributed the nine-month delay in the management's response to the workers' petitions of 1937 to the clumsy supervisory structure and management insensitivity. At this time the manager was directly supervised by the general manager of the Nigerian Railway, who in turn reported to the governor's office. Administrative and financial authority over the colliery was held by the general manager. In 1936 the Transport Directorate was formed and the director of Transport was his immediate supervisor. The management lacked final authority even in the recruitment of labor, let alone over conditions in the camps and workplace, and the settlement of grievances. The Resident of Onitsha, the Chief Commissioner, Southern Provinces, the District Officer of Udi, and the Local Authority of Enugu each had the right to interfere in these labor matters and to overrule the manager. Thus, when he negotiated with workers, the manager could not make binding decisions, leading them to identify agencies outside the industry for the resolution of their grievances.[7]

Socially, the colliery workers began to raise the problems they confronted in their homes, trying to bring the benefits of wage labor to their families. Most of the men were proud, self-improving, responsible, family men and they had clearly defined ideas about the use of their income for self, family, and community betterment. They considered the investment in the education of their children to be one of the most important uses of their income and poured money into scholarships, school construction, and salaries of teachers. They also worked with pride to bring significant improvements in their home villages. Even the Owerrians and Onitshans, who lived permanently in Enugu, funneled their income through their "improvement" unions to home villages to help build roads, supply pipe-drawn water, and construct churches and schools at home. The state assumed its paternalistic model of "developing" the village, but the men had long established their priorities. They had their own ideas of what constituted "development," and they often objected to state policies that they felt were not adequately preparing them for independence. In 1946 they opposed the government's mass literacy program, and echoed the nationalist demand that compulsory education was the most adequate preparation for independence.[8]

They were also motivated by evolving gender ideologies that drew on their own and other traditions. Their demand for more housing and a family wage embarrassed the Colonial Office at a time when state ownership was being criticized by Britain's major capitalists who were interested in West Africa. This led to the first attempt to create the social environment to nurture urban family life.

## RACE, MASCULINITY, AND THE CHANGING CONTEXT OF INDUSTRIAL RELATIONS: INDUSTRIAL COMMONALTIES WITH METROPOLITAN LABOR

The industry's supervisors and colonial authorities still saw the men as "African workers," with all the deprecating implications that the term carried. However, the workers felt that they were part of a brotherhood of coal miners with close linkages with the miners of England. They resented the racialized system of industrial authoritarianism that subjected them to demeaning forms of address and brutality. They understood, through their personal experiences, the racialized power that enforced colonial production regimes, in which "one racial group dominates through political, legal and economic rights denied the other."[9] However, they also considered themselves to be working men, men employed in an industry—coal mining—that everywhere symbolized the struggles workers waged for workplace power and against increased supervision. The culture of coal, with its celebration of male physical strength, endurance, bravery, and seldom recognized skill, encouraged them to construct identities of proud men belonging to an international brotherhood. Information from radio reports on British and American miners, and interactions with expatriate staff who came largely from Britain's north coal fields, encouraged them to appropriate European and American models to develop their own ideas about what they deserved as workers and as men. David Frank, a Canadian labor scholar, captures the essence of the universal brotherhood of coal miners in the eloquent opening to a review essay on coal mining:

> The country of coal is a discontinuous land. Like the black coal seams that outcrop on both sides of the Atlantic, it runs from the mining settlements of Scotland and Wales to the coal towns of West Virginia and Illinois. Its course carries us from the earliest stages of the Industrial Revolution to the most recent battles for economic democracy. The power of coal has been a founding force in the development of industrial capitalism, and the people of this relatively unrecognized country have shared much history in common.[10]

It was the commonalties of coal mining that fueled the colliery's most turbulent period of unrest from 1938 to 1949. Physical strength and the mastery of specific skills, some intuitive, others learned, were celebrated wherever coal was mined. In Europe and America, the miner's skills were his "property" which he learned through apprenticeship or training under his father's supervision. These skills were an important component of working class masculinity.[11] In Enugu's mines, which offered little formal training, men nonetheless understood that their work required specific skills as well as an unflinching bravery, given the fearful context of mining deep in the earth.[12] The same qualities required of mining that marked Western norms of manliness were in synergy with the indigenous Igbo male ethos which explicitly valued power, aggression, perseverance, and stoicism in the face of danger.

Comparisons with European and American coal miners were a dominant thread that informed demands and shaped worker militance. From 1938, the struggles they waged showed a heightened political sensitivity to the issues of racial discrimination and workers' rights. At this time they explicitly raised issues of dignity, respect, social justice, and racial parity, and brought customary and insulting industrial practices into the public eye by using the nationalist press and calling their supervisors before the courts. They argued that their low wages made it impossible for them to fulfill the male breadwinner norm, an ideology that did not reflect their domestic reality in which wives worked and held their own income. As men they could not protect their families from the indignities that they were forced to endure because of overcrowded and unsuitable housing.

The boundaries between metropolitan and colonial industry, British "working men" and "native" laborers, were more "imagined" than real. The physical imperatives of coal mining projected metropolitan production regimes into the colonial industry. Recruitment of management and their models of workplace discipline, decisions about extractive systems and production techniques, the procedures for disputes management and the standards of safety, accident compensation, and workmen's compensation were transferred from the British coal fields. But in their adaptation to the colony they were transformed to accommodate British ideas about the deficient character of African labor, ideas that were framed within the discourse of colonial racism.

Arbitrary physical violence was an important part of this racialized industrial power, and took a form that deliberately challenged the masculinity of working class men. Beatings were common as was the occasional, and deprecating slap in the face. This coercion was not gratuitous but a strategy to solve a seemingly intractable problem that confronted management daily. Getting the worker into the mine was only one part of the process. The second part was converting his labor-power into labor; i.e., making him work with sufficient energy during the period that he was being paid. Wages paid for his labor time, it was management's responsibility to convert this time into useful labor.

But on the eve of World War II there was a noticeable change in the state's treatment of physical abuse in the workplace. Court cases began to appear in which workers successfully sued European staff for these assaults. The political environment of change and reform, emanating from the Colonial Office, gradually trickled down to the local level of the colliery, and it disturbed the racial protocol of the workplace. It affected European and "native" staff, and more importantly, the men themselves. Emboldened by this new environment and armed with a sharpened awareness of their role in the imperial economy, they began to push for rights that they felt entitled to as working men with families. Their quest would fuel the ripples of unrest that rocked the colliery during and after the war.

For the average expatriate "boss," the shift in state policy on the eve of World War II must have been an unsettling experience. Until the late thirties assaults against workers were protected by the state's refusal to give Africans the right to contest this treatment in the courts. Suddenly, the racial protocol of the workplace that gave supervisors so much power over their African workers was unacceptable to the state. Practices that had been enshrined in the systems of industrial discipline, such as assault against workers, the use of insulting forms of address, and management's dismissive attitude towards worker complaints were changed. Realizing that the state no longer sanctioned colonial production regime, the workers frequently violated the moral economy of race in the workplace and confronted their bosses. "Customary" forms of colonial discipline were regarded as dangerously provocative and led to several lightning strikes in 1938.[13]

The men's activism forced Britain to push the negligent colliery management to intervene in the colonial workplace, to supervise the conditions under which the men worked, and to improve conditions in the "native" townships and labor camps that structured working class life. The Nigerian government began to regulate the terms under which African labor-power was being appropriated and reproduced. To miners this intervention was a vindication of their existence as "industrial men" rather than the "primitive" and undisciplined "African workers."

Moreover, following the 1937 strike, the colliery began a wide-ranging program of reform. But a consensus on the extent and nature of social reform proved elusive and colonial authorities debated issues of policy and experimented with societal models that had evolved to contain class contradictions in British society. Some involved a series of changes that undermined the arbitrary control Europeans had over the men. They established representative councils rather than trust the "boss boys" or Europeans to articulate the grievances of their men.

The council members had been leaders in the colliery *Nzuko* and these new appointments legitimized these worker associations as negotiating bodies rather than creating a pliant advisory board that merely conveyed managerial directives to the men. Both management and European staff as well as rural leaders were angry that the government insisted on using the representative councils as consultative bodies for the workers. Underground "native" and expatriate staff were especially attuned to their loss of power to enforce colonial discipline. The councils successfully lobbied to eliminate the interpreters, a significantly powerful group that extorted the workers and frequently assaulted them as well. Finally, in 1939, after a particularly disruptive, but from the workers' position, successful period of negotiation, the manager ended the councils.[14]

Expatriate colliery and government staff were divided on the use of workers' councils and the propriety of improvements in the labor camps. Some felt that it would only encourage the men to be even more critical of "tribal" authority, and settle in town where the state had little control over their behavior. Others felt that the best way to forestall future colliery strikes was to apply the most enlightened managerial policies developed in Britain. Nonetheless, the impending war in Europe required that the colonial working class be sufficiently appeased to prevent their interrupting production during such critical times.

Nonetheless, it was important that the state establish control over the various aspects of the industry in which workers had considerable autonomy: the labor market or supply of labor to the mines, the power that various categories of workers held over the mines' output, and the urban sprawl and disorder of the mines' labor camps. These initiatives would preoccupy the state and management for the duration of the colonial period. Policies to control the labor market involved several innovations. First, in 1938, a decision was made to restrict all future hiring to the adjacent villages. This would prevent overcrowding in Enugu and also allow the industry to pull in and dismiss workers without causing social unrest. Secondly, the employment cards were updated, and superfluous men were retrenched and evicted from the overcrowded camps. Because mine work had become an important part of male strategies to marry and achieve status, there were thousands of men in adjacent villages who had worked at some time in the industry. These constituted an important pool of labor with a level of skill that could not be attained by "green" labor. Thirdly, when the men objected to retrenchments, the state began a system called "rostering," through which the mines' daily requirement of jobs was shared by a much larger workforce. The name "rostering" came from the work roster, the sheet that announced the names of men who would work the next day. The advantage to management of having a large number of redundant workers available for periods of increased production was clear. However, to the workers, this meant the weakening of their ability to develop their own combinations of mine and farm work, and an inability to work when and as often as they wished.

It proved more difficult to identify the points in production over which managerial control, never effectively exercised, could now be applied. The state tried to make labor more efficient, dependable, and intensive. Before the introduction of mining machinery in Europe, the problem of managerial control over coal miners confounded managers for centuries. But gradually, with the introduction of coal-cutting machinery, European and American owners were able to reduce, though never totally to eliminate, the controls that workers had over production. In Enugu, such mechanization never occurred. The dispersal of worksites under the *pillar and stall* system, the shortage of European managers during the war, and the inability to use machinery in these mines, all made this a difficult task. Nevertheless, in 1938 the government would attempt to set production targets and attendance requirements to bring the miners under more direct supervisory control. However, the events in Enugu demonstrated how productivity, far from being a quantitative or "objective" term, is a managerially defined concept whose meaning can be manipulated in a number of ways to justify incursions into the workplace autonomy of coal miners.

These attempts to instill closer supervision met resistance from the workers who, like coal miners everywhere, jealously guarded their autonomy and preferred to work at a self-regulating pace. The piece-rate system encouraged Enugu hewers' independent self-identity. First, they were the only workers whose wages were based on piece rates, a factor that reinforced their sense of skill "since their earning depended ... on their ability to use a wide range of hand tools, and to interpret the geological and other conditions under which they worked."[15] Secondly, because of the high worker-to-supervisor ratio, and the dispersal of work faces under the *pillar and stall* system, they functioned with little direct supervision but for an

occasional visit by a "native" or European supervisor. While this degree of autonomy was typical of non-mechanized coal mining in the United States and Europe,
in Enugu the degree of workplace control was even stronger. The "sanction of the
sack," the ultimate managerial weapon, was of moderate effectiveness to miners
who integrated farming with bouts of mine work. Until 1937 the hewers were labor
contractors who created, directed, and paid their own work group of "apprentice"
hewers and "tubboys" similar to the "butty" system in England.[16] They also appeared to have incorporated many of the butty's abuses, as the hewer's was the
only name on the colliery payroll and he paid the work team from the output of his
group. Like the "independent miner" of England and Scotland, Enugu's hewers
nursed a vision of themselves as proud, self-improving men whose masculinity
was strengthened by their skill and their ability to dispense jobs as patronage to
their family and friends in the village. This power tapped into ideologies of reciprocity ingrained in Igbo leadership norms and contributed to the influence and esteem with which these men were viewed in the village.

In fact, because the Derbyshire system divided up tasks, all jobs were important
for production. Hewers and other groups of underground workers—tubmen, railmen, haulage workers, timbermen—developed a consciousness linked to discrete
tasks. Although many of these jobs were designated as "unskilled," workers realized that they required an expertise and intuitive knowledge. This gave them considerable pride that was expressed in their arguments for improvements on the eve
of the war. By 1936 underground workers had several decades of experience with
successful agitation organized by the *Nzuko Ifunanya*. As noted in the previous
chapter, they attracted the attention of the highest levels of the nation-state and beyond that, the Colonial Office.

## MODERNIZING INDUSTRIAL "INDIRECT RULE":
## TENTATIVE STEPS OF LABOR REFORM

The colliery management was as negligent as a landlord as it was in the workplace. Although the industry ran several labor camps with over 4,000 inhabitants,
it put few resources into housing. Even under the best of economic conditions, housing in the camps was unsanitary, overcrowded, and substandard. After the depression, it became even worse. Most workers lived in very rudimentary range-style
housing designed for individual men as indentured workers in the colonies. They
were a row of rooms 12' × 12' × 10' separated by partial partitions and topped
with corrugated roofs. They were insufferably hot during the day and held an average of 5.5 people.[17] The overcrowding violated Igbo (and western) marital norms
by requiring parents and children to share a common sleeping space. The men found
the housing to be demeaning, immoral, and incompatible with family life. But for
those who were far from home it was the only option to housing in Enugu.

In 1938 only 30 percent of the men in the camps were married, and most of these
were from Owerri.[18] The overwhelming majority were either unmarried junior men
or "local" men who had left their wives in the village. The preponderance of male-

headed households is suggested by the number of servants. Of the total camp population of over 4,000, 741 were servants, more than women (685) or children (584). This was an average of one servant for every three laborers.[19]

The industry's required labor redundancies, casual daily recruitment practices, and the men's own gender ideologies about male domesticity all exacerbated the housing crisis. The labor camps, "native" location, and unregulated squatter camps reflected the imprint of colliery chaos. To accommodate the men's erratic work habits, the colliery had to keep 100 percent more workers on their books than were daily necessary, and house them as well. Many Agbaja and Nkanu men stayed in town, commuting home on the weekends, because daily work assignments depended on selection by the "boss boys" who made up their crews at the pit mouth. In 1938 the colliery employed 2,650 workers daily, with approximately 600 commuting from neighboring villages each day. The total population of the four labor camps, was 4,316, of which 2,326 were laborers. Thus the colliery was housing approximately 500 people not employed in the mines.

Because most adult and junior men lived in villages a reasonable distance from the worksite, they commuted daily or weekly to work in the mines. This allowed them to be a social force in their communities where often their status in the hierarchy of production was recognized. Their communities benefited from their income and progressive outlook and regarded them as powerful "modern" men. District officers called them "coal gentlemen," who were recognizable by their flashy clothes, bicycles, and air of jaunty self-confidence.[20] Their proximity to home allowed them to remain involved in the social, political, and economic life of their village. This was especially important since farming, not just an economic necessary, was ideologically important as a source of prestige for Igbo men.[21] Because there were no labor contracts, the men made individual determinations of the time and duration of their work, thus having the flexibility to respond to the demands of rural society.

To the industry, the adult male population in adjacent villages, labor camps, and the "native" locations of the city constituted a labor reserve of experienced mine workers who could be called upon to supply labor when the fluctuating market required. But these men elected to sell their labor power in small and unpredictable units, often leaving the colliery short on workers. To some extent this rural "straddling" relieved the state of the problem of maintaining workers and their families during slack coal periods. But it still gave the men far too much control over the industry's labor market.

The connection with rural life was also encouraged by the colliery's contined pattern of incorporating rural leaders, chiefs, and elders in the industry's affairs. This practice was even less successful than the chiefs were in controlling the men in their villages and regulating their responses at work. In the countryside, the men crafted their own model of the "responsible" worker, and he was not an industrially "disciplined" man. Rather he used colliery work to construct the type of rural existence that made him feel important and fulfilled as a man.

Differential access to and the importance of mine jobs became a defining element of "clan" identity, a concept legitimized through the paramount chieftaincy system. "Clan" was being redefined as a colonial category of political power during the thirties. In 1929, when officials surveyed Igboland in preparation for taxation, the women of the southern region, fearing that they would be taxed, rose up and pulled down Lugard's elaborate paramount chief system. During the uprising, the Women's War of 1929, they destroyed unpopular Native Courts, attacked chiefs, and brandished symbols of war.[22] Finally, government realized its own ignorance of the people it claimed to govern and commissioned a rash of intelligence reports on most village-groups in Igboland.[23] Armed with "scientific" evidence from their intelligence reports, officials decentralized rural political structures but retained "clan" as a concept of political organization. Thus, the post of paramount chief was abolished, but Chief Onyeama became *Okuru Awha*, or clan head, of a council of "traditional" leaders selected by village-groups. Because of Onyeama's power, the Agbaja "clan" reorganization proceeded relatively uneventfully until 1933 when he committed suicide.[24]

For the colliery the implications of rural reform were threefold. First, it emphasized an invented category, "clan," as a valid category for the organization of state power. Secondly, by limiting particular jobs to specific "clans," it used "clan" as an organizational principle for access to mine jobs. Consequently, the differential role of mine work in local economies made mining an important element in the definition of "clan" identity. Thus, work in the pit became a characteristic of "Agbajaness" while a resistance to mine work or preference for unskilled surface jobs became a characteristic of "Nkanuness."

By the 1930s, over 60 percent of Agbaja men were working or had worked in the mines, making these villages similar to the militant coal-mining communities in England.[25] A stint in mine labor became an important dimension of becoming a mature man. Not only did it provide these villages with resources that came to signify progress and modernization—bicycles, schools, health centers, zinc roofs—but it also permitted the men to acquire the prestige goods that signified male power.[26] While some "foreigners" from Owerri and Onitsha held the most skilled "pit boy" posts underground, their educational levels led them to dominate all clerical posts. Thirdly, officials still believed that rural, clan-based leaders were the most effective means of controlling the working class, and developed a mutually beneficial relationship in which they allowed the councils to recommend men for colliery posts. This gave rural leaders a power that became a new basis for patronage and political influence.

As an "invented" colonial category, "clan" identity was unstable, and contentious, especially when it was evoked to mask exploitative practices that victimized the men in the mines. Although "clan" affiliation became a base of some struggle among workers in the thirties, it is unclear if it had any significant claims on workers' affiliations. Nonetheless, management and the state evoked "clan" as a counterpoint to all other forms of workplace association—be they *Nzuko* or the

Representative Councils that management created in 1937. The clan councilors, while reliant on the income of the miners for village improvements, watched suspiciously as these men brought new, and threatening, ideas about democracy, social development, equality, and political representation into the village. The *Nzuko* mobilized members by job category and legitimized competing groups of leaders who had the confidence and loyalty of the village's miners. For most of this period, the rural leaders could not understand *why* their men would listen to, let alone follow, a man from another area of Igboland.

During the late thirties conflicts over access to jobs at various levels in the work hierarchy pulled at the fragile unity that "locals" and "foreigners" had created, and plunged the workforce into a frenzy of clan bickering. For the Agbaja men, masculinity was very bound up with coal mining, and they had clear ideas about entitlement and the responsibilities of the state for their welfare. These ideas were strengthened by the strategic importance of the industry during the war and the consummate attention they received during this period of unrest. By now the old system of industrial "indirect rule" had outgrown its usefulness and new, more scientific managerial methods were required. The Colonial Office pushed Nigeria's central administration and the industry's officials to use these new systems. But the workers still retained considerable control.

Management encouraged "clan" differences, which they considered primordial, by selective hiring practices, but it is unclear how much these differences meant to the underground workers. They were thrown into sharp relief when the first state-endorsed workers' organizations, the Representative Councils, stepped to the forefront of the workers' struggle.

New currents of colonial labor policy were felt in the Enugu area in 1935. The Secretary of State for the Colonies W.G.A. Ormsby-Gore dispatched a circular on the question of the supervision and treatment of colonial labor which may have been prompted by questions from the Labour Party, now in opposition, to embarrass the conservative ministry on the treatment of labor in the colonies. The Ormsby-Gore Circular required both reports on the existing machinery for inspection and supervision of colonial labor, and proposals for remedies where inadequacies were found. The circular drew special attention to new industries such as mining and suggested the creation of a permanent administrative position to report on and monitor labor conditions. He identified several conditions requiring special attention: (a) housing, sanitary arrangements, hospital facilities; (b) observation of labor contract laws and regulations; (c) application of English inspection procedures to mines; (d) application of English inspection systems to factories.[27] In Nigeria the governor could use the Labour Ordinance of 1929 which gave him wide-ranging powers to monitor conditions in places that were designated as "Labour Health Areas," and Enugu was so designated in 1935. This required that the Residents include in the annual provincial reports those steps they had taken to implement the directives. Ormsby-Gore also appointed labor inspectors for industrial and plantation areas. The senior medical officer in Enugu made frequent visits to inspect labor camps at the colliery but both the management and the local administration lacked a coordinated plan to supervise the treatment of Udi miners.[28]

Late in 1935 the colliery made several timid attempts to form a coherent labor policy and to undertake direct supervision of the recruitment and conditions of service of the working class in a manner that circumscribed some of the powers of the "boss boys." These moves, initiated in the environment of increased Colonial Office scrutiny at local levels and major strides in England toward a colonial labor policy, were related to the separation of the Enugu colliery from the administrative hegemony of the Nigerian Railway following an important strike in 1937.[29]

These bureaucratic innovations did not mean that the older, more stereotyped views of the "African worker" were completely abandoned however. Not all policymakers were convinced that colonial workers were sufficiently "civilized" and economically "responsible" to be trusted to form or run their own trade unions. But the strategic location of the small colonial working class in the political economy indicated that a system of consultation and grievance resolution was needed. Therefore, at the end of the decade the Colonial Office pushed the Nigerian government to legalize trade unions, which it envisioned as institutions of colonial order. They had no intention of their functioning as effective vehicles of workers' interests, and the unions labored under all types of restrictions such as compulsory registration. But initial manpower shortages in the colonial service prevented officials from guiding the direction of these unions, and many of them functioned in their initial years with very little direct intervention by authorities. Later the exigencies of the war forced the Colonial Office to overcome initial suspicions of the British Trades Union Congress and to invite the congress into a partnership to promote "responsible" trade union activity in the colonies.[30] By 1942 the BTUC and the Colonial Office experts were institutionally joined in a new Colonial Office committee, the Colonial Labor Advisory Committee, which together with overseas employers' federations, coordinated colonial labor policy.[31]

However, during the thirties, distrust of the TUC led the Colonial Office to "go it alone." At the colliery the activism of the "pit boys" and the prospects of war led the Colonial Office to question the competence of management and its ability to contain the aspirations and expectations of the workers. In effect, the government became more concerned with the social reproduction of the workforce and sponsored several local investigations into the world of work and family life at the colliery. These studies became the basis for a comprehensive experiment in social engineering and increased industrial discipline. This experiment continued during the war and into the postwar period. In the city it included extensive social policies that differentiated a core of the most skilled men in the workforce, gave them housing, attempted to restructure their families, and claimed to make their families more healthy and better educated. These policies also attempted, though less successfully, to make these men more reliable, efficient, and productive workers. The men, on the other hand, had their own ideas about their work and family lives, and they articulated these ideas explicitly, through petitions and demands placed before management and the central government, through workers' associations, and in their struggles at the point of production.

These social and industrial reforms did not meet overwhelming support from either the Nigerian government or the Enugu industrial and political authorities, who often subverted them. But by the end of the decade Britain was at war and the pressure on the Nigerian state to modernize its labor policies was expressed in a corpus of labor laws that attempted to direct worker unrest into controlled channels of expression, and to position the state as custodian of the social and economic welfare of its workers. Although these laws were derived from British labor practice, they never fully extended to colonial workers the rights and privileges of British workers. However, they did encourage a generalized discourse on workers' rights that led the miners to measure their own conditions against those of British and American coal workers. This worker awareness of metropolitan and international labor standards, and sensitivity to the racially based differences between their conditions of work and their European supervisors, drew upon the men's experiences in defining their demands and strategizing to attain them. Their desire to bring their conditions on a par with those of workers in Britain pushed the colliery into the throes of persistent unrest which outpaced the war. The imperial state was now confronted with an internationally conscious working class.

## WORKERS' VISIONS OF THE WORKPLACE AND HOME: THE AGITATIONS OF 1937–1940

From the spring of 1936 until late 1940 the colliery workers maintained a period of unrest and worker agitation. It all began in the spring of 1936 when, despite the economic recovery, redundancies in the workforce led to retrenchments of a further 600 men.[32] Even in the midst of these retrenchments (a labor surplus), the "pick boys" felt sufficiently confident to initiate an industrial crisis by demanding the restoration of wages to the pre-1931 level. On 9 March 1937 they sent a petition to the colliery manager for increased pay, improved working and camp conditions, and other demands. Three days after the petition was presented, it was forwarded to the general manager of the railway, then direct supervisor of the colliery. On March 15, the day the general manager received the petition, giving no further notification, the miners stopped work. The manager tried desperately to get the men back to work. A worker described how the *Nzuko* leaders came to represent the strikers:

> The Management wanted to find a way to get the workers to resume work, so they sent for the District Officer, the Police Superintendent, and the Resident for Onitsha Province. These men went from camp to camp trying to talk to workers and get them to return to work. They finally decided to ask the workers to select two hewers, two tubmen, two railmen, two timbermen, and two surface workers to meet with the Management to discuss the strike.[33]

The men selected those most identified with colliery protest—the *Nzuko* leaders. It was decided to summon the Director of Transport G.V.O. Bulkeley. Immediately, Governor H.T. Bourdillon dispatched Bulkeley by special train to investigate, and the chief commissioner for southern provinces to alert the miners of Bulkeley's task.[34] While he was to inquire into their grievances, he complained: "I considered their action in striking without giving time for consideration of their demands to be unreasonable."[35] Warning that the administration was not responding to their "beck and call," he noted that should any increase in pay be decided upon, it would take effect from the date of their return to work.[36]

His warnings were futile. Unintimidated, the "pick boys" agreed to work on March 20 and warned him that he had until Tuesday the twenty-third or they would resume the strike.[37] At the meeting Sunday, March 21, they clarified their demands:

Increased wages retrospective from July 1931, an increase in the amount paid to men certified as unfit to work owing to injuries received while working, the appointment of more European overmen underground, and improved housing arrangements in the camps.[38]

The governor noted in his report to Colonial Secretary Ormsby-Gore, that the strike appeared to have been influenced by "an increase in the rates of pay to labor employed generally in the Onitsha and Warri Provinces."[39] Beyond their attempt to restore wage concessions made during the Depression, the "pick boys" were aware of the normal systems of workmen's compensation. The demand for more and improved housing was important for the married men with families as well as for single men and local married men living in Enugu without their families. All needed to be in the camps to be selected by the "boss boy" for work daily.[40]

When the Director of Transport, G.V.O. Bulkeley, visited the pit site, he was shocked by the dangerous, cramped, and grueling conditions of work and reported that the demands were justified. Bulkeley concluded that the underground work was "probably more onerous than those of any other government employees" and "the nature of the labor compels them to effect much of it in cramped positions and in a hot humid atmosphere."[41] Nonetheless, he was mindful of the importance of the industry to the region's economy and the historic difficulties with its troublesome workforce, and he initiated a wide-ranging government attempt to bring the coal miners under closer managerial control. At a meeting on March 22, he announced his conclusions.

First, he changed the pay system. He restored the 1d cut for all workers but he proposed a change which further underscored the unique skill and power which the pick men held in production. He recommended that they be paid a fixed rate per day in addition to amounts they earned at present piece-work rates.[42] Before the strike the hewers' piece-rate earnings averaged between 2/3d and 2/9d per man. Under Bulkeley's award the hewers had a fixed rate of from 10d to 1 shilling depending on their seniority, with additional tonnage rates of 3d per tub in *robbery* and 5d in *development*. Although the new wages gave the hewers an average of 3 shillings per day, a mere 1d increase, this special payment further underscored the pivotal role of hewers. The proposal was a saving. It added £4,576 per annum at the given rates of production, while the hewers' original demands would have cost the colliery an additional £8,100 per year in addition to the retroactive increase.[43]

While Bulkeley considered this day-rate as compensation for harsh underground conditions it did not conform to the complex incentive system necessitated by the variable effort—costs of particular jobs in the mines. From the standpoint of management, the combined tonnage and time-wage system reduced the incentive for production. In the specific circumstances of Enugu, where few workers were proletarianized, even the tonnage wage system was a poor alternative to direct supervision. Secondly, given the fragmentation of jobs under the Derbyshire system, the hewers' combined day and tonnage rate did not encourage the coordination of tasks and provide incentives necessary to integrate the various categories of workers involved in the actual coal production.

The miner relied on the tubmen to supply him with tubs that he filled with coal. If the tubman was on a day rate, there was no incentive for him to supply those tubs expeditiously. Furthermore, the pay system actually encouraged conflicts between workers who interacted in production. From the standpoint of the hewer, a tubman's failure to provide him with tubs had a direct impact upon his wage packet, which was based solely on tonnage rates, reflecting his daily output. Similarly, the hewer also depended on the timbermen to open a new coal face for his operations. Thus, in most mines, the hewers, tubmen, timbermen, and those special labor workers who ripped the road would be paid piece-rates. This would encourage them to work quickly creating the conditions under which the main coal getter—the hewer—could produce. In Enugu, however, even the tubmen, those most obviously involved in daily production, were on day rates. Soon after the award, hewers complained that the tubmen were not providing them with sufficient tubs to maintain their output.[44] Certainly, when the hewer-contractor system existed and the entire group functioned as one production unit—hewer, tubmen, each with his assistants—the tonnage rate encouraged coordination of energy and effort. This, however, ended with Bulkeley's day rate.

In coal-mining practices, management usually put hewers on a day rate when mining moved to machine production. In the United States and Europe it was resisted by workers because it threatened increased supervision and scientific management. U.S. miners complained that it "will 'factoryize' the mine ... [and] make a Ford plant out of every coal mine."[45] Although Enugu's mines were never thoroughly mechanized, one cannot dismiss the possibility that Bulkeley and his superiors anticipated the movement into mechanization as a way of reducing dependence on a recalcitrant and unreliable workforce. Further, by requiring that every hewer be paid a day-rate, the director pushed the industry to keep accurate records of the men working daily. This was because each worker was, at the very minimum, entitled to wages based on the day-rate. This increased managerial supervision eroded some of the autonomy that the "boss boys" had in determining their daily work crews and the informal hewer contractor system became obsolete. But having released the hewers' earnings from its dependence solely on his productivity, the industry had to restructure its management to create the supervision necessary to insure output. This would prove far more difficult than anticipated.

Secondly, Bulkeley launched a financial investigation into the fiscal condition of the industry. In June, in further testimony to negligence at the highest political level, the colliery's accounts (see Table 5.1, p. 200) showed that there was no financial reason why wage improvements and amenities in the labor camps could not have been implemented earlier.[46] After allowing for depreciation and other charges, both absent from the colliery accounts, the governor found that the annual surplus of revenue over expenditure was approximately £20,000, a sufficient amount to permit both the wage increases and improved labor camps. The mines could have financed improved working conditions and wages in nineteen of the twenty-one years of its existence.[47]

Thirdly, Bulkeley improvised a grievance system that he hoped would reduce the power and autonomy of the *Nzuko*. Management was to appoint workers to an industrial council that would meet regularly with management to discuss problems. This new system, which closely resembled the existing system of consultations with *Nzuko* leaders, tacitly acknowledged the failure of the "boss boys" to resolve grievances. The men did not trust the "boss boys" and in many instances, the "boss boys" themselves were the problem.[48] Authorities were also concerned that the *Nzuko*, the only organized worker bodies, were secretive, violent, and operated outside the control of management. Leck appointed the *Nzuko* leaders to the new councils, attempting to coopt them into a body where they could be monitored openly by management. The impact of these new appointments on the coercive systems of industrial discipline is examined below.

## THE COLONIAL OFFICE RESPONDS WITH IMPATIENCE

While the Nigerian government bungled on the ground, Colonial Secretary Ormsby-Gore, became alarmed at yet another example of governmental incompetence being exposed by worker activism. These conditions embarrassed the government at a time when proposals to bring the troublesome British coal industry under state control were again being debated. Every instance of managerial neglect and archaic or coercive labor policies offered the possibility of being thrown into the national debate.[49] The Secretary, aware of political vulnerabilities, noted his misgivings about the condition of the industry:

> I was not too easy in my mind about this example ... of state socialism when I
> visited Udi eight years ago, and financial considerations are not the only ones to
> be borne in mind in an industrial undertaking of such character.[50]

Previous Colonial Office appeals for governments to develop systematic provisions to monitor African labor went largely unheeded.[51] Now with the economic recovery, perhaps something could be done to improve their conditions. He therefore responded to the March strike with bewildered exasperation that a state-owned colonial industry could prove as insensitive to workers' lives as a private one. Ormsby-Gore felt that it was the responsibility of the imperial state to be an exemplar of enlightened labor policy for the colonial working class, especially when it had not organized into trade unions to protect the workers' interests. Moreover, as a state-owned industry the Enugu colliery was open to public scrutiny in Parliament, and internationally to the criticism of the ILO which was tentatively intruding into the world of colonial labor relations. The Secretary complained:

> The conditions at Iva Colliery revealed in connection with this strike occasion me considerable concern. The existence of a colliery owned and managed by Government in a territory where there are no effective Trade Unions or other associations for safeguarding the interests of the workmen calls for a more vigilant government supervision than would appear to have hitherto been exercised in this case and if the facts were revealed in your dispatch under acknowledgment were widely known, I should find great difficulty in defending the Nigerian Government from the criticisms which would inevitably be provoked.[52]

He further noted that because the colliery was administered by the Nigerian Railway, critics might speculate that wages were kept low and conditions poor to cheapen transport costs. J.B. Sidebotham correctly assumed managerial disinterest in the conditions, and he noted that Leck, the manager:

> ought ... to have been aware of the unsatisfactory conditions in the labor camps and the lack of certain amenities, and certainly should have seen that regulations were properly complied with. ... The question of wages, too, if admittedly inadequate, as the Director of Transport considers, is again a matter which should have come under review earlier.[53]

Subsequently, Governor Bourdillon was notified:

> From the facts before us it is rather difficult to understand how it is that the unsatisfactory conditions revealed at the Labour Camps should not have come to light until attention was directed to them as a result of the strike last March. We do not of course wish to pre-judge the question in any way but we shall be glad to learn whether you are satisfied that the management of the Colliery is in fact being efficiently carried out. I see that Leck, who went on leave in January and so was absent from Nigeria when the strike occurred, is quite well reported on.[54]

Despite this increased scrutiny the Nigerian government still misread the signs of eminent worker protest. When Bulkeley announced that he would investigate the other demands but only restore the depression pay cut at a mass meeting on March 22, all classes of workers were dissatisfied with their increases. The Colonial Office and Nigerian government refused to recognize that the cost of living had increased above the pre-depression level. Four months later, the Nigerian government still had not responded. It was left to the workers to shake them out of their reprise.

## WORKING FOR "LABOUR-LOVE": THE CRISIS
## OF FAMILY AND WORKING LIFE IN THE 1930s

The protests came initially from the urban-based workers. Although Enugu was an Igbo town, the majority of its permanent inhabitants were "foreign" Igbo from Owerri or Onitsha, areas that workers considered more "civilized." To the "civilized" Owerrians, many of whom were the industry's first workers, housing was an intolerable affront to their status as working men. Although they retained contact with their villages through the Owerri Improvement Union, eastern Nigeria's earliest urban union, Enugu was now their home, the place where they established their families and raised their children. Their arguments were rooted in the dignity of their work, the uniqueness of their skill, and the consciousness of themselves as a cultural and economic elite. C.H. Croasdale, local authority, Enugu, noted:

> These long-service labourers have gradually come to regard themselves and the "coal people" generally as "different" from the other inhabitants of the township and entitled to all kinds of special privileges and consideration.[55]

These "foreign" workers saw themselves as pioneers who helped to carve the mines and city out of the "bush" at a time when the *indigenes* were still "cannibals." Many of them still considered the "locals" to be *wawa*, a derogatory term that means "backward" and "primitive." These sentiments were especially strong among the Owerrians who, being close to coastal society in the Niger Delta were indeed better educated and more familiar with the "white man's ways." This elitist attitude was further encouraged by their possession of highly technical skills required in mining, skills which were far more specialized than any of the tasks performed in the indigenous economy. They, like the railway workers, considered themselves to be a breed apart and the reaction of the government to their demands further encouraged this self-perception.

Four months after the workers met with Bulkeley, the Nigerian government had still not responded to their demands. They, on the other hand, had kept their agreement to return to work pending a decision on their grievances. When no decision was announced, the various *Nzuko* contracted professional letter writers to compose petitions stating their demands.[56] Although encumbered with a clumsy and self-deprecating language, the petitions exhibit a discourse about work and family life that reveals a moral universe in which the workers judged their treatment by the state, the value of their work, and the importance of their home life in the colliery camps. They based their case for improvements on the morality and justice of their cause and not just on the conditions of the coal market. Each petition explained the importance of their work for the safe and economic operation of the mines, emphasized the skill inherent in the job, and argued that their wages made it impossible for them to be male providers.

They considered the poor facilities available for their families to emulate an immoral lifestyle and to expose them to unhealthy, substandard conditions beneath their status as working men. Although the colliery camps were free, and to the "foreign" workers an important alternative to high-cost rental housing in Enugu, they were unsanitary rural slums. The camps were built in the style of range-type housing an imperial housing style originally developed for indentured workers, but now declared unacceptable for family life by the ILO and the British government.[57]

For "pick boys" at the top of the hierarchy in production, these conditions were an insult to their status as workers. They were especially outraged because occasionally they were forced to board a single "pick boy" with their family or to share a room with another family. Reminding the administration of the conditions under which they had returned to work in March, they asked for only one family to share a room or in the case of single men, only two "pick boys." In July, they demanded:

> new construction of quarters with more accommodative rooms that [sic] the present ones enough to live in, that is to say, quarters of providency [sic] of sufficient rooms each of which may be able to accommodate a workman and his wife alone meaning either a pick boy coupled or a coupled tub-boy without to be tampered with, by an uncoupled workman or without two couples to occupy or share one room without a party wall or partition as this mode of living is often unbecoming.[58]

In a dramatic testimony to their awareness of "modern" ideas of hygiene, the hewers saw that such overcrowding violated colonial sanitary conventions and complained that "our current mode of living is rather an inconvenience and far out of sanitation so well."[59] Conditions were especially unpleasant for polygynous families. In this case a rural symbol of masculine status that many men embraced as a validation of their power clashed with the spatial constraints of urban living. Some rooms had an employee, three to four wives, seven to ten children, and one or two servants.[60]

The "tubboys," as the other coal face workers, also based their claims on the dangerous conditions at the coal face. They were paired with a hewer and were exposed to many of the same risks of cave-ins and injury. They reflected the historic awareness of underground workers of the uniquely dangerous and skilled nature of their work. Like coal workers everywhere, they argued that they deserved compensation for the risk they confronted every time they entered the pit. Given that all men worked barefoot with no protective equipment in poorly lit stalls, it is no wonder that haulage injuries, especially mutilation of fingers and feet, would lead the list of accidents. The "tubboys" cite these accidents as reasons for their raises:

> That your humble petitioners beg to inform you that we are the people who always got accident in the Mines for this reason the amount of 1/3d (one shilling and three pence) we are receiving per diem is not sufficient for us. Many of us have got wives and children, after receiving our monthly wages is not enough to support ourselves and them.[61]

Similarly the "timberboys" and "railboys" called attention to the risks they encounter when they lay rails and timber at a new work face, or removed them after *robbery* to allow a cave-in. Although both jobs are considered unskilled the men recognized that this was not the case. It was skill ("in the obvious knowledge") that enabled them to recognize a hazardous roof ("where a crackling noise is heard") and their bravery to perform their job when others fled fearing a cave-in ("where from the workers of the place suddenly sally out"). Their petition, more than the others, explicitly states the pride, "labor love," they feel for their job:

We would point out the hardest work we laboriously undertake which is unquestionably in the obvious knowledge, and that is that every work in the mine which looks fearful is not undertaken by us willingly, not for the stead of avarice but for the labour-love, and in required order such as the opening of a novel place of the mine of fear and danger before any man could venture make entry into that part by first firing at it by means of rockets, as fixing timbers to support the infalling crevices of layers, and is repairing and reconstructing a place where a cracking noise is heard and where from the workers of the place suddenly sally out.[62]

Even the twenty "boss boys" evoked allegations of the danger of their jobs, their indispensable skill, and their bravery to support their claims. Working as supervisors of the hewers, they considered their functions to be "comparable to any other works of industrialism and intelligences in the mine." They had to inspect work sites to determine if they were safe:

considering the amount of difficulties and periods we have to daily encounter. That all places of perils and dangers resulting death if suddenness called the fatal accidents are those to which we are exposed to open for all workmen of all ranks and files to pass freely out of fear.[63]

Furthermore, as status-conscious headmen they were concerned that their living arrangements reflect their ranking in the mines. They noted that their families "must needs be fed adequately as families of men holding employs."[64]

The "tub headmen," next in rank to the "boss boys," complained that their pay was not substantially higher than that of the tubmen they supervised. Their petition emphasized the importance of the tubmen to the hewer:

We are next in rank to the Boss–Boys and that our work in the mines is super-abundantly incomparable in its own special way, considering that by our super-visions and controls consistent of both physical movements hither and thither vocal sounds, the work in the mine enhances and pushes on and forward.[65]

Under the Bulkeley award the "tubboys" received a 1/3d daily wage while the headmen had 1/4d, a mere 1/d difference. The "boss boys," on the other hand, received 2/6d. The petitioners complained:

The big difference is a conspicuous indication by their wages of 2/6d earned per diem by each and, by subtraction process, we find that what they earn almost doubles our per diem by an outstanding odd remainder of 1/2d while the difference of our wages from that of the tub-boys, our ruled subordinates, only shows 1d, the two different wages being then almost tantamount.[66]

## THE END OF THE CONTRACTOR SYSTEM: THE OBSCURITY OF PRODUCTIVITY

The Bulkeley award unwittingly restructured relations of power in production eliminating the system that allowed the master hewer to create and supervise the

**Table 5.1** Colliery Accounts, 1915–1937

| Year | Revenue | Total Expenditure | Deficit/ Surplus | Amount of Surplus or Deficit |
|---|---|---|---|---|
| 1915/16 | 208900 | 360480 | Def | 151580 |
| 1917 | 1201950 | 511910 | Sur | 690040 |
| 1918 | 990020 | 608500 | Sur | 381520 |
| 1919 | 927360 | 853470 | Sur | 73890 |
| 1920 | 1054540 | 1336890 | Def | 282350 |
| 1921/22 | 1566080 | 1314480 | Sur | 251600 |
| 1922/23 | 776980 | 721440 | Sur | 55540 |
| 1923/24 | 919840 | 754160 | Sur | 165680 |
| 1924/25 | 1033530 | 823970 | Sur | 209560 |
| 1925/26 | 1196840 | 853440 | Sur | 346400 |
| 1926/27 | 1715200 | 1060360 | Sur | 654840 |
| 1927/28 | 1535530 | 1126580 | Sur | 408950 |
| 1928/29 | 1456910 | 1227180 | Sur | 229730 |
| 1929/30 | 1449340 | 1057660 | Sur | 391680 |
| 1930/31 | 1246410 | 945150 | Sur | 301260 |
| 1931/32 | 1005750 | 786930 | Sur | 218820 |
| 1932/33 | 944300 | 671170 | Sur | 273130 |
| 1933/34 | 892090 | 619050 | Sur | 273040 |
| 1934/35 | 923350 | 615400 | Sur | 307950 |
| 1935/36 | 872940 | 603400 | Sur | 273700 |

|  |  | | Surplus | 5507330 |
|---|---|---|---|---|
|  |  | | Deficit | 433930 |
|  |  | Surplus over 21 years | | 5073400 |

*Source:* C.O. 583/216 Governor to Ormsby-Gore, 24 June 1936, Appendix B, "The Colliery's Financial Position."

basic production unit—the work group. He could no longer coordinate the production process. It was the final blow to the contractor system which government had begun to attack when it instituted direct recruitment.[67] Under the new wage system, every hewer at the coal face was to be paid at the day rate. Therefore, the names on the central labor registry had to be reconciled with the timekeepers' books, leading to the retrenchment of a significant number of redundant workers at the mines. By eliminating the redundant men hired by the hewers, the management assumed responsibility for the creation of the work team. Now, for the first time, the output attributed to a single "master" hewer was accurate. The statistics suggested the full extent to which actual output per man (OMS) was obscured by the hewer's work group. At first glance it appeared that the award of a day rate led hewers to become less productive. The men's productivity plunged between 1936 and 1939, but in actuality, these figures were the first reliable reflection of the workers' capacity since 1920 (see Table 5.2).

Although management knew that the OMS figures before 1939 were actually a product of a team, as labor and management locked horns around issues of production control neither the state nor management ever acknowledged the underlying causes of this statistical drop in hewers' output. Both used the statistics to support their argument that wage increases had led to dramatic drops in the hewers' output. Conveniently, this subjective measurement of "productivity" was never articulated. As long as labor was plentiful, cheap, and paid piece-wages, management could reach the goal of increased production by allowing hewers to hire more unskilled labor from the pool of villagers in the area. But as the price of labor-power went up with each worker being paid what amounted to an underground allowance, and as the skills demanded by production prevented the facile replacement of militant miners with unskilled recruits from the "reserve army of labor," the colliery was forced to examine the production process more scientifically. No longer able to hire unlimited numbers of men, the colliery now had to find alternative methods of effecting savings in the cost of production and to increase the output of the miners. This interest in a more systemic examination of labor productivity was a local response to the concerns of labor managers at the Colonial Office level as imperial labor policy began to take shape during the war.

As they plunged into the "hidden abode of production," colonial authorities and management found that the Enugu miners had so shaped the culture of work and workplace traditions that their intervention would be largely ineffectual in recon-

**Table 5.2** Output per Man-Shift, 1928–1940[68]

| | |
|---|---|
| 1928 | 70 CWT |
| 1930 | 80 CWT |
| 1932 | 110 CWT |
| 1934 | 116 CWT |
| 1936 | 130 CWT |
| 1938 | 60 CWT |
| 1940 | 50–60 CWT |

figuring both power relations and achieving the control they wanted over the labor process. The ramifications of these innovations for the colliery will be examined in a subsequent chapter.

By August, 1937, the administration still had not responded to the workers' demands, putting the mines on the verge of another strike. The governor, hoping that a personal appeal for more time to evaluate the claims would forestall a strike, visited the mines at the request of the men, and held a mass meeting on September 4.[69] He thought he had secured a pledge from the miners not to strike until the government had responded. However, six days later, on September 10–11, production stopped when the "tubboys" went out after a European boss man assaulted one of them.[70] The case will be detailed below. The strike should have been interpreted as a sign of worker impatience and an unwillingness to accept the old racist forms of colonial discipline. However, the Transport Director and the national government still deliberated and stalled giving no response to the workers' petitions.

## COLLIERY REFORM AND THE SHIFTING STRUCTURES OF INDUSTRIAL POWER IN ENUGU, 1937–1940

The men had embarrassed the colliery's management by voicing complaints in public that raised questions about the true nature of colliery operations. The entire system of discipline was pushed into the public arena, and was subject to discussion by the various layers of the state as well as the general population of the city. This was a new political environment, and official and unofficial abuses that were hidden from the public eye could no longer be concealed. Management became uncomfortable with this new attention and the industry slowly moved toward reform. The workers celebrated, realizing that they had the industry "on the run."

By early 1938 the contours of the government's reform process were becoming visible. The District Officer of Enugu, C.H. Croasdale, was commissioned to conduct a study of the mines on the order of the intelligence reports then being written about rural communities.[71] From November 1937 until April 1938, Croasdale visited the mines, camps, and neighboring villages conducting a census of the camps, investigating the *Nzuko*, and meeting with the men. His recommendations, however, were controversial. Croasdale clearly understood the relationship between "spatial organization" and the workers' agitation.[72] He explicitly warned the government that in improving conditions they could be encouraging a class consciousness and creating a working class.

He understood the political threat posed by a mine working class and deplored any effort to improve the camps. He felt this would cause the men to "lose contact with their homes and native authorities, learn new wants, become dependent on the colliery for a livelihood, and thus be liable to destitution and discontent in the case of a slump in the coal market; such has been the experience elsewhere."[73] Ignoring the prominence of poor housing in the men's complaints, he argued that most people were quite happy with the accommodations, though the "untidy and congested appearance of the camps gives to the temporary visitor a quite erroneous impression as to the actual material welfare of the inhabitants."[74] Nonetheless, should the government go forward with its plans to improve housing, Croasdale felt that their layout and location had to be carefully planned. They should be near the "native" location and kept small "to facilitate ease of control and to prevent the growth of a 'mining village' spirit."[75] Further, he suggested that only the labor master determine who lived in the camps, thus the colliery could use access to housing as a reward to reinforce good work habits, encourage discipline, efficiency, and long service for the industry.[76]

Despite his misgivings about the propriety of colliery reforms, Croasdale accepted a position as the colliery's first Labour Master. Working with F.J.W. Skeates, a former headmaster of a Salvation Army's Boys' Industrial School in Yaba, who became the social welfare officer, his first task was to examine the labor registration system at the mines. While the colliery's daily labor needs averaged 2,600 underground and surface workers, Croasdale found over 4,000 workers' names in the registration file.[77] A number of men had identical tally numbers while others listed on the more accurate time books had no card at all. Several "dead men" were still on the list. At the conclusion of the study, the registry had 54 percent more names than the mine's daily requirement, which far exceeded the 20 percent redundancy rate that the management kept to accommodate the miners' irregular attendance and railway fluctuations.[78] The staff welfare officer assumed responsibility for the updated files and was charged to report monthly to Lagos on conditions.

Croasdale's arguments notwithstanding, the colliery could not avoid making improvements in housing in the labor camps. In these interventions into the domestic sphere, the industry tried to reshape African single and married households to facilitate social control and industrial discipline. Croasdale's camp census found that many men lived with two or more servants, and in other rooms one employee lived with 3–4 wives and 7–10 children with servants. The industry began by setting occupancy at 5.1 persons per room and restricted the number of servants to one per room, thereby restructuring the domestic arrangements to comply with state health standards. When evictions began in 1939 the greatest resistance came from the most prestigious men, those with two or more servants. Almost 1,000 were cleared in six months.[79] New houses of the "range type" were still constructed and roads, drains, kitchens, and latrines were improved.[80] Showers were installed at the mine entrances, and became immensely popular. Two sports grounds were laid out as were some five "social shelters," where the inhabitants could hold meetings and arrangements were made to establish a large market.[81]

Administratively, the colliery was pulled from under the railway and became a separate department under the Transport Directorate. While the accounting, marketing, and stores remained with the Nigerian Railway Manager Leck now reported directly to the Transport Directorate in Lagos on administrative matters.

It was hoped that this arrangement would improve communications between Lagos and the management. The manager also had full control over production concerns. But employment and control of labor was still not vested in the industry but was under the Chief Commissioner, Eastern Provinces, who was not an industrial official. He was designated the head of labor welfare at the colliery. This again suggested that the state had difficulty in seeing the men as fundamentally industrial workers. To permit closer supervision of the conditions at the colliery, the Colonial Secretary demanded that monthly statistical and narrative reports on the mines and camps be sent to the governor and thence the Colonial Office.[82]

From the standpoint of the men, one of the most significant changes encouraged by this period of reform was the erosion of "colonial despotism" by which the state withdrew its support for the bosses—white and black—to use violence as part of industrial discipline.[83] Both African and European staff found that they could no longer exert the same forms of authoritarian discipline on their workers. With the Colonial Office focusing on reform, the Nigerian state could not endorse the most abusive aspects of colonial production relations.[84] Caning by interpreters and "boss boys," extortion, and assault, were all used frequently to enforce mine discipline. A previously noted incident illustrates the impact of this change on the workers. In September 1937 a European foreman, R.V. Kerr, struck a leader of the "tub-boys' " *Nzuko*, one Lawrence Amukenebe of Agbaja. In an unusual act of solidarity against this common form of discipline, the "tubboys" struck in protest. Kerr was apparently known for his abusiveness and Leck noted that "he is inclined to be impetuous in his handling of the boys."[85] Although the police initially refused to prosecute the case, Amukenebe insisted on pressing legal charges against Kerr, and the Secretary of the Southern Provinces agreed that the case should be heard.[86] He assigned his assistant to prosecute even though there was no significant injury. The magistrate publicly criticized the victim, but found Kerr guilty of a "technical assault" and ordered a minimal fine and compensation.[87] The incident embarrassed the management, which admonished Kerr for being so impulsive. To the men who were daily subjected to these forms of discipline, the message was that physical violence would not be tolerated in the workplace and Africans could count on support from the courts to insure that they were no longer victimized by this type of abuse. Furthermore, Amukebe's victory raised the prestige of the *Nzuko* as an institution capable of resolving workers' grievances.

## MANAGEMENT'S *'NZUKO'*:
## THE REPRESENTATIVE COUNCILS

Further erosions of the powers of European bosses came in October 1937 when the Director of Transport instructed the manager to appoint three consultative councils to represent the underground, surface, and camp workers. Although the councils were not elected by workers, management appointed the men, all *Nzuko* leaders, who were selected by the workers during the March strike.[88] The Councils implicitly challenged the authoritarian, paternalist ethos that governed colliery operations until this point, leading to contentious encounters with management. Leck was clearly annoyed that government felt that these men could be trusted to articulate coherent demands and be truly representative of the men, but he was forced to accept them. To Leck the men were still irrational "boys," insufficiently knowledgeable of their own needs to warrant serious consultation, and too untrustworthy to engage in fruitful negotiation with colonial management.

Despite Leck's misgivings about the leadership of the underground *Nzuko*, these were the men who were recognized as leaders. They had become very experienced in mobilizing support among the hewers, tubmen, and special labor gangs for many strikes. The men who assumed leadership had many of the characteristics that were so valued in rural politics. They were articulate men who had "good mouth,"[89] "energy, personality and slight extra knowledge of affairs."[90] Oratory skills were an important leadership quality in village politics where decisions were taken by consensus and one's ability to sway others often proved crucial. Strong men were valued for having *Ikenga*, that is, a moral determination, physical strength, and a willingness to champion a cause that put their own positions in jeopardy.[91] Men with *Ikenga* stood up against unjust authority and persistently attacked problems until they were resolved. By confronting racist abuses by men like Kerr, *Nzuko* leaders increased their stature in the eyes of the men. As in the village, a leader's authority over the workers depended on his ability to "deliver" what the men demanded, be that increased wages, prosecution of an abusive boss, or better housing. In this crisis these leaders found new strategies of protest that utilized the "rights" extended to colonial subjects. They secured the assistance of professional letter writers to formulate their grievances in a rhetoric understandable by colonial employers.

In the eyes of the workers, the appointment of these leaders to the Representative Councils legitimized the *Nzuko* as an officially recognized organ of worker representation, and elevated its leaders to positions of power as brokers between the state, management, and the workers. This was resented by the clerical workers, "native" staff, rural clan councilors, and the European bosses, all of whom recognized that it reduced their power over the workforce. The "foreign" clerical workers, who were contemptuous of the manual laborers, were outraged that the management gave a forum to these "unschooled" men when they themselves, as educated men, should have been allowed to represent them. Underground supervisors realized that the Councils undermined industrial discipline. The "boss boys" felt that the Councils violated the job hierarchy and elevated men who were their subordinates to a position of undeserved privilege. Further, culturally, they considered such leadership to come only with seniority, a seniority that they had acquired through their years of work at the mines and which was validated by their appointments as "native" staff.[92] Village "clan" leaders could not understand the new forms of affiliation that ignored village-based authorities. The president of the influential underground council, Daniel Iwagu, was from Owerri, and Agbaja's village elders could not understand how a "stranger" could be "chief" of their men working in mines that were located on their grounds.[93] European supervisors were outraged that African "boys" were given a status within the industry that gave them access to many echelons of the state that were denied them. Moreover, they recognized that the Councils violated the racialized hierarchy in the industry and their arbitrary use of coercive disciplinary forms. Conflicts between white bosses and the Council members occurred with increasing frequency as the "bosses" struggled to preserve a racially based system of industrial authority in a political environment in which this was a liability.

In appointing the Councils, the government tried to coopt the *Nzuko* into the officially recognized channels of industrial relations. In so doing they hoped to push an autonomous, secretive, and militant organization into the open where it could be more closely monitored. Leck and others in the Enugu administration did not agree that government should endorse *any* type of worker organization, and although they had to follow the policies, they nonetheless worked to undermine the Councils. The workers' leaders, on the other hand, seized the legitimacy granted by their appointment and basked in the prestige that it conferred upon them. They astutely used their appointments to manipulate the conflicts between the various layers of the state and to gain power and influence among the workers. Even from the first meeting, it was clear that they were not going to function within the narrowly defined terms of reference of the national government. Rather, they used the Councils as negotiating bodies and seized the opportunity to challenge the arbitrary and brutal powers exercised by the various European and "native" staff. Many of their demands called for management practices that would bring the colliery in tune with the standards of industrial relations used in England.

The Councils were determined to function as a bargaining unit, despite the governments' instructions that they were to be merely consultative bodies to alert the government to problems before they erupted into a work action. At their first meeting in Port Harcourt with the Director of Transport on 9 November 1937, they presented a list of seventeen demands. As a document the list called for standardized disciplinary and promotion procedures, institutionalized safety equipment and measures, the adoption of annual increments that accepted the principle of seniority, overtime pay, workmen's compensation, and the establishment of wage-bargaining machinery. The demands called for procedures that, if followed, would prevent "native" and European "bosses" from using promotions or infliction of punishments to exercise their power. The men tried to insinuate the Councils into the disciplinary process by asserting their right to review and receive written notice of any punishment. They argued for due process in disciplinary actions such as fines, degrading, and dismissals, which would prevent "bosses" from victimizing workers.[94]

The demands were the first comprehensive critique of the deplorable work conditions that existed at the colliery for many years. They had never been aired in public because disinterested European staff and political authorities had managed to intimidate the men individually to hide them. But now, an air of relative transparency prevailed. The men demanded criteria be established for promotions so that advancement within scales was no longer at the discretion of corrupt supervisors and also sought to systematize advancement within scales. They demanded that gratuities be granted routinely when long-service employees left their posts, and criticized the indefinite period for apprenticeships, where many men remained for many years. The workers also attempted to adjust the wage system to permit a more effective coordination of tasks in production by demanding that "tubboys" be placed on piece-rates to give them an opportunity for increased pay and to provide an incentive for productivity. Finally, they asked for wage increases for all categories of work.[95] While the government deliberated, the Councils held negotiations with the management. The state did not respond until January 1938.

As state workers, the men felt that they had specific rights which related to how they conceptualized the responsibilities of political authorities. Some of this arose from Igbo concepts of the obligations of leadership. Others, to new ideas that they had crafted from their understanding of western political hierarchies and industrial regimes. They knew that political officials had jurisdiction over the industry's management so they paid attention to the conflicting bureaucratic levels of the state and continued to take grievances to the highest officials—violating the chain of command.

In the meetings of late 1937 the Councils again revealed a sharper awareness of sound managerial procedures than either the management or state authorities. To resolve a problem with "tubboys" not supplying tubs, they suggested that by putting them on piece-rates, the colliery could use the wage system to coordinate the tasks, as in the Derbyshire system.[96] Secondly, they were concerned with the large number of minor but debilitating accidents sustained by the hewers, haulage workers, and tubmen. To management, accustomed to the high mortality rates of Britain's gassy mines, Enugu's number of injuries was insignificant. To the men, on the other hand, these accidents were intolerable. They attempted to get management to issue some protective footwear to the hewers to replace that which the men had to improvise. For example, the hewers placed a shovel near their bare foot when hewing to protect it from falls of roof. The men made their own form of shin protection from rags. (See Photo 3.8.) Management's careless disregard for the men's industrial safety, and cynical sentiments that these workers did not deserve equipment granted British miners, was evident in its response:

> There is no doubt that many minor accidents due to coal flying from the face when hewing would be obviated if boots and protective leggings were provided. If protective footwear were given to one class, the other classes would ask for boots. I regret I am unable to form any idea of the costs. This idea I suppose, is based on the home practice of providing underground face workers with protective helmets.[97]

The Council meetings continued through 1937 and 1938 with the men reasserting the issues first presented in the earlier petitions. The meetings with government officials in Lagos and the complex legislation that the state was creating during the late thirties encouraged the men to seek professional representation, and they hired a Lagos lawyer to assist them with Lagos officials.[98]

## THE EVANS AGREEMENT: ABORTIVE ATTEMPTS TO REDUCE JOB CONTROL

On January 28, the government finally responded to the demands. The acting Director of Transport, F.D. Evans, went to Enugu to announce his decision.[99] The administration thought that they could use the dispute to introduce more supervision over the underground workers by making employment contingent upon performance on the job, regularity of attendance, and ability to make production targets. Evans hoped to exert more control over the men's erratic work habits. He tried to restore the hewers' wages to piece-rates by offering: "If the hewers are prepared to willingly forego the shift rate of 10 pence (or 1 shilling) per shift, Government will be willing to pay a piece rate only of 8 pence per tub from development and $4\frac{1}{2}$ pence per tub from robbery."[100] The average hewer would earn $40\frac{1}{2}$ to 45 pence per day regardless of his years of service. Under the daily plus piece-work wage rate, those with less than ten years' service would average $37\frac{1}{2}$ pence in *development* and 24 pence in *robbery*. The director argued that "rates of pay to employees on daily pay must be decided by grading according to qualifications and the principle of time scale increments cannot be admitted."[101]

On the issue of poor and overcrowded housing, Evans had little sympathy for the men because he argued that overcrowding was caused by the industry's need to compensate for poor work attendance, and the men's housing of unauthorized persons. Further, he argued that government could not provide housing for all. Additionally, he deprecated the "pick boys'" request that two men and not three be housed in a single room, but agreed that only married couples should share a single room. Nevertheless, the colliery had already begun to improve the most horrendous of the camp conditions.[102]

For many years the men had argued for yearly increments as an indicator of seniority, and the Director of Transport had always rejected them. Evans struggled to reconcile his goal of encouraging long-term employees with his refusal to acknowledge time increments. He tried to make a hairline distinction by introducing a grade scale with a rough time dimension: those who had worked less than ten years and those who had worked more. Under this system a man with more than ten years' experience would not normally have a ranking lower than grade three. Undoubtedly one reason Evans rejected seniority-based increments was because at Enugu, seniority did not indicate that a man had worked consistently over a period of years. When the records indicated that a man had begun working, say, ten years ago, it said little about how many days during those years he had actually worked. More likely than not, the local Agbaja would have had erratic work habits, but they were nonetheless seasoned workers.

The men had also questioned the indefinite period of most apprenticeships. Incredibly, Evans denied that *any* official apprenticeship program ever existed before 1938, and claimed that the title "Apprentice Fitter," "Apprentice Carpenter," etc., were only job categories and not training programs. His assertion that these titles were "no more than a classification for rates of pay" was perhaps one of the most blatant examples of his underestimating the sophistication of the men. But while he did begin time-scale rates for so-called apprentices, he argued that they had little to do with time worked, but with skill, reliability, and capacity. However, he did agree to consider longevity as one criteria that could lead to promotion to a higher rank.

Evans tried to simplify the colliery's system of over seventy grades by grouping jobs into several new categories for skilled labor: artisans, carpenters, electricians, fitters, turners, and helpers to whom he also gave graded wage scales. In his reluctance to accept seniority as an employment principle, he created an elaborate ranking pay system with promotions based on job performance rather than time worked. His revisions became yet another attempt to bring the workers under industrial discipline.

Evans was as annoyed as were other authorities with the way that the Councils had evolved. He rejected any suggestion that they be incorporated in the disciplinary process and asserted that such matters were only under the purview of management, not the workers. Further, he arrogantly suggested that in granting his award he had practically eliminated most of the questions that they would raise with the management. Moreover, he proposed that to prevent "prolonged and unnecessary discussions," the men should submit any discussion subjects prior to the meeting and he would reply in writing to any question. He also tried to redirect the Councils from pressing the case of individual workers by instructing them to raise issues of "general" interest, and instructing them to encourage the men to submit individual cases directly to the manager. Further, he informed them that the Lagos office would only entertain their visits in exceptional circumstances. Normally, therefore, they should present their grievances to the manager. Aware that disruptive grievances could nonetheless arise, he outlined a structure of visitations by the Director of Transport, Resident, Onitsha, and other political authorities during which he hoped the men would present problems to the authorities.[103]

A number of issues such as workmen's compensation were deferred pending government legislation or further consideration. The Governor was still considering legislation on injuries and would notify the men when it was introduced. There would be no consideration of any retirement program for men too old to work.

Despite the debilitating effect of frequent accidents, in 1939 the mines changed the method of compensating injured miners for accidents, granting less pay. Formerly, the accident pay had been based on the total number of working days per month. Under the new reorganization, an injured miner's pay was determined by the number of days he had actually worked the previous twelve months. This system penalized those men who worked infrequently. Resident D.P.J. O'Connor noted that this had resulted in a "drastic reduction in pay for a large number of poor and indifferent workers." F.D. Webb, of the Colonial Office, was amazed that the miners accepted the terms, noting that it was a "drastic measure, but the men appeared, surprisingly, to have accepted it."[104]

Evans' Agreement was rejected by the men. Having waited nearly a year for the state's response, the workers were enraged that he had dismissed so many of the issues that they felt strongly about. The next day, 2 February 1938, the men again went on strike. The Colonial Office was frustrated with the cavalier way that the Nigerian government had handled the entire crisis from March 1937. J.B. Sidebotham commented:

It was pretty obvious after the strike of March last that wages and conditions generally wanted looking into, but it has taken nine months to do this, and the upshot is another strike.[105]

The Evans Agreement managed to alienate every category of labor in the mines from "boss boy" to unskilled screen workers, thereby creating the conditions for worker solidarity. A Colonial Office official remarked:

On this occasion it looks as if the pick boys took action not so much on their own account as with the object of assisting their grades of workers in obtaining greater improvements in their pay and conditions.[106]

The degree of worker frustration was expressed in the violence of the strikers who dealt roughly with "scabs."[107] They picketed the roads and forcibly removed men from the 5:30 A.M. shift. This unusually violent response reflected their moral indignation that they had patiently waited for 11 months, agreed to an endless succession of meetings to discuss their grievances, and had refrained from striking only to be presented with an offer that, in some cases, granted workers lower wages than they currently made. But by now the state had put legislation in place to protect its interventions at the point of production. The men could not oppose the Evans Agreement by strikes or interfering with men who chose to work. They were offered the opportunity to enter arbitration, but they demurred and ended the strike. However, it was clear that the issue was far from resolved. The Colonial Office was not pleased.

## THE DIVISIVENESS OF 'CLAN'

Thwarted in their attempt to interrupt production, the Councils refocused their efforts on corrupt "native" and European staff who victimized the workers. Their meetings with the manager became more contentious. In so doing they reopened the clan issue in a divisive way. On 28 April 1938, the Underground Representative Council demanded that largely Agbaja interpreters be dismissed, arguing that they were responsible for "bad treatment," caused "most of the confusion," and demanded bribes.[108] The accusation had sufficient truth to attract the Transport Director's attention. He realized that they often caned the men, intentionally distorted translations, and dismissed workers who failed to bribe them. Moreover, he suspected that some of the European staff may also have been implicated in the abuses. Nonetheless, Leck stalled and asked for a formal complaint naming specific interpreters, but before the case was presented he decided to abolish the position of interpreter, only to reverse himself several weeks later. The turnabout was in part a response to the protests of the interpreters who demanded to see evidence of their offenses:

We understood that the Colliery Manager said that Interpreters are receiving bribes. We beg to know from whom? We should like to know why we are treating as un-known workers. ... Is it right that we should be blamed, when

Colliery-Manager, Under-Manager or Overman dismiss boys or suspend them. Sir, if they are not accusing us, maliciously, we beg to have concrete understanding in this matter.[109]

The Agbaja interpreters used this opportunity to plant seeds of division among the men. They were influential men in their natal villages and utilized the pre-existing suspicions held by their clan councils to defend themselves from what they characterized as an unfair "foreigner" attack. The impact was clear at the May 27 meeting of the Underground Council when one Joseph, an Agbaja "pick boy," asked for total separation from Owerrians.

Originally we wanted to be one but owing to palavor [sic] and indifference shown by Owerrians we do not now want anything to do with Owerrians. We had a meeting last night and the Abajas said they didn't want to mix with Owerrians. If I have anything to say to tell them separately. Why we say so, we do not want palavor [sic]—owing to this regular trouble we come to make money not trouble—we want the wise men to go and make their own council and we made ours. We should be divided into two parts in every case or part—the only part we wish to join is on one pay table.[110]

The more the "foreign" Underground Council pressed for the elimination of the interpreters, the more ethnic quarreling flared. In the turmoil that followed, the surface workers also endeavored to go beyond the limits set by employers and became aggressive. Confronted with this behavior, Leck emerged as increasingly authoritarian in the minutes of meetings held in early May 1938. He arbitrarily manipulated the rules governing the Councils to reduce the powers of the representatives. One particularly thorny point was the type of cases that the representatives could raise in the Council meetings. Leck summarily dismissed inquiries concerning the grading of specific workers. Assuming that this applied only to individual workers, the councilors raised a grievance on behalf of four workers who had been demoted to a lower pay scale. When he refused to entertain the cases, they requested clarification: "how many persons will be in a case before it can be called general as to come to council?" Arrogantly, Leck argued that it was self-evident. Nonetheless the councilors eloquently asserted their solidarity:

We want to let you know sir that we fight for the new grade together and that we are not going to take the case as individual case; as we know some people have not well graded we are going to fight together for justice in every case. Our letter to Government about the omissions will be forwarded with name of people who get bad grade, when ready or any other way we like.[111]

In June 1938 when the hostility at the Underground Council meetings made them ineffective, the men took matters into their own hands and followed the pattern of colliery protest. Although the Councils were blocked from encouraging strikes they increasingly used legal redress to press cases of corruption. The Underground Council sued one C.H. Matthews, a European, and Joseph Okpokwu, his interpreter, for depriving them of their livelihood alleging that they replaced them with men who had paid bribes. This use of the judicial system to prosecute workplace corruption was a new tactic. The Council also sent a delegation to Lagos to appeal to the Director of Transport. Armed with numerous petitions from workers, they hired a Lagos barrister to represent them. The delegation included three representatives from Owerri and one from Agbaja. They were Ben Duru, a "pick boy" from Owerri; Lawrence Amukenebe, the same man assaulted by Ken, a "tubboy" from Ebe, Agbaja;[112] and one Nwankwo, a "pick boy" from Owerri. The fourth member, Gabriel, a "machine boy" of Owerri, joined the group a week later and apparently brought £17 collected from the miners to pay the barrister, Ogunyemi Ajose.[113]

The group summarized the major issues in their position paper.

1. Dismissal without notice. There were several cases in which miners had been asked to go on leave by their supervisor or were absent in the hospital for several months only to return and find that their jobs had been taken by another worker.

2. Removal of Interpreters. While once necessary they now were irrelevant in many of the work areas and were guilty of taking bribes. Those work groups who wished to retain them should be permitted to do so.

3. Filling of Vacancies. "Boss-boys" and under managers seldom promoted miners to fill vacant posts and preferred instead to recruit from outside the work force usually in the villages of the "boss boys."

4. Second Increment. On December 27, 1937 "tub" and "pick boys" were promised a 2d increment if they agree to work a new shift from 6:30 AM to 2:30 PM. Having done so, they had not received the promised increment.[114]

Several Agbaja "boss boys" and interpreters were named in the complaint. The powers these men had over translation have been noted above, but they were also given other functions. They were often sent back into the mine by a European foreman to see if the men followed his orders.[115] In one petition the men asked that Augustine Ude of Umuaga, Udi, and Joseph Okpokwu of Abor, Udi, be kept out of the mines for making unauthorized dismissals for bribery.[116] The complaint claimed that these interpreters' actions had been the major grievances for a number of past strikes and warned of recurrent strikes if they remained in place.[117]

Although the Councils had violated the procedures laid out in the Evans Agreement by circumventing the colliery manager, the Director of Transport nonetheless took seriously the threat that interpreters would be the cause of further strikes. He suggested that they be disbanded and assigned to "harmless clerical" positions. Lastly, he put his finger on what may have been the heart of the matter, the way in which the European overmen were allied with interpreters.[118] Clearly the reliance on interpreters had encouraged a relationship of convenience between European and interpreter. The Councils recognized that Europeans were involved in corruption and interpreters wielded considerable power in their Agbaja villages. On several occasions European overmen had been convicted with their interpreters of conspiracy to extort bribes, but the sentences were commuted. The Director had little sympathy for interpreters and criticized the European staff's reluctance to eliminate them:

> I understand that these men live in the compounds of the European officers. ... It appears that too much reliance is placed by the European officers on their interpreters. ... I am not satisfied with the bald statements of the Under Manager and some of the Overmen that the mine would be unsafe without the interpreters, or that they themselves could not be responsible for safety were they withdrawn. Such statements have the appearance of superficiality and a dislike of change which may be stubbornness.[119]

The Director agreed to meet the deputation despite the restrictions of the Evans Agreement. It was difficult for the manager, Leck, to understand the necessity for organized worker consultation. Perhaps because he had proven himself to be disinterested in those conditions that were so disruptive in the colliery, or incapable of running his industry in an efficient manner, Leck found little sympathy in the central administration. The Director continued to lend credibility to the Councils even at the price of undermining the manager's authority. Leck tried to question their authority with claims that the other council members disagreed on the issues raised. But his efforts were unsuccessful. The colliery was too strategically important to risk an additional strike. Despite the manager's claims that "these men represented no one," the Director met with them and heard the grievances. Nominally sympathetic to the manager's complaints, he wrote Leck on June 8:

> Every representation must pass though you and be commented on by you before we will agree to discuss it here and I made this clear.[120]

But the Director nonetheless received the delegation, further underscoring the fragility of the manager's authority in the face of resourceful maneuvers by the representatives. Leck pleaded:

> I beg to strongly insist that paragraph 2 of your D. T. S. 334/1384 be adhered to most rigidly—otherwise I can see that any authority the CM has, at present, will be entirely lost. This is a principle on which it is not possible to give way in the slightest.[121]

It was subsequently revealed that the group had openly defied Leck, who had denied them leave and passes to go to Lagos. When he warned the men that the Director would not decide on their complaints without consulting him, the men merely "laughed and went away."[122] When the men returned Leck attempted to fire the delegates, arguing that they had dismissed themselves by being absent without leave. The Director's response revealed the extent to which he deprecated Leck and wished to avoid another strike. Saying that while the delegation should have obtained formal leave, the fact that they were absent without leave was not inconsistent with the normal behavior of men in the colliery where a high degree of absenteeism was normal:

As I understand there are many more men on the colliery books than are ever at work at the same time, and that these men are in the habit of absenting themselves for a period after working for a period. In any case, the men at present concern should not be penalized on their return to work but you should make the position clear to them.[123]

Clearly, the Director felt that it was more important to prevent a strike than to reinforce the authority of a manager whose record was of dubious quality. On July 12, the Director intervened to finally abolish the interpreter position and assigned them to other posts at the mines. He suggested using "graded Lamp Boys" as interpreters and established that demands for bribes would be punished by dismissal.[124] The interpreter conflict brought ethnic divisions to the forefront at a time when the Councils were proving most effective in attacking coercive systems of authority in the workplace. While some Agbaja were pitted against Owerrians, it is unclear if this was a generalized response or a manipulation by "clan" leaders and resentful Agbaja interpreters. In May, prior to the first termination of interpreters, some of the Agbaja had demanded their own clansmen on the Representative Council. Moreover, they suggested that they be given a separate workplace in the mines distinct from the Owerrians.

> We have the honor most respectfully to forward this our humble application before you. Again to notify you that Agbajie under Colliery Mine wished to have their own meeting different from Owerre people. And in working place, we Agbajie beg you with honor so that you may look us with money and divied [sic] mine work section by section, and let Agbajie section get their own working separately. Likewise to Owerre let them get their own section difference.[125]

The management exploited and encouraged this type of divisive ethnicity, encouraging the Agbaja headmen who promoted this decision to mute the militancy vocalized by the Owerrians. The Owerrians, understandably, opposed any ethnic rationale in determining worker status. But the position of another Agbaja group asserted that the proposal for separate working places was a maneuver by the "boss men" to exploit their own workers.

> Two or three of our headmen often make meeting without our knowledge and they come and speak in favour of Agbaja, witsh we know nothing about the whole matter. ... If the division is to be made, now tell as in which side the Europeans at our head will be? then, have we to have two Managers, one of Agbaja and one for the other part. Consider this case properly for a great riot will come out if the division is being made. Those head-men that come to you are planning for another way of bribing themselves after the division is made.[126]

The demand for separate councils was a call to institutionalize clan cleavages in the workforce at a time when clan was a declining category of alliances. The manager agreed to "seriously consider" the proposal and immediately began to communicate with the two groups of representatives separately. The Agbaja representative agreed with the manager's criticism of the June delegation and claimed that it was a fundamentally Owerrian scheme.

> The petition sent to Lagos and which was not passed through the Colliery Manager shows how the Owerrians despised both the Abajas and Colliery Manager. If Abaja want anything they will first approach the Colliery Manager.[127]

While clan affiliation was undoubtedly important given the persistent links between mine and village, it is difficult to determine how much support the Agbaja proposal had among the miners. But at least one group of Agbaja saw the demands for segregated workplaces as a scheme to permit corruption of Agbajas by Agbaja interpreters. The signatories of the May petition from "Agbaja People" attacking the interpreters were all from Ukana, Ebe, and Amaokwe towns of Agbaja, but they all lived in colliery labor camps. They clearly spotted the opportunism of their clansmen who manipulated the clan sentiment of the miners. While we do not want to make a mechanistic correlation between residence and clan-based behavior, it would appear that the experience in the camps removed them from the manipulations of the village leaders and allowed them to be more focused on their interests as workers.

The fragility of clan affiliation was made clear by the people of Ngwo, an Agbaja village-group who lost most of their farmland to the mines. Seeing that management was favorably disposed to clan-based work groups and representation on the Councils, they put forth their demand for Ngwo work districts, supervisors, and representation. The Ngwo demands were undoubtedly stimulated by recent reorganization of the Agbaja Native Court, separating it from that of the other Agbaja, in an act that apparently authenticated their existence as a distinct group.[128] At the base of the demand lay Ngwo's long-standing grievance that they had been cheated of their land by the fraudulent "chiefs" who signed the original agreement with the government for the colliery, and may have represented their expectation that they would receive royalties for the lands. They saw jobs in the mines as compensation for this injustice. In July 1938 G.O. Ugwo, secretary of the Representative Council, wrote Leck that the Ngwo workers were still waiting for him to honor his agreement to place two Ngwo miners on the council. They argued that Ngwo was the most underrepresented group in the higher positions at the mines and buttressed their arguments by asserting that Ngwo was not an Agbaja group.

> We learnt that the division of work amidst the workers of the undermine will take place on Monday showing each town its own part or position. ... In Abaja there are 136 Headmen or Heads of Labourers etc; and in Owerri there are many of these kinds mentioned. We have often quoted, and should say, we spoke in many occasions of time that Ngwo is a separate entity, in this regard we mean that Ngwo is neither Abaja nor Owerri, and can Ngwo go for nothing ... Ngwo has no Bosses and so on. Are we late in the Coal field? ... There are no men of argument in this Town, but we now want to put points after point and arguments on argument that Ngwo should with countless reasons have its own foremen of

works, its own Bosses, its own Heads of labourers etc. In the office the Agbaja and the Owerri are the only town in which clerks and Interpreters were being engaged; in Ngwo there is none.[129]

The separation of Ngwo from Agbaja court was cited as evidence to support the claim for separation. The call for Ngwo preference and representation was an important issue for the miners of that village-group, because they had lost so much of their land to the colliery and to the forest reserve that was opened in the thirties. The effort was undoubtedly championed by the Ngwo council in the Native Court. While there is no written record of direct intervention by the Ngwo councilors, there is evidence that they attempted to use the courts to enforce solidarity among the Ngwo miners. In August 1937 the Ngwo chiefs attempted to prosecute one miner, Samuel Mba, who had been promoted to "boss boy" on their recommendation, but had later refused to support Ngwo demands. The incident underscored the claims of several miners that often work-related conflicts spilled over into the villages.[130]

The clan leaders' intervention to enforce Ngwo unity was a natural consequence of the management's use of Native Authority officials to control workers at the mines. The overlapping of political influence in the villages with labor control in the mines created an environment in which village leaders assumed that they could lead the workers' movement. The contradictory positions taken by various sectors of the Owerrian and Agbaja workforce revealed the conflicting allegiances held by the miners. Some disregarded clan affinity and argued against the exploitative interpreters, while others continued to assert that the major contradiction was between the Owerrian and Agbaja clan groups. But the fragility of clan identity and the capacity for infinite kinship fragmentation was evident in the defection of the Ngwo group from the Agbaja position. Even clan cohesion became tenuous when the village political leaders lacked the mechanism to enforce it. It could be possible that in segmentary societies such as the Igbo, the possibilities of fragmentation are infinite and could theoretically break down to the base of the household unit or extended family.

The entire dispute over the interpreters, the charges and countercharges by the Agbajas and Owerrians, and the Council's relatively successful struggle to become a functioning organ within the constellation of forces at the colliery led the manager to suspend the Underground Council in late 1938. He had written in July of his frustration as the entire system collapsed into a series of suits and countersuits: "Personally, I think this Underground Council has gone too far and I propose to dismiss them as a Council for this season."[131] By the end of 1939 the colliery, despite the many efforts at reform, was nonetheless tottering on the brink of another wave of worker action. With improvement being made in the camps, the men began to feel the impact of yet another new system which nonetheless kept redundant workers on the books. The management did not continue the series of retrenchments begun in 1938. Instead of reducing the size of the workforce, the colliery complied with the request of the Iva Valley miners in August to allow them to share work in a system called "rostering," after the work roster containing the names of workers on a day's assignment. "Rostering" created a regulated pool of workers that were trained, although they only worked infrequently and could be engaged more or less regularly depending on the coal market.[132] The system benefited the management by keeping on the books all the qualified miners, which reduced the time and cost required for new recruitment. The "roster" gave the state and not the men control over the composition of the work group. But as workers discovered how infrequently they would work, they became more disgruntled. In the last three months of the year most of the men worked only eight or nine days per month, although they had expected that retrenchments would increase their number of working days.[133] Further, posting a "roster" did not protect the men from new systems of fraud and corruption. A group of men petitioned the manager about two "boss boys," again Augustine Ude, a former interpreter, and Jacob Aniogbo, for assigning them to a "hard" coal face:

> We members of pick-boys in No. 1 Coal mine require your visit to our list-board. Our intention ... was that many of us attend good places where they can ... fill at least about 10 tubs (ten) of coal while others who were hated attend to bad places where they cannot fill 3 tubs (three) of coal before it was time. We ask your honour to take away Mr. Jacob Aniogbo from our part, and let him become ordinary travelling staff; and put either Mr. Peter or Mr. Maduke in his instead, or Mr. Anithony [sic] the Staff take the whole shift.[134]

As war approached, the Colonial Office was less willing to allow Leck to use his old methods of worker consultation and control. The post-depression recovery had generated a frightening rash of colonial labor protests. In both the English-speaking Caribbean and on the Zambian Copperbelt workers with trade unions and without launched a wave of strikes that came dangerously close to challenging the existence of colonial rule and property relations of capitalist production. In Jamaica unions attacked the existing system of land ownership.[135] In Zambia workers attacked Europeans and went on a rampage at the mine site. These strikes moved beyond workers' actions and became broad militant populist movements that made political demands on the colonial government.[136] The dangers of the alliance between colonial workers and an independence movement with leaders whose political motivation often flirted with communism, provided the stimulus for a more serious consideration of imperial labor policy.

The eminence of war reinforced the Colonial Office's responsibility to modernize labor policy. These initiatives were a demonstration to the private sector, which often created messy social crises in their myopic quest to maximize profits, and to colonial subjects who now, more than ever, needed proof of the benefits of continued British rule. In Enugu, as elsewhere, the policy involved a number of initiatives. On the one hand, there were modest improvements in urban living and working conditions in the colonies to diffuse discontent. Colonial labor experts assumed that by acculturating African workers to the industrial and urban environment they could create a disciplined working class capable of reaching increased levels of productivity.[137] On the other hand, officials nonetheless developed more elaborate schemes to thwart the activism of the colonial working class.[138] After the last series of West Indian riots,[139] the Labour Party successfully got the Tory government to bring the British Trade Union Congress (TUC) into the main policy-making body on imperial labor policy—the Colonial Labor Advisory Committee, a tripartite organization with members of the Colonial Office, the TUC, and overseas employers' federations.[140] The Congress proved especially cooperative in encouraging apolitical trade unions, and even seconded their members as colonial agents to be labor advisors to many of the colonies to oversee the creation of "responsible" colonial trade unions.[141]

In order to insure the levels of production needed to supply sufficient colonial resources for the war the workforce had to become stabilized and made more productive. Stabilization, if handled reasonably, could avoid proletarianization, a process that many in the Colonial Office viewed with foreboding. At Enugu this meant "rostering" which created a labor pool from which daily workers could be drawn according to requirements without completely separating the men from their farms. To control urban overcrowding officials had decided to recruit locally from the adjacent Agbaja villages. Nonetheless, the city grew by 400 percent during the war, creating a social problem that subjected urban workers' lives to more government attempts at control and monitoring. But this new population entered an increasingly radicalized city. New immigrants were socialized into city life by the improvement unions (so-called "tribal" unions) in which the restive clerical population played a crucial leadership role. Their significance in generating discontent was enhanced in 1938 when the city became the regional capital of southeastern Nigeria, attracting more literate Africans seeking government jobs. This generation of clerks were as disenchanted as their counterparts after World War I with the inequities in colonial life that pulled them between the expectations of a westernized elite and the harsh racial realities of the life of a native civil servant. This discontent made the clerks pivotal players in the rising forms of political agitation on the eve of war. Given their interactions with the city's workers in the improvement unions and the rising levels of nationalist discourse, they were bound to have an influence on the many government workers in railway, colliery and other employment areas.

In the mines, managerial control had been considerably compromised by a heritage of corruption, neglect, and incompetence. Now, with legislative provisions to supervise colonial labor, workers continued to shift their tactics into the courts, using the state's laws in quite unintended ways. Their Representative Councils, that overlapped considerably with the *Nzuko*, had been dismantled, but it is probable that they continued to meet informally. The attempt to replace the *Nzuko* with government-endorsed councils had failed to subsume colliery unrest. Further, because they were not worker controlled, the men only showed them guarded support. The clan fighting that proved so divisive would not succeed in breaking workers' solidarity when the war began. However, the underground workers would look suspiciously at any organization introduced by the management. During the war, they would continue to struggle to be treated as modern industrial men. This time their struggle would pit them against the colonial state with tragic consequences.

## NOTES

1. NRUCAR, 1933/34.

2. NNAE, Onprof 1/32/110, "Onitsha Provinces Annual Report for 1931."

3. Richard Sklar, *Nigerian Political Parties: Power in an Emergent African Nation* (Princeton, 1963), 165–67.

4. NNAE, UDDIST 3/1/5, "Divisional Annual Report: Udi Division, 1937," 9.

5. In my interviews in the "unofficial" camps of Ugwu Alfred and Ugwu Aaron respondents emphatically stated that they did not allow "traditional" rulers to establish any control in their camps. Similarly a former tubman stated "the miners always stand for democracy." Interview in Ugwa Alfred, 5 July 1975.

6. On the Copperbelt, see Ian Phimister, "Early African Leadership: The Copperbelt Disturbances of 1935 and 1940," *Journal of Southern African Studies* 2 (1975): 83–97; Ibid., "Wage-Earners and Political Protest in Colonial Africa: The Case of the Copperbelt," *African Affairs* 57 (1973): 288–99; Charles Perrings, *Black Mineworkers in Central Africa: Industrial Strategies and the Evolution of an African Proletariat in the Copperbelt 1922–41* (London, 1979). On the British Caribbean, see Arthur Lewis, *Labour in the West Indies: The Birth of a Workers' Movement* (London, 1977); Ken Post, *"Arise Ye Starvlings": The Jamaican Labour Rebellion of 1938 and its Aftermath* (The Hague, 1978).

7. Agwu Akpala, "Background to the Enugu Colliery Shooting Incident in 1949." *Journal of the Historical Society of Nigeria* 3, 2 (1965): 343.

8. NNAE, Uddist 9/1/1, Annual Report, 1947.

9. Burawoy, *The Politics of Production,* 226.

10. David Frank, "The Country of Coal." *Labour/Le Travail* 21 (Spring 1988): 234.

11. Tosh, "Masculinity," 186.

12. Aniakor, *Igbo Arts*, 30.

13. During this particularly volatile period of worker unrest, following the economic recovery from the depression, a European overman known as being "rather impetuous with the 'boys'" was charged in court with slapping one of the leaders of the *Nzuko* and the Representative Council. The magistrate was disgusted that the case was taken seriously, but under instructions of the Secretary of the Southern Provinces, had to levy a fine against the "boss." ONDIST 12/1/1562, Manager to Transport, 6 July 1938.

14. Among other things the Councils hired a Yoruba lawyer in Lagos to represent them in negotiations with the Transport Directorate, the governmental agency that supervised the colliery and railway.

15. Campbell and Reid, "The Independent Collier in Scotland," 57.

16. The "butty" is a master hewer who contracts with the colliery owner to mine a particular area at a certain price. He then brings in his own work crew and they extract the coal under his supervision. The pay is by the tonnage and given to the master hewer who in turn pays the work team. In Yorkshire this led to many abuses. See Douglass, "Pit Talk in County Durham," 309.

17. CO 583/263/30544, Colonial Office Press Section, "Model Villages for African Miners," 11 May 1943.

18. Croasdale, "Enugu Colliery," 55.

19. Ibid., 7.

20. NIGCOAL 2/1/94, Colliery Manager to Director of Transport, 20 June 1938.

21. See discussion in Chapter 1.

22. Judith Van Allen, "'Sitting on a Man': Colonialism and the Last Political Institutions of Igbo Women," *Canadian Journal of African Studies* 6, 2 (1972): 168–81.

23. In the Udi area there were reports for both Nkanu and Agbaja regions. See NNAE OP/1070, "Agbani-Akpugo," Beaumont.

24. There are many theories as to the cause of his death. Some claim that he was being investigated for a murder while others say he was despondent because of his demotion. At any rate he died as dramatically as he lived. He shot himself in the mouth while traveling on a train. Onyeama, *Chief Onyeama*, 123–26. Also see file CSO 26/1 for the accusations of his involvement in several murders.

25. Croasdale, "Enugu Colliery."

26. See Chapter 1. This included title societies, many wives, etc.

27. UDDIST 3/1/4, "Circular from the Secretary of State to the O.A.G.," 9 November 1935; Bourdillon to Ormsby-Gore, 1 October 1936.

28. UDDIST 3/1/1. 1931, 17.

29. Annual Report on the Colliery Department for the Year 1938.

30. For an attack from the left (British Communist Party), see Jack Woodis, *The Mask is Off! An Examination of the Activities of Trade Union Advisers in the British Colonies*, (London, 1954).

31. Although the committee was only established in 1942, informal meetings had been held in the colonial office since 1931 to discuss labor policy. The documentation is available in the Public Records Office, Kew Gardens, England. File series CO 323/1117 and CO 888/1. Files CO 888/2-11 contain the documents of the committee.

32. UDDIST 3/1/4, "Udi District Annual Report 1936."

33. Unfortunately, Smock does not identify the respondent. Smock, "Village to Trade Union," 125.

34. CO 583/216, According to Governor Bourdillon's report to Ormsby-Gore on 3 April, 1937.

35. Ibid.

36. Ibid.

37. Ibid., Bourdillon to Ormsby-Gore, 20 March 1937.

38. Ibid., 3 April 1937.

39. Ibid.

40. Croasdale, "Enugu Colliery," 36–37.

41. Ibid.

42. Ibid.

43. Ibid.

44. NIGCOAL 2/1/94, Minute of Meeting, Port Harcourt with Surface and Underground Representatives, 9 November 1937.

45. United Mine Workers of America (UMWA), Proceedings, 1927 Convention, 442–45, cited in Keith Dix, *What's a Coal Miner to Do?: The Mechanization of Coal Mining*, (Pittsburgh, 1988), 165.

46. The mines' books also showed ineptitude and outdated accounting methods. Rather than using a costing system which would permit a more accurate calculation of the fiscal status of the colliery, a simple receipts expenditure system was used. The mine had to meet

capital expenditure from its revenue under the heading of "Special Expenditure." There was no renewals account so the depreciation of plant and machinery was estimated by the government in its review in June. Finally, while the costs of African employees' Provident Fund were included in expenditure figures, the funds for European pensions, a substantially larger sum, were absent. CO 583/216, Report of Acting Colliery Manager to Colonial Administration, 8 June 1937, Appendix A, enclosure in Bourdillon to Ormsby-Gore, 24 June 1937.

47. Maybin in the Colonial Office noted that profit might have been slightly less than the figures if calculated using the system of commercial enterprises. However, clearly there was sufficient surplus to permit a wage increase. Ibid., Maybin to Ormsby-Gore, 24 June 1937.

48. Croasdale noted that the "boss boys" were resented by the men and seldom interacted with them socially. They were called *Nduku* or "Big Man." Croasdale, "Enugu Colliery."

49. See Supple, *History of the British Coal Industry*, Chap. 11.

50. Ibid.; CO 583/216 Ormsby-Gore Minute, 26 April 1937.

51. Cooper, *Decolonization and African Society*, 61–62.

52. In the original draft he had written "some" concern, but he crossed this out and wrote "considerable." CO 583/216, Ormsby-Gore to Bourdillon, 13 May 1937.

53. Ibid., J. Sidebotham Minute, 20 April 1937.

54. Ibid.

55. Croasdale, "Enugu Colliery," 40–41.

56. Professional letter writers were a critical element in the multifaceted strategies of urban colonial workers. They were somewhat like paralegals, having some knowledge of the laws and assuming the role of community protectors for both villages and urban groups. Several of them frequently wrote petitions of this period: J. Beresford Jarrett, whose name appears on several of these petitions and wrote for slave *ohu* communities from Nkanu during this same period, and M.O. Ogbenika. NIGCOAL 2/1/94, See letters #1, 7, 9, 10. District Officers complained bitterly of the "number of semi-literate youth who, rather than return to hard manual work, set themselves up in the profession of letter-writer." NNAE, ONPROF 1/32/110, "Onitsha Province Annual Report 1931."

57. Major G. St. J. Orde Browne, *Labour Conditions in West Africa*, Cmd. 6277 (London, 1941).

58. NIGCOAL 2/1/94, Letter from Colliery Department, Iva Valley to the General Manager, Railway, Lagos, 12 July 1937 and Colliery Manager.

59. Ibid.

60. This information followed a survey of the camps during the period of labor force stabilization in 1939. CO 583/237, Bourdillon to MacDonald, 30 August 1939.

61. Ibid., "Petition from the Southern Native Location, Enugu Township to the Colliery Manager, Colliery Department, Enugu through the Under Manager, Iva Valley Coal Mine, Enugu," 21 August 1937.

62. Ibid., "Letter from Colliery Department Iva to Colliery Manager, Enugu," 30 August 1937.

63. Ibid., "Letter from Colliery Department, Iva Special Headmen to Colliery Manager, Enugu," 30 August 1937.

64. Ibid.

65. Ibid., "Letter from Tub Headmen, Iva to Colliery Manager, Enugu," 31 August 1937.

66. Ibid.

67. Akpala, "African Labour Productivity," 236.

68. Ibid.

69. Croasdale, "Enugu Colliery," 70.

70. Lawrence Amukenebe of Ebe, Agbaja, chairman of the Haulage and Tubboy *Nzuko*, was slapped by a European "boss." ONDIST 12/1/1562, Manager to Transport, 6 July 1938.

71. This study has been a key source for information on early worker collective action as well as details on the labor camps. See Croasdale. "Enugu Colliery." A series of such studies was made of every village-group in southeastern Nigeria following the Women's War of 1929. See Van Allen, "Sitting on a Man."

72. Frederick Cooper, "Urban Space, Industrial Time, and Wage Labor in Africa." In *The Struggle for the City: Migrant Labor, Capital and the State in Urban Africa*, edited by Frederick Cooper, 35. Beverley Hills: 1983.

73. Croasdale, "Enugu Colliery," 70.

74. Ibid.

75. Croasdale, "Enugu Colliery," 53.

76. Ibid., 50.

77. Federal Ministry of Labour Archives, Yaba, Lagos, Nigeria (hereafter FMLA), Labour Ministry Files, no. 3, vol. 4, Croasdale to CM, 17 September 1938.

78. CO 583/232/30331/K/3, Bourdillon to Ormsby-Gore, enclosure in D.P.J. O'Connor, "Colliery Labour General Reorganization."

79. CO 583/237/30046, Governor Bourdillon to MacDonald, 30 August 1939.

80. Range housing was a line of single rooms, each with an entrance on a common porch. Kitchens and bathroom facilities, rudimentary, open sewers, were usually detached in the back.

81. CO 583/266/30046, Governor to Ormbsy-Gore, 27 January 1938.

82. CO 583/216/30046/12, Governor to Ormsby-Gore, 24 June 1937; CO 583/227, Bourdillon to MacDonald, 30 August 1938; CO 583/216, Ormsby-Gore to Bourdillon, 9 August 1937; Akpala, "Colliery Shooting," 324.

83. Michael Burawoy, *The Politics of Production*, 226.

84. Ibid., 236.

85. NIGCOAL 2/1/94, Colliery Manager to Director, Transport, 20 June 1938.

86. ONDIST 3/1/5, "Udi Division Annual Report for 1937."

87. CO 583/229/30159, Bourdillon to Ormsby-Gore, 2 March 1938. Kerr was a particularly abusive supervisor. In 1940 "boss boys" accused him of making false charges against them and "slapping and knowking (sic) us in the mind and disgracing us in many other respectsd." NIGCOAL 2/1/126, "Boss-Boys to Colliery Manager," 6 January 1940.

88. See Croasdale, "Enugu Colliery," for a list of members, 30–32.

89. Uchendu *The Igbo of Southeast Nigeria*, 90–91.

90. Croasdale, "Enugu Colliery," 29–30.

91. See earlier discussion in Chapter 1.

92. Croasdale, "Enugu Colliery," 32–33.

93. Ibid., 33.

94. NIGCOAL 2/1/94, "Representation and Deputations from Surface/Underground Colliery Staffs," 9 November 1937.

95. Ibid.

96. NIGCOAL 2/1/94, Director of Transport, "Minutes of Meeting at Pt. Harcourt with Surface and Underground Representatives," 9 November 1937.

97. NIGCOAL 2/1/94, CM to Dir. of Transport, 20 January 1938.

98. NIGCOAL 2/1/94, Transport to Leck, 6 July 1938.

99. Nigerian Coal Corporation (NCC), New No. 1, "F. D. Evans: Complaints and Petitions by Colliery Employees," 2 February 1938.

100. Ibid.

101. Ibid.

102. Ibid.

103. Ibid.

104. CO 583/237/30046/21, D.P.J. O'Connor, "Colliery Labour General Reorganization," enclosure in Bourdillon to MacDonald, 30 August 1939.

105. CO 583/233/30037, Sidebotham minute, 8 February 1938.

106. Ibid.

107. NIGCOAL 2/1/94, F.P. James to Chief Secretary, Lagos, 7 February 1938.

108. NIGCOAL 2/1/94, "Meeting of the Underground Council," 29 June 1938. Memorandum from Director of Transport to Colliery Manager, 22 July 1938.

109. NIGCOAL 2/1/98, Underground Interpreters to Colliery Manager.

110. Ibid., "Meeting of the Underground Council," 29 June 1938.

111. Ibid., "Meeting of the Surface Council," 5 May 1938.

112. The was the same man in the assault case that caused the lightning strike in September.

113. NIGCOAL 2/1/94, Ogunyemi Ajose to Transport, 6 July 1938.

114. NIGCOAL 2/1/98, "Grievance of the Underground Council," 14 June 1938.

115. Ibid. Memorandum, 8 June 1938.

116. NIGCOAL 2/1/94, Director of Transport to Colliery Manager, 12 July 1938; "Memorandum," 8 June 1938.

117. Ibid.

118. There was at least one court case implicating a European supervisor and interpreter. An ex-tubman, Eugene Onu of Ebe, Agbaja, claimed £100 damages against C.E. Matthews, underground supervisor of all colliery operations and his interpreter Augustine Ude of Umagua, Udi, for depriving his work gang employment in the spring of 1938. NIGCOAL 2/1/94, DO Enugu to Secretary, Southern Provinces, Enugu, 9 August 1938.

119. Ibid., Director of Transport to CM, 22 June 1938.

120. Ibid., Director to CM, 8 June 1938.

121. Ibid., CM to Director, 20 June 1938.

122. Ibid., CM to Director, 17 June 1938.

123. Ibid., Director to CM, 4 July 1938.

124. Ibid.

125. NIGCOAL 2/1/98, Joseph E. Ekowa et al., to CM, no date, May(?) 1938.

126. Ibid., Agbaja People to CM, no date.

127. NIGCOAL 2/1/94, "Meeting of the Underground Council," 29 June 1938.

128. CSE 1/85/6411, "Intelligence Report on the Ngwo Clan of Agbaja Area, Udi Division, Onitsha Province," H.J.S. Clark, Assistant DO, 1933.

129. NIGCOAL 2/1/98, Ngwo Town through Under Manager to Manager, Enugu, 10 June 1938.

130. NIGCOAL 2/1/94, CM to DO Udi, 20 July 1938.

131. Ibid., CM to Director, 22 July 1938.

132. N.C.C. Files, P. 1/9, O'Connor to Secretary, Southern Provinces, 6 September 1939.

133. UDDIST 3/1/7, "Udi District Annual Report for 1939."

134. Ibid., Pickboys to Underground Manager, Iva Mine, 15 September 1939.

135. Peter Weiler, "Forming Responsible Trade Unions: The Colonial Office, Colonial Labor, and the Trades Union Congress," *Radical History Review* 28–30 (1984): 370; K.W.J. Post, "The Politics of Protest in Jamaica: Some Problems of Analysis and Conceptualization," in *Peasants and Proletarians: The Struggles of Third World Workers*, ed. Peter Gutkind, Robin Cohen, and P. Brazier (New York, 1970).

136. On the Caribbean, see A. Lewis, *Labour in the West Indies*, and Post, *"Arise Ye Starvlings."* On Zambia, see Charles Perrings, "Consciousness, Conflict, and Proletarianization: An Assessment of the 1935 Mineworkers' strike on the Northern Rhodesian Copperbelt," *Journal of Southern African Studies* 4, 1 (1977); Ibid., *Black Mine Workers in Central Africa* (London, 1979).

137. Frederick Cooper, "From Free Labor to Family Allowances," 753.

138. Weiler, "Forming Responsible Trade Unions," 371.

139. Sir Walter Citrine was appointed to the Royal West Indian Commission, and during his visit to Jamaica, made acquaintance with Alexander Bustamante, the Jamaican nationalist and trade union leader. Under Bustamante's aegis the TUC pressed the Colonial Office over the conditions of colonial labor. In their annual congress in 1938, they discussed colonial labor conditions and passed a resolution that the Colonial Office pressure governments to introduce trade unions, collective bargaining machinery, and improve labor conditions. They touched on political issues by asking the government to "give natives responsibilities in government by extending the franchise and adopting ... democratic principles." CO 323/1536/1751 "Resolution Put Down for Discussion at the 70th Annual Congress of the TUC, to be Held at Blackpool, September 5–11, 1938."

140. See Frederick Cooper, "Rethinking Social Policy: Colonial Bureaucrats and African Labour in the Age of Decolonization," unpublished paper, 1990. The Committee's documentation is in PRO, CO 888.

141. For a communist critique of this practice, see Jack Woodis, *The Mask Is Off!*

# 6

# THE POLITICS OF "PRODUCTIVITY": UNIONS, THE WAR, AND CHANGES IN THE POLITICAL APPARATUS OF THE MINES 1940–1945

Please note that in [the] future the designation "men" must be substituted for "boys" in all communications referring to the Colliery labour either collectively or individually. No person employed by this department must be addressed as "boy."[1]
—Announcement by Colliery Manager, 23 December 1941[2]

The governments which ruled French West Africa and British Africa during the early war years had one characteristic in common: both were planning for futures that did not exist.
—Frederick Cooper, *Decolonization and African Society*[3]

Britain declared war in September 1939 but it was not until 1940 when Italy's declaration for Germany closed the Mediterranean route to the Middle East and Asia that Nigeria was drawn directly into the fight for the very survival of England. When France's West African governors declared for the Vichy government, the exception being Felix Eboue, the West Indian governor of Chad who supported free France, Britain's colonies, Nigeria, the Gold Coast, and Sierra Leone, were the only secure territories from which military operations could be launched in the

Mediterranean and Far East. These colonies became "strategic highways for Allied military movements" and this initiated a series of radical changes in the Nigerian economy and society, which sharpened the contradictions of colonial rule.[4]

At the center of these changes and Britain's involvement in Nigeria was the recruitment and control of Nigerian labor. Thousands of Nigerian men, and women, were pulled into the massive construction projects that built and maintained airfields, constructed barracks, roads, harbors, and railways. All the major cities experienced population explosions with Enugu growing 400 percent in 1939. The demand for labor both stimulated and undermined food production. Initially, the rapid urbanization of the civilian population and the stationing of thousands of military personnel expanded the market for locally grown produce. In Enugu the people of Nkanu became flush with cash from this market but by 1943 the attractions of the expanding labor market caused manpower shortages in the agricultural economy. This in turn translated into severe food shortages that plagued the entire colony. With imported foodstuffs in short supply and normal trade networks interrupted, these shortages further exacerbated the inflationary spiral confronting urban workers. It was only a matter of time before urban workers were pushed to protest these economic conditions, a fact being watched with dread by the Colonial Office.

The previous chapter outlined the tentative changes in colonial labor policy which recognized the social nature of colonial labor. But under the strain of war these timid measures barely papered over the deep, structural problems confronting colonial peoples and splitting colonial society. Moreover, in Nigeria the government proved particularly inept in answering the political challenges being voiced by the nascent nationalist movement. It made few political concessions although the Nigerian people professed their loyalty to the Allies, sent several hundred thousand men to battle in the Middle East, Ethiopia, and Burma, supplied agricultural and mineral exports at low prices, and voluntarily contributed more than £100,000 to the war. Government insensitivity to the Nigerian people was expressed in its refusal to even appoint any Nigerian personnel to the Nigerian Air Squad Empire Training Scheme or the Royal Air Force. When nationalists demanded to know what benefits Nigeria would receive after the war, Governor Bourdillon callously responded "survival."[5] In Nigeria, as throughout the Empire, putting old wine in new bottles failed to stop the inevitable surge for political participation. These critiques were alive in Enugu where nationalist politics flourished among restless, agitated government employees.

Meanwhile, the opening of hostilities caught work relations in disarray at the colliery. The grievances that sparked the 1937/38 protest were still unmet. Moreover, the one organization that represented the miners' interests, the Underground Representative Council, had been disbanded by management. But war conditions mandated some type of worker representation and a reluctant administration would accede to the Colonial Office demand that it establish the industry's first trade unions.

The "best" ways of controlling Nigerian workers had not yet been determined and the labor "experts" in the Colonial Office fumbled along, experimenting with the shell of British industrial relations institutions and processes—i.e., trade unions, collective bargaining, and disputes procedures—distorted by colonial authoritarianism. Thus unions were legalized but required to register, and laws specified the procedures of wage bargaining but locked in strike prohibitions. The right of workers to select their own representatives, a precondition for effective unions, was practically nonexistent as trade union leaders were often targeted by the state. For example, Michael Imoudu of the Railway Workers Union was summarily arrested and deported when he attempted to lead a job protest. Others, like the colliery's most charismatic leader, Isaiah Ojiyi, were subjected to sustained official harassment.

Between 1941 and 1943 Nigerian workers, particularly in Lagos, challenged fiscal policies that restricted imports, fixed depressed prices of agro-exports, created food shortages, and froze wages. The state responded aggressively with legislation that circumscribed workers' rights to strike, persecuted workers' leaders, and burdened the functioning of trade unions. These laws, collectively known as the Nigerian Defense Regulations, rapidly provoked resistance by the most organized sectors of the nation's working class. Railway workers and government employees engaged in several agitations between 1941 and 1943, culminating in 1945 in a 50-day general strike which brought the economy to its knees. However, until 1945 the new legislation secured relative peace in the coal industry. But there were many signs of discontent. Conflict erupted on several fronts: for the right to work under "rostering," against customary racist systems of industrial discipline, for wage increases, to secure recognition of workers' organizations, for improvements in conditions underground, etc. But the conflict that would plunge the industry into its most severe wartime crisis would occur when a new manager altered the organization of work and the system of pay.

For miners the depredations of the war occurred just as they became more aware of the struggles of British and American coal miners. The war emphasized the commonalties of coal mining whether in England or Nigeria, and the men were even more interested in how their wages, conditions of service, and living conditions compared with those of British and American miners. Increasingly, they behaved as part of an international brotherhood, a brotherhood of miners acutely aware that they produced the primary energy resource for the nations fighting the war. Despite colonial racial policies these comparisons came easily with the information available in the wireless broadcasts of government propaganda.

Between 1939 and 1942 the cost of living increased 75 percent in Nigeria. The coal miners endured low wages, deplorable housing conditions, and were increasingly unable to save resources to transfer to their villages for "development" projects. In this way, the economic crisis threatened their role as modernizers in their village and as patriarchs in their homes. Nonetheless, they made extraordinary sacrifices to build schools, educate their children, and improve health care in their villages because they could *see* a future. But to construct it, they had to struggle for the income to lay its foundation. This expenditure, which was never included in any of the government's assessments of the "cost of living," implicitly challenged

British assumptions that Africans were incapable of conceptualizing, let alone executing, their own model of development.[6] While authorities recognized that the workers were putting a tremendous amount of energy into "improvement"—both of self and community—the state felt that only the government had a coherent plan for the future.

Although weakened by restrictive laws, newly established colliery trade unions exploited provisions of the new labor legislation to engage in a discourse on their rights as working men, as subjects of the Crown, and as loyal supporters of the imperial war effort. They astutely continued to manipulate tensions among the layers of the state on social and labor policy to leverage more power. They raised these issues in a series of disputes during World War II, which led the state to circumvent the management and to further force a comprehensive transformation of colliery labor regulations. Many of these changes intensified earlier interventions into the social dimension of workers' lives—the composition of the African family. Would men with several wives be allowed to occupy government housing? What of other relatives who compose the extended family? Or would they have to accept the model of the nuclear family to have access to modern housing built for workers during the war?

The war intensified management's determination to force the colliery's workers to attain production targets needed to support England. Industrial struggles at the colliery pitted a working class staggering under the weight of spiraling inflation against a management intent upon ending its traditions of militance. The nexus of this conflict was productivity—a seemingly objective calculation that measured the ratio of output against the number of workers. But it was precisely the deceptive nature of this simple calculation that led Enugu's miners to wage their most intense struggles against the industry. In doing so, they revealed their recognition of those production conditions impacting output that were under their control and those that were under control of management. The state still used as an index the deceptive output figures before 1938 when the tonnage of a work-group was attributed to a single hewer. Such eschewed measurements of current production were politically advantageous for securing state support. Thus, it was to management's advantage to define productivity as narrowly as possible, ignoring the underground conditions or the composition of the work-group. But, for workers, it was important to identify those conditions that reduced their ability to produce and to recognize that many, such as the ratio of productive to nonproductive workers, were management's responsibility alone. These wartime disputes about productivity plagued the industry until the close of the decade. They also give us an opportunity to situate a managerial concept—productivity—within the contradictions of the colonial capitalist workplace.

These reforms were especially critical because, as West Africa's only coal mines, the industry was crucial for the economic and military role the region played in the war. Industrial unrest continued after the war in the volatile political context of radical nationalist agitation. The men eventually challenged the legislation that legalized restricted trade unions, introduced collective bargaining, prescribed disputes procedures, and mandated various forms of consultation. The chapter describes this difficult period in which workers struggled to retain their prominent positions as "modern" industrial men.

## THE CHALLENGE OF THE WAR: CONTROLLING NIGERIA'S NEW WORKING CLASS

Like the working class throughout Nigeria, the men at the colliery were profoundly affected by the war both economically and ideologically. They watched the vicissitudes of Britain in the early years of the war when the German Blitzkrieg dumped 20,000 tons of bombs, killing 42,000 and injuring 50,000.[7] The men's realization of the vulnerability of England further underscored the strategic importance of their labor to the survival of the metropolitan state and undermined the myth of British superiority. From June 1940 until June 1941 Britain could only stand alone against Germany with U.S. help.[8] She had exhausted most of her hard currency reserves purchasing war matériel from the United States. Conditions worsened in 1941 when the German invasion of the Soviet Union gave the Japanese an opportunity to push to the south in Asia. And in the summer of 1941 they entered Indochina, threatening Britain's access to Malay's rich rubber and tin resources and the oil reserves in North Borneo and Brunei. By January 1942 the threat had become a reality and Singapore fell, followed soon thereafter by Malaya, the Philippines, and the Dutch East Indies. The Japanese occupied Burma and threatened India. This gave Japan three-fourths of the world's rubber, two-thirds of its tin and enough oil for its needs.[9] By the late summer of 1942 the future of the British war effort looked very grim.

It was in this context of savage bombing raids, humiliating defeats at the hands of the non-white Japanese, and the rapid depletion of the treasury that officials in the Colonial Office searched for a policy to increase colonial labor productivity and prevent collective worker action. Propaganda became an important instrument for the extremely complex task: to secure the loyalty of colonial subjects without making major concessions to the most vocal critics—the nationalists. For the first time, wartime propaganda emphasized *colonial peoples'* importance to the imperial war effort and "*appealed* for the loyalty of their subjects" rather than assuming it as a right.[10]

Additionally, after the Japanese victories in Southeast Asia in 1942, West Africa became Britain's main supplier of tin and tropical food products.[11] Colonial exports were critically important as supplies for British factories, to earn hard currency in trade outside the sterling area, and to buy war matériel from the United States.[12] Colonial exports helped Great Britain to earn over £3,000 million in sterling balances.[13] It was therefore critical to push production to its highest levels, a process requiring increased managerial control of the workplace. In Nigeria's tin mines, the only source available to the Allies, the state violated the ILO Forced Labour Convention of 1930 by using forced labor to recruit workers for private companies.

Africans also watched the debate between Allied nations about colonialism. The Soviet Union and the United States were highly critical of Britain's imperial sta-

tus. American politicians engaged in well-publicized debates with British government apologists over the propriety of colonies in a world in which Germany and
Japan's acquisition of colonies had become a central focus of the Allied critique.
Roosevelt's opposition to colonialism put Churchill on the defensive but other
members of his government appeared to have acknowledged the contradiction between the Allies' principles and practice.[14] The tension focused on the application
of Article II of the Atlantic Charter, signed in August 1941, to Britain's tropical
colonies. Conceived as a statement to Nazi-occupied Europe, it was quickly embraced by Africa's nationalists.[15] It floated many "dangerous" ideas such as the
right of self-determination, which declared:

> the right of all peoples to choose the form of government under which they will
> live; and they wish to see sovereign rights and self-government restored to those
> who have been forcibly deprived of them.[16]

Churchill's interpretation notwithstanding, it became increasingly more difficult
to argue convincingly that this clause did not apply to the "darker races," and the
Charter gave ideological direction to the growing dissatisfaction with colonial expressions of racial superiority.[17] In Nigeria there was an air of anticipation that
since the country had remained loyal to England and had proven so indispensable
to the war effort, major improvements, both political and economic, were in the
offing. Moreover, working class men expected that they would have the income to
assume new leadership roles as family heads and modernizers. Unlike the Nigerian government, they were planning for a future that would exist.[18] Personal, village, and family improvement became ever more compelling goals as workers
expressed their expectations of a better *future* when hostilities ended. In Enugu,
workers' understandings of these ideological changes were enriched by the discourse of the nationalist movement, which was particularly popular in this, the
"city of clerks." The influence of literate nationalists on Enugu's miners made
Britain's goal of depoliticizing colonial unions more difficult. Moreover, because
miners either lived in the village or, in the case of locals who boarded in the city,
returned there on the weekends, they brought the ideas and debates of the nationalists into Udi Divisional politics. After the war a district officer noted:

> Divisional politics in Udi Division are always strongly influenced by the views
> of the intelligentsia in Enugu as interpreted by the illiterate colliers, who, com-
> ing home at weekends, and particularly at month-ends with cash wages, are able
> to pay the piper and call the social, and to some extent the political tune.[19]

Workers also continued to target racialized systems of industrial authority. The
privileges of superior "colonizer" over inferior "native" caved in under the weight
of propaganda and Britain's dependence on colonial human and material resources.
Racial discrimination became an important signifier for the undemocratic nature
of imperial rule. In the colliery workplace, white bosses were under increased pressure to end the abusive forms of colonial discipline as workers challenged racist
traditions. The more the workers tested the new reality, the more incidents of white

bosses assaulting workers occurred.[20] British bosses found it very difficult to adjust to the changing racial reality, and their outbursts were the last expressions of a dying racial work culture incompatible with the realities of the war.

But much of the war's impact was to levy more burdens on a restive colliery workforce. Real wages were pounded by double-digit inflation, exorbitant rents, and food shortages. Moreover, the state imposed price controls on agro-exports which further encouraged rural farmers to flee to Enugu to join the unemployed and the working class.

Reforms begun before the war were carried forward with increased speed. Urban overcrowding still threatened political stability. Croasdale's evictions and the enforcement of public health standards and occupancy rates continued. But the state secured Colonial Office funding for a major labor estate project that became a platform for interventions into the working class home: home visits by social welfare officers, maternal and child health projects, regulation of the size of the family, schools, clinics, etc. The project reinforced the male breadwinner norm, forbidding women from opening trading tables on the estates, attempted to reduce polygyny, a rural male status signifier, and to stop the phenomena of government employees' households being larger than those of the private sector workers. These estates also separated "responsible" workers from the "riff raff" of the slum yards where many coal miners had to live or board.

Secondly, legislation was developed to prevent labor disputes from interrupting production and escalating into social disorder. In short, this was the application of the elaborate industrial-relations machinery that was gaining currency in England. The Colonial Office knew far too well how disruptive coal miners could be because of the problems with British miners during the war.[21] There was a "correct way" to handle labor disputes and an "incorrect way." The "correct" way was to acknowledge that workers had grievances, but to prevent those grievances from seriously jeopardizing the production process. The key element in this process was collective bargaining; "the great social invention that has institutionalized industrial conflict and ... created a stable means" for its resolution."[22] The problem was whether colonial social relations, a racialized state, and the oppressive workplace could permit the formation and existence of the core institution for its functioning—trade unions—as legitimate social institutions representing employees' interests.

Trades disputes machinery was introduced with mandatory arbitration, conciliation, and a series of industrial relations bodies imported from England.[23] But should that fail, the Nigerian government introduced Essential Works Orders which restricted the right to strike of all workers in industries deemed "essential" for the war effort. Although this law resembled its counterpart in England, the definition of "essential" industry was so liberally applied in Nigeria that it included most of the small working class.[24] Colonial governments had to be coached away from a knee-jerk reaction to quash every protest and taught to use cumbersome consultative procedures and intricate disputes processes to slow down and, it was hoped, moderate most industrial actions. In effect, this legislation governed production by locking in a process that would allow management to intervene in the point of production to increase output while denying workers the ability to exercise a right to strike.

Employers had to admit that despite their generally deprecatory assessments of African workers, they were not interchangeable. There were differential levels of skill, commitment to jobs, and importance to colonial industries. Colliery workers who had made their arguments in grievances before the war would continue do so with increased determination during the war.[25] Now, some even argued for inclusion in the senior staff.[26] The Colonial Office acknowledged that segmentation of the labor force could be the best antidote to those huge, political general strikes that shook the West Indies and Copperbelt in the 1930s. This meant dropping the color bar and admitting some Africans to the senior service. Specialized training programs were initiated to put Africans into the "pipeline" for supervisory positions. Differential privileges and elaborate grading systems were envisioned as a way to encourage men to be productive, diligent workers.

In order to make informed decisions about colonial labor, in 1939 the Colonial Office appointed Major Granville St. J. Orde Browne, a former colonial official in East Africa, as the first colonial labor advisor. He toured the colonies, reporting on labor conditions and making recommendations to the Colonial Labour Advisory Committee. His visit to Enugu in 1940 and again in 1942 led to a round of reforms that targeted the health and working conditions of the workers and their lack of representation.[27] Undergirding most of the reforms was the assumption that British industrial relation systems and trade union structures could be transferred to the colony and would work there just as they had in England. This assumption proved flawed in Enugu. Laws developed for fully proletarianized workers will not have the same impact on stabilized workers who move in and out of the workforce and are *committed* to this pattern. Moreover, the colony was not a *tabula rasa* upon which English organizational and disputes patterns could be imposed with little interference. Enugu's miners had established work patterns, forms of protest, organizational cultures, and leadership styles that shaped their responses to industrial reforms. Any "foreign" institutions or disputes management systems were deflected through the prism of these experiences, often with unpredictable results.

The labor disputes during the war were in reaction to the insidious ways that management and state officials manipulated this new legislation to reassert control over the workplace, the labor market, and the character of urban working class family life. However, these same reforms also gave workers the tools with which to resist the arbitrariness of the boss's power in the workplace, such as preventing lockouts. The new laws constituted a framework for the conduct of labor relations and workers were less subjected to the whims of authoritarian supervisors and management. Moreover, with the implementation of wartime Africanization policies some colliery men received training in these laws, which they subsequently manipulated in their struggle against colliery management. This was the case with the industry's first modern trade union leader, Isiah Okwudili Ojiyi.

In many respects this is the story of two models of "development." One was envisioned by colonial officials and policymakers trying to give an embattled colonial state a new raison d'être but refusing to recognize the essential nature of Nigerian coal miners as industrial men. The other was held by Enugu's working men and women who, caught in the vise of rampant inflation on the one hand and wage freezes on the other, were squeezing their meager incomes to support their own visions of progress and development. Labor unrest during this period was driven by the men's visions for their future, as well as their sense of entitlement to a respectful and decent life. Moreover, most of Enugu's workers, like colonial workers elsewhere, were compelled by a deep-seated sense that the state was treating them unjustly.

## THE SEVERITY OF URBAN LIFE: THE CITY DURING THE WAR

The political importance of Enugu was associated with both the strategic value of Nigerian tin, tropical products, and the opening of the theatre of war in North Africa.[28] Enugu coal was the fuel for the Nigerian Railway, its transporter which brought Nigeria's exports to the coast.

In North Africa Allied fortunes swung back and forth until May 1943, when all Axis troops were expelled from the region. From September 1940 when the Italians began their desert campaign until the coordinated Allied surprise attack at the end of 1942 many West African cities became important staging areas for British, colonial, and American troops. Under the Trans African Air Base Program, American and British airplanes were assembled in and deployed from newly constructed airstrips.[29] Consequently more than 100,000 British and several thousand Americans came through such cities as Lagos, Kano, Ibadan, and Enugu.[30]

The British stationed thousands of troops from the West African Frontier Force (WAFF) in Enugu. The presence of these troops, and the government projects they stimulated, created an economic boom in the city. Villages in the Nkanu area supplied food to the city's ever-growing population. The township report noted that "Enugu ... became a Mecca for those who set out from home to seek their fortune."[31] Men seeking jobs found posts in construction. The population grew from 13,000 in 1930 to nearly 40,000 in 1945.[32]

The colliery workforce tripled during the war from an average of 2,500 in the thirties to 3,600 in 1940, and 6,800 in 1945.[33] Despite the earlier plan to recruit only from adjacent villages to reduce urban settlement and overcrowding, many colliery workers still relocated to the city, if only as weekly boarders. With "rostering," one needed to present oneself at the mine daily to secure a post for the day. The colliery's estates could only accommodate 1,640 workers and an additional 3,100 miners lived in private housing. Three thousand living in the villages walked daily to work, a distance of from two to ten miles.[34] Although the state was preoccupied with African labor productivity, the industry still refused to plan a subsidized transportation system to bring the men to the mines.

But the boom strained scarce housing resources. Until 1943 the government still had not assumed responsibility for providing housing for urban workers and most lived in deplorably sub-standard hovels. The various sectors of the city were sep-

arated by bush and in some areas, particularly Ogui, a settlement on the fringes of
Enugu town and Abakpa Nike, an adjacent village, there was no regulation of housing construction.[35] Many Africans just erected shacks and rented them out to desperate workers. Soon Ogui became known as the residence of the "dregs" of society
with the unemployed and casual workers, prostitutes, and criminals. This was the
type of cross-class social intermingling that Orde Browne warned of. Proximity of
workers to the lumpen proletariat encouraged poor work habits, undermined industrial discipline, and reinforced "criminal" forms of worker protest.[36] This social contact between important sectors of the working class and the "dangerous"
(lumpen proletariat) classes, was a recipe for insurrection that could threaten both
administrative and commercial functions in the city.[37] In 1944 the local authority
gave a snapshot of the city's social composition:

> Meanwhile because of the war and the large RWAFF (Royal West African Fron-
> tier Force) garrison here, contractors, sub-contractors, all their labourers, garri-
> son labourers, loose women and out-of-works, besides legitimate workers, had
> continued to swell the population of the Township where accommodation was
> limited.[38]

The overcrowding and inflation increased government's concern with urban
order.[39] Generalized poor living and working conditions encouraged a solidarity
between "committed" workers and the urban "riff raff," those casual labourers and
lumpen proletariat whose work habits were unpredictable and undisciplined.[40] Such
solidarity could transform industrial disputes into broad popular uprisings. Moreover, the proximity of a large, discontented population to the commercial and administration agencies in Enugu heightened its threatening character. As early as
February of 1939 one official observed a marked change in the level of political
sophistication of the miners:

> I have some fears. The miners are very agitated and under influential leadership.
> We must not assume that they are docile and [un]willing to take risks which might
> result in unemployment for a prolonged period. While a sense of determination
> is not widespread, the fact remains that enough of them are prepared to go on
> strike. It must be recognised that *as miners* [emphasis added] they have devel-
> oped an aggressive turn of mind which some of them are able to convert into po-
> litical protest. The days seemed to have passed when we can assume that fair but
> firm negotiations with the natives will produce honourable results. I see no way
> of avoiding the observation that these men are far from politically naive.[41]

The Local Authority complained of the colliery's lax housing policies. Singling
out two other problem areas, the "informal" camps of Ugwu Alfred and Ugwu
Aaron, as "slums of the worst description," he noted:

> The stench from refuse thrown indiscriminately about is frightful, the alleys be-
> tween the houses are about three feet, and the houses are of mud wattle and mat
> roofs with totally inadequate ventilation even when opened up. If any sanitation

is at present being carried out by the Colliery then it is totally inadequate. Nothing except demolition will improve the space between the houses and the ventilation of the houses themselves.[42]

Like the households of other government workers, colliery employees' homes had higher occupancy rates than those of workers in private employment. Over 63 percent of government quarters were overcrowded compared to 41 percent for non-government quarters.[43] This disparity reflected the increased familial responsibilities of men whose wage stability in government employment attracted the attention of their extended families. With their meager but regular wages, government employees were under considerable pressure to accommodate relatives seeking jobs in Enugu.

Overcrowding was a threat to health, as the men had noted in their protests of 1937/38. Their warning proved prescient and in June/July 1943, a serious outbreak of cerebro-spinal meningitis originated in Abakpa Nike, and spread to other parts of the township followed several months later by a smallpox epidemic that spread throughout the city.[44] Ironically, the state was less aggressive on public health than the miners themselves. Coal employees in Agbaja villages included health concerns in their development patterns in their villages. Industrially, their preoccupa-

**Photo 6.1** Entrance to Ugwu Alfred, July 1975 (Carolyn Brown)

tion with these issues was evident in their requests for medical care and accident prevention training among the demands raised during many disputes.[45] A man's concern with the provision of good health for his family was also an indicator of "modernity" and masculine responsibility.[46] The village of Ngwo, the primary area of mine recruitment, built and maintained its own maternity home, employed a midwife, and contracted with the colliery to have a doctor and nurse visit periodically.[47]

As a regional government center, Enugu attracted young male clerks whose frustrations with the pace of political change fueled nationalist politics, transforming Enugu into an exciting center of nationalist agitation. An informant described this group:

> A "new middle class" of government employees and men of initiative in the professional, business, and service fields, drawn from all parts of the region, settled in the burgeoning city.[48]

With incomes higher than the working class, they financed political movements and were avid patrons of radical nationalist press. The *West African Pilot*, the flagship of Dr. Nnamdi Azikiwe's newspaper empire, avidly covered colliery affairs, seizing every opportunity to attribute to this state industry the abuses of the imperial order. These young men and women honed their organizational skills in the urban improvement associations demonstrating to the city's railway workers and coal miners[49] strategies that would prove useful in organizing government protest. Government clerks were as outraged, as were their predecessors in the First World War, with the disparity between their wages and conditions of service and that of

**Photo 6.2** Ugwu Alfred: Charles Ugoji, Gabriel Mbalemlu, Michael Nwakuache, and Clement Egbogimba, 5 July 1975 (Carolyn Brown)

their white coworkers. They, like the workers, found it difficult to support their families in a style to which they felt entitled. Moreover, it was critically important for their status that they be able to consume those products that symbolized "civilization" and status. Their expenses reflected their heavy dependence on imported goods, and the importance of the social distance that it reflected between themselves and the urban working class. Overcrowded "native" locations pushed them too close to these "lower" classes forcing them to live below their perceived "station" in life.

Urban associations also put workers in contact with Nigerian businessmen who were hurt by the new forms of monopoly control the expatriate firms held on internal trade, which excluded them from government bulk purchasing agreements administered by these firms. It was no coincidence that Nigeria's first nationalist party, the National Council of Nigeria and the Cameroons (NCNC), was formed from a coalition of these groups.

## TOWARD A COLONIAL LABOR POLICY: ORDE BROWNE IN ENUGU, 1940 AND 1942

In February 1940, Major Orde Browne investigated labor conditions in Britain's four West African colonies—Nigeria, Sierra Leone, Gambia, and Ghana. The visit aimed to assist governments in preventing labor disturbances that would jeopardize Sierra Leone's vital port of Freetown, Ghana's bauxite, gold mines, and port city, and Nigeria's ports, tin, and coal mines. Since miners, railway, and dock workers were crucial groups in the region with long traditions of disruptive militance, Orde Browne included the colliery among the "trouble spots" to visit in 1940. While he considered the colliery to be "a great asset to the country," he noted with considerable understatement that conditions "cannot be considered satisfactory." The workforce remained disgruntled because conditions that led to the 1937 strike had not changed, and in some cases had worsened. Orde Browne identified as the major problems an "acute shortage of housing," and low wages made worse by the "rostering" or sharing work system.[50]

As a military man, Orde Browne was particularly concerned that urban and industrial disorder not interfere with the region's wartime functions. He concentrated on those areas of major employment—mines, railway, docks, and plantations. His preoccupations were with "detribalization," labor migration, diet, housing, wages, education, and medical care.[51] In addition to recommendations for improvements in these areas, he also suggested appointing administrative personnel to allow the supervision of workers in the jobs and communities.

To his credit Orde Browne recognized that many broad social problems, such as urban overcrowding, were actually labor problems arising from insufficient wages, and he made suggestions for improving the social conditions under which workers lived.[52] The general thrust of Orde Browne's recommendations was the social and not industrial experiences of labor. Most of his suggestions concentrated on housing which he linked to family policy and social order. He noted with astonishment that most colliery housing was single-sex dwellings that violated ILO standards and discouraged family life.[53] He believed that an "industrial man" headed a nuclear family so employers would find that investments in family life produced diligent and contented workers. He recommended additional construction near the mines of adequate bathing, washing, and latrine facilities, and argued strongly against the colliery's outmoded "range" style quarters with six to ten $12' \times 10'$ adjoining rooms which also facilitated the spread of infectious diseases.

However, Orde Browne had remarkably little to say about improving the *conditions under which Africans worked*. He commented, here and there, on how horrible these conditions were but did not offer any guidelines to management or the state, save improving wages, housing, nutrition, and family life. It was apparently easier for him to comprehend miners as a social category than as an industrial one. His comments after visiting the worksite suggest the extent to which his own reformist ideas were imprisoned by his racialized assumptions about African workers:

> Working conditions on the mine are also very trying; I went as far as the coal-face and watched the men at work under conditions of damp heat, cramped space, poor ventilation and very little light. I could not help feeling surprised that men could be induced to work regularly under such conditions. Small wonder therefore that they are discontented. Indeed, I doubt *if anyone but Africans* would have been as patient as they have been [emphasis mine].[54]

Although the men's productivity was deeply compromised by these conditions, Orde Browne ignored the specific working conditions and located the cause in indigenous culture—the deficient nutritional habits of the Igbo. Noting that the diet was extremely starchy, he was apparently convinced their lack of stamina came from protein deficiency, rather than harsh underground conditions.[55] Correctly anticipating opposition from the men, he suggested a gradual introduction of food rations, beginning with cocoa and saline solutions, and culminating in a hot stew.[56]

While recognizing that problems endemic to the railway, the seasonality of its supply of rolling stock, created objective conditions for an unstable pattern of labor deployment, Orde Browne deplored "rostering," and recommended gradual dismissals coinciding with the planting season, accompanied by a repatriation bonus. He also cautioned against retrenchments at short notice, suggesting improved mine site storage facilities to bridge the periods when railway bottlenecks prevented removal.[57]

He was also concerned about the political transformation of Nigeria, most especially, the accommodation of the African elite. After his second visit to Enugu, Orde Browne emphasized, in his discussions at the Colonial Office, the importance of a development policy that included the "plantation owner, mining prospector, shopkeeper, factory manager, skilled mechanic." He noted that:

> The development of this class would go far to give the African the feeling that he owned his country and exploited its resources, instead of seeing these constantly in the hands of the white man.[58]

Orde Browne was attuned to the political attention race was getting throughout Nigeria. His instincts were quite correct. Nigeria's first nationalist party, in fact, emerged as a coalition of the urban improvement unions controlled by this elite social strata. But the biggest challenges during the war would come from Nigeria's organized working class—the trade unions in Lagos.

The political environment of change and reform sweeping Nigerian society emboldened colliery men to push for rights they felt entitled to as working men with families. Their initiatives in utilizing income, forming associations, and tapping into a generalized nationalist discourse of the period encouraged the industrial turbulence of the war.

## THE NATIONAL TRADE UNION STRUGGLE, 1939–1943: THE COST-OF-LIVING AGITATION IN LAGOS

Between 1941 and 1943 the Nigerian economy registered the full consequences of the wartime restrictions on the economy. The colonial government intervened into the economy in unprecedented ways. The war required a level of central planning largely absent in the earlier years. The Colonial Office established a number of coordinating bodies in West Africa to facilitate the centralization of policies concerning the economy in general as well as labor. For the first time the Colonial Office appointed a Cabinet-ranked Resident Minister for West Africa with full authority to make decisions without consulting Whitehall.[59] He headed a West African War Council in which the various governors and military officials coordinated economic policy over the region. Labor policy was coordinated through a series of West African Labour Conferences in which policy was discussed, production targets set, and strategies for containing working class unrest developed. Similar efforts were initiated within the colonies themselves. Wage-fixing boards were founded in Onitsha Province as were similar urban initiatives in Enugu. Concern with the escalating prices of essential goods led the state to experiment with controlled market schemes, which were largely ineffective and only succeeded in mobilizing marketing women against the state.[60]

Given these inflationary pressures, the Colonial Office looked to collective bargaining as the favored method for forcing unrest into predictable and less disruptive forms of collective action. Although colonial trade unions were an important precondition for this process, this *was* war and these *were* African workers. These two factors—the urgency of war and the "difference" of African workers—would influence the paramaters that would be drawn around "legitimate" collective action, the powers trade unionists would be allowed to exercise, and the forms of protest tolerated by the state.

By 1939 the Colonial Office had pushed governments to allow unions to operate as "the surest means of securing industrial stability and the removal of extremist tendencies."[61] As Colonial Secretary Ormsby-Gore noted, not allowing unions to develop would "encourage the formation of illegal organizations which may easily develop into 'secret societies' and extend their operations into the political field."[62] But colonial unions did not have the full rights of metropolitan unions. They had to be registered, which was granted at the discretion of the government, follow a six-months' waiting period, and submit their books to a close monitoring of finances.[63] After an initial period of distrust for what were, after all, state-introduced institutions, workers tried to use them as vehicles of mobilization and came up against managerial restrictions.

There was no consensus among expatriate department heads and colonial officials over the value of trade unions as vehicles to contain worker militance. At the colliery management smarted under the conflict in the Underground Representative Council and was loath to authorize yet another worker-chosen consultative body. Even though the new unions were burdened by bureaucratic restrictions, management was not convinced that they would be useful in securing the industrial peace necessary to meet war demands. But under pressure of war, management could utilize all of these restrictions to circumscribe trade union leaders and, when these failed, could withdraw recognition of the union. Thus, in its first experience with government-imposed unions, the workers' movement would be subjected to the full weight of repressive legislation.

Nigeria legalized trade unions in 1939, extending the restrictions suggested by the Colonial Office of compulsory registration and the six-month waiting period. Throughout Nigeria, workers responded rapidly to the opportunity to form unions. Forty-one unions representing more than 17,000 workers were registered in 1939 and 1940.[64] But between 1941 and 1943 the state chipped away at the rights of these unions through a series of wartime legislation covering "essential industries," a rather broad category which, in an economy so dominated by the state, covered the majority of Nigeria's workers. Soon thereafter, in 1942, the Nigerian General Defense Regulation prohibited strikes and lockouts,[65] mandated disputes procedures that included binding arbitration, waiting periods, and prohibitions of the right to strike.[66]

The coal miners' struggles during the war occurred in a national context of escalating conflict between Nigerian workers, employers, and the state. Two major worker mobilizations occurred, one in 1941 and another in 1943. In July 1941 the Railway Workers' Union took a leading role in forming a federation of government workers, the African Civil Servants and Technical Workers Union (ACSTWU) in Lagos. Following its registration in July 1940, the Railway Workers' Union, under the leadership of Michael Imoudu, and the African Locomotive Drivers' Union successfully waged a struggle against the replacement of the daily-wage system by an hourly system of pay.[67]

The transformation of the pay scale, which divided the workers into established staff and laborer, followed the Colonial Office strategy to reduce worker solidarity by segmenting the workforce into distinct sectors with different pay scales, amenities, and conditions of work. The policy aimed to co-opt skilled and semi-skilled workers and to transform them "into differentiated, segmented workforces organized along the principles of British-style trade unions."[68] This revision of the pay structure became the basis for generalized reforms for government workers issued in a circular of 6 October 1941.

In late 1941 the Colonial Office's new strategies received their first test when the ACSTWU agitated for a cost-of-living increase, which it considered a "war bonus." The Colonial Office response was to ignore inflation, which had steadily spiraled from 1935, and argue that any hardship was only temporary as it was caused by war conditions. It therefore held base wages constant and added various allowances. Special attention was given to the lowest paid workers. The standard pattern of response was clear: a state-appointed commission that used new social science research techniques (especially the household survey) to determine living costs and indices to locate these costs relative to "normal" 1939 prices. By selecting 1939 as the base year the Colonial Office underestimated the decline in real wages which began in the mid-thirties.[69] Finally, some type of bonus would be granted.

In response, the government appointed a Commission of Inquiry headed by A.F.B. Bridges, formerly Resident, Onitsha Province. The composition of the commission was unusually representative for a state-appointed body. The majority of its members were Nigerians with a significant number representing trade unions, including an official of the ACSTWU. There were also several women and representatives from the major government departments concerned with social welfare. The Commission deliberated for some eight months, but in December 1941, recognizing the urgent nature of the crisis, asked the government to make an interim award of a 3d (pence) per day pay to all government employees on annual wage or salary of less than £36 (pounds). The Commission's investigation found that there had been a 150 percent increase in the prices of selected, domestically produced food items in Lagos from 1939 to 1942.[70]

While protests and negotiations were going on in Lagos, the colliery workers were distracted by leadership struggles following the collapse of the Representative Councils. In 1940, the Udi District Report noted that the prices of selected food items in Enugu showed a 30–50 percent increase over those in 1938.[71] They did receive some wage adjustments from national negotiations. Under the Bridges Award, Enugu was grouped with the northern cities of Jos and Kaduna and received a 9d increment. All daily-paid workers received a 3d per day increment provided that the increase did not place them over 7/6d per month. The cost-of-living allowance (COLA) increase was 100 percent for those on the 5d daily rate and 50 percent for all other daily-paid workers making from 5d to 1s 6 1/2p. Those on monthly pay schedules of 15s to £2 and on an annual schedule of £48 received a 50 percent increase. Colliery workers received a further increase in April 1942, when the 1938 Evans Award was revised with a 1d increase to most grades of daily-paid labor and a 1d increase in the daily-rate of hewers. Their piece rate for tubs was raised to 6d in *development* and 3 1/2d for *robbery*.[72]

In granting these concessions, local authorities reflected the concerns of the "men on the spot" who had to confront the accumulating rage of workers in pivotal industries who felt that they deserved far better wages. This concession and the commitment to future review, taken without consultation with the Colonial Office or the West African War Council, established to coordinate labor policy, earned Governor Bourdillon a pointed reprimand by the Colonial Office which "questioned the competence of sectors of his administration."[73] The Colonial Office tried to formulate and implement economic strategies on a regional basis and encouraged all the West African governors to follow the same policy. However, the particularities of worker militance in Nigeria led Governor Bourdillon to break ranks and grant a wage increase retroactive to October 1941 and commit his government to periodic cost-of-living reviews.[74] The pattern was set for future negotiation and worker agitation.

In May 1942 the government gave another increase that highlighted the patently discriminatory nature of economic policies. Governor Bourdillon relieved the hardship of his European employees by giving "separation allowances" to those expatriate men whose wives were not in Nigeria, followed in November 1943 by additional increments for other dependents.[75] The award was a recognition that the war's economic pressures undermined a man's role as provider. Blatantly discriminatory, the award supported the responsibilities of white men to their families, while leaving African working men barely able to meet their individual, let alone family, obligations. Incredulously in October 1942, Governor Bourdillon naively reported to the West African War Council that he doubted that these increases would incite "the more highly paid African grades who did not receive this allowance at present."[76] He was wrong.

## ENUGU'S MINERS "FEEL" THE WAR: ECONOMIC CRISES AND THE CONDITIONS FOR SOLIDARITY

Although the demand for coal would increase during the war, initially labor requirements were not significantly higher. The state decided to use this period to establish rational labor practices in preparation for anticipated increased demand. When hostilities began, Enugu's miners were in a particularly vulnerable position. Management had refused to recognize their only organization, the Underground Representative Council, and although the Council had succeeded in forcing the Director of Transport to eliminate the interpreters' post many of these same people had simply moved to other positions of authority. Additionally, the Staff Welfare Officer evicted thousands of people from the labor camps and upgraded the housing for the families of the core workers.

Croasdale's retrenchments in 1939 and the introduction of "rostering" made colliery employment less reliable and secure. Moreover, workers found it difficult to keep their name on the employment lists for future jobs unless they bribed village leaders.[77] Management extended "rostering" to all mines to accommodate the men's erratic work habits to the variations in the railway's ability to transport the coal, exacerbated by the frequent shortages of railway rolling stock during the war.

Unlike the period before rostering, the men now had less choice over the days that they would present themselves for work. This substantially reduced the local men's ability to integrate mining with bouts of farming. Additionally, rostering had a drastic impact on income. Optimally hewers should have earned 17s 6d per week based on a rate of from 2s 11d to 3s 6d per shift. Other underground workers should have made from 1s to 1s 4d per shift, and surface workers from 1s to 1s 5d. However, with "rostering" most men worked only three days a week, earning barely half. With food averaging between 3d and 4d per day and rent from 4s to 10s per month, most workers could barely survive.[78]

Moreover, because of corruption a man couldn't even be sure that daily selection of workers was fair. Timekeepers tampered with the lists, even after they were posted in glass cases, and "native" bosses still replaced those whose names were on the roster with workers from their villages who, most often, had paid them bribes.

Local men thrown out of work who returned to farming could not benefit from wartime price increases of primary products because bulk purchasing agreements held down the prices of their palm products to subsidize metropolitan production. The Association of West African Merchants, an organization of the major expatriate commercial firms in West Africa, formed a group in 1937 to set prices and divide markets among themselves. As an entity they totally controlled all West African trade during the war because they contracted with the state to process all bulk purchasing agreements of commodities allegedly held by marketing boards.[79]

As farmers, Enugu miners were cheated out of the just prices that their goods could get on the world market. As workers, they were hurt by the price-gouging in consumer goods. And African merchants, squeezed between their customers' low wages and the exorbitant wholesale prices charged by the firms, struggled to keep afloat. As the cost of living escalated with the prices of imports controlled by these firms, they became politically vulnerable to generalized African critiques of the abuses of colonialism. Again, economic policy set the conditions for a political alliance that could challenge colonialism.

Workers, farmers, African merchants, and market women also suffered from food shortages, import restrictions designed to conserve gold and dollar resources and the use of British goods to earn foreign exchange. Furthermore, these policies were experienced against the backdrop of heightened expectations that life would improve, especially after the depression. But the net result of these policies was a deepening plunge into poverty. The three prongs of British fiscal policy—price regulation of colonial exports, reductions of metropolitan and foreign imports to the colonies, and the accumulation of sterling and dollar reserves—worsened the economic conditions of Enugu's workers before they could recover from the depression.[80]

The severity of economic conditions and the importance of colonial resources for the war required that colonial labor policy be more systematic and professional, and local administrators, usually a conservative force, could not be trusted to avoid provoking industrial conflict. Nigeria moved rather rapidly to establish labor administrators. In 1939 and 1940, C.H. Croasdale and W.G. Wormal were appointed labor inspectors. Subsequently, Wormal became Inspector of Labour for the colliery, and P.H. Cook of the BTUC, seconded to the Labor Department, became Industrial Relations Officer. Because of his experience, Cook was given the responsibility of supervising the Staff Welfare Officer's work, advising the manager on labor organization, and educating the colliery workers on the principles of "responsible" trade unionism.[81] Finally, in October 1942 the Labour Department was established and by the end of 1943 had grown to include over twenty officers.[82]

## CONSTRUCTING THE FOUNDATIONS OF "REFORMED" COLONIAL INDUSTRIAL RELATIONS: THE TROUBLED GENESIS OF TRADE UNIONS

> When maltreatment became so much we started going into the bush to have meetings. It was during this meetings that we discussed about go-slow and strike. It was then that we were put into light and registered our union. Before we were not allowed to talk. Because the whites did not want us to discuss together. When they met us together discussing they would call in a police to arrest us. Now that we registered and discussed about go-slow and strikes the Government started hearing our voices. Then whites agreed to talk with us. Then all African workers were titled boy e.g. timber man was called timber boy, peak called peak boy, tub man called tub boy everything, boy boy. Only the Europeans were called overman and foreman.[83]

Orde Browne had disparaged the formation of colliery unions, arguing that the men were "mainly of a primitive and uneducated type, and the formation of any kind of trade union is for the time being quite beyond their powers."[84] Unions did not fit into his vision of industrial paternalism, despite the long history of worker-management consultation and the relatively effective role played by *Nzuko* in organizing earlier forms of protest. While most of Orde Browne's suggestions became the blueprint for the colliery's social welfare reforms, the industry rejected his advice and followed the national trend which encouraged trade unions. The experiences of the colliery's first unions, established in 1940, illustrated the hostile context in which African workers organized. The unions were banned the very first time they were used in a major dispute.

In the early period of union organization management and state officials used the new labor legislation to restrict effective union activity. Although they held on to old assumptions about the "primitive" African workers it was management, and not the underground workers, who pushed to form the first unions. Having disbanded the Underground Representative Council, the manager responded to pressure from the Colonial Office by selecting trusted workers from the survey department, several former interpreters or supervisors, to establish the Enugu Workers Trade Union (EWTU) to represent underground workers.[85] He was ill-disposed to permit effective African trade unions after his bruising encounters with the Underground Representative Council, whom he felt received far too much attention from the central government.

In March 1941 the government issued a certificate of union recognition to the EWTU, but several members of the Surface Workers Representative Council seized the document from the post office and held it for several weeks before detection. When the culprits, Eze Ozogwu and Jacob Aniogbo, both "boss boys," were found and subsequently punished by the management, the surface workers threatened a strike. Under management encouragement the clerical leadership of this council formed another union, the Enugu Surface Improvement Union (ESIU), and secured recognition in November 1941.[86] Neither union enjoyed the support of the *Nzuko*, and the workers were resistant to participation.

The leaders of both unions regarded the laborers with contempt. The clerks felt that as literates and leaders in the urban improvement associations, they should run the industry's organizations as well, and they did in fact run the surface union. The Agbaja "boss boys" assumed that they had acquired the right to lead the underground union as a reward for their long-term loyalty to management. Now, both resolved to seize command of these new government-sponsored organizations and not be eclipsed as they were with the Representative Councils. The underground workers watched with suspicion as management tried to bring in new organizations to replace the militant councils. One respondent noted:

> Management tried to bring unions into the Colliery to replace councils. The men refused it completely. They felt that trade unions were government's organizations. Not for workers. Because the ordinance allowed five persons to form a union, Okpokwu and Ude could bring as many people from their areas as they wanted to form the union.[87]

The improvements in living conditions and labor reforms at Enugu were unmediated by the exigencies of private capital. They came into operation around an industrial dispute that began in 1943, a time of major significance at the national and industrial levels. By 1943 the full weight of imperial wartime economic policies was unleashed on colonial workers and they were pushed even further into poverty. In Lagos the working class mobilized against 150 percent inflation. In Enugu the trade unionists likewise pushed for relief. This year was also crucial for the industry because the colliery was called upon to compensate for the crisis in the British coal fields where worker protests, manpower shortages, and absenteeism exacerbated fuel shortages. Management made several administrative decisions that, while they enabled the industry to respond quickly to this demand, ultimately reduced output. And finally, this was the year when Isaiah Ojiyi became General Secretary of the new Colliery Workers Union (CWU), and launched the colliery workers into Nigerian labor history.

Despite the bickering between the leadership of the two unions, the complexity of the evolving labor legislation and the continued decline in real wages encouraged underground workers to become involved in the unions.[88] Their early experiences were discouraging and they were not at all convinced that these new government-sponsored institutions were worthy of their involvement. On several occasions former interpreters, now in union leadership positions, manipulated the men at one mine into breaking a strike by falsely claiming that workers in another mine had returned to work.[89]

As the war progressed the mines' output reached unprecedented levels, climbing from 330,000 tons in 1940 to over 500,000 in 1943/44 after doubling the workforce to nearly 7,000.[90] On 1 April 1943, the colliery began a second shift following recruitment of a thousand new miners through the Native Court clerks and Clan Councilors, exposing workers to further corruption and bribes. By the summer of 1943, the men, like their counterparts in Lagos, had grown impatient with management's refusal to raise wages and improve living conditions. They were overworked, burdened by inflation, and restricted by Nigerian Defense Regulations from exercising their right to strike. The government, having just granted a COLA award, was unable to control the spiraling of food prices, and turned to anti-inflationary policies that while used successfully in England, further impoverished the population in Nigeria. Fearing that higher wages would lead to spiraling prices the government lowered the minimum annual salary for income tax from £24 to £18 allegedly to pull money out of circulation. The national trade union movement became restive. In June 1943, the ACSTWU in Lagos petitioned the government to make a comprehensive review of salaries, wages, and other conditions of service.[91]

The CWU submitted petitions to the acting Chief Commissioner of the Eastern Provinces, restating many of the demands raised in 1938 but this time they compared their situation with other coal miners in the United States and England. Now the grievances included, for the first time, a demand for an underground allowance, recently granted to European supervisors but denied to African supervisors. The men became more conscious of the colliery's discriminatory practices when they heard a "wireless" report that the same had been granted to American miners.[92] The initial demand for a 10 (shillings) per day underground allowance was subsequently reduced to 6d. The union also requested a war bonus of 1/6d for all daily-paid workers and increased allowances of 6d per tub for *robbery* and 1 (shilling) for *development*. Other demands were for annual increments on basic wages and free boots for each underground miner.[93] Rebutting the union, the manager returned the petition for further clarification, dismissing it as "incomprehensible." But the miners refused further clarification and from August 13–16, the same controversial Augustine Ude, the president, called out the CWU on strike, apparently without informing other officers or attempting to coordinate the action with the leadership of the CSIU. The remaining CWU officers subsequently disassociated themselves from the action and resigned in protest.

The Manager used the Nigerian Defense Regulations, the new legislation prohibiting strikes in essential industries, and served notice that all strikers would be prosecuted as of August 18. Two days before that deadline he began recruiting new workers. By August 19, most workers had returned to the mine and production proceeded at a normal pace. One hundred new workers, hired during the strike, were retained to fulfill the demand for increased output. The government and management thought the issue was settled.[94]

In Lagos, O.A.G. Grantham in the Nigerian Secretariat deprecated the seriousness of the strike by attributing the unrest to the peculiar cultural characteristics of

Igbo workers rather than the normal response of industrial workers feeling the impact of wartime inflation. Articulating a racialist perspective of the man-on-the-spot who *knew* his "natives," Grantham assured the Colonial Secretary that the Igbo workers

> attempt to see whether Government could be coerced into granting unwarranted concessions. It is desirable to emphasize, in connection with the Colliery, that the majority of the employees [were] drawn from primitive communities, and that past events have repeatedly shown that their *temperament is unstable* and that their *reactions are often unpredictable*. They have a natural predilection for demonstrations, and their *excitable character* renders them ready tools for astute leaders who may believe that show of force will influence Government. The mass organisation of bluff on a large scale amongst the Ibos is not necessarily so serious a phenomenon as it would be in other countries and amongst other people [emphasis mine].[95]

Thus, just beneath the discursive facade which described Africans as "industrial men" lurked the essential "tribesman," shrouded in irresponsible backwardness. When all other explanations failed, this was just the type of racist analysis that colonial field officers often directed to Whitehall. The strike was "settled" and a record quarterly output of 138,314 tons ensued, but the issues that generated the discontent were left simmering beneath the surface. The workers' movement was still too weak from its recent internecine conflict to unite against the management and the state.

The responses of the state to wartime colliery protests clearly indicated that this was an entirely different context for industrial negotiation. Disputes management machinery was being put into place, labor personnel were more closely monitoring workers on the job and at home, and the state no longer trusted local managers to resolve colliery problems. Nonetheless, the workers still understood their power over the industry, although they were somewhat disoriented by the Nigerian Defense Regulations and the chaotic management-sponsored unions. The severity of the economic conditions forced them to recognize that they needed to engage some of the state's institutions and procedures. Their belief that their 1937 grievances were largely unmet fostered a simmering outrage, made all the more ironic by the sacrifices they were making to support Britain in the war. The war encouraged a sense of their importance, which was especially acute with the hewers. They were restive, and to some extent outmaneuvered by the state, but as their grievances accumulated, an industrial crisis was inevitable. The context for this crisis arose in 1943, when the colliery was asked to increase production to compensate for workers' restriction of output in the British coal industry.

## THE EMERGENCE OF A NEW LEADER: ISAIAH OJIYI AND THE UNDERGROUND WORKERS

By 1943 the miners' union, CWU, was in disarray, at a time when the workers were squeezed by inflation. They found a leader from among those Africans being prepared to "Nigerianize" the industry. Among the contradictions unleashed by the Colonial Office labor reforms was the ascent of the industry's first modern trade union leader, a product of their programs to train Africans to move through the color bar. The Nigerian state and the Colonial Office reconceptualized colonial labor within an existing context of improved social welfare, increased worker productivity, and controlled systems of representation. The elaborate legislative structure that bureaucratized worker protest encouraged workers to seek out their own "interpreters" of this administrative maze. Most often these "interpreters" were charismatic, contemptuous of white bosses, relishing a role in leading the "masses," sufficiently educated to comprehend and simplify the labor legislation, and usually very much attracted to the nationalist movement. Nigeria had many such leaders—Michael Imoudu of the Railway Workers Union, Nduka Eze, and A.A. Adio-Moses of the Amalgamated Union of United Africa Company (UAC) African Workers (UNAMAG), to name a few.[96] The colliery produced its own leader— Isaiah Okwudili Ojiyi.

Ojiyi was a former schoolteacher from Amawbia, Awka, near Onitsha. He began at the colliery in July 1938 as a temporary clerk and was quickly recruited for a pilot program for underground "mine improvers," and later for Junior Technical Staff, both supervisory positions to integrate Africans into the established staff. Ojiyi entered into union politics just as the workers' movement had become demoralized by the resignation of the officials of the two unions.[97] He responded to a request by some underground workers to assist them with establishing a new union.[98]

Ojiyi made a bid for leadership in the context of the union crisis in 1943. As a "foreigner," from Amawbia, he rejected clan-based policies and targeted the Agbaja hewers and other underground workers as his constituency. Unlike many of the other African staff who saw their posts as opportunities for personal advancement, he used his training in Nigerian labor law to develop demands that fully exploited the legal parameters set forth by the state. His contempt for the racial culture of the mines and his arrogance toward his European superiors made him a natural hero of the workers and a *bête noire* of European bosses. One informant recalled:

> This age is also known as the turkey getting age because without being able to give present of turkey and possibly money and pay inhuman adoration to the European Over manager one cannot aspire to have a penny increase on his salary.[99]

While the CSIU floundered in disarray, Ojiyi strengthened the CWU by solidifying his base among the underground laborers. By the end of 1943, he had pulled the organization away from Augustine Ude and had become General Secretary of the Colliery Workers Union.

Unlike the educated clerks, he did not look down on the miners and other laborers, but relished his role as their leader. He was a populist, quite similar to many trade union leaders of the period, men whom the Colonial Office viewed with suspicion. Whitehall concluded that the major problem in West Africa's labor relations was irresponsible, inexperienced, and "politically minded" leaders.[100] To the men Ojiyi had *Ikenga*, a willingness to confront an unjust adversary even at personal risk, a stubbornness in attacking a problem, and a strength to take a stand for what was morally good.[101] As he struggled against his detractors from within the CSIU as well as within his own union, he deliberately challenged the types of racial authoritarianism exercised by white underground staff.

While Ojiyi was popular and loved by the men, he was incorrigible, egotistical, and arrogant. He practiced many aspects of Igbo leadership. For example, he used gifts of snuff when he visited the mine to share his income with his members.[102] He also cultivated a speaking style that excited his listeners among the labor force. Politically, he had nationalist sympathies and enjoyed challenging European bosses who were accustomed to near total power over their workers. To European staff the erosion of their privileges to physically and verbally abuse Black workers was viewed as the loss of work discipline and they complained to management that "their boys" were exhibiting a new, and dangerously recalcitrant attitude. Ojiyi typified these intolerable forms of "cheeky" behavior which he appeared to have enjoyed. However, he became a target of management retribution himself.

In his confrontations with the state and the colliery management he often startled them with his knowledge of pertinent trade union ordinances and his awareness of the gains of the national trade union movement. Further, like a true nationalist rebelling against the racial practices of colonial society, he failed to observe the protocol of colonial deference to his European superiors both in the industry and in the state at large. This made him a lightning rod for persecution by European bosses angry that the state was intruding into the workplace and restricting the forms of discipline and subordination formerly customary in the colonial workplace.[103] By 1943 management complaints of his behavior were so vociferous that they drew the attention of the Chief Secretary.[104] But attempts to fire him for insubordination were blocked by the new legislation concerning trades disputes. When the manager tried to serve notice Ojiyi cited the new labor regulations to argue that he needed three months' written notification and an opportunity to answer the charges before any dismissal.[105] He persisted in believing, quite correctly, that he was being persecuted because of his union activities and for vigorously representing the union's case. He noted in a letter to the manager:

> I agree that, at trade dispute interviews held between the Manager and the Unions, I always possess strictness in my discussions, and that is a matter of duty, and should not be reckoned as evidence of unruliness and conduct to the Manager.[106]

Ojiyi's political inclinations led him to frame the workers' struggle in the discourse of radical nationalism. As a union leader, he articulated industrial grievances within the context of colonial exploitation. He saw the relationship between the workers' political status as colonial "subjects" and the intolerable conditions in which they worked and lived. These connections were even more obvious for workers in a state enterprise such as the colliery. Ojiyi clarified the political contradictions in his presentation of the colliery workers' demands. For example he used allegations of racial discrimination to link the workers' industrial struggles with the general nationalist campaign against colonial racism. A key component of his ideology was the expectation that those in authority—the state—had a responsibility for the social development of their employees. These themes of racial discrimination and state responsibilities were echoed throughout the nationalist movement.

## RESISTANCE TO RACIAL DISCRIMINATION AMONGST BROAD SECTORS OF THE POPULATION

Racial conflicts between British "bosses" and the workers were pushed to the surface. The colonial labor process, with its racial forms of control, was unsustainable now that the political apparatus was being reshaped to accommodate independence.[107] Officially, the state could not protect what white bosses did to "native" workers in the dark recesses of the mines. The frequent resort to corporal punishment and the dehumanizing racial discourse in the mines became indefensible. The whole political apparatus that supported the colonial labor process was being chipped away as old conventions were being discarded and replaced with "new" systems of industrial control. The colliery's European staff were not convinced that the new systems could work but they were fighting a losing battle to retain the old.

Charges of racial discrimination filtered into public discourse and colliery racial tensions increased as bosses tried futilely to preserve the colonial labor process. Workers reported incidents to the press, throwing into public view abuses that were formerly hidden in the mines, protected by "white skin" privilege. Through the nationalist press, they reached a receptive audience among the clerical workers so dissatisfied with the direction and pace of political change. Most incidents of assaults occurred when Africans refused to be subservient. Such was the case with Ojiyi.

Later, in August 1945, Ojiyi had the opportunity to present himself as a "hero" in the eyes of those workers who had felt the brunt of violent discipline in the mines. In this instance, as was often the case, the British supervisor was a man from the British working class probably attracted to colonial service by opportunities to earn more money and live better than at home. The underground manager, T. Yates, claimed that Ojiyi refused to follow his instructions and then laughed at him. This was more than Yates could take and he slapped Ojiyi. He gave this account of the incident in the grammar of an undereducated English worker who enjoyed a privileged status in the colonies:[108]

> Then Isiah started to laugh so I told him that it was not a laughing matter, he persisted on laughing so I warned him a second time that he need not laugh about it. He still laughed so I slapped him across the mouth with the back of my hand. He laughed again so I slapped him again, then he seemed to go mad at the thought that he had been struck and went and called two hewers to witness the fact that I had severely flogged him when all the time the only witness was my cloth boy.[109]

Ojiyi insisted that the assault was not due to insubordination but because management was trying to "level false accusations on me" to prevent his receiving his annual salary increment. He also claimed that Yates had previously tried to influence him to vote in the May election for the manager's representative committee to replace the union.[110] In a letter to the manager Ojiyi claimed:

> I was beaten to distraction this year [by] the Overman, Yates. Previous to the beating incident, Mr. Yates advised me to take part in the voting of the people who would constitute the Manager's New Organization. In my reply, I told him that that would be impossible as far as I remained a Secretary in the Union.[111]

This was just the incident to permit Ojiyi to demonstrate his militant posture as a leader. Ojiyi rejected government advice to settle the issue privately and insisted on taking the case to the magistrate, where he was awarded a fine.[112] The trial made him a hero and reinforced his image as a brave leader, confronting historic practices that had terrorized underground workers since the industry opened. But his personnel file indicates that official harassment never stopped and European staff were ever looking for any opportunity to persecute him.

## INDUSTRIAL PATERNALISM AND STRUGGLES OVER SOCIAL REPRODUCTION: THE COLLIERY VENTURES INTO THE AFRICAN HOME

In addition to the rise of Ojiyi, the increased demands for coal, and the spiraling cost of inflation, 1943 was also the year when the Nigerian government finally made strides toward a coherent housing policy. Furthermore, with unions being formed, the adoption of Major Orde Browne's recommendations, and the welfare reforms suggested by the Bridges Committee the government came to use the colliery as a model site to test industrial reform. For example, the Social Welfare Officer developed programs to reduce the accident rate,[113] giving special attention to provision of boots, safety helmets, and locally made leg protectors. Classes on first aid and accident prevention were held using films provided by the British Safety in Mines Research Board under the supervision of the Colliery's Inspector of Labour W.G. Wormal. Although the industry had no doctor, an assistant medical officer from Enugu visited daily.

Heeding Orde Browne's assertions about nutritional impediments to production, saline beverages were provided at various spots underground, and an experiment using cocoa drinks began with plans for implementing a food ration system in the future.[114] As Orde Browne anticipated, the men resisted any attempt to supply food rations arguing that if they had more pay they could buy their own food. He lamented the fact that the colliery would not be able to use rations in Enugu, which he noted had been so effectively introduced in both South African and Copperbelt mines.[115]

In keeping with Orde Browne's suggestions and Colonial Office policy, the colliery's reforms were directed at the social wage rather than at increasing the base salary. This was because officials expected that by improving certain amenities workers would not request increased wages.

While before the war many officials were concerned about encouraging a stable mining community, now they saw such communities as an important context in which to cultivate disciplined workers.[116]

As anticipated, when Orde Browne's report was made public in late 1941, it led to queries in Parliament that embarrassed the Colonial Office and the Nigerian government.[117] Nonetheless, it was not until March 1942 that the Nigerian government applied for a loan under the Colonial Development and Welfare Act to finance an ambitious housing scheme to correct many of the abuses mentioned in Orde Browne's report.[118] In the interim the Nigerian government had tried to upgrade some of the housing and continued evicting what they considered to be superfluous people from the camps. This act itself tampered with the structure of family life and met with considerable opposition from the men. To them these evictions, while logical from a health standpoint, were an unwanted invasion into their homelife. The ability to head a large household, a rural norm expressed in the "Big Compound," was a sign of male prestige.[119] Although it presented difficulties in the city, the status connotations did not necessarily disappear. As noted above, many government employees were expected to open their homes to rural relatives, and apparently did so to such an extent that their rates of overcrowding exceeded those of privately employed men.[120] Colliery men relished this role, provided they could negotiate sufficient wages to endure the economic stress of the war. Their opposition to the occupancy restrictions indicated the cultural character of the social wage.

By November 1942 the British Treasury had approved a loan of £104,000 for the construction of 461 semi-detached houses, providing 922 rooms.[121] From its inception, the project was envisioned as a model of state ownership for critics in Britain and a demonstration to Africans of the correct, "modern" way to construct houses. Construction began in February 1943. Orde Browne, like many in the Colonial Office, perceived the project as an "object lesson on the possibilities of government ownership, both as a business proposition and in maintaining satisfactory conditions for working people."[122] In Enugu, a colliery "Housing Committee" had finalized the plans in a series of meetings held as early as October 1940. Membership in the committee touched all major government agencies involved in land use and social welfare, as well as labor officials and colliery welfare staff.[123] At no point did the committee bother to consult with the unions or the workers. It was assumed that they would be impressed by the superiority of British planning. Again, they were wrong.

The three estates were an excellent example of an "imagined" English mining village, an illustration of the fantasies colonialists entertained in the world inhabited by African workers. Not surprisingly, they reflected the frustrations of controlling the British coal miners. Two-room cottages on plots 40 by 60 feet were built with a verandah, electric lights, and a small garden. The camps had wide roads, open spaces, bathrooms, social halls, and chlorinated water. It was to provide the spatial context for a new, more cooperative workforce.

Although officials saw these estates as mining villages, they were not the rowdy type of English village that for centuries, and even in this war, fostered militant

**Photo 6.3** Garden City Housing Estate (MMS.AFR.s. 1507 Fol. 24–Bodleian Library, Oxford)

worker unrest. Rather, they modeled the camps on an idyllic pastoral mining village that followed the "Garden City" model of town planning: ordered bright and airy houses, with sufficient vegetation. In fact, the Udi Siding Camp was called Garden City.[124] But it was one thing to design the physical space that workers and their families occupied, and quite another to make them occupy it according to the priorities of colonial labor experts.

Officials ignored the miners' own preference in modern homes built with zinc roofs in the village. It was assumed that once the communities saw how beautiful and modern these buildings were, they would modify their own construction in the villages.[125]

The plan was that once in the estates the women and children would be supervised by female welfare officers who operated children's clinics and visited the homes, teaching nutrition and health. Initially the wives of the Staff Welfare Officer and Deputy Manager held these posts. They also visited adjacent villages.[126] The unions resented these intrusions and asked that the women welfare officers stop "supervising and molesting their wives when they went to work."[127] The men interestingly underscored this by reminding the officials of "the substantial quota the colliery workers were contributing towards the war effort."[128]

Despite the attractiveness of these new homes the men put up a formidable resistance to the more subtle but invasive dimensions of this project. Many of the urbanized men were polygynous and insisted on having adequate housing for their families, and servants as well. The unions organized a boycott of the estates and fined people who agreed to occupy them.[129] It was apparently effective, as in November the Colonial Secretary noted that only one hundred people had consented to live in them.[130] He noted that while they looked "very nice," they were "hog wash" and they cost over £100 per room as compared with £30 per room in Accra before the war. Moreover, he commented with disgust that "no one had apparently attempted to find out the sort of accommodation which, while satisfactory from the health point of view, would be acceptable to the Africans."[131]

To the men the central conflict was the impact of the houses on the family's autonomy. At a meeting with the Senior Resident and Acting Manager, Augustine Ude, of the Colliery Workers Union, complained that under the occupancy limits of $3\frac{1}{2}$ people per room in Garden City, they would have to leave part of their family "behind or throw them away."[132]

## THE COLLIERY AND THE LABOR CRISIS IN THE BRITISH COAL INDUSTRY: MANAGERIAL MANIPULATION OF "PRODUCTIVITY" STATISTICS

One further change occurred at the Colliery in 1943. William Leck, the colliery's only manager, retired. He was replaced by Russell Bracegirdle, a thirty-one-year-old mining engineer with no experience in Africa.[133] Bracegirdle "inherited" the summer dispute just as the Combined Production and Resource Board of London asked the Nigerian government to increase the output at Enugu by some 250,000 tons per year to supply the Allies' West African railways. For a young, inexperienced manager faced with this challenge so early in his tenure at Enugu, tensions were bound to be exacerbated. The request reflected the failure of the metropolitan state to resolve the endemic problem of the British coal industry—a slow but determined decrease in worker productivity and serious decline in manpower. By August 1939 the British coal industry had already lost 65,000 men to better paying jobs in war manufacturing and the armed forces. By 1943 this crisis had become full blown. That November the British government was forced to take extreme measures: it began compulsory recruitment of men for the mines. Twenty percent of all drafted men, 18–25 years old, were sent underground.[134]

In Enugu, Bracegirdle calculated that he could increase the monthly output to 60,000 tons with minor alterations in the colliery's railway facilities and the hiring of an additional 1,000 miners. The previous year's output had averaged 530,000 tons. The size of the workforce expanded to 4,000 in 1943/44 and 7,300 by 1945/46 (see Graph 6.1). The additional staff permitted an output of 668,148 tons making Enugu coal the staple throughout West Africa (see Table 6.1).[135]

In the process of reaching these production goals the new management made technical decisions that, while increasing production, both reduced the output per

**Photo 6.4** William Leck with deputy colliery manager, district officer, and unidentified prominent African men (Courtesy of P.E.H. Hair, personal collection)

**Photo 6.5** Isaiah Ojiyi, Amawbia, July 1975 (Carolyn Brown)

**Table 6.1**[136] Sales of Coal to African Colonies, 1944/45 to 1945/46

| Colony | 1944/45 Sales | 1945/46 Sales |
|--------|---------------|---------------|
| Gold Coast | 89,403 | 84,510 |
| South Africa | 6,149 | — |
| Belgium | 17,156 | — |
| Sierra Leone | 14,882 | 17,020 |
| Gambia | 602 | 1,502 |
| Dahomey | 541 | — |
| Free France | 83,033 | 46,341 |
| Spanish Gov. | 6,559 | 785 |
| TOTAL | 218,325 | 150,158 |

man shift (OMS) of the total underground workforce and increased the cost of production.[137] As the colliery trade unions became more successful in securing wage increases they confronted increasingly "scientific" counterarguments by management and the state. Workers' productivity became a central point of contention. Because calculations of output per man shift were often considered "objective" measurements of worker effort, it is important to contextualize them and subject them to an intensive examination of the labor process. Productivity measurements can be used to obscure, rather than expose, the real constraints on worker output.

According to management, worker productivity had been on a steady decline from the 1937–1938 strike when the Bulkeley Award gave hewers a minimum wage as noted in Chapter 5. While output statistics showed a drop in OMS (see Graph 6.5) the underlying cause of this decline, the collapse of the hewer contractor system, was obscured by the nature of mine work. In 1943 management assigned the bulk of the new workers to *robbery*, removing pillars of coal in previously *developed* mines. The impact on output and labor costs was dramatic. Governor Bourdillon bragged to the Colonial Office that even after drastic reductions in the numbers of workers the Colliery reached a 220 percent increase in output with a 40 percent lower price per ton.[138] While this may have persuaded the Colonial Office that Enugu's management and the Nigerian state were *finally* observing rational management practices, and bringing their workforce under industrial discipline, the illusion was short-lived. Inevitably, extraction reached the limits of existing *devel-*

*opment* and it was necessary to redeploy men to carve out new pillars for future extraction. Instead of retrenching workers who were no longer able to perform *robbery*, they retained them, and the number of men exceeded "the demands of *development* and got out of proportion with the strict needs of the circumstances."[139]

The technical deployment of labor in production was of crucial importance during the war because of changes in the pay system that was instigated by wartime strikes. As shall be seen in Chapter 7, management's concern with productivity increased when all face workers (hewers and tubmen) successfully won a basic underground allowance in addition to tonnage or piece rates. Previously, under the Bulkeley Award, only the hewers had both basic and piece-rates, while the tubmen were only on time rates. As noted previously, this aspect of Enugu's pay system— the payment of time rates to tubmen—defied the logic of productive coal payment systems. Tubmen, whose supply of tubs determined the output of hewers, should have been paid by the numbers of tubs pushed (piece-rate) as an incentive for them to supply tubs expeditiously. Interestingly, as early as 1937, the Representative Council raised the issue of putting the tubmen on piece-rates (i.e., payment per tub supplied). It took fully ten years before management applied this basic component of production incentives. The issue of worker productivity, in all its mystified existence, obscured more than it revealed and sparked more critical struggles in 1945.

In this deployment of hewers to *robbery*, management diverged from the "ideal" ratio of jobs that mine managers used in deploying workers to *robbery* and *development* tasks. Only 1 hewer was assigned to *development* for every .7 hewers in *robbery* as against the ideal ratio of 1 in robbery for every 2.26 in development The estimated costs of this imbalance was over £17,000 per year.[140] Conveniently, management ignored these calculations when linking any future wage gains to increased productivity. Since the hewers were the actual coal getters, any deployment of labor that decreased their numbers in relation to other classes reduced OMS.

In this case, several changes led to a radical decline in the number of hewers— the producers—in relation to other workers underground. Reorganizing the work-group management followed what had become a customary pattern of underground deployment, which was supposed to compensate for harsh underground conditions and the alleged inferiority of "native" labor.[141] Work-groups were composed of one railwayman, two timbermen, eight tubmen, and eight hewers. The primary coal extractors, the hewers, were less than half of this nineteen-man group. In fact, this decline in hewers relative to other underground workers became a fatal trend during the war. The hewers' proportion of the total workforce declined from 20.54 percent in 1940/41 to 14.43 percent in 1946.[142] Additionally, the large number of auxillary underground workers was a natural consequence of the large number of worksites under the *pillar and stall* system. As the management opened new work districts or "robbed" those in *development*, more and more men were needed for "deadwork," i.e., the maintenance of roadways, pumping of water, and replacing timber. Moreover, as additional men were deployed for surface tasks, the hewers' proportion of the workforce fell even more drastically.

**Table 6.2**[143] Hewers as Percentage of Underground Workforce

| Year | Total Undng. | Hewers | Hewers % Undgnd. | Total | Hewers % of Total |
|------|-------|--------|-------|-------|-------|
| 1940 | 1,365 | 461 | 34% | 2,244 | 21% |
| 1941 | 1,461 | 503 | 34% | 2,377 | 21% |
| 1942 | 1,822 | 658 | 36% | 2,928 | 36% |
| 1943 | 2,470 | 920 | 37% | 4,070 | 23% |
| 1944 | 2,986 | 1,046 | 35% | 6,625 | 16% |
| 1945 | 2,766 | 931 | 34% | 7,370 | 13% |
| 1946 | 2,940 | 955 | 33% | 6,660 | 14% |
| 1947 | 3,465 | 1,187 | 34% | 6,704 | 18% |
| 1948 | 3,422 | 1,355 | 39% | 7,134 | 19% |

The impact of this declining proportion of coal extractors was dramatic because "productivity" was calibrated by dividing the number of workers into the total output, or similarly, the number of underground workers into total output. The smaller the number of actual producers—hewers—the lower the productivity. This is demonstrated below (see Table 6.2 and Graphs 6.1–6.5).

This unfavorable ratio of productive to non–productive face workers reduced output by 30 percent, and added 9d to the total cost of production per ton. Hewers' wages were only 3.9d of this amount, while the remaining 5.1d was paid to other underground workers. The financial impact was obscured while wages were low, or when only the hewers received a basic daily tub-rate. The full consequence of this decision would become obvious after the war when, in 1946, the tubmen, as well as hewers, received daily rates. In this case the hewers' output was not high enough to compensate for this large number of workers, and it distorted the productivity calculations. However, as a postwar study noted, the costs of hewer output was obscured:

> It is obvious that any decrease in Hewers' O.M.S. must correspondingly result in an increase in the production cost of their coal. However, the whole significance of this rise in cost of production is not so apparent, and is due to the incidence of the fixed daily wage, not of Hewers only, but of the whole group of face workers.[144]

**Graph 6.1** Hewers in Relation to Other Categories of Workers

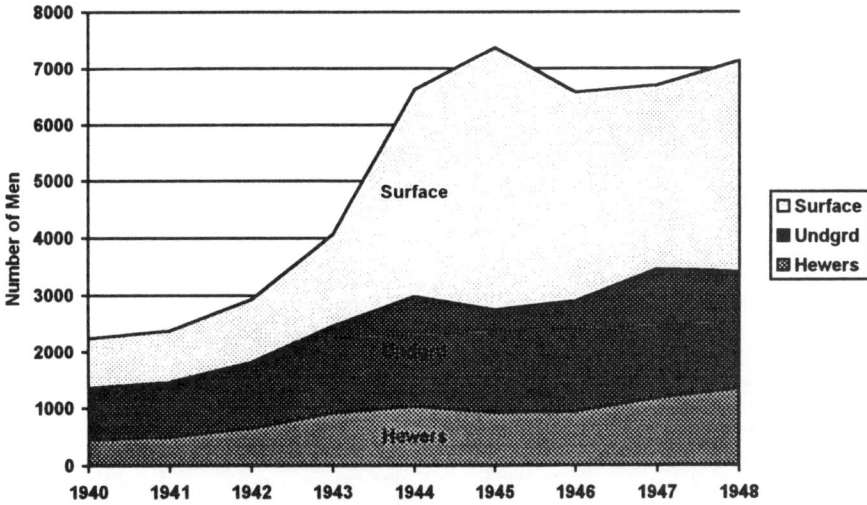

Source: Great Britain, Colonial Office. *Report of the Commission of Enquiry into the Disorders in the Eastern Provinces of Nigeria.* C.O. No. 256, London, 1950, Table IV, 57.

The deployment of workers was but one factor impacting production. The severe underground conditions that reduced worker stamina, discussed in Chapter 3, did not improve appreciably during the war, and in fact worsened.[145] The haulage system collapsed under the strain of this surge in production, creating costly delays in the supply of tubs. Outside the mine shortages of replacement parts for trains also caused costly delays in availability of rolling stock to evacuate coal, as well.[146]

From the standpoint of the miners, any pay system that made their income fully dependent on production made them carry the burden of wasteful managerial practices, poor environmental conditions underground, and delays in the supply of tubs underground and of railway cars on the surface. Their attempts to prevent this shifting of managerial responsibility characterized the industrial struggles towards the end of the war.

## THE LONG AWARD, AN "ILLEGAL LOCKOUT" PAVES THE ROAD TO IVA VALLEY, 1944–1945

Wartime industrial policy was largely successful in preventing work stoppages at Enugu. However, by late 1945 the conflicts between the two trade unions, the CWU and the CSIU, clashes between Ojiyi and Bracegirdle, and the crushing weight of inflation brought the colliery to the brink of another crisis. Several elements converged: the state's use of the new Nigerian General Defense Regulations to curtail strikes,

**Graph 6.2** Percentages of Workers by Category

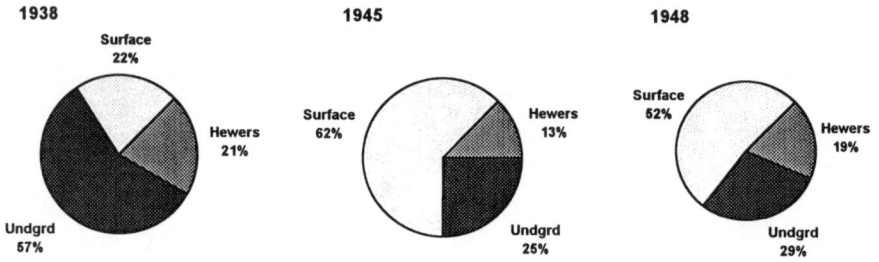

Source: Great Britain, Colonial Office. *Report of the Commission of Enquiry into the Disorders in the Eastern Provinces of Nigeria.* C.O. No. 256, London, 1950, Table IV, 57.

**Graph 6.3** Output per Man Shift, 1945–1951

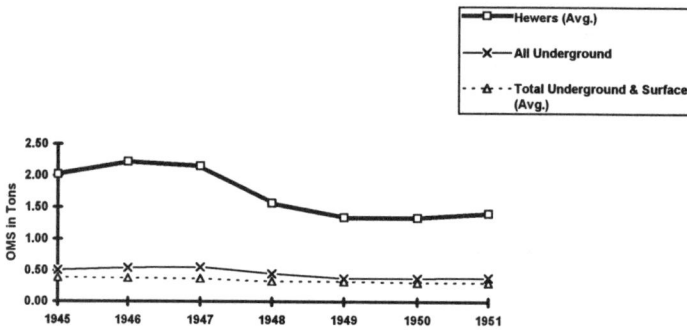

| | | Absolute Figures of Output per Man Shift (OMS) | | | |
|---|---|---|---|---|---|
| Year | No. of Days | Output (Thou. Tons) | OMS (Tons) | | |
| | | | Hewers | Other Undgrd | All |
| 1945 | 267 | 668,158 | 2.02 | 0.506 | 0.383 |
| 1946 | 280 | 505,565 | 2.22 | 0.543 | 0.376 |
| 1947 | 260 | 633,852 | 2.16 | 0.551 | 0.374 |
| 1948 | 297 | 551,706 | 1.57 | 0.45 | 0.33 |
| 1949 | 307 | 610,283 | 1.35 | 0.375 | 0.327 |
| 1950 | 230 | 526,613 | 1.34 | 0.38 | 0.308 |
| 1951 | 307 | 583,433 | 1.41 | 0.39 | 0.312 |

the struggles with union leadership to secure the confidence of the workers, and the attempt by a new manager to regain managerial authority over the labor process.

The crisis began in August 1944 when Ojiyi submitted an extensive memorandum that raised a number of grievances that reflected the gains of British coal miners. Referring to conditions in English mines, he demanded: a seven–hour working

**Graph 6.4** Total Output of Coal in 100,000 Tons, 1940–1948

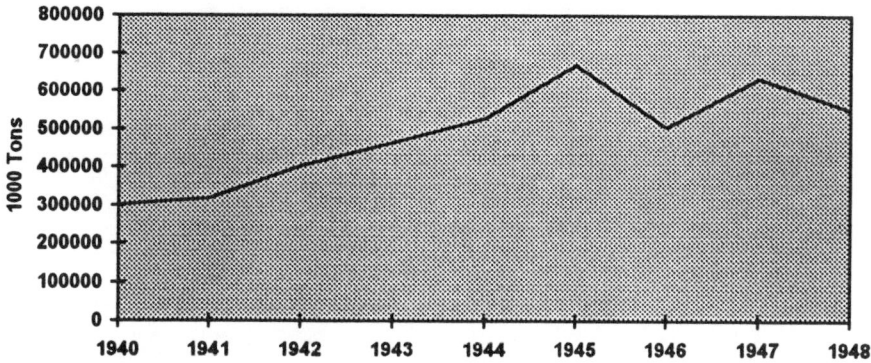

*Source:* Powell Duffryn Technical Services, "First Report to the Under-Secretary of State for the Colonies, Colonial Office, Dover House, Whitehall S.W.1., on the Government Colliery, Enugu. The Characteristics of the Coal Produced and the Investigation into the Other Coal and Lignite Resources," London, 1948, D–2.

day, an underground allowance of 2/6, and improvement in underground conditions to prevent occupational diseases—rheumatism, consumption, lockjaw, and other infirmities. He also asked for free mining equipment (i.e., shovels, picks, etc.), a divergence from British practice, arguing that tools should be supplied by the state because Enugu miners worked for the Nigerian government which represented the people. Further, in a personal attack against the new manager and an attempt to curry favor among surface workers, the memorandum complained that conditions for the surface workers had deteriorated, and wages had fallen since the coming of the new manager.[147]

When management did not respond, Ojiyi threatened a strike, in violation of the Defense Regulations. It appears that Bracegirdle may actually have set up the confrontation to create an opportunity to change both the pay system and further tighten managerial control over the labor process. He made two proposals which he argued would give the increased pay the union demanded. The first grouped the men into syndicates of sixty—30 hewers and 30 tubmen—to be paid an aggregate wage that they could divide equally between them. Tubmen were to fill rather than push tubs, a clear fragmentation of the hewers' skill. The second option used the same work groups, but with piece-rates based on individual work.[148] Both terminated all time payments (i.e., daily pay rates) and put the key underground workers—the hewers—fully on tonnage-rates (i.e., piece-rates). With hewers, special labor, and tubmen on piece-rates, he argued, they could earn the money in the union's demand.[149]

From the perspective of management it was a brilliant but naive proposal. Since the Bulkeley settlement the hewers had earned both day and tonnage rates, giving

**Graph 6.5** Productivity Charted Against Wage Awards

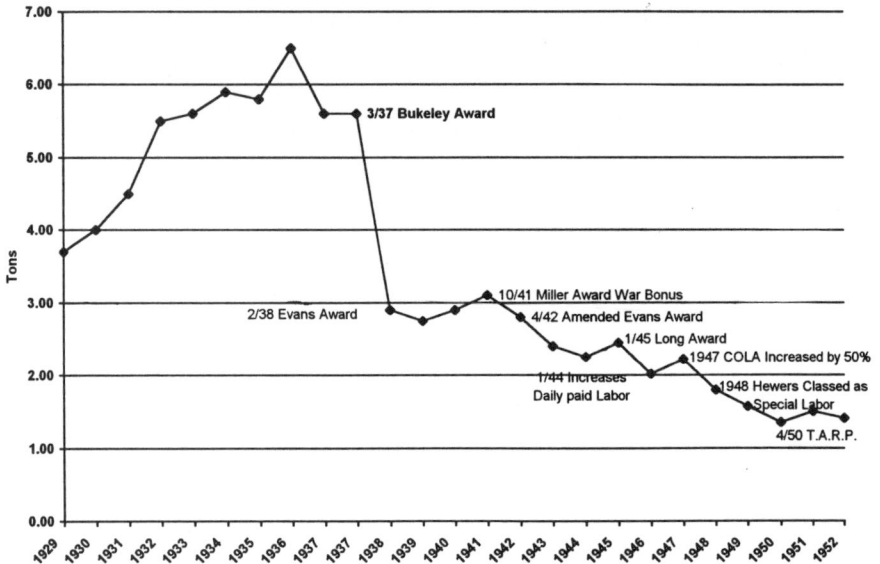

*Source:* NNAE, 5/6 (2) Nigerian Coal Corporation "Output Per Hewer Per Day."

management little control over the pace of work or of productivity. Each hewer was entitled, in the very minimum, to the day-rate and this he would be paid for only showing up to work even if he sat down throughout his shift. Moreover, by paying a daily rate the colliery was in essence shouldering the cost of productivity caused by deplorable conditions underground.[150] Putting all workers on piece-rates forced workers to carry the economic burden of these conditions on their wage packets. Were all workers on *only* piece-rates, management could increase productivity simply by hiring more workers, as they had done before the 1937 changes.[151] Thus the manager's proposal to restructure work relations was far more than an attempt to enable the men to make more wages. It was a desperate move to recapture managerial control over the labor process at a time when Enugu coal was of strategic value to the Empire. Workers recognized it as such and responded accordingly.

Bracegirdle was fully aware of the powers he now held under the new labor legislation. Thus on 22 September 1944, he dismissed several hewers when the unions responded with a trade dispute.[152] The unions rejected both options, and the dispute went to arbitration under the Nigerian Defence Regulations (1941). This— like Britain's Essential Work (Coal Mining Industry) Order of 1941—prohibited strikes in strategic industries and mandated compulsory arbitration in trade disputes. But the law also offered some protections to workers—protections from lockouts, for example. Bracegirdle's action looked curiously like a lockout, an *illegal* lockout. Ojiyi, representing the underground workers, anticipated an unfavorable outcome of arbitration and attempted to withdraw the demands and deal directly with the Chief Secretary. He asserted that if forced to arbitration, the union would not accept responsibility for the workers' response. He submitted his letter to both the Chief Secretary and to the nationalist press, attempting to alert the larger community of an impending confrontation.[153] Surface workers, on the other hand, under advisement from Nnamdi Azikiwe, the nationalist leader, refused to participate.[154]

Thus, in its first major protest, the union became ensnarled in the compulsory arbitration requirements of the Nigerian General Defense Regulation (1941) giving it firsthand experience with the laws then being targeted by the national trade union movement.[155]

As Ojiyi anticipated, the arbitration under Harold H. Long, a chartered accountant from Lagos, was far from impartial. Although Long was extremely unsympathetic to the union's case and Ojiyi, he was locked in by the restrictions of the Defense Regulations. The union presented its case, demanding return to individual pay and the maintenance of the daily wage with piece-rates and underground allowance, and argued for further increases and upgrading of the staff. The management offered its two alternatives.

The arbitration award, announced in January 1945, rejected the union's demand and ruled in favor of the management's first proposal, syndicate work with group pay. The union was dissatisfied with the ruling but was mandated to comply under the Defense Regulations. The new system was to begin April 1. To the manager, the men were finally put under the full incentive program. The possible earnings under the Long Arbitration are summarized in Table 6.3.

**Table 6.3**[156] Wages of Hewers and Tubmen Based on Long Award, 1945

| Hewers | Robbery | Development |
|--------|---------|-------------|
| 1 tub | 2/2 | 2/5 |
| 2 tubs | 3/6–1/2 | 4/9d |
| 10 tubs | 5/3 | 7/8 |
| | | |
| Tubmen | | |
| 1 tub | 1/3–1/2 | 1/5 |
| 5 tubs | 2/1–1/2 | 2/9 |
| 10 tubs | 3/1 | 4/5 |
| 15 tubs | 4/1d | — |

The manager decided to conduct an experiment in March to determine the best timekeeping methods to use. When output during the trial period dropped drastically—one tub per hewer—it was clear that the miners were in dispute against the award. There may have been other reasons why the system was unworkable but the manager did not think them through. Rather, Bracegirdle decided to force the miners to accept his new system, demanding that they all sign individual agreements to follow the award. Refusal to sign was interpreted as resignation.[157] Under Part 8 of the Nigerian Defense Regulations, he could argue that the arbitration award was compulsory.[158]

Of the over 2,000 underground workers confronted with what the manager defined as "the new terms of service," only 117 headmen/supervisory staff and six hewers agreed to sign. Among the signatories were former officials of the CWU—Augustine Ude, Joseph Okpokwu, Sam Ude, and Jacob Ahamefule—men with previous histories of sympathy with management. On March 23 the management announced that 1,800–1,900 miners were considered to have resigned and immediately recruited replacements in Owerri. A trade dispute was declared and Captain D.H. Holley, acting commissioner of Labour, came from Lagos and made an unsuccessful attempt to break the miners' resistance.[159]

The tenuous position of the CWU under the new labor legislation was clear on April 3, when the manager Bracegirdle, the Secretary, Eastern Provinces, and Labour Commissioner declared the CWU unrepresentative of the workforce, thereby revoking the union's recognition. In a classic example of circular reasoning they cited the miners' refusal to comply with the arbitration award, which the Defense Regulations had made mandatory, as proof that the union was not representative of the miners.[160] Thus, while the union tried to express the resistance of the men to the new arrangements, they were nonetheless held responsible for making this unpopular arrangement palatable to the resistant workers. In destroying the union, the manager, the Secretary, and the Labor Commissioner had created the very conditions that the legalization of unions was designed to prevent—working class militance organized secretly beyond the watchful eyes of the state. Thus management was surprised when they mobilized the Agbaja villages to support their position.

While initially the management's actions appeared to have "solved" the problem of a militant union, it nonetheless created two new difficulties—the recruitment of replacement men and the need for a representative body for the workers. As punishment for confronting the management, recruitment bypassed those Agbaja villages that were previously given preferential access to jobs to prevent overcrowding in Enugu, leading village leaders to complain vociferously against the exclusion of their people.[161] Despite their dismissal the miners remained adamant in fighting for their jobs. They launched a vigorous offensive to discourage and forcibly obstruct new recruits. The DO Udi, reported that they crowded recruitment sites and prevented the enlistment of new labor. Moreover, miners also refused to assist him in locating workers who had robbed a recent recruit from

**Table 6.4** Number of Workers 1938–1948 (Annual Average)

| Year | No. of Workers (Annual Ave.) | | | | Hewers as % | |
|---|---|---|---|---|---|---|
| | Hewers | Others Undgrd | Surface | Total Undrgrd & Surface | Of Undgrnd | Of All Labor |
| 1938 | 507 | 1387 | 528 | 2422 | 27 | 21 |
| 1939 | 564 | 1599 | 601 | 2848 | 26 | 20 |
| 1940 | 461 | 904 | 879 | 2,244 | 34 | 21 |
| 1941 | 503 | 958 | 916 | 2,377 | 34 | 21 |
| 1942 | 658 | 1164 | 1106 | 2,928 | 36 | 36 |
| 1943 | 920 | 1550 | 1600 | 4,070 | 37 | 23 |
| 1944 | 1,046 | 1940 | 3639 | 6,625 | 35 | 16 |
| 1945 | 931 | 1824 | 4615 | 7,370 | 34 | 13 |
| 1946 | 955 | 1958 | 3660 | 6,660 | 33 | 14 |
| 1947 | 1,187 | 2278 | 3239 | 6,704 | 34 | 18 |
| 1948 | 1,355 | 2067 | 3712 | 7,134 | 39 | 19 |

*Source:* Calculated from Nigerian Government Colliery, "Annual Report for the Colliery Department, 1938–1948" and Nigeria, Federal Ministry of Labour, "Udi Colliery Quarterly Report and Staff Welfare Officers: Quarterly Reports 1938–1948."

Nsukka, leading Bracegirdle to suspend all recruitment in Ukana, Ebe, and Aboh, the offending villages. Nonetheless, miners canvassed other Udi villages advising non-cooperation with recruiters.

The workers' campaign was quite effective and forced government to focus most of the recruitment in Owerri Province, the area in the palm belt that had contributed so many "foreign" workers in the industry's early history. This reincorporation of the "foreigners'" group, which in 1925 the management considered too militant, was one of the ironies of the industry's history. The "backward" Agbaja, once heralded for their industrial docility, were now the "militants" who were to be distrusted.[162] By May of 1944 the industry had between 1,800 and 1,900 new men.[163]

The banning of the union was greeted with pleasure by Ojiyi's detractors from among the clerical and underground supervisory staff as well as the elite of the urban improvement unions. Both they and the rural clan councilors resented Ojiyi because he deprived them of their "rightful" role as leaders. In the void left by the union, the urban district unions and village councils stepped forward claiming to represent the miners. At a meeting of the Enugu Division Union on 16 April 1945, Thomas Noisike, a colliery interpreter, blamed the dispute on the problems of translating the proposal into the local dialect of Igbo. The Division Union offered to translate the award into the Agbaja and Nkanu dialects of Igbo and tried to position itself as a representative body for the workers. They asked to be notified of impending disputes so they could mediate.[164] Although the miners were members of these associations dominated by clerical and "native" staff, they did not trust them in industrial issues. And they had always considered village leaders to be too unsophisticated to understand the complexities of workplace issues. In essence they distrusted these leaders.[165]

As workers rebuffed initiatives by alternatives to the union, management realized that by stripping the CWU of recognition, it was confronted with a disgruntled workforce with a long history of successful use of industrial disruption with no organized group to represent them. The search for an alternative representative body divided the manager from the Labor Department and the "old" from the "new" approaches to managing colonial labor. Bracegirdle, clearly bruised by his encounters with Ojiyi and the CWU, subsequently argued that he was sure the men would accept the leadership of the village authorities and urban tribal unions. Although a newcomer to the colony, he felt that he "understood" native labor:

> Having had some experience of Ibo labour brought directly from 'bush' into the mine I am not still satisfied that representation of workmen by a Committee comprised of their Native Authorities and Tribal Unions with a leavening of Colliery workmen would not be in the best interest of all concerned.[166]

On the other hand, the Commissioner of Labour, Capt. Holley, who recognized the signs as labor discontent, argued for a worker-elected body. He proposed the election of an interim committee of delegates who could become the nucleus of a new and perhaps more controllable trade union.[167]

The debate was a local reflection of discussions within the Colonial Office on the principles for establishing organs of employee representation. To Bracegirdle, the men's status as workers was less salient than their existence as rural and urban "tribesmen." On the other hand, Holley recognized that the miners, as industrial workers, were unlikely to accept representation by men who were outside the industry. This debate, which would pit one view of African labor against another, prevented a consensus within the state on worker representation. Workers recog-

**Table 6.5** Accident Rates, 1943–1946

| Period | Labor Force | Output | Fatal | Non-Fatal | # Days Worked | Per 100,000 Man Shift | | | Foot | Type of Injury | |
| | | | | | | Fatal | Non-Fatal | Sick | | Hand | Leg |
|---|---|---|---|---|---|---|---|---|---|---|---|
| Oct.-Dec. 1943 | 4,574 | 136,052 | | | | | | | | | |
| Jan.-March 1944 | 4,995 | 124,101 | 0 | 248 | | | | | | | |
| April-June 1944 | 4,914 | 164,127 | 0 | 292 | | | | | | | |
| July-Sept. 1944 | 5,356 | 173,494 | 1 | 413 | 72 | 18.56 | 6,182.13 | 1,280 | 36.0% | 27.5% | 19.9% |
| Oct.-Dec. 1944 | 6,020 | 179,822 | 0 | 484 | 72 | | 6,699.98 | 1,471 | 34.0% | 24.4% | 23.4% |
| Jan.-March 1945 | 6,142 | 151,664 | 0 | 439 | 68 | | 6,451.55 | 1,553 | 34.4% | 28.1% | 20.0% |
| April-June 1945* | 6,348 | 100,540 | 0 | 438 | 58 | | 5,106.24 | 1,326 | 33.1% | 31.9% | 16.1% |
| July-Sept. 1945* | 6,400 | 96,611 | 1 | 322 | 67 | 16.82 | 5,400.40 | 1,236 | 39.4% | 28.3% | 14.6% |
| Oct.-Dec. 1945* | 7,306 | 16,576 | 3 | 538 | 23 | 42.16 | 5,973.30 | 1,848 | 32.5% | 30.8% | 19.9% |
| Jan.-March 1946 | 7,173 | 142,650 | 0 | 413 | 63 | | 4,503.45 | 1,308 | 36.4% | 31.0% | 17.0% |
| April-June 1946 | 7,384 | 134,431 | 2 | 410 | 63 | 26.67 | 4,371.50 | 1,723 | 42.4% | 25.4% | 16.9% |
| July-Sept. 1946 | 7,130 | 157,316 | 2 | 344 | 77 | 13.94 | 3,527.61 | 1,997 | 32.3% | 29.9% | 23.2% |

*Long arbitration dispute leads to drop in output and eventual strike.

*Source:* Ministry of Labour 3/5.2 Vol. 1., *Colliery Manager Quarterly Report.*

**Table 6.6** Classification of Causes of Injury, 1944

| | JAN | FEB | MARCH | APRIL | MAY | JUNE | JULY | AUG | SEPT | OCT | NOV | DEC |
|---|---|---|---|---|---|---|---|---|---|---|---|---|
| Total Accidents | 585 | 917 | 723 | 796 | 991 | 114 | 90 | 105 | 136 | 122 | 133 | 134 |
| At Fall Of Roof | 5.9% | 7.7% | 8.3% | 7.60% | 9.1% | 5.3% | 10.0% | 11.4% | 61.5% | 4.9% | 8.3% | 6.7% |
| Haulage Accidents | 22.4 | 31.8 | 29.1 | 20.25 | 33.4 | 28.9 | 24.4 | 25.7 | 28.6 | 31.2 | 28.6 | 30.6 |
| Derailments | 9.4 | 14.3 | 7.0 | 8.86 | 12.1 | 4.4 | 5.6 | 4.8 | 11.0 | 9.0 | 6.8 | 8.2 |
| Accidents Caused Whilst Material Handling | 3.5 | 2.2 | 7.0 | 3.80 | 4 | 4.4 | 5.6 | 1.9 | 3.6 | 0.8 | 1.5 | 3.7 |
| Accidents From Tools | 11.8 | 4.4 | 9.7 | 11.39 | 6.1 | 7.0 | 7.8 | 7.6 | 5.1 | 4.1 | 1.5 | 4.5 |
| Falls Of Coal From Face | 19.0 | 17.6 | 19.4 | 20.25 | 19.2 | 23.7 | 22.2 | 23.8 | 18.3 | 19.7 | 16.5 | 23.2 |
| Erecting and Withdrawing Supports | - | - | 1.4 | 2.53 | - | 0.0 | - | - | - | - | - | - |
| Miscellaneous-Not Classified | 15.0 | 8.8 | 13.9 | 13.92 | 10.1 | 19.3 | 16.6 | 16.1 | 16.1 | 22.1 | 22.5 | 14.9 |
| SURFACE | | | | | | | | | | | | |
| Haulage Accidents | 2.4 | 5.5 | 1.4 | 1.27 | 1 | 1.7 | 1.1 | 1.0 | 0.7 | 1.6 | 4.5 | 1.5 |
| Handling Materials | 5.9 | 4.4 | 2.8 | 7.60 | 4 | 4.4 | 5.6 | 4.8 | 1.44 | 3.3 | 6.0 | 2.2 |
| Screen Accidents | 1.2 | - | - | 2.53 | - | - | - | - | 0.7 | - | - | 1.5 |
| Miscellaneos | 3.5 | 3.3 | - | - | 1 | 0.9 | 1.1 | 1.0 | 2.2 | 0.8 | 2.3 | 2.2 |
| Falling Objects | - | - | - | - | - | - | - | 1.0 | 2.2 | 2.5 | 1.5 | 0.8 |

*Source:* File no. 794 Nigcoal 2/1/80.

nized this fracture in the armor of imperial labor policy and seized upon it when-ever possible.

The resulting Representative Committee was an uneasy synthesis of the two per-spectives: delegates were elected by the workers, but representation was based on both job (industrial) and clan (i.e., "tribal") categories. In late May, P.H. Cook, a BTUC labor adviser to the Department of Labour, who became the colliery's in-dustrial relations officer was charged to call the election. Voter turnout proclaimed the workers' dissatisfaction: only 5.2 percent of the workers participated.[168] Blind to this reality, management and the state insisted that the forty-six member Rep-resentative Committee was the new "representative" body for the workers. From its inception the miners refused to accept them, as reported in their first meeting on 27 July 1945:

> After explaining to the workers our object of convening the meeting, Mr. Joseph, Tubmaker, who replied on behalf of the workers said that the workers were not prepared to discuss anything with us as the workers do not in any way associate themselves with our selection as Committee Members. After Joseph's reply all the worker shouted on us and dispersed.[169]

Moreover, workers also blocked managerial attempts to exclude the union from participation in other committees. When management attempted to appoint a hous-ing committee to supervise the labor estates, one worker responded by asserting his faith in the defunct union:

> We have heard what you told us about starting a Housing Committee. After ex-amining ourselves, we find that we are not competent enough to make any de-cision in the matter. We have a Union. ... You will allow us time to discuss the matter in our Union meeting and you will hear from us in the course of time. If the Manager wants a Housing Committee, he should notify our Union and reach a decision with them.[170]

The management's incorporation of rural leaders failed to recognize the "pro-gressive" role that miners felt they played against authoritarian village leaders. Au-gustine Ude, CWU, noted:

> The miners were most modern and power[ful]. Because they were always after democracy. And they don't allow the chief by opposing him to harass his peo-ple. And [they] always succeeded in opposing him.[171]

Management had created a leadership vacuum which it proved incapable of fill-ing. Every option was tried—the urban unions and the village councilors—and nei-ther was able to secure any legitimacy with the workers.

Underground, meanwhile, the Long Award was no more popular with the new workers than with the old. On 8 June 1945, confronted with a drastic decline in output, Bracegirdle decided to revise the award by instituting his second alterna-tive of syndicate work with individual pay of piece-wages.[172] It was unclear if he had the authority to do so, given the legal standing of the arbitration. But he

**Table 6.7** Total Colliery Output, 1916–1951

| Year | Tons |
|------|------|
| 1916 | 24,511 |
| 1917 | 83,405 |
| 1918 | 145,407 |
| 1919 | 137,844 |
| 1920 | 180,122 |
| 1921/22 | 194,073 |
| 1922/23 | 112,818 |
| 1923/24 | 175,137 |
| 1924/25 | 220,161 |
| 1925/26 | 242,582 |
| 1926/27 | 353,274 |
| 1927/28 | 345,303 |
| 1929/30 | 347,151 |
| 1930/31 | 327,681 |
| 1931/32 | 263,548 |
| 1932/33 | 259,860 |
| 1933/34 | 234,296 |
| 1934/35 | 258,893 |
| 1935/36 | 257,289 |
| 1936/37 | 310,308 |
| 1937/38 | 391,159 |
| 1938/39 | 323,266 |
| 1939/40 | 300,090 |
| 1940/41 | 318,594 |
| 1941/42 | 402,640 |
| 1942/43 | 463,978 |
| 1944/45 | 668,158 |
| 1945/46 | 505,565 |
| 1946/47 | 633,852 |
| 1947/48 | 551,706 |
| 1948/49 | 610,283 |
| 1949/50 | 526,613 |
| 1950/51 | 583,433 |
| Total | 11,645,128 |

*Source:* Powell Duffryn Technical Services, D–2.

nonetheless placed his modification before the newly elected Representative Committee which of course endorsed his revision of the original Long Arbitration Award.[173] Immediately, Ojiyi, on behalf of the CWU, challenged the endorsement as a violation of the arbitration provision of the Nigerian Defense Regulations since the committee was not party to the original arbitration. The manager countered that since the new committee and not the CWU represented the workers, its members' approval was sufficient compliance with the law. Despite this attempt to wrap the committee in a cloak of legitimacy the men refused to accept the Representative Committee and ignored every attempt to impose its powers on them.

When the former miners saw resumption of individual pay, more of them demanded to return to work. Management was besieged by petitions from ex-miners requesting reinstatement. Although most were reincorporated into the colliery where they worked with scabs, they were far from admitting defeat. Even when the first group of miners demanded reinstatement, the struggle for higher wages had moved from outside the colliery to the workplace itself. Their displeasure was graphically illustrated in the output figures. By the second quarter, output had dropped from 151,664 tons to 100,539. In the July-September quarter, it plunged to 96,611 and reached an all-time low of 16,576 CWT in the final quarter.[174]

Managerial control over production was contested every day. First, the reinstated tubmen would not cooperate with newly hired hewers and disregarded instructions of tub headmen.

> I find that instead of assistance being given to hewers there is a strong tendency on the part of reinstated tubmen to malinging (sic) in the ordinary course of a tubmen's work ... I have also noticed that the tubmen disregard the headman tub completely to the extent of sitting laughing at him when trying to chase them to work.[175]

At the Obwetti mine supervisors recognized a general air of insolence and complained of malingering and deliberate sabotage by the old miners. In response, the miners blamed their poor performance on unfavorable working conditions or obstructions presented by other groups of underground workers. Collaboration between hewer and tubman was evident in reports from British bosses who alleged that the hewers claimed:

> the coal was hard or they were waiting on the tub-boys. The tub-boys when asked ... stated they were waiting on coal. The tub-boys are definitely not giving the hewers any assistance but at the same time they are being supported by the hewers regarding assistance to be given while waiting on coal.[176]

By the final quarter of 1945, output dropped to a record low of 16,546.[177] This declining output was a devastating statement of the workers' resistance to the Long Award, and a testament to their ability to maneuver around the government's Defense Regulations. The purposeful restriction of output, which constituted a "go slow," did not violate the law because it was not technically a strike. Although "officially" the union did not exist, it continued surreptitiously. Ojiyi held meetings usually in the villages or at "Seven Mile Corner," a road junction between Udi and Enugu.[178] Moreover, even without the union, the miners proved that they shared Ojiyi's aversion to the Long Award and could act against the system without overt leadership.

## THE POLITICAL POTENTIAL
## OF ORGANIZED COLONIAL LABOR

While the coal miners labored under restrictive industrial relations machinery, the Lagos working class demonstrated political consequences of unresolved labor problems. From 22 June to 6 August 1945, over 40,000 workers downed tools.[179] The years of negotiating with largely unresponsive colonial department heads as well as the Colonial Office had proven unbearable. But it did give the nationalists an audience among important sectors of the working class, and the independence movement, which had expanded beyond its regional divisions, coalesced into a mass-based national movement.[180]

Thus the coal industry lumbered through the armistice with the seeds of the next phase of miners' struggle deeply embedded in the patterns of industrial relations. Despite the progressive intent of the new labor reforms both management and the state were deeply wedded to the old systems of authority and control in which Africans were marginalized from substantive areas of decision making in the industry. It was not just local political and industrial authorities who tried to undermine the development of strong trade unions but officials at the national and Colonial Office levels. The progressive vision was to have unions function as a means of mobilizing labor for development, but the meaning of development was defined by the colonial state.

"Development" itself was being reconceptualized and narrowed, now that the war had ended. Britain had to confront the reality of its money shortages in United States dollars, shortages that, given the destruction of its industrial infrastructure, it had few possibilities of resolving. Formerly characterized as a process that emphasized improvements in social welfare and raising the living standards of colonial people, "development" was now defined as an economistic construct which emphasized those projects that facilitated the redirection of colonial products to metropolitan reconstruction and, naturally, made African labor more productive.

The explanation of this shift lay in the particularities of Britain's postwar economic quandary. Now African products were even more valuable to the economic reconstruction of Britain. After the war, an unfavorable balance of trade drained Britain's monetary holdings borrowed from the United States during the war.[181] British productive capacity was dwarfed by that of the United States which was now the world's major manufacturer. With her industry in shambles, dependence on American imports depleted her dollar reserves. Moreover, members of the Commonwealth who had agreed to restrict their imports during the war began to relax this policy and ran import deficits that required that they convert their sterling currency to U.S. dollars.[182] While Britain could not control these decisions among the dominions—Australia and newly independent India—they could enforce import controls in the remaining colonies to retain their sterling balances.[183]

Additionally, Nigeria was important because postwar shortages drove up the prices of primary goods. Nigerian groundnuts and palm products now commanded prices higher than during the war. They were wonderful sources for earning hard currency, i.e., U.S. dollars, and by getting them from the colonies within the sterling area, Britain needn't spend already scarce hard currency purchasing them on world markets.[184]

When the Labour Party came to power in July 1945 it was confronted with this desperate postwar fiscal reality. The previous concerns in organizing African trade unions, shaping industrial relations through the application of "modern" process and institutions, and raising the productivity of African workers by improving the social welfare of the colony, gave way to a narrowed concern with output-productivity.[185] The role of colonial resources was clear. The Labour Party planned to "incorporate the postwar colonial hinterland, now predominantly Africa, as a source of food and raw materials to replace imports from dollar sources."[186]

As long as Britain needed Nigeria's resources, the Nigerian Railway needed Enugu's coal. But few officials trusted that African workers were able to be sufficiently productive to supply these goods. Those old images of the backward primitive were so familiar they proved resilient. Moreover, officials were locked into the notion of "the peculiarity and backwardness of the African."[187] They were illiterate, unsophisticated laborers who were an easy "mark" for unscrupulous, "warped" trade union leaders, like Ojiyi.[188] Few would accept that the workers had developed their own critiques of the conditions of work and systems of remuneration. But no trade union movement could develop strong roots in this type of hostile political environment.

Management's struggle to control production—couched in the terminology of "productivity"—was an industrial expression of the "productionist" development project. Almost immediately upon his arrival Bracegirdle had met the challenge. He had led the industry to produce unprecedented coal tonnage, thereby responding favorably to the Combined Resource Board's request. But he had done so at the expense of future operating costs. Once this target was met and *robbery* exhausted all *developed* areas, he should have reorganized labor deployment to prepare for future extraction. The failure to do so only accelerated the decline in productivity. This was either managerial ineptitude or inexperience. Nonetheless, it was the workers who shouldered the burden of this managerial decision and who were judged "guilty" in state investigations of the industry. It appeared that they reduced productivity with each successive wage award. Productivity statistics became the "objective" proof because the "truth" was hidden underground in the abode of production.

Could Enugu's unions be "partners" in "development" or were they doomed to be pawns of the "demagogue" Ojiyi? The labor experts were trying to convince colonial employers and officials that it was better to have workers' activism contained by structures like trade unions who could be partners in negotiations and the numerous industrial relations institutions than to be confronted with wildcat strikes and industrial violence. But even these "experts" were held captive by the imagined "African worker" who appeared so "different" as to call into question the word "worker." Just how much of a "worker" were they? Or were they just "tribesmen," in which case should the "tribal" councils and unions be sitting at the negotiating table? In 1945 the pendulum was inching towards the "tribesman" side. With the manager arguing for the essentialism of "clan" and the new Labor Department gingerly pushing for an "elected" representative committee, neither recognized the significance of the men's loyalty to the CWU and Ojiyi, because, after all, the men were incapable of responsible behavior.

The hewers were deeply troubled by these attacks upon their power over the labor process. Like their cohorts in England, the Enugu miners well understood the pressures they could bring to bear on the nation's economy to underscore the terms under which they were willing to sell their labor power. The tragic consequences of this knowledge will be the subject of the next chapter.

## NOTES

1. Nigerian Coal Corporation Files (hereafter NCC), New No. P.1, "Letter from Colliery Department to All officials and staff—European and African," 23 December 1941.

2. Ibid.

3. Frederick Cooper, *Decolonization and African Society*, p 110.

4. J.O. Olusanya, *The Second World War And Politics in Nigeria* (London, 1973), p. 48.

5. Ibid., p. 56.

6. Frederick Cooper notes that even the Labour Party could not conceive of African society being able to generate its own plan for the future. Cooper, *Decolonization*, 122.

7. R.A.C. Parker, *The Second World War: A Short History* (Oxford, 1977).

8. France had fallen in June 1940 and now had the Vichy government, which declared its neutrality in the war. This denied Britain security of valuable air bases with which to attack German submarines in the Atlantic and Mediterranean.

9. Parker.

10. Michael Crowder, "The 1939–1945 War and West Africa." In *History of West Africa*. Vol 2, For an interesting discussion of another colony, the Gold Coast, see Wendell Holbrook, "British Propaganda and the Mobilization of the Gold Coast War Effort, 1939–45," in *Journal of African History*, 26, 4, 1985. edited by Michael Crowder and J.F.A. Ajayi, 612. London: Longman Group, 1974.

11. Michael Cowen and Nicholas Westcott, "British Imperial Economic Policy During the War," in *Africa and the Second World War*, ed. David Killingray and Richard Rathbone (London, 1986), 44.

12. Ibid.

13. These were export earnings in excess of expenditures. For colonies these earnings increased during the war because of the restrictions on imports. Before the Lend Lease Act with the United States, these balances financed half of the United Kingdom's deficit and 15 percent in 1929. These restrictions of imports, raised prices and created scarcities. Ibid., 28, 29.

14. Deputy Prime Minister Clement Attlee commented to the West African Student Union (WASU) that "You will not find in the declarations made on behalf of the Government any suggestion that the freedom and social security for which we fight should be denied to any of the races of mankind." *West Africa*, 23 August 1941, p. 818, as cited in Hakim Adi, *West Africans in Britain, 1900–1960: Nationalism, Pan-Africanism and Communism* (London, 1998). During the war the Union was an important political force representing Africans in the United Kingdom and lobbying for political change in Africa. See also Coleman, *Nigeria* 239–243.

15. For the fullest discussion see Adi, op. cit. The nationalists were prolific writers leaving a generous record of their thoughts on the charter. For one discussion, see A.A. Nwafor Orizu, *Without Bitterness: Western Nations in Post-War Africa* (New York, 1944).

16. William Roger Lewis, *Imperialism at Bay: The United States and the Decolonization of the British Empire, 1941–1954* (New York, 1978), 124.

17. Winston Churchill tried to argue that the clause should only be applied to European nations invaded by the Axis Powers. Attlee met with the West African Students' Association and clarified that the right to self-determination did in fact apply to "coloured peoples, as well as white." Lewis, 125.

18. This is a paraphrase of Frederick Cooper's introduction to Chapter 4 of *Decolonization and African Society*, 110.

19. UDDIST 9/1/1/, "Annual Report 1947—Udi Division."

20. Such behavior led to a lightning strike in 1937. See Chapter 5.

21. Supple, *History of the British Coal Industry*, 558.

22. Richard Hyman, *Industrial Relations: A Marxist Introduction* (London, 1975), 191.

23. As part of the standardization process in operation during the war, the Colonial Office used a set model of trades disputes law and sent it throughout the colonies. The most popular model was the Trinidad Trades Disputes Law which was drafted with the help of Orde Browne by the Colonial Labor Committee. See PRO, CO 859 Social Services Department, CO 323.

24. The Nigerian working class was so small, and in such narrow areas of the economy— with a large percentage being state employees—that it was rather easy for the law to effectively eliminate the possibility of strikes for the majority of the working class.

25. See petitions in the 1937/38 strike in which men note the quality of their skill and their importance to the production process. See Chapter 5.

26. For examples, see petitions submitted to Orde Browne on his visit to Enugu, see NNAE, NIGCOAL2/1/126, "Boss Boys-Colliery," 1940–1947.

27. Orde Browne's report was so critical of the Nigerian Government Colliery that the Colonial Office considered withholding publication until after the war. For a discussion and critique of Orde Browne's recommendations, see PRO, CO 554/125, 129, 130, 132. Orde Browne, *Labour Conditions in West Africa*, 162–167.

28. For an account of the tin mines' response to the defeat, see Chapter 5, Bill Freund, *Capital and Labour in the Nigerian Tin Mines* (New Jersey, 1981). Orde Browne, that beacon of "progressive" labor policies, helped the Colonial Office to contravene the ILO 1933 Forced Labour Ordinance, which Britain had signed, that forbade the use of forced labor for private industry.

29. The story of the Airbase Program concerns a seldom acknowledged role played by West Africa before Pearl Harbor and the United States entrance into the war. Forbidden by neutrality clauses from selling airplanes to Britain, Roosevelt contracted with Pan American Airways to lease their trans-Atlantic routes from Natal, Brazil, to West Africa and to have their pilots deliver airplanes to British forces in Libya and Egypt. The project required construction and maintenance of airbases along the West African coast. Following the Takoradi route, named after a terminal city in the Gold Coast (Ghana), and crossing the Sahara at Chad, declared for Free France by Felix Eboué, France's only Black governor, hundreds of pilots became an important lifeline for besieged Britain. When the United States did enter the war, the Pan Am bases were militarized, giving the Americans a route across Africa through Ethiopia to access the Pacific. The full story of this fascinating episode is found in Deborah W. Ray, "Pan American Airways and the Trans-African Air Base Program of World War II" (Ph.D. diss. New York University, 1973) and her article "The Takoradi Route: Roosevelt's pre-war venture beyond the Western Hemisphere," *Journal of American History*, LXII, 2 (September 1975).

30. Coleman, *Nigeria* p. 253.

31. ONDIST 12/1/1207, "Annual Report of Onitsha Province, 1940."

32. NNAE, NIGCOAL 2/1/138, Local Authority to Resident. 20 March 1945

33. NIGCOAL 2/1/138, Dewhurst, Local Authority, "Census of Enugu," 1945, 57.

34. Ibid., 57.

35. UDDIST 9/1/1/, "Udi Division Annual Report 1942."

36. For a discussion of crime as a form of worker protest, see Robin Cohen, "Hidden Forms of Consciousness."

37. In 1939 Enugu had become the seat of the Eastern Provinces Secretariat and it was the headquarters of many of the large expatriate trading firms who were the purchasing agents of palm products and other goods designated as critical for the war effort.

38. ONPROF 8/1/4902, "Annual Report—1944."

39. Orde Browne feared that the economic crisis would spill over into a political challenge to the state. He argued with those in the Colonial Office who did not share his sense of the urgency of labor reform, that such discontent formed a "permanent basis for political agitation of the unscrupulous type." Such challenges were more likely in cities. CO 554/132/33718, Orde Browne, Memorandum, "Labour Problems in Relation to Development in West Africa," 31 March 1943.

40. For a similar example of a pivotal urban working class whose industry encouraged casual labor and the colonial government recognized its dangerous consequences, see Frederick Cooper *On the African Waterfront: Urban Disorder and the Transformation of Work in Colonial Mombasa* (New Haven, 1987).

41. 314/39/PE 476, DO Enugu to Provincial Commissioner, 24 February 1939, cited in Gutkind, "The Emergent African Urban Proletariat," 32. Peter Gutkind, *The Emergent African Proletariat*, Centre for Developing-Area Studies, Occasional Paper Series, no. 8, Montreal, 1974.

42. NIGCOAL 2/1/138, Local Authority to Colliery Manager, 20 June 1944.

43. NIGCOAL 2/1/138, Local Authority "Census of Enugu," 56.

44. UDDIST 9/1/1/, "Udi Division Annual Report, 1942."

45. Recall 1937/38 demands.

46. Lisa Lindsay makes this point in her study of Lagos-based Yoruba employees in the Nigerian Railway. She argued that the provision of health care was an expression of a man's responsibility to his family and a reflection of his status as a "big man." Lindsay, "Shunting Among Masculine Ideals," 6. Paper presented at the annual meeting of the African Studies Association, Orlando, Florida, 1995.

47. Interview with B.U. Anyasado. Mbieri, Owerri, 23 July 1975.

48. Richard Sklar, *Nigerian Political Parties* (New Jersey, 1963), 208.

49. Women were extremely prominent in the nationalist movement but they also had their own organizations. One was a mutual aid and dance group called *Igboenwezu* which was founded in Coal Camp, Enugu, by Mme. Janet Okoye. They performed at political rallies of the NCNC to attract followers. NNAE, Box 202, *Life Profile and Mass of the Resurrection for the Late Madam Janet Matagu Peter-Okoye*, MBE, 25 July 1991, p. 5.

50. Major G. St. J. Orde Browne, *Labour Conditions in West Africa*. The report was so critical of the government that the Colonial Office engaged in a lively debate over the wisdom of publishing it. See C.O. 554/132 for the correspondence.

51. Ibid.

52. For an index of the recommendations, see [Ibid.], 78.

53. CO 554/125, Orde Browne to O.G.R. Williams, 15 February 1946.

54. Ibid.

55. See Chapter 3.

56. Orde Browne cited the experience in South African and the Copperbelt mines as evidence that increased protein would affect productivity. Orde Browne, *Labour Conditions in West Africa*, 61–62.

57. Ibid, p. 57.

58. CO 554/132, Orde Browne, "Labour Problems in Relation to Development in West Africa," 31 March 1943.

59. Michael Crowder, "The 1939–45 War in West Africa," 608.

60. Market women were angered by Conditional Sales, in which they were required to sell slow-moving goods with more desirable products. In 1943 government initiated the Pullen Marketing Scheme in which government established markets in Lagos that sold food at below market prices, the state attempted to restrict price gouging, distributing consumer items to market women, and prohibiting high profits. The scheme failed for several reasons, including families who cheated on their quota, reselling acquired foodstuffs at 100–300% above purchase prices. Riots at these markets also deterred housewives from attending. See Wale Oyemakinde, "The Pullen Marketing Scheme: A Trial in Food Price Control in Nigeria 1941–47," *Journal of the Historical Society of Nigeria* 6 (1973): 413–23.

61. Royal Commission on disturbances in Trinidad as cited in Weiler, "Forming Responsible Trade Unions,": The Colonial Office, Colonial Labour, and the Trades Union Congress, *Radical History Review* 28–30 (1984). 374.

62. PRO, CO 1766/37, Ormsby-Gore, "Circular," 24 August 1937 as cited in Weiler, "Forming Responsible Trade Unions," 372.

63. CO 554/132/33729, Sec. of State Oliver Stanley, to H.V. Tewson, Assistant Secretary, BTUC, 8 July 1943.

64. Nigerian Department of Labour Annual Report, 1941.

65. Robin Cohen, *Labour and Politics* (Nigeria, London) 1974, 159.

66. Ibid.

67. Tokunboh, *Labour Movement in Nigeria*, 32; Ananaba, *The Trade Union Movement in Africa*, 27ff; Robin Cohen, "Nigeria's Labour Leader No. 1: Notes for a Biographical Study of M.A.O. Imoudu," *Journal of the Historical Society of Nigeria* 5, 2 (1970): 303–08.

68. Timothy Oberst, "Cost of Living and Strikes in British Africa, c. 1939–1948: Imperial Policy and the Impact of the Second World War," Ph.D. diss. Columbia University, 327.

69. For a thorough discussion of this flawed process, see Ibid.

70. The fact that the committee was so representative of the various government agencies and had a Nigerian majority may explain why its recommendations expressed sensitivity to a broad range of issues that affected the working class. The committee members were A.F.B. Bridges (Chairman), W.G. Wormal, Inspector of Labour (Secretary); Mrs. O.M. Abayomi; Miss T.O.A. Pearce; W.H. Biney; C. Enitan-Brown; H. Chapman; G. Cotgreave; Rev. T.O. Dedeke; E.J.B. Gahan, Agricultural Chief Engineer, Nigerian Railway; E.G. Garrity, Works Manager, Public Works Department; Dr. J. Hamilton, Ag. Deputy Director of Health Services; R.J. Hook, Food Controller; C. Macdonald, Principal Assistant Secretary, Nigerian Secretariat; Honorable Jibril Martin; J.A. Ojo; Hon. H.S.A. Thomas; Lamidi Thompson; and A.E. Normal Williams. Tokunboh, *Labour Movement in Nigeria*, 32.

71. UDDIST 3/1/8, "Divisional Annual Report-Udi Division, 1940"; Wogu Ananaba, *The Trade Union Movement in Nigeria* (New York, 1969), 27, 29.

72. Powell Duffryn Technical Services, "First Report to the Under-Secretary of State of the Colonies, Colonial Office, Dover House, Whitehall S.W.1., on the Government Colliery, Enugu. The Characteristics of Coal Produced and the Investigation into the Other Coal and

Lignite Resources," London, 1948, D–165. The discussion of the Evans Award is in Chapter 5.

73. C.O. 554/129, "Minutes of the West African War Council (47)," 17 October 1942.

74. Department of Labour Annual Report 1942, pp. 16, 17 as quoted in Ananaba *Trade Union Movement in Nigeria* (1969), 28–29.

75. Robin Cohen, *Labour and Politics in Nigeria*, 159; Ananaba, *Trade Union Movement in Nigeria*, 1969, 47–48.

76. CO. 554/129, Secretary of State to O.A.G. Nigeria, 10 July 1942; "Extract of Minutes of the West African War Council (47)," 17 October 1942.

77. Interview with Charles Morris, 19 June 1975.

78. Orde Browne, *Labour Conditions in West Africa*, 58.

79. AWAM included the largest firms in West African trade such as the United Africa Company Ltd., G.B. Ollivant Ltd., John Holt and Co. (Liverpool) Ltd., and Companie Française de L'Afrique Occidentale. This was but one example of monopolistic practices during this period. The AWAM was also involved in shipping cartels, allocation of import licenses, and the distribution of American goods. P.T. Bauer, *West African Trade: A Study in Competition, Oligopoly and Monopoly in a Changing Economy* (New York, 1967) 67, 172–73, 189–91.

80. Cowen and Westcott, "Imperial Economic Policy," 20, 21.

81. CO 583/261,/30425, Secretary of State to Governor Nigeria, 22 March 1943. For a discussion of the Colonial Office attempts to contain trade union activism, see Peter Weiler, "Forming Responsible Trade Unions."

82. T.M. Yesufu, *An Introduction to Industrial Relations in Nigeria* (Oxford, 1962), 23–25.

83. Interview with Eze Ozogwu, Udi 2 June 1975.

84. Orde Browne, *Labour Conditions in West Africa,* 60.

85. Akpala, "Enugu Colliery Shooting Incident," 348.

86. Smock and Akpala have different names for the unions. Akpala referred to them as the Enugu Workers Trade Union and the Enugu Surface Improvement Union. This writer will use Smock's nomenclature, The Colliery Workers Union and the Colliery Surface Improvement Union. See David Smock, "From Village to Trade Union in Africa" (Ph.D. diss. Cornell University, 1964), 129; and Agwu Akpala, "Enugu Colliery Shooting Incident," 348.

87. Morris referred to Joseph Okpokwu and Augustine Ude, two former interpreters from Agbaja. Both featured prominently in the dispute following the Representative Council's attempt to eliminate interpreters in 1939, discussed in Chapter 5. Interview with Charles Morris, a "foreigner" clerk from Owerri, Ogbete, Enugu, 19 June 1975.

88. Akpala, "Enugu. Shooting Incident," 358.

89. Interview with Isaiah O. Ojiyi, Amawbia, Awka, Nigeria, 27 July 1975.

90. NIGCOAL 2/1/138, Dewhurst, Local Authority, "Census of Enugu," 1945.

91. Ananaba, *Trade Union Movement in Nigeria*, 32.

92. CO 583/261/30425, O.A.G. Grantham to Colonial Secretary, 30 November 1943.

93. Ibid.

94. Ibid.

95. Ibid.

96. Ananaba, *Trade Union Movement in Nigeria* 75; Cohen, "Michael Imoudu"; Wale Oyemakinde, "The Nigerian General Strike of 1945," *Journal of the Historical Society of Nigeria* 7, 4 (June 1975): 693–771.

97. The resignations followed a disagreement between the union leadership over the 1943 strike. CO 583/261/30425, Grantham to Colonial Secretary, 30 November 1943.

98. Interview with Isaiah O. Ojiyi. 27 July 1975.

99. Personal Collection of David Smock, Jacob A. Diewait Typescript.

100. CO 554/129/33636 "Record of a Meeting Held on 23 June 1942."

101. For an extensive discussion of this concept, see Chapter 1.

102. Interview with Dr. Agwu Akpala, London, 14 February 1975.

103. The correspondence in his personnel files strongly suggests that there was a conspiracy against him. In some cases management actually documented their attempts to coerce him into leaving the union, arguing that it would interfere with his career. See NNAE, P/2/1/1 "Personal Papers of Mr. O.I. Ojiyi."

104. One European supervisor complained, "This Isaiah is either a mental case or an impossible person." NCCF, P.2/1/1, Angus Kerr to CM, 30 March 1942; B.S.S. to CM, 14 July 1938.

105. P.2/1/1, Ojiyi to Colliery Manager, 19 October 1944.

106. Ibid.

107. For a discussion of the "political apparatus" that sustained the "colonial labor process" see Michael Burawoy's *The Politics of Production.*

108. The educational gap between British managers, such as Yates, and many of the men whom they supervised, such as the Junior Technical Staff (JTS), was glaring. Many Nigerian managers in training commented that some of these men could barely write. The educational requirements for JTS service put these men far above them. This also contributed to the feeling of injustice.

109. P. 2/1/1, T. Yates to Colliery Manager, 21 August 1945.

110. P. 2/1/1, Ojiyi to Chief Secretary, Eastern Provinces, 16 November 1945. For discussion of this election, see p. 259ff.

111. Ibid.

112. In a remarkable coincidence Ojiyi was defended by one "Mr. Onyeama." One of the chief's sons was a lawyer and became involved in the proceedings following the shooting in 1949. P. 2/1/1, P.W. Holm, "In the Magistrate's Court of Nigeria," 13 November 1945.

113. See Table 6.5, "Accident Rates, 1943–1946," 266.

114. CO 583/261/, O.A.G. Grantham to Stanley, 27 July 1943.

115. Orde Browne, *Labour Conditions in West Africa*, 61–63.

116. Frederick Cooper, "From Free Labour to Family Allowances," 753.

117. Having read Orde Browne's report, C.W.W. Greenridge, Secretary of the Anti-Slavery and Aborigines Protection Society, questioned the government on redundant labor and housing accommodations. Private employers used the scandal to comment that government housing was worse than private. Lord Trenchard raised this in the House of Lords. CO 583/263/30544, C.W.W. Greenridge to Secretary of State for Colonies, 30 December 1941.

118. Ibid., Burn, O.A.G. to Lord Cranborne, Colonial Secretary, 18 March 1942. The Colonial Development and Welfare Act was the imperial state's response to the West Indian riots of 1935–1938 strikes in Rhodesia, Gold Coast and Dar es Salaam between 1935 and 1939. It purported to mandate reforms in the workplace and living conditions of colonial labor and to mandate systems of worker representation—trade unions. It included a modest amount of funds for housing construction, as well as improvements in health and general social welfare. For a discussion of the debate in Parliament and the Colonial Office, see Cooper, *Decolonization and African Society*, 113–121.

119. For discussion of this concept see Chapter 1.

120. See NIGCOAL 2/1/138, "Census of Enugu."

121. CO 583/263, "Report of a Committee Appointed to Review the Question of Housing Accommodations for the Employees of the Government Colliery, Enugu," 27 September 1941.

122. CO 583/261, Orde Browne Minute, 4 March 1943.

123. Members include the Resident, Onitsha, Manager Leck, and F.J.W. Skeates, the Colliery's Staff Welfare Officer. "Report of a Committee."

124. According to an informant it was better placed than the others. People were encouraged to beautify their compound, and they held competitions on the best-looking garden. The district officer and colliery manager awarded prizes. Interview with B.U. Anyasado.

125. CO 583/263, Gerald Wormal, "New Homes in Old Africa" n.d.

126. Hansards, *37th Parliament. Debates 1942–43*, 11–17 November 1943, 344.

127. They also asked for a woman who was not married to be the Lady Welfare Officer. The current officer was the wife of the Staff Welfare Officer, Skeates. UDDIST 3/1/104 "Enugu Colliery Workers and the New Housing Scheme." *The Eastern Sentinel*, 21 May 1943.

128. Ibid.

129. Ibid.

130. CO 583/261, "Notes on Points Arising in discussions with the Secretary of State on Wednesday 27 October and Thursday, 28th October 1943."

131. Ibid.

132. "Enugu Colliery Workers and the New Housing Scheme."

133. Colonial Office, "Enquiry into the Disorders in the Eastern Provinces of Nigeria: Proceedings of the Commission," vol. 1 (London, 1950), 78.

134. Supple, *History of the British Coal Industry*, 558.

135. NIGCOAL 2/1/175, Paraphrase of cypher telegram Lagos to Secretary Eastern Provinces, 15 September 1943.

136. Nigeria, *Report on the Accounts and Finances for the Years 1944/45 and 1945/46* (Lagos: Government Printer, 1947).

137. However, it was not until the 1948 publication of a monumental report on the colliery by the Powell Duffryn Technical Services, that the question of declining productivity was adequately and systematically examined. The report indicated that the war period was crucial in determining the full causes of the phenomena, specifically from 1942 through 1945/46. Since during this period the workers' struggle for a representative organization intensified, it is important to look most closely at the dynamic of the work process. Powell Duffryn Technical Services, "Characteristics of the Coal," 18.

138. C.O. 583/261/30425 23, Governor Bourdillon to Stanley in Colonial Office, January 1934.

139. Ibid.

140. This ratio is an ideal that cannot be attained given the real conditions in the mines. However, by approximating this ratio the management could significantly reduce labor costs, and thence, costs of production. Powell Duffryn, "Characteristics of the Coal," D-12, D-14, D-15.

141. In 1947, Dr. W.S.S. Ladell of the Hot Climate Physiological Research Unit in Lagos made the first scientific study of the underground conditions at Enugu. In 40 percent of his observation sites, the temperature exceeded 85 degrees Fahrenheit, a totally unacceptable level for effective work. Under such conditions it was necessary to double up the hewers, permitting one to rest and fan himself while the other worked. W.S.S. Ladell, "Applied Physiology in Nigeria," *West African Medical Journal* (March 1952): 35–37; Ibid., "Some Phys-

iological Observations on West African Coal Miners," *British Journal of Industrial Medicine* 5, 16 (1948): 16–20.

142. Powell Duffryn, "Characteristics of the Coal," D.18.

143. Calculated from the *Report of the Commission of Enquiry into the Disorders in the Eastern Provinces of Nigeria*, Report. C.O. No. 256 (London, 1950), 59. The Powell Duffryn report used more exact figures and thus had slightly different calculations.

144. Powell Duffryn, "Characteristics of the Coal," D.18.

145. See Chapter 3.

146. Powell Duffryn, "Characteristics of the Coal," D.20.

147. NCCF, P. 2/1/1, Ojiyi to CM, 16 August 1944.

148. Great Britain, Commission of Enquiry into the Disorders in the Eastern Provinces of Nigeria. *Proceedings of the Commission*, vol. 1, 12 December to 19 December (London, 1950); Testimony of R. Bracegirdle, Proceedings, vol. 1, 79.

149. *Report of the Commission of Enquiry*, pp. 18–19.

150. This is explained in the American example in Priscilla Long, *Where the Sun Never Shines*, 76.

151. Ibid.

152. NIGCOAL 2/1/77, "Minutes of the Meeting," 12 December 1945; Testimony of P.H. Cook, "Proceedings," vol. 2, p. 13.

153. Ibid.

154. David Smock, "From Village to Trade Union In Africa," 137.

155. Cohen, *Labour and Politics in Nigeria*.

156. NIGCOAL 2/1/182, Long Award Development-Hewer; Long Award Development Tubman; Long Award, Robbery Tubmen; Long Award Robbery, Hewers., n.d.

157. *Proceedings of the Commission,* vol. 1, Testimony of P.H. Cook, Proceedings, 14.

158. Ibid., Testimony of R. Bracegirdle and P.H. Cook, 14, 78.

159. "Coal Miners Tender Wholesale Resignation," *Nigerian Eastern Mail*, (7 April 1945).

160. *Proceedings of the Commission* P.H. Cook, 78.

161. NIGCOAL 2/1/182, Agwu Branch to DO Agwu, 11 April 1945; Deputy CM, "Interview with Awgu District Union, Enugu Branch," April 1945(?).

162. Ibid., DO Udi to CM, 18 April 1945; Telegram, Coals to Executive Owerri, 9 April 1945; Sealey-King to Executive Udi, April 1945.

163. *Report of the Commission*, p. 19.

164. NCCF, P.2/1/182, Enugu Division Union to CM, 16 April 1945.

165. Ibid.

166. NCCF, P. 2/1/3, 1949. R. Bracegirdle to Secretary, Eastern Provinces, 15 September 1945, Labour Dispute; Fintgerald Commission of Enquiry Representations, Attachment III.

167. Bracegirdle to Secretary, Eastern Provinces, 15 September 1945; NIGCOAL 2/1/21, Capt. Holley to P.H. Cook, 24 April 1945.

168. NIGCOAL 2/1/182, "Notice of Election Results," 30 May 1945; P.2/1/3, 1949 Labour Dispute; Fitzgerald Commission of Enquiry Representations, Attachment III, R. Bracegirdle to L.T. Chubb, Secretary, Eastern Provinces, 15 September 1945.

169. P. 2/1/3, 1949 Labour Dispute: Fitzgerald Commission of Enquiry Representation, Attachment II, J.C.M. Durake, 20 December 1949.

170. NIGCOAL, 1/1/21, M. Oba, Staff Representative to Manager, 29 November 1945.

171. Interview with Augustine Ude, Umuaga, Udi, August 5, 1975. Ude, of which more is written in earlier chapters, began at the colliery in 1919 as a messenger at age ten. In 1922 he became an interpreter and was the subject of many complaints by miners. His name was raised many times in my interviews.

172. Smock "From Village to Trade Union In Africa," 137.

173. NIGCOAL 1/1/3, "Minutes," 30 June 1945.

174. Ministry of Labour Archives, 3/S.2, vol. 1, Colliery Manager Quarterly Reports, 1945.

175. NIGCOAL 2/1/182 George Barclay to Colliery Manager, 3 May 1945.

176. NIGCOAL 2/1/182, Paton to Bracegirdle 3 May 1945.

177. Federal Government of Nigeria, Ministry of Labour Archives, 3/S.2, Vol. I, "Colliery Manager Quarterly Reports, 1945."

178. Interview with Isaiah O. Ojiyi, July 1975, Amawbia, Nigeria.

179. For the most recent analysis of this strike, which emphasizes the manipulation of the male breadwinner norm by strikers, see Lisa A. Lindsay, "Domesticity and Difference: Male Breadwinners, Working Women and Colonial Citizenship in the 1945 Nigerian General Strike," *The American Historical Review* 104, 3, (June 1999): 783–812.

180. With the exception of a few articles and references in the general histories of the nationalist movement there is little investigation of the event. See Wale Oyemakinde, "The Nigerian General Strike of 1945," *Journal of the Historical Society of Nigeria*, 7, 3 (December 1975). For two classic studies of nationalist politics see Richard Sklar, *Nigerian Political Parties* and James Coleman, *Nigeria*. For the relationship between labor and the movement see Robin Cohen, *Labour and Politics in Nigeria, 1945–1971*, (London, 1974).

181. Kenneth O. Morgan, *Labour in Power: 1945–1951* (Oxford, 1984), 339–40.

182. Partha Sarathi Gupta, *Imperialism and the British Labour Movement, 1914–1964* (New York, 1975), 305–09.

183. Cowen and Westcott, "British Imperial Economic Policy," 59.

184. Cooper, *Decolonization*, p. 203; see also P.J. Cain and A.G. Hopkins, *British Imperialism: Crisis and Deconstruction, 1914–1990* as cited in Cooper.

185. Cooper, 204.

186. Ibid, p. 59.

187. Ibid., p. 202.

188. P. 2/1/3, DO Udi to Colliery Manager, 12 February 1946. E.R. Chadwick, DO Udi argued that Ojiyi was "warped ... by that section of the African press that makes it appeal to the semi-literate on the grounds of racialism."

# 7

# THE IVA VALLEY
# MASSACRE OF 1949:
# TRADE UNION
# STRUGGLES IN THE
# COLD WAR

Officer Ormiston: ... We were completely hemmed in by miners.
Quashie-Idon: How many miners?
Officer Ormiston: The whole place was black with them.
                              —Testimony at the Commission of Enquiry.

I am saying that the workers never knew they would open fire because there
was no cause. There was no struggle of any kind. There was no fighting with
the police. They were all just there.
                    —Constable M. Ogbonna, Iva Valley Detachment.[1]
                              Testimony at the Commission of Enquiry.

A manifesto ... shows that they are becoming increasingly subject to Communist influence. It is clear ... that those who prepared it have not only read
[a] considerable amount of Communist propaganda but must also have made
some study of Communist organization.
                    —Nigerian Government Secret Report on the
                              Zikist Movement, December 1948.[2]

The colliery workers had never experienced the naked hand of state violence until
18 November 1949. On that day troops fired eighty-seven rounds of ammunition
at a peaceful gathering of miners occupying the Iva Valley Mine to prevent a lockout in an industrial dispute.[3] When the shooting stopped twenty men lay dead on

the site and scores were wounded. Within a few days the death toll climbed to twenty-two. Riots erupted in all the major cities of Eastern Nigeria and crowds attacked those expatriate trading firms that had profited so greatly from the war. Zikists, the most radical wing of the nationalist movement, were prominent among the crowds in the streets of Port Harcourt, Enugu, and Calabar where soldiers shot more victims. In the United States, W.E.B. Du Bois and Paul Robeson of the Council of African Affairs dashed off a protest to the Colonial Office and miners' unions throughout England, Scotland and Wales voiced their indignation. The nationalists had their dramatic moment and briefly, a workers' dispute occupied the center stage of the political debate over the future of Nigeria. Today, despite the complex factors contributing to the success of the nationalist movement, most Nigerians cite the Iva Valley Massacre as the primary event ending British colonialism in Nigeria. In Enugu the memory is even more intimate and many of the older generation can cite at least one person who died or was wounded. The tragedy is embedded in popular memory as the sacrifice coal miners made to the birth of the Nigerian nation. An imposing bronze statue commemorates the shooting from a central crossroads in Enugu.

Something had gone terribly awry. The Labour Party's ambitious plans to contain and reform colonial labor had collapsed into a paroxysm of terror more befitting a Conservative government. The legalization of trade unions, the deployment of cooperative BTUC advisers to coach "responsible" trade unionism, the prodding of colonial governors to modernize labor policies, the endless proposals and convoluted procedures designed to diffuse industrial conflicts, the various "enlightened" social welfare policies—all had failed to prevent this tragedy. Rather, they had led to the type of embarrassing excesses of brute force that Colonial Office policies had sought to prevent. The shooting occurred under the government of the same Labour Party that, in opposition, had promoted workers' rights (albeit circumscribed) during the war. It now was responsible for shooting unarmed colonial workers in cold blood, not unlike an authoritarian "throwback" to early colonial times. But pushing a package of labor rights while custodian of the imperial state had its contradictions and these contradictions bubbled up and slapped Labour in the face. Colonial workers were not imbeciles and they proved able to manipulate the cumbersome industrial relations machinery in unanticipated ways, most often under the leadership of sophisticated men. These men, whom state officials considered "demagogues," manipulated the new laws, exploited the new industrial institutions, unraveled the cumbersome procedures, and skillfully navigated the minefield of state legislation to secure their membership's demands.

The Iva Valley tragedy is a lens that captures the obstacles confronting colonial workers who viewed the new forms of employee representation, institutions of industrial relations, and processes for disputes management with skepticism. It was caused by a constellation of events rooted in the historical evolution of worker protest, management, and state intervention in the colliery. The transference of British industrial management techniques, being excitedly applied to the postwar British working class, proved ill-suited to the explosive context of the postwar

colonial workplace. This chapter argues that many of the industry's most significant postwar conflicts actually evolved *because* of government's labor reforms.
Most often the state's interventions, far from resolving industrial conflicts, sharpened these conflicts and pushed them to the surface. This had been demonstrated
in the crisis over the Long Agreement of 1945. The social legitimacy of trade unions
as organizations of worker representation was undermined when management and
the state's labor officers used compulsory arbitration to manipulate the union to
accept a settlement that neither the workers nor their leaders supported and then
disbanded it as non-representative when it failed to win the workers' support. There
followed a lockout of questionable legality in which management tried to
reorganize the labor process in ways that reduced the miners' autonomy. And although the state succeeded in imposing this system, it finally had to recant because
no sector of the workforce felt it had been treated justly. The industrial climate
steadily deteriorated and the industry lumbered to its next crisis.

Now that the war was over, the Colonial Office could hone in on industrial policies introduced during the war to sharpen their effectiveness in preventing industrial unrest. Colonial resources were still of importance to rebuilding the British
economy, and work stoppages by "native" laborers were of no small consequence
to the possibilities of metropolitan economic growth. These policies were never
designed to give real power and authority to African unions but to channel discontent into directions that were least disruptive. Now the state concentrated on an
elaboration—the promotion of collective bargaining—as the only legitimate context for expressions of worker grievances. Legalized but restricted trade unions,
cumbersome consultative machinery, and joint consultative processes were all refined to weaken worker power.

But all these attempts failed in their purpose to derail worker militance. The
biggest labor disputes erupted in the postwar period, when Enugu miners attempted
to address the depredations of the war, to get their union reinstated, and to secure
the same types of amenities and wage allotments as British miners in England. The
effectiveness of reforms crafted in London by Colonial Office experts in mediating the levels of conflict in the colliery were undermined by their ignorance of local
conditions and a blind assumption that any mechanism developed for the English
working class could certainly be used to good effect with "native" labor. Rhetoric
to the contrary, the Colonial Office was still locked into old racialized notions of
African labor which made it impossible for them to conceptualize Africans as modern, industrial men. This led officials to see every outburst of worker protest, every
memorandum listing demands, and every argument raised in consultations with
management as the insidious result of the capricious "demagogue" Ojiyi's manipulation of "illiterate manual workers." Surely Enugu's workers were incapable of
recognizing the problems in their own condition and organizing around their solutions.

There was a blatant contradiction between the ideological foundations of the
new policies and the reality of colliery industrial relations. On the one hand, the
exigencies of the war and the militance of colonial workers encouraged officials

to view them as "universal industrial men" not totally dissimilar from the British working class. Hence they assumed the relevance of British industrial relations structures and processes for Nigeria. On the other hand was the resilience of "old" conceptions of African workers held by officials in all echelons of the state, from labor advisors in the Colonial Office to the manager in the colliery. Could the irresponsible militance of the "primitive African worker" be mediated by structures and procedures that enjoyed success with most sectors of the British working class? Did Enugu's workers *deserve* to have the rights "won" by struggling British working class men? Were these men capable of forming the type of unions that would stabilize the Nigerian economy and assist the state in the development project?

While officials pondered these questions they ignored the fundamental question. It was not: *Could* Africans form unions? But, would state officials and the industry's management *allow* meaningful trade unions to develop? The interval between the disarray of the 1945 Long Award lockout and the 1949 shooting suggests not.

On the ground, labor policy vacillated between—the "industrial" man and the "native" worker—reflecting the ambiguities of authorities themselves. This was manifest in a number of ways, most fundamentally in a paternalistic refusal to believe that the key workers, the miners, were capable of analyzing their own work situation and formulating grievances *without* the manipulation of allegedly "demagogic" labor leaders like Ojiyi. Concomitant with this assumption was the state's persistent attempt to replace the union with either rural or urban leaders of "ethnically" based associations, be they the rural village council or the improvement unions. After all, they felt that beneath the skin of the Enugu miner you found a rural "tribesman" on whose consciousness "tribal" leaders had a deep primeval claim even if he "appeared" to be an industrial worker. Yet at the same time, some state officials, especially the labor professionals, promoted British industrial relations procedures that structured industrial conflict as if the men were "true" workers. Clearly there was ambivalence within various layers of the state and, in many cases, within the same official. This ambivalence confronted the daily reality of the men's activism.

This final chapter brings forth these themes in a complex narrative that begins with attempts by workers to restore their union and to settle claims first raised before the war. It chronicles a flawed process of state intervention into the workplace during a period of uncertain political change. To the metropolitan state this was a political context of dangerous possibilities. Many local officials saw Communist conspiracies behind every nationalist strategy and most believed that African workers were too unsophisticated to recognize when they were being used. But the colliery was racked by industrial struggles over the nature of power in production, not the general political disposition of Nigeria. To the industry's workers this was a time of exciting possibilities which they had "paid" for with their labor during the war. They were poised to demand wages that allowed them to prepare their families, villages, and communities to accept more political responsibility for Nigeria. The postwar struggles reflected the aspirations of workers, which informed their determination to settle unresolved claims and to revitalize their union, hobbled by the manipulations of the metropolitan and colonial state and the industry's management.

The resolution of industrial conflict became more and more complicated by state-mandated procedures of consultation and arbitration. This was the ritualization of class conflict, and its intricacies emphasized the critical role of the shifts in relations "in production" for explaining the more public collective displays of worker activism.[4] This bureaucratization of the class struggle generated a body of trade union and disputes management legislation that was applied, insidiously, to the labor disputes during this period.[5] Ironically, the types of men who became leaders were those who were valued for their ability to weave through the entanglements of this legislation and use this or that aspect of the law to articulate historic workers' grievances.

These realities gave the workers' struggles of this period a complexity that was largely absent in the pre-war period. Now many of the conflicts were over interpretations of regulations, regulations which quite often management and local authorities did not understand nor support. These fluid complexities are reflected in the detailed narrative. Although intricate, the narrative recaptures the texture of the daily struggles of African workers in a historical period of sharpened aspirations and hope. It documents their sophisticated understanding of the nature of the challenge launched by the state and the ways they devised to circumvent it. The reader can therefore understand the emotional and political context in which labor was being reformulated and was asserting its integrity amidst the chaotic process of decolonization.

Unlike most studies of the shooting, which rely heavily on the conclusions and recommendations of the Fitzgerald Commission Report, the government's investigative body, this chapter draws upon eyewitness accounts in testimony before the Commission, interviews with victims, and a contextual analysis using archival sources.[6] While most sources explain the crisis by echoing the Commission's conclusion that Ojiyi "misled" the workers, this study examines the relationship between consciousness, positionality in the labor process, and the changing responsibilities and self-image of Igbo men. By centering on the miners we can explore the ways that the hewers' power in production was affected by changes in the organization of work and how this sharpened their awareness of the industry's importance to the national economy. Additionally, the chapter demonstrates how the adoption of British labor union structures could be problematic when it ignored indigenous organizational traditions. Thus, the chapter centers on the hewers and suggests that their realization of their power and entitlements, rather than the manipulations of Ojiyi, drove the crisis of 1949.

The narrative follows a prescient series of conflicts in which the successive resolution of one only "papers over" the deeply rooted problems in the industry and planted the seeds of successive and more severe phases of conflict. The chapter identifies two waves of conflict: in 1946/47 and 1948/49. In both cases, the state underestimated the sophistication of union leadership, the determination of the rank and file, and the level of political consciousness of the miners. For these reasons, state policy was never able to successfully create an environment in which management could get substantial control over the labor process. Secondly, both the union leadership, Ojiyi in particular, and the management failed to understand the sense of power and leadership that the hewers felt as the producers who "drive" the industry.

The deteriorating industrial environment at the colliery severely compromised the policies of labor reform drafted in Lagos or London. All the various instruments of "responsible" worker-management dialogue were burdened by this reality. The chapter then locates the genesis of the 1949 shooting in a dispute in 1946/47 when management failed to consult with the union on the application of a national wage award to the colliery's workers. Finally, it chronicles the series of events in late 1949 that catapulted the colliery into the center of nationalist consciousness. At that time, the hewers ignored both management and the union leadership and plunged the industry into a crisis in which a confused and paranoid state proved incapable of distinguishing a "political" from an "industrial" conflict.[7]

## AN "ATTITUDE OF SUSPICION AND HOSTILITY": LEVELS OF INDUSTRIAL CONFLICT, 1945–1947

The war changed the housing patterns of the workforce. Almost half of the workers now lived in the city, rather than commuting daily or weekly from adjacent villages. This was partially caused by recruitment of Owerri strike breakers during 1945 and partly by the more general urbanization which affected most African cities during the war.[8] The city's expansion was also related to military establishments which housed several thousand troops stationed there during the war. The demobilization of troops after the war also had an impact as there were over 600 in the Udi district alone.[9] These men often unemployed were a radicalizing force in national politics and exhibited a certain impatience with the slow pace of political change.[10] Many were "Boma Boys," some of the 30,000 Nigerian troops who fought in Burma.

Politically, Enugu's inhabitants were swept into the nationalist mainstream by the formation of the National Council of Nigeria and the Cameroons (NCNC) in August 1945. It was through this Council that the political energies of the discontented urban elite found expression. As a federation of urban improvement unions, trade unions, and political associations of the Nigerian educated elite the Council further enforced the transmission of nationalist ideologies to broad sectors of the population. Although the NCNC leadership was multi-ethnic, its strongest base was among the Igbo and it was very popular in the cities, like Enugu, of eastern Nigeria.[11] While the NCNC was a mass-based organization, its ideology was not necessarily radical nor its programs activist. In 1946 a group of "angry" young men and women dissatisfied with the pace of change towards self-government formed the Zikist Movement using Nnamdi Azikiwe (Zik), the NCNC leader, as its symbol but not its leader.[12] The Zikist advocated a strategy of "positive action" or civil disobedience similar to that being used by Nkrumah in Ghana and espoused an eclectic ideology of radical nationalism.[13] The movement appealed to the restless junior clerks in government service whose opportunities for occupational and political advancement were circumscribed by the racial hierarchies in the civil service and the state's proclivities towards "traditional" rural rulers. Many of the more socialist Zikists sought to create viable links with trade unions that they considered to hold potential for political mobilization.[14] The movement's militant nationalist ideology and tactics appealed to a sector of the national trade union leadership who similarly relished mass action. One of its founding members, Nduka Eze, was the secretary of the United Africa Company Workers Union (UNAMAG) and Ojiyi claimed to be a member of a local chapter established in Enugu. As a member, Ojiyi, like Eze, was a *realization* of the government's greatest fear—a leader who linked an important workers' movement with an unpredictable radical nationalist party.

As was the case throughout the Empire at this time, the European community had long been alarmed with the breakdown of colonial privilege and the transgressive behavior of African men which reached considerable frequency during the war. This insubordination was conceptualized as a dangerous disorder. As noted earlier, industrially it appeared as acts of insubordination in the railway and Public Works departments. "Abusive" graffiti appeared on coaches; strikes and "go slows" were frequent. The comments of one Norman Smith exemplified the alarmist position of some in the European community. Complaining about the state's tolerance of nationalist agitation he was appalled by the

> aggressiveness of the Africans and the licenses allowed them by higher authority to pursue a policy of vilification of the British or indulge in strikes and go slow methods which, in the opinion of many, were quite unjustified.[15]

It is difficult to assess the extent of social hysteria among the European population. Nonetheless, if not a dominant sentiment it did reflect an air of uncertainty, instability, and concern among European colonials, many of whom would be in crucial decision-making positions over the colliery. Despite Colonial Office claims that such allegations were exaggerated, local officials were more sanguine about their significance and could not afford to take them lightly. Many of the police commanders at the Iva Valley strike recalled feeling claustrophobic, surrounded by "hysterical natives," and being in eminent danger of being attacked by weapons, and by "dangerous dancers."[16]

The postwar period was a time of industrial contraction reflecting a decreased coal demand and the railway's inability to evacuate the full output of coal.[17] The railway's secondhand rolling stock had been pushed to its limits during the war and collapsed afterwards under the strain. Equipment was not immediately repaired because of the condition of British industry after the war. Additionally, Nigeria also had to resettle ex-servicemen. Some 600 were registered in Udi Division and absorbed into an already surplus mine workforce.[18] As a political group they further radicalized Nigerian politics in general and colliery industrial relations in particular. Nine hundred of a total surface and underground workforce of 6,325 were redundant at 1946 production levels.[19]

Under these uncertainties Bracegirdle reinstated "rostering" to keep surplus workers "on the books" and fully mobilized but underemployed. As noted earlier, "rostering" was a long-standing grievance and despite condemnation by labor experts such as Orde Browne, the manager felt he needed the flexibility of having workers available at a day's notice. But it disadvantaged workers because it prevented them from being able to plan their finances and to meet their obligations to their families and communities.

The timing of "rostering" after the war was provocative because relations between workers and management were at their worst and there was no union to present the men's feelings to management. Postwar inflationary pressures continued to mount and it was difficult to earn a living wage when working so few days. The men saw the system as another indication that management had little concern for their conditions and abilities to carry forth their roles in their communities and families. This was all the more important because this was a time of excited expectation and seemingly endless possibilities for a better future. Although the Nigerian government was slow to seize the initiative in proposing a model of political transformation, everyone knew that some form of majority rule was eminent. This pressured colliery men who felt responsible for insuring that their children and their villages were positioned to take advantage of the new Nigeria.

Now colliery jobs were even more important in financing the large number of development projects being organized in the villages. District Officers frequently commented on the miners, echoing the opinions of the "intelligentsia in Enugu." For example, they, like the intelligentsia, rejected the government's Mass Literacy programs as inadequate in favor of compulsory education.[20] When the state proved reluctant to expand education they created

> a quite phenomenal outburst during 1946 and 1947 of building of large stone-built primary schools, paid for to a large extent from the wages of colliers and wage earners living in Enugu.[21]

As men of considerable stature and prominence, colliery workers were also committed to support maternity clinics, build roads, and to bring potable water to the village. These commitments were based on stable wages which were eroded by inflation and undermined by "rostering." To be unable to meet these responsibilities was a source of considerable shame. The hewers' resentment was deeply felt because the financial solvency of the industry depended on their skill and labor and they did not feel that they were being treated fairly.

Perhaps the deepest source of worker resentment was the refusal of the management to accept "their" union. Although workers' support of the union was not unconditional, they did feel that Ojiyi had more than proven his sincerity in confronting management and political authorities on behalf of their demands. But the debate over the propriety of "modern" metropolitan industrial relations practices and institutions with colonial workers continued between local management, state officials, and the Colonial Office labor experts. Not even the "labor experts" were convinced that African workers were responsible enough to select good leaders.

Workers confrontations with management often incorporated personal conflicts that symbolized a masculine confrontation between Africa and Britain. Such was the case by late 1945 when relations between Ojiyi and Bracegirdle had reached their lowest point. In addition to those disputes arising from the union/management struggle, the two men were locked in a personal conflict. They hated each other. To Bracegirdle, Ojiyi was an "uppity native" who certainly didn't "know his place" and was hell bent on antagonizing every European underground. To Ojiyi, Bracegirdle was a disrespectful and arrogant young person who would not give him the respect he was due as his senior. Additionally, as a young man new to Nigeria (1943) Bracegirdle was already having problems establishing his legitimacy among the older, more experienced European staff, some of whom were apparently passed over in the selection of manager.[22] These tensions further poisoned labor/management relations during the period when the union was not recognized. Like many labor-management conflicts in the colonial workplace this one had racial dimensions.

The end of the workers' tolerance for the most violent forms of workplace authority in the mines was an industrial expression of the prominent role that racial discrimination was playing in the mobilizations of the nationalist movement. The Nigerian government was slow to proclaim opposition to the most offensive vestiges of racial privilege among the colonial service although racist employers had sparked more than one strike among industrial workers.[23] Officials underestimated the capacity of these blatant inequities in wages, conditions of service, and job promotion to mobilize broad sectors of the population.

Thus the nationalist and trade union movements seized the racial issue and "ran." In 1946 the NCNC toured the country using racial discrimination as a mobilizing tool to generate support in their campaign against the constitutional proposal of Governor Arthur Richards, which blocked consultations with nationalists in deference to "traditional rulers" and gave no substantial concessions for political participation.[24] The team included the most prominent and respected nationalist and trade union leaders: Nnamdi Azikiwe, Herbert Macaulay, who died early in the campaign, and Michael Imoudu, President, Railway Workers Union and leader of the 1945 General Strike. For eight months the team toured and organized public meetings which met enthusiastic crowds, especially in the east. Administrators noted, in dismay, the heightened political discourse in Enugu where the NCNC was especially strong. Here Zik had used his press, especially the *West African Pilot*, to give voice to the concerns of clerks, artisans, and teachers. Giving "the social and recreational pursuits of the common clerk or artisan who, flattered to see his name in print or his picture in the paper was inspired to support Azikiwe politically and to become a habitual reader of his papers."[25] This was especially the case with the Udi improvement unions which had a large number of coal miners and clerks.[26]

Despite this "warning" of the incendiary possibilities of colonial racism, it wasn't until a more embarrassing event that the government made a public proclamation against racial discrimination. In April 1947 an official of the Colonial Office, of African descent, was denied accommodation at the Lagos Bristol Hotel.[27] The nationalists organized mass meetings, forcing the governor to issue a circular banning discrimination in all public facilities.

At the mines, the colliery's African clerical staff and laborers were also concerned with racial discrimination. They evaluated their conditions of work against the allowances and privileges reserved for European employees. Miners were especially rankled by the separation allowances given to British employees whose wives remained in England. Others alleged that Europeans even had allowances for their dogs! Despite the exaggerations, clearly broad sectors of the African population had embraced the idea of equality and self-determination. The underground allowance, granted only to Europeans, symbolized this racial difference and would become a target of union action.

Moreover, there was a particularly insidious practice that symbolized the racial environment at the colliery—the hammock tradition—which now was an intolerable symbol of racial privilege. Despite the availability of cars, African "hammock boys" carried white bosses to work in hammocks from their homes perched on the hill.[28] The practice was accompanied by other, more brutal examples of racial privilege. Decades later, one informant described the humiliation of this tradition to the worker:

> A section of the workers were designated hammock boys who carry their European bosses to and from the mine. When on the execution of this carmel (sic) and never eating (sic) duty, they are subjected to beating, spitting upon, kicking about by boots for any shake their boss could receive while in his hanging home build (sic) on the head of human being; this offence (sic) earned a worker so employed immediate dismissal and loss of all benefits.[29]

Conditions were far from auspicious for Ojiyi in the union as well. He was under attack by a clique of clerical and supervisory workers, many of whom had a long history of cooperation with management at the expense of workers. The attacks came from many quarters. The former interpreters and other staff from the Agbaja village-group resented the influence Ojiyi had over their men. Men like Joseph Okpokwu, a leader in Aboh, and Augustine Ude, former CWU President, from Umuagua were active. Some were in leadership in the Surface Improvement Union.

On the political front, national, regional, and local authorities were not predisposed to help diffuse the hostile environment at the mines, which, in any case, they had helped to create. They had not been confident supporters of the reforms being dictated by the Colonial Office and they were not entirely convinced that they should trust the new cohort of BTUC labor advisers to "understand the native workers" sufficiently to make any useful suggestion for resolving industrial conflict. At any rate, political officials were deeply implicated in the intrigues against Ojiyi personally and the union in general.

The Colonial Office and its labor experts made an abstract distinction between economic and political disputes and tried to control each with appropriate mechanisms. The "man on the spot," the political official in the field, found this distinction to be rather contrived. To those state functionaries charged to administer Enugu and adjacent villages, every industrial dispute was potentially a political crisis. In one respect, they were quite right because the distinction between politics and colonial industry was more imagined than real. But, to the Colonial Office, there were "correct" ways of handling industrial disputes that could channel broad workplace issues—issues that questioned the very foundation of colonial society—into manageable economistic solutions. And there were ways of coopting nationalist leaders to "win" them away from radical ideologies.[30] But the state could hardly make these distinctions without the assistance of the labor advisers regarded with suspicion by many of the "old hands" and stumbled from crisis to crisis in the minefield of Nigerian domestic politics.

Even the local state officials had long-standing misgivings about Bracegirdle's competence and the extent to which his apparently "difficult" temperament would provoke conflict. Confronted with an ineffective Representative Committee in 1946 he revived his suggestion to replace it with a body including representatives from the village and urban unions.[31] But E.H. Chadwick, D.O. Udi, and L.T. Chubb, Secretary Eastern Provinces, deprecated his suggestion and Chadwick noted that any attempt to stamp out the union was sure to create suspicions among the urban ethnic unions that they would be next. But the Resident, D.P.J. O'Connor, similarly critiqued Chadwick's suggestion that as an alternative the Colliery Management "keep in touch with the men as at present through notices."[32] O'Connor noted sarcastically:

> With all respect to the Colliery Management and with no desire to wound feelings ... "keeping in touch" ... is precisely what the Management for long years has signally failed to do. I doubt whether the Management will ever acquire that trust and confidence which has been reposed in Administrative Officers in the past. The mere fact that for so many years before 1943 little or no attempt was made to establish this "touch" will occasion deep suspicion of any attempt to attain it, now or in the future.

He then made a surprisingly prescient comment, that he would leave management alone "until the last possible minute when troubles have become a definite political issue."[33] The manager sensed this lack of confidence and harbored great resentment against officials who often overstepped his authority or undermined his decisions by negotiating with workers behind his back.

Political officials also had larger concerns. Regional authorities were disturbed by new political developments in eastern Nigeria. First, there were rumors that explosives had been stolen from the coal mines and construction sites.[34] This was especially serious because there were some 600 ex-servicemen in Udi district alone.[35] Many had been trained in guerilla warfare in Southeast Asia and were among the most vociferous critics of the slow and unenlightened pace of political change.

The role of the 1948 Gold Coast ex-servicemen's riots in stimulating Kwame Nkrumah's "positive action" campaign made the Nigerian government even more concerned about the political radicalism of this group.[36] Many of them lived in

Enugu where postwar resettlement policy integrated them into the national working class, by requiring government departments to fill 5 percent of their positions with veterans.[37] At the colliery they entered the workforce as "supernumeraries," i.e., excess workers hired preferentially and absorbed into an already surplus mine workforce.[38] As a social group they further radicalized Nigerian politics in general and colliery industrial relations in particular. They were especially antagonistic towards the village leaders and played an important role in initiating challenges to the various management schemes to "trick" workers into ignoring the union.

In late 1948, the Zikists appeared to be teetering dangerously close to inciting a similar demonstration of "positive action" in Nigeria. On 27 October 1948, Osita Agwuna, a member from Onitsha District, delivered a speech called "A Call for Revolution" which made thirteen proposals for civil disobedience. The government became alarmed and rapidly arrested the major members of the group.[39] By the time of the colliery's November 1949 crisis the government anticipated the possibilities of radical disruptions through the Zikist linkages with the trade union movement.

## LURCHING TOWARD TRAGEDY: THE "VICTORY" 1947 SETTLEMENT AND THE ROOTS OF THE 1949 CRISIS

While state officials in British West Africa muddled through the political transition to representative government management, the local authorities stumbled from crises to crisis at the colliery, arrogantly ignoring the indicators of impending disaster and confidently assuming that they could find a more "cooperative" alternative to Ojiyi and his Union. The Nigerian General Strike and the rash of wildcat strikes in various government departments led the Colonial Office to recognize that the deplorable state of labor-management relations within government subverted/jeopardized the productionist thrust of postwar colonial economic policy. The Colonial Office sought to diffuse the volatile industrial environment by using various forms of joint consultation which in the United Kingdom fostered a "respectful *can* in handling civil service associationism."[40] The promotion of concilliation processes became a keystone of government labor reform, but it presupposed a set of institutions and practices that management did not accept. Specifically, it required independent forms of employee representation and at the colliery, as in many colonial workplaces, it was difficult for employers to acknowledge this principle. The underlying problem was that this "culture of consultation" required that expatriate department heads treat "native labor" as employees within the rubric of industrial relations. But they so resented having to treat "the native" as an industrial worker that they infused these meetings with such invective that they became yet another site of racialized conflict. Nigerian workers' representatives were sensitized to a racialized managerial culture that subjected them to dehumanizing and emasculating behavior. In sum, cooperative consultation could not bear the weight of colonial racial and class contradictions.

As the conflict in 1945 showed, state commitment to labor unions was clearly contingent upon their rejection of militance. When they proved problematic at the colliery management and the state used compulsory arbitration, launched court challenges, withdrew union recognition, encouraged union dissidents, and even resorted to personal harassment. Ojiyi had resisted personalized management attacks for several years, alleging throughout, and quite vociferously, that he was being singled out because of his trade union activities. The archive fully supports his contentions.[41] In April 1946 management finally succeeded in hounding him out of his position and he submitted his resignation. From this time onward he was a full-time labor organizer. But Ojiyi, who had trained in Nigerian labor law within the Junior Technical Staff, was a capable adversary. He was just the type of leader workers counted on to demystify the complex bureaucratic procedures that characterized postwar industrial relations. In an undoubtedly coordinate effort, Lagos officials sued the leadership for failing to follow the financial provisions of the trade union law.[42] But Ojiyi responded, pointing to the absurdity of suing a non-existent union:

> If the Government does not recognise the Unions, why then did the Government sue the very Unions in the Magistrate Court of Lagos for failing to abide by some of the Trade Union Ordinance?[43]

The 1947 dispute did more than any single event to push the industry towards the tragedy of 1949 and underscored the difficulties of transferring British industrial relations procedures to the colonial workplace. The colliery had an environment of unresolved and long-held grievances, dissident challenges to the credibility of union leaders and official harassment from local state officials and management. Ojiyi adopted a two-pronged strategy. First, he continued to lodge the men's grievances. In January 1946, Ojiyi, besieged by detractors, revitalized the unresolved demands that had generated the 1945 Long crisis. But this time he drew upon the anti-discriminatory discourse of the nationalists and challenged the management to extend the recent award of a £5 underground allowance for expatriate staff to African miners.[44] He shrewdly argued:

> The workers ... believe that the approved Underground allowance is not only applicable to European Underground workers, but also to the African workers. If the Colliery Manager allows only the European workers to get their allowances ... then he is showing a grim discrimination in that respect.[45]

Ojiyi had identified an issue capable of politicizing industrial grievances in a form that resonated with the deeply rooted resentments workers harbored against the racism of the colonial workplace. Workers responded with a brief protest, which will be discussed more fully below. His strategy was to undermine management's withdrawal of recognition by ignoring local officials and placing these demands before various government agencies, a tactic that briefly succeeded in manipulating the administration in Lagos.[46]

Like many early trade union leaders throughout Africa, he had rapidly mastered the rhetoric, legalities, and structure of the Colonial Office's labor reforms, and manipulated them against the state. For example, citing provisions of Regulation

156 of the same Nigerian Defense Regulations that management used to enforce the Long Arbitration he argued that the dismissal of the workers was a lockout and hence prohibited by law.[47] He succeeded in sparking a debate between regional and national officials over the interpretation of the law.[48] The state could bureau- cratize labor relations in many complex ways, but this would encourage workers to secure educated trade unionists to assist them in understanding these realities.

The union unleashed a brilliant tactic that circumvented the Defense Regula- tions prohibition against strikes and drew upon the protest traditions of Britain's militant coal miners. In February 1946 the workers launched a brief "go slow" which Ojiyi called a *ca'canny*.[49] *"Go ca'canny"* was a Durham term for "go slow" or "work to rule."[50] Ojiyi indigenized the term by calling it *"welu nwayo"* in Igbo and spent many days in the mines teaching the men.[51] Although the demonstration quickly folded in the face of a lockout, it nonetheless should have been seen as a barometer of the levels of discontent simmering beneath the surface of industrial calm.

Events were brought to a head by the management's handling of a national wage negotiation in 1946/47. At that time Ojiyi was asked to make presentations at two state investigative bodies appointed to propose adjustments in national wages for established and unestablished government staff. Despite the legal position of the CWU they could not omit the colliery from their investigations. It is unclear whether these commissions were ignorant of the union's status or were simply ac- knowledging the reality of the union's strength among the workers. Ojiyi gave tes- timony at both the Harragin Commission,[52] that examined the wages of established staff, and the Miller Commission,[53] of unestablished staff. Perhaps emboldened by the reality of the union's importance to national government wage-fixing bodies and the necessity of their meeting with him, amidst challenges to his leadership, Ojiyi chastised the Manager:

> That the Government Colliery refuses to negotiate with the Colliery Unions does not, in any way, mean that the unions do no longer exist and will no longer exist legally. That will not also be a necessary ground to deprive the Unions of their legal rights to act and function for the members within the ambit of Trade Union laws as approved. ... So no-recognition has very little to do with the existence and functions of the Unions.[54]

Because of the numbers of manual workers at the colliery, the Miller Commis- sion was the more relevant for the mine workers. The Commission only consoli- dated wages and did not grant wage increases, a distinction the men failed to make. The Commission's purpose was misunderstood and caused unfulfilled expectations of further wage increases. Because the colliery operated with such a complex wage system (i.e., time wages, tonnage rates, various allowances, and seniority pay) the manager was asked to develop his own wage consolidation proposal in consulta- tion with the workers' representatives—Ojiyi. Relations between management and workers were at their lowest and, as should have been expected, Bracegirdle was ill-disposed to consult with either the workers or the banned union. Thus, when he announced his adjustment in October 1947, several months after the national award, he met with angry opposition.[55] Within days the industry was in the throes of another industrial crisis.

In November 1947 workers launched another "go slow" to underscore the grievances of 1944, to protest against racial discrimination in wages, and to demand improved conditions of service. Management attempts to use the village leaders, improvement unions, and supervisory staff to mobilize workers failed again when the men refused to even discuss their grievances with outside groups.[56] But when Bracegirdle followed the same procedure as in 1945 and began firing hewers, J.G. Pyke-Nott, the Chief Commissioner, Eastern Provinces, intervened and attempted to channel the dispute into conciliation, but with a decidedly colonial twist.[57] Normally, conciliation uses an impartial party to assist labor and management in settling differences. However, in this case, the conciliator came from the same Labour Department that had helped to create the problems requiring negotiation. The Labour Department violated the spirit of the conciliation system when its Senior Labour Officer, P.H. Cook, met with management and the Secretary (Finance) Eastern Provinces, to plan strategy for the conciliation. The violation of the principles and conventions of conciliation was yet another example of the colonial corruption of industrial conflict procedures.

Conciliation hearings were held from 3–20 December and were highly contentious. The minutes reflect Ojiyi's initial concerns to enlist management in crushing the union dissidents who had become increasingly disruptive when the union lost its registration. Under attack, Ojiyi had to reassert his position against management in order to retain the support of his men. Additionally, Bracegirdle was even more insulted that he had to meet with a man he considered to be a scoundrel and charlatan. Despite administrative collusion and the challenges to leadership, they did reach an agreement that favored the union.[58]

The settlement expressed elements of a broader postwar colonial labor policy to break up the solidarity of the working class that was reflected in the wave of general strikes, which had been encouraged by undifferentiated work areas in which the commonalties of economic hardship created a strong incentive for collective protest.[59] Clearly the state had to offer the prospect of some parity with expatriate workers for at least the higher skilled and clerical sectors of the workforce. But again, a policy promoted to diffuse industrial conflict was hobbled by colonial contradictions. Many strikes during this period were focused around the regrading of jobs which often expressed workers' challenges to the ways that management assessed the level of skill required by their job. This was the case with the 1947 strike. All labor was reclassified into three groups: established staff, special labor, and general labor with corresponding amenities and wage increases.[60] The underground allowance that symbolized racial discrimination was extended, although in a much smaller amount to all underground workers. The hewers regained the daily rate lost under the Long Arbitration. For the clerical workers, the agreement upgraded many staff posts and extended to them fringe benefits that were formerly restricted to Europeans, such as leave and holiday pay. Hewers were given overtime pay for holidays and supervisory staff were given a six-hour workday comparable to European staff.

The most important provision of the agreement was its wage award which granted over £150,000 in back wages from 1 January 1946. The amount was based on the retroactive application of the councillors' findings and was both a dramatic indication of the benefits accruing to workers if they accepted the state's industrial relations procedures and evidence of the benefits of a strong trade union.

But while a victory in wage terms it also planted the seeds of controversy that would prove fatal to the stabilization of the union. This principle of retroactivity became the Achilles' heel of the agreement because it only applied to certain groups of workers. The union leaders argued that if the agreement was retroactive, then all provisions held within were likewise retroactive. If certain groups of workers were given salary awards based on retroactivity, then all had to be. Ojiyi immediately recognized the implications of the retroactive provision and raised it again in 1949. Moreover, a second problem came when the men received their pay. Ojiyi and the union executive collected a levy from each worker, a sum of £2,000 which was apparently distributed to the negotiating team in payment for their securing the award.[61] The exclusion of the clerical staff leaders from the levy infuriated them and stoked the fires of resentment which encouraged them even more to challenge Ojiyi's leadership among the rank and file and his compliance with the state's trade union legislation. They would hound him for most of this period, forcing Ojiyi to stave off their challenges. Additionally, the Agreement left a number of issues pending further discussion. These included safety equipment, transport facilities, and ending the unpopular system of "rostering." These issues would be sufficient to prolong the conflict.

Finally, the Colonial Office commissioned a comprehensive industrial study by a major Welsh mining company, the Powell Duffryn Technical Services, Ltd. The company had extensive operational experience with African coal mining and ran the infamous Wankie Colliery in Zimbabwe.[62] Their report, released in 1948, was to provide a blueprint for the reconstruction of the industry in preparation for restructuring under decolonization.

## RECREATING THE COLLIERY UNION:
## IGBO VERSUS BRITISH ORGANIZATIONAL CULTURES

The Agreement initiated a process to reinstate the colliery union but to reorganize it to insulate the workers from the influence of Ojiyi. Both the new labor experts and state officials were caught in the mythologies that characterized much of colonial labor policy during the period of decolonization. They had imagined a polarity: the irresponsible, demagogic trade union leader and the cooperative "responsible" tribal elders. Therefore, Ojiyi—who manipulated the legitimate grievances of the workers—could not be trusted. He was a literate African exerting control over the unschooled masses which he incited for his own benefit.[63] Because the clan/village councilors and the leaders of the urban improvement association

sympathized with the position of management, the workers refused to acknowledge their leadership. The workers understood which among these contenders could
successfully win them gains.

The state used a bureaucratic solution to attack this problem. In November,
Robert Curry, a labor adviser from the British TUC, restructured the banned CWU
in preparation for restored recognition.[64] Curry used a model of union organization,
the branch structure, which he hoped would reduce the direct control Ojiyi appeared to exercise over the workers. However, this model was interpreted in a way
that reflected the different cultural meaning of the Igbo labor force. This had tragically unintended consequences.

The previous CWU structure was united with all classes of labor relating directly to the executive committee. There were mass meetings, largely dominated
by Ojiyi's charismatic oratorical presence. In many respects Ojiyi exemplified the
patterns of leadership exercised by powerful and influential men in the village.
Ojiyi's style resonated culturally with that of Chief Onyeama at an earlier period:
If a leader observed the principles of reciprocity, dispersing goods or patronage in
his community, he could exert considerable power. Consequently, while Ojiyi enjoyed the workers' support his power was contingent upon his fulfilling these patterns of leadership.

Curry divided the union into five branches, each with its own officers dealing
independently with management. These branches were for surface workers, hewers, mechanics and fitters, general underground workers, and clerks. The new Executive Committee was composed of elected branch officers who formed a
Representative Committee from which the union's Executive Committee was
elected for negotiations with management. Such negotiations, however, would only
occur if branches were unable to resolve grievances with management. Thus, these
various branches assumed many of the functions formerly held by Ojiyi and the
union executive.

There was nothing in Igbo organizational culture that resembled the federalist
representative structure implicit in the branch trade union model. For purposes of
comparison the most relevant voluntary organizations were the urban improvement unions. Enugu was filled with these unions that both influenced village politics and assisted the state in securing urban order. Although they were organized
by village, each urban improvement union operated with relative autonomy from
the village of origin and the central executive. The single instance of coordination
and centralization was the annual or biannual conference in which decisions taken
at the home village were passed to constituent branches. But the basic principle of
representation was individual and in no case did one have the right to represent the
interests of his particular branch of the union.[65] Most colliery men belonged to
these unions, which were their point of reference for "modern" organizational structure. Curry's intention had been to create structural barriers that isolated Ojiyi from
his base, the rank and file underground workers. However, to the men he had actually created five independent unions.

The impact of the reorganization was to change the dynamics between Ojiyi, the union dissidents, and the underground workers, his base. The new union structure did drive a wedge between Ojiyi and the workers by creating a new level of branch officials authorized to negotiate their sectional interests/concerns with management. But it also reduced the accountability of all officials, branch and central, to the membership and to each other. Secondly, it gave the clerical branch and the mines supervisory staff, the center of opposition to Ojiyi, an organizational base— their own branch—from which to continue their campaign against Ojiyi. Moreover, in the new union executive these clerks had equal representation with the more numerous miners. Doing so reduced the relative power of the largest and most productive sector of the workforce, the hewers, within the union executive. Thirdly, the reorganization gave dissenters an accepted organizational base, it also gave the underground workers an independent expression. The hewers assumed that they now had an independent union with more local decision-making power to formulate strategies. The reorganization had created a setting for industrial chaos.

On the other hand, the settlement undermined Bracegirdle's position in the industry because officials clearly rejected all of his proposals for resolving the crisis. The men could see that he had little power; one minute officials invested him with the authority to deal with the workers, the next they were overriding his decisions. He was outraged by the settlement.

> The fact that Government deemed it wise to concede on practically every point was omitted in the Conciliator's Report. The Management does not agree that the workmen's grievances were to some extent justified ... I should be grateful if it could be placed on record that the management realized Government's difficulties and for that reason and that reason only, were we prepared to concede to the rate of pay and conditions of service which ... were unreasonable when considered in light of the work performed, the skill required and the rates in existence for other workers in the Eastern Provinces.[66]

Complain he might, but he had no authority to reject any concession. It was a hard pill to swallow and Bracegirdle was angry and felt betrayed. *This* was the person the government entrusted to participate in joint consultative systems.

Despite the impressive wage award, the Agreement also contained a number of erroneous wage calculations that left the key underground workers—hewers and tubmen—feeling that they had been cheated. In actuality, they had. Some groups were improperly graded or put into incorrect wage systems. Tubmen, who had been on piece and daily rates of pay were converted to only a daily-wage. Increments for most apprentices were incorrectly determined and failed to incorporate previous COLA increments in their overtime calculations.[67] There were errors of calculation with some wages and the hewers' increases ignored seniority increments made in 1946 and 1947 settlements. The state also used the Agreement to make yet another attempt to change work rules by setting minimal performance levels as a prerequisite for continued employment in the mines. For tubmen, it was six tubs pushed per day; for hewers it was eight in *robbery* and four in *development* with provisions for review at the end of 1948. Moreover, the grading of a number of groups was yet undetermined.

Almost immediately there were signs that the award was unacceptable. Tubmen refused to push the minimum number of tubs and stopped using their tokens, the only way their output could be assessed. Hewers, dissatisfied with the revocation of seniority pay, slowed down and refused to fill the required number of tubs. And management still had no organization of employee representation accepted by the workers. Moreover, despite its role in negotiating for the workers, the CWU was *still* not recognized as the authorized union to represent the workforce.

The 1947 agreement was a bold application of the new framework for resolving industrial disputes—cooperative consultation—which the state hoped would foster a new culture of submissive acquiescence. The settlement clearly indicated with whom the state was willing to negotiate when disputes occurred, within what institutional context such discussions would occur, and what procedures had to be followed when crises occurred. In order to complete the model, the colliery union had to be legitimated and reconstructed as the primary institution through which employees participated in cooperative consultation. From the state's perspective, "responsible" unions required that workers understand the need for discipline and "sound" trade union principles.[68] To the workers, it was not completely clear if these new state-instituted bodies were of any value to them.

The basic institutions for workplace consultations varied with each department. At the colliery the system of consultation was quite complex, utilizing Whitleyism, of which more will be discussed below. As in the United Kingdom, consultation assumed independent trade unions whose existence "preempted more radical challenges" to managerial power over production. The basic framework of the Whitley process was outlined by T.M. Cowan, of the U.K. Ministry of Labour and National Service of which more will be featured below.

As negotiations continued into April, the union pressed grievances representing the complaints of the dissatisfied groups. Again, Ojiyi was able to use an interpretation of the laws regulating industrial disputes to raise yet another demand on behalf of a group of workers. In this case, he targeted the Joint Technical Staff, those men, who like himself, were training for managerial responsibilities now relegated to Europeans. This was a group whose support he undoubtedly sought to win, against the machinations of union dissidents. In this case he used a brilliant manipulation of the principal of reciprocity that was popularized in the generous wage award. Ojiyi argued that the Junior Technical Staff was owed additional arrears under the new trade union legislation of 1946. Although the Agreement gave the Junior Technical Staff a six-hour workday, they had previously worked in excess of six hours. Since the agreement was retroactive to 1 January 1946, Ojiyi claimed additional pay for all Junior Technical Staff (JTS) who had worked in excess of six hours before 7 December 1947.[69] The demand showed Ojiyi's sophisticated understanding of the law, confused management and sowed seeds of anticipation among the JTS.

Ojiyi prepared the case to reject the 1947 pay scales amidst an expanded campaign by the union dissidents. The nucleus of dissent was in the clerical workers' branch of the newly organized union and may in fact have been caused by the exclusion of the dissidents from the distribution of the more than £2,000 which the negotiating team collected in the levy after the 1947 agreement.[70] In 1948 they succeeded in getting government to call a new election to contest Ojiyi's position as General Secretary but the scale of Ojiyi's victory—4,604 votes to 9[71]—clearly indicated that the reorganization had failed to undermine his popularity.

In late 1948 the anti-union group appealed to the manager to investigate several grievances that they attributed to Ojiyi's mismanagement: 1) the Union's poorly held accounts; 2) failure to account for the 20 shillings of the £2000 levy; 3) self-promotions by the General Secretary; 4) consistently misrepresenting the workers' and managers' positions in negotiations; and 5) the union's refusal to hold meetings since the last election of official union members.[72] In October the dissidents could only secure the signatures of 165 workers protesting Ojiyi's misappropriation of union funds. On 11 November 1948 he unsuccessfully tried to get management to dismiss these dissidents, claiming that they caused most work stoppages.[73]

Despite this internal conflict, the union's recognition was nonetheless restored in December 1948 following an agreement brokered by M.E. Tokunboh, a Nigerian staff member of the Ministry of Labour. In the agreement, additional arrears were given to screen and haulage workers, screen foreman, token collectors and hangers, shouters, and clerks. Recognizing that outstanding claims might still remain, it set a deadline date of March 1949 for any further adjustments. It was the Tokunboh Agreement that finally recognized the Colliery Workers Union as the sole representative of the workers. The 1948 agreement decreed that any further disagreements arising from this or any previous awards be resolved through joint consultation machinery.[74]

## THE COLONIAL INTERPRETATION
## OF COOPERATIVE CONSULTATION

In confronting the 1948–1949 crisis, the colliery continued to use the system of joint consultation, although conditions were so hostile as to make it fatally flawed. This implied frequent meetings between labor and management to discuss potential problem areas *before* they become grievances or managerial demands. Official advocacy of joint consultative machinery came in the Tudor Davies Commission Report after the 1945 Nigerian General Strike but this was its first application in Enugu.[75] In 1948 the Cowan Commission Report suggested appointment of Whitley Councils,[76] a particular form of joint consultative body which was used by government agencies in the United Kingdom to encourage "cooperative consultation" rather than "adversarial bargaining." Again trade unions were the only institutions of employee representation.[77] Additionally, the Commission made several proposals to insure that Nigerian unions were following a "responsible path"—increased numbers of British trade unionists were to serve as labor advisers and the accelerated educational programs in England and Nigeria were to train Nigerian unionists in acceptable trade union practices.[78]

The Nigerian state was following the principle that states usually promote joint consultation "when political considerations made the direct repression of some organized section of the wage-earning population impossible or impractical."[79] This was most certainly the case in 1948. The postwar intensification of nationalist agitation thrust each industrial confrontation into the political arena and there had been several explosive developments. In June 1947 a group of United Africa Company (UAC) employees were shot by police in Burutu, northern Nigeria, during a strike. The event popularized an effort to federate all UAC unions into the Amalgamated Union of UAC African Workers of Nigeria (UNAMAG) under the leadership of a Marxist and radical Zikist, Nduka Eze. To the government, Eze was a dangerous radical influence in the national trade union movement.[80] Clearly, any further labor incidents like Burutu would likewise strengthen the hand of other militant nationalists like Eze. This, the state did not want.

The Whitley Councils were promoted as an alternative to confrontation. Three national Whitley Councils were established in Lagos: one was for senior staff, and two for junior supervisory staff and clerical workers. A separate council was set up at the colliery because of the particularities of mine employment, the distance of Enugu from Lagos—the venue of the National Whitely Council meetings—and because the CWU was not affiliated with a national labor organization that could represent it at the Lagos Councils.[81] The Councils were charged to: 1) promote cooperation between the government as employer and the CWU to improve efficiency and promote "well-being of those employed"; 2) provide grievance-handling machinery, and 3) to provide a forum for communication between representatives of all sectors of the colliery workforce. They were not to consider individual cases but to make decisions on general principles of conditions of service such as recruitment, promotion, tenure, hours, remuneration, and superannuation.[82]

In the industrial environment at the colliery, it was not surprising that the Councils were being improperly used as a forum for negotiations and collective bargaining. Even under the best of conditions it is difficult to distinguish between joint consultation and collective bargaining. Consultative machinery was useful

> to exchange information and consider suggestions ... of common interest rather than as in collective bargaining, on a basis of divergent interests and demands.[83]

Predictably conditions at the colliery could not sustain this level of "cooperative" discussion. Most especially, Whitley Councils could only work when there was a broad consensus on industrial issues. At the colliery, they were unable to survive the personal and racial contradictions between the manager and Ojiyi. Moreover, management was unable to make decisions to settle inevitable conflicts without referral to Lagos. On the staff side, the dissidents had begun to bear fruit. The union leadership was confronted with an increasingly skeptical rank and file that required that Ojiyi demonstrate his integrity as a leader to represent the workers' interests. In these ways, the realities of the colliery industrial relations strained the capacities of the new Whitely Council to a breaking point.

The Whitley Council was but one part of the consultative system at the colliery. There were bi-weekly sessions between the CWU and the personnel manager allegedly to air grievances in a less formal manner. A labor officer could also be called in when there was a deadlock but he lacked statutory power and his decisions were non-binding. The next level of appeal was to the colliery manager, who more than likely had been a party to the original disagreement. Failing these internal bodies, a conciliator could be requested.[84] The system was severely compromised, slow, often involving disgruntled officials with no authority to reach binding agreements, and stymied by the tension in the industry. There were only three Whitely Council meetings in mid-1949. A fourth, scheduled for November 7, was postponed to the fourteenth. By that time the crisis had reached such major proportions as to make it irrelevant.[85]

Given the complex instability of the colliery, the unions' incorporation in such extensive management consultations generated suspicions of collaboration among the workers that were encouraged by the dissidents.[86] To the workers, Ojiyi's frequent meetings with Bracegirdle suggested that he had become "friendly" with management and perhaps could not be trusted. The underground workers' branch of the union, led by the hewers, increasingly began to act as an independent union. Trade unions had not earned the confidence of these workers, who considered them to be state-sponsored institutions of worker control.

In the fall of 1949 the manager violated the "rostering" prohibition of the 1947 agreement and unilaterally announced that he would resume "rostering" to compensate for shortage of railway cars that required reduced production. He further argued that because of labor costs the increase in the cost of production from 11/6d in March 1947 to 25 shillings in May 1949 threatened the colliery's market. Moreover, he alleged that unless costs were reduced it was inevitable that the mines would be closed.[87] He placed this ultimatum on the table.

The union executive countered that "rostering" placed the burden of the railway wagon shortage on the colliery workers who had no responsibility for the problem. This they said was a management problem. Further, they argued that the unilateral institution of "rostering" violated both the 1947 and 1948 Agreements. But the management's ultimatum placed Ojiyi in the unenviable position of having to convince the workers to support the same "rostering" system which the union had previously attacked, just at the time when his credibility as a leader was under question. Now the dissidents were joined by the Udi Clan Council, ever watchful for an opportunity to discredit Ojiyi, who offered to assist the manager in convincing the miners to accept "rostering." They claimed that Ojiyi's influence among the workers had declined since he had become the manager's "friend" and they offered to play the same collaborative role as they had unsuccessfully offered during the 1945 crisis.[88]

## "ROSTERING" AND THE PRINCIPLE OF RETROACTIVITY: THE UNION'S MANIPULATION OF THE 1947 AGREEMENT

Confronted by challenges to his integrity, Ojiyi placed fourteen demands before the management on May 18. The demands clearly represented an attempt to refute rumors that he had become a stooge of management. The resumption of rostering opened a new dispute. Rumors were circulating among the men that the colliery owed an additional £180,000 in back pay to compensate for hours of work lost by men denied the opportunity to work during the interval between the outlawing of rostering by the June 1946 Trade Union Ordinance and the colliery's suspension of rostering under the 1947 Agreement.[89] These rumors were a logical interpretation of the principles of retroactivity so prominent in the 1947 Agreement.

This demand for additional back pay came from an interpretation of Sections 31 and 36 of the new Trade Union Ordinance, effective 1 June 1946. These sections prohibited "rostering" and established penalties for employers who persisted in using it. Section 31 stated that an employer was obligated to give all workers on oral contracts seven days' notice *before* their contract could legally be terminated. Under Section 36 employers failing to follow the period of notification must provide work for all physically fit employees who show up for work or *pay wages equivalent to the amount they would otherwise earn.*[90] Ojiyi had a new issue, an issue arising from a sophisticated interpretation of the law.

The claim caught the government by surprise. Neither the personnel manager nor officials in Lagos could determine if "rostering" fit within the definition of "termination" in the Ordinance.[91] Given the contentious environment at the mines, word of additional arrears spread like wildfire fanned by the workers' deep suspicions that management was not to be trusted. Dropped into the contentious interactions between Ojiyi, the clerical dissidents, and the hewers in the mine, the promise that an additional £180,000 were owed to the hewers fell on receptive ears. The rumor became another element of the leadership struggle to represent the hewers. Ojiyi was later to claim that he was pressured to accept this demand. As evidence of mischief he alleged that the dissidents were circulating a paper to the local chiefs that claimed that £2,000,000 had been set aside to improve workers' conditions if they removed him from leadership.[92] Later, he subsequently placed an article in a local newspaper, *New Africa*, claiming that the government owed this additional amount. Ironically, this became a crucial piece of evidence to substantiate the state's claim that Ojiyi had manipulated the hewers.[93]

While authorities deliberated, Ojiyi pressed the other demands designed to counter the dissidents' propaganda. He called for a regrading of all categories of labor: hewers, tubmen, timbermen, railmen, haulage men, machine laborers, pipe workers, and even cocoa workers were to move to artisan status. Protective equipment was to be supplied to all working with acid, electricity, and haulage. A transportation allowance of 5 shillings was to go to all living more than nine miles from work another demand arising from a provision of the 1946 Trade Union allowance.[94]

Discussions at the Whitley Council turned into negotiations. On July 11 and 12 considerable progress was made on the fourteen demands in meetings at the Whitley Council. Among the most significant concessions was the management's agreement to extend payment of seniority arrears awarded to the hewers to other categories of workers.[95] This decision opened a Pandora's box when payment was made later in the summer. Although they had received their increased pay, the hewers revived their claim for additional payments. Ojiyi, of course, endorsed their claim.

For much of September and October 1949 the hewers were restive. In November the CWU Executive raised the issue of the hewers' seniority arrears and illegal "rostering" at its bi-weekly consultative meeting with the Assistant Personnel Manager, E.J. Scanlon, but it was rejected. In response, on November 8 the hewers initiated a "go slow" which appeared to be a "wildcat" strike. While it may have been encouraged by the union dissidents, it was solidly rooted in the hewers' belief that the union could not be trusted to pursue their demands.

Curry's 1947 reorganization, with its loosely federated structure, had now spawned a semi-autonomous hewers' executive which was operating without consultation with the central executive.[96] Throughout the mines' history the hewers had perceived themselves as powerful and distinctly different from other workers. Now their distinction was institutionalized in their branch organization. They no longer accepted the central executive as their representatives. In fact, even the rank-and-file support for their representative was tentative. When the hewers' representatives agreed to terminate the strike, the underground workers persisted. The underground workers were in a complete state of insurgency against both layers of leadership—branch and central. The decline in the union's control was graphically illustrated in a meeting the night of November 8 which was broken up by the union dissidents.[97]

The crisis continued to escalate on November 12 when Bracegirdle suspended fifty workers. The strategy had just the opposite effect from its objective and the tubmen joined the hewers in the "go slow." The strikers had now become an independent force physically attacking several of Ojiyi's staunchest supporters in the mines. The manager recognized the hewer's insurgency and determination:

> The average hewer who has carefully nursed his imaginary grievances during the past four days, is still convinced that Government will agree to his demands before the next pay day early in December and the dismissed workers, who continue to go underground each day, are confident they will be reinstated. There is no tendency to follow leaders as the men now prefer to rely on their own efforts rather than to entrust their case to any would-be champion of their rights.[98]

In the midst of this crisis the state began to implement the recommendations of the industrial study by Powell Duffryn Technical Services. Specifically, it established the Enugu Coal Board as a statutory body to oversee the administration and policy of the industry.[99] The Board constituted a government divestment/distancing from the troublesome management of the colliery.[100] Among its six members were a lawyer and two prominent Nigerian businessmen, Louis P. Ojukwu and L.N. Obioha. However, it had scarcely a chance to organize when the crisis occurred. Their attempt to intervene was unsuccessful.

The men then occupied the mines launching a sit-in which became a "go slow." Output dropped from 922 tons on November 13 to 500 tons on November 14. The men sabotaged the chain conveyor. While the night shift men left, the day shift remained underground two hours after the third shift.[101] On the fourteenth the Personnel Officer transported a large group of new recruits from the Colliery Office to the Labour Office in Enugu. Two hundred were examined by the doctor. This confirmed the men's fears that the government had determined to replace them and hardened their resolve to retain control over the workplace.[102]

## "AN ATMOSPHERE OF A WAR COUNCIL": THE STATE PREPARES TO CONFRONT THE WORKERS

As the trouble in the mines escalated, the management and the state took actions that indicated a break with past state responses to colliery unrest. The government had obviously decided that the crisis should become a showdown and was more of a political than an industrial dispute. They began to prepare for the immediate coal shortages by requesting coal from the Gold Coast Railway and cutting back passenger and goods traffic. From the sixteenth to the eighteenth a group of state and industrial officials held a series of daily meetings. They included J.G. Pyke-Nott, Chief Commissioner, Eastern Provinces; Dr. Raeburn, Board Chairman; Bracegirdle, the manager; and other state officials.[103] The African members of the Coal Board were conspicuously absent. The tenor of these meetings was of impending violent confrontation. No offers to diffuse the crisis were seriously entertained. In fact, the group rejected assistance by the only person trained in labor relations: H.J. Honey, the new Senior Labour Officer. Any mediation was considered to be a sign of weakness. Honey subsequently characterized the atmosphere of the meeting on November 16 as that of a "War Council," more concerned with the deployment of police and armed forces than in reaching a settlement.[104] The government likewise rejected an offer by the Ngwo Clan Council on the sixteenth to mediate.[105]

While the miners continued the "go-slow" and the management and CWU deliberated, the government made preparations for a military confrontation with the miners. One hundred fifty policemen came to Enugu from the northern provinces. They were Hausa Munshi soldiers, whose black uniforms distinguished them from the local police. By the seventeenth there were 900 policemen in Enugu, 150 were armed with rifles.[106] The government alleged that it feared that the explosives would be seized by the miners and fall into the hands of "terrorists." Government intelligence in Lagos had been alerted that "extremists" had been attempting to acquire arms and explosives to be distributed to "terrorist parties" (i.e., Zikists?) to use in a "positive action" campaign. Some thefts had evidently occurred, including 30 cases of colliery explosives. Eleven had never been recovered.[107] On the seventeenth the government decided to arm the police to remove all mine explosives on November 18. The decision was made by Pyke-Nott, in consultation with the manager, the Coal Board Chairman, the Secretary of Finance, Eastern Provinces, and the Assistant Commissioner of Police. It appears that the government assumed a connection between the Zikists and the miners, perhaps in the person of Ojiyi himself. At this point the dispute ceased to be an industrial crisis and had become a serious political one.

The strategy adopted was two-pronged. While refusing to open any avenues of communication with the union, the government activated District Officers to propagandize the villages, to create public pressure on the miners to end the strike. The efforts were unsuccessful. One political officer visited the major villages in the area—Enugu Ngwo, Ngwo Uno, Eke, etc.—and met with suspicion and distrust. Even the clan councilors were uncooperative because they resented not being consulted when strategy was being decided.[108]

## THE WIVES' DEMONSTRATION, 15 NOVEMBER 1949

The first confrontation involving the police was with the miners' wives. When the "go-slow" became a sit-in the informal network of miners' wives was activated and the women congregated to discuss the crisis. Their primary concern was with the men's failure to return from the night shift on the fourteenth. While they were aware of the issues involved, they seemed not to know that the conflict had escalated during the night. According to the spokesperson of the group, Alice Afamuefuna, wife of a blacksmith residing in Coal Camp, emissaries were sent to all the camps to bring the women to a meeting. The decision was taken to seek clarification from the manager the following morning and to take food for the husbands in the mines.[109]

On the morning of the fifteenth, 200–300 women met fifty baton-wielding police when they visited the manager's house. A confrontation ensued when the group failed to disperse and the women were beaten. Undaunted, one group doubled back and wrecked the manager's office where they were joined by some youths stoning the police vehicles. Later that afternoon the group reached Obwetti Mine and one contingent held four European staff in their office while a second raided the storehouse. From the descriptions of the affair, the demonstration appeared to have many of the characteristics of the traditional "sitting on a man."[110] Efforts by the Local Authority to peacefully disperse the women failed and the police used batons in a charge to secure the release of the European staff. Mrs. Afamuefuna claimed tear gas was used to disperse the women.

The following day at a meeting in Udi Siding, 200 women put forth their grievances to the Local Authority. The two spokeswomen, Alice Afamuefuna and Christina Amadi, asserted that their husbands' back pay was important because they were poorly paid and couldn't afford the taxes. They also complained that the colliery's European employees' wives received pay, free coal, and allowances for their dogs, obviously an allusion to the family allowance allocated to European employees.

They also resented the rough treatment they received at Obwetti. The Local Authority responded that Europeans were not responsible for holding down their husbands' pay but the Coal Board was. The Coal Board had African members on it, and so they could not say, as they had suggested earlier, that the European colliery officials were trying to deceive them.[111] He discounted Ojiyi's announcement in the Zikist-controlled (but not Zik-owned) *New Africa* newspaper that arrears were owed to the miners.[112]

At a subsequent meeting with the women addressed by the Resident Onitsha, V.K. Johnson, on the seventeenth, Ojiyi reasserted that arrears were owed to the workers. The women were disappointed with the Resident because he didn't sympathize with their complaints against treatment by the police. To Mrs. Afamuefuna, "he came to abuse the women," not to help them.[113]

## THE SHOOTING OF 18 NOVEMBER 1949: THE MARTYRDOM OF COLONIAL LABOR

The events at the Iva Valley Mine that culminated in the shooting of striking coal miners was a snapshot of the escalating contradictions in colonial Nigeria on the eve of independence. On the one hand were anxious political officials fearing workers' contacts with potentially violent radical nationalists and disgruntled local officials highly critical of what they felt was government's conciliatory tone towards "undisciplined" workers. On the other was an expectant group of state workers sensitized by their role in a crucial wartime industry and a trade union leadership under siege. The elements for a tragedy were clearly present. Two official documents provide some insight into the motives, expectations, and tragic decisions that led to the massacre—the Fitzgerald Commission Report and the Commission's "Proceedings."[114] Both are a rich, and largely unplumbed, source for scholars documenting the personal and political tensions between European and African during this period of rapid change. By comparing the testimonies of "colonizer" and "colonized" we can see how conflicting assumptions and racialized stereotypes led to a dangerous escalation. Space will not allow a thorough treatment; however, we can get a suggestive glimpse of this fatal dynamic through the testimonials of participants. Despite conflicting claims and evidence, a tentative reconstruction of events follows.

The shooting occurred at Iva Valley Mine when the police commander panicked during an attempt to remove mine explosives. The officers realized that they had underestimated the amount of explosives. The miners, believing that the removal of the explosives signaled a "lock-out," appeared hesitant to permit the operation. Several eyewitnesses, Emanuel Okafor and Peter Afamuefuna among them, said that the miners crowd was not unruly but only curious about the commotion of the police arrival and the unusual color of their black uniforms. Neither witness considered the crowd to be hostile.[115]

The process began when Mr. Moran, the Personnel Manager, visited the mine and attempted to encourage the men to help him remove explosives from an adjacent store. When he met with their refusal, he assumed that they intended to retain the explosives. However, the testimony of J.E. Nzerogu, a screen foreman, suggested that the refusal had more to do with job hierarchies.

> What they said was that they were not carrying men. They are tubmen and pickboys and have nothing to do with the carrying of the magazine. ... This job is for timbermen, some special laborers. He should call them.[116]

Moran then left, leaving the men to face the Hausa policemen alone.

The first contingent of police arrived at Iva Valley Mine around 11:30 that morning under the direction of O.P.S. Jones, Assistant Superintendent of Police (Jos). When he arrived there were no men outside the mines but some soon gathered out of curiosity. When the initial plan to remove the explosives proved unworkable because there were more than anticipated, officials then secured a train to transport the explosives. In the interval one worker was given the key to lock the magazine and did so with no resistance.[117] Seven to eight hundred men had gathered at the mouth of the mine to watch.[118] The actual tenor of the crowd is subject to conflicting interpretations. One constable said the crowd was so relaxed it was eating lunch, chattering cordially, and even brought bananas to share.[119] Constable Okolie described friendly discussions between the workers and the constables. In fact he overheard one saying,

> We do not come to shoot you people. You are demanding your rights from the Government. The Government will pay you people this money.[120]

To this he alleged that a worker replied "We are glad you people know this, but you people should remember we be brothers."[121] The men had little indication that they were in danger.

However, this was *not* the scene that greeted E.J.R. Ormiston, the Senior Assistant Superintendent of Police, Enugu. The chatter, singing, and fraternizing appeared threatening to him. He felt hemmed in by the miners who were so numerous that "the whole place was black with them."[122] Similarly, Captain F.S. Philip, Senior Superintendent of Police, saw only menace. These were not industrial men conducting a protest but savage, hysterial natives, doing "dangerous dances," screeching unintelligible noises, poised to attack his troops. He had been anxious since he brought his troops through the Iva Valley Camp which seemed suspiciously vacant. Only a few women and children were about and these angrily shook their fists at him as he passed in the lorry with his men. Earlier, he had removed the explosives from the Obwetti mine with no incident. Iva Valley Mine, however, was shaping up as quite dangerous. At about 1:30 P.M. he got to Iva Valley Mine and became worried about the numbers and the mood of the crowd. They seemed to be "pouring" out of the mines on to the grounds by the hundreds. Nonetheless, he felt sufficiently confident to try to enlist their support in removing explosives from a nearby magazine.[123]

Ignorant of the language and unfamiliar with the traditions of colliery protest, Captain Philip panicked. Within fifteen minutes the workers were in an angry mood, brandishing "weapons—bows, arrows, machetes, long steel bars."[124] Curiously, many of the men had red pieces of cloth tied to their miners' helmets, wrists, or knees which Philip assumed to be the signs of "some organization along military lines."[125] As the minutes passed the men began to sing hymns and songs of solidarity—"We are all one!"[126] Philip only heard a "tremendous howling and screeching noise going on"[127] to which several men danced in a "dangerous" way.[128] After giving the order to shoot, Philip himself aimed his revolver at a dancer immediately in front of him who "was jumping up and down and his eyes were popping out of his head—like a lot of the others."[129] Within a second he had shot Sunday Anyasado in the mouth.[130]

Sunday Anyasado had been among the miners who came out of the mines when the train approached the explosives stores. He was a hewer and the brother of B.U. Anyasado of Mbieri, Owerri, a prominent clerk and union dissident during the forties, and was in the forefront of the crowd outside Iva Mine. He was a young man, recently married, who had come to Enugu to earn a living. He occupied the mine to prevent a repeat of the 1945 lockout and had come outside when the black-shirted Mushi troops from northern Nigeria disembarked from their transport lorries. And they were prepared to risk everything to prevent the removal of explosives, which would be a sign of a lockout. Sunday joined his brother miners chanting, singing, and dancing in front of the crowd facing the troops and their commanding officer, F.S. Philip. He probably did not hear the warning shots, nor did he expect that the police would fire. Philip aimed his revolver at Sunday and shot him in the mouth. He died immediately. He then shot Livinus Okechukwuma, a machine man from Ohi, Owerri, killing him as well. Hearing the noise, Okafor Ageni, an Udi tubman, ventured out of the mine, asking "Anything wrong?" A bullet killed him on the spot.[131]

The shots were inaudible over their singing and the men pushed closer and closer to the action. Philip saw "an avalanche coming down from the back, rolling on top of us."[132] But as it became clear that shots were fired and men were dying they ran in horror. Many were shot in the back.[133] The volley kept coming for a good two minutes and some eighty-seven rounds were spent.[134] R.A. Brown, Assistant Superintendent of Police, Kano, shouted the order to stop shooting and went along the line of fire and deflected the rifles into the air. But Superintendent Philip was still shooting, having completely lost his wits, after being terrified by the native "with the machete, ... dancing round and round, and slowly coming towards us, circling round and round."[135]

The men fled in all directions as the dead and wounded collapsed on the ground. Many fled into a nearby stream, while others retreated back to the mines. Many anticipated more shots. Emmanuel Okafor asked Philip to take him to the hospital, "I surrender. Take me to the hospital." He alleges that Philip answered, "I don't care," and left him behind.[136]

After the barrage, the troops calmly fell into formation and marched back to their depot in Enugu. The commanding officers made no arrangements to care for the wounded and the dead remained on the ground for the rest of the day. Villagers in Iva Valley Camp hearing of the slaughter, lay in wait to ambush the troops as they returned but lost their courage. Sunday would become famous as the first one shot. Nationalist leaders said the shots were the inaugural bullets of Nigeria's nationalist struggle. The days of colonial rule were numbered.

The tragedy reflected a hysterical reaction of British non-commissioned officers when confronted with African men "out of place." E.J.R. Ormiston had even forgotten to load his revolver.[137]

Despite the terror of the moment the people of Iva Valley Camp, along the road to the mine site, reacted in bold hostility. They felled trees and put debris on the road to prevent another incursion by troops. Word reached the Ngwo clan councilors as they negotiated with the management behind the backs of the union leadership, trying to get the men to leave the mine. In Agbani a group of women armed with sticks targeted the rural symbol of state repression and African collaboration—the local court—and confronted their elders and councilors who had been supporting management and the state.[138]

A virtual panic ensued as a mixture of fear and anger swept Enugu, the mines, and the villages in Udi. Ojiyi claimed that he spread the word nationally with the help of a telegraph operator in Enugu who was a Zikist sympathizer.[139] Testimony of hospital personnel at a subsequent investigation revealed no substantive reason for an untimely delay in the removal of the wounded. But to the miners it was a further attempt to intimidate them into breaking the strike. The account of one of the wounded appears to indicate that the delay was more than coincidental.

> When white men came to visualize the shooting I told them to shoot me to death for I was then on the verge of dying. They refused. I told them to give me drinking water. They refused. One Mr. Nnanji Nwa Ozor Onyia gave me water and I became unconscious after drinking the water. When I recovered I was in the hospital.[140]

Emmanuel Okafor, a blacksmith, was also attracted to the outside by the singing. Sensing that the men were in trouble, he "had to go there" because "I am a worker." As he ran towards the noise he saw Felix Nnaji, an electrican apprentice from Agbani, lying on the ground with a chest wound. Felix begged: "Please Emmanuel, can you give me help?" When he bent down to comfort him he took six shots in his leg. Nonetheless, he tried to carry Felix to safety but collapsed after only a few yards. He rested Felix's head on his chest to comfort him but watched in alarm while blood trickled "through the nose and mouth." Felix died there on his chest and Okafor gently laid him down and removed the undershirt soaked with Felix's blood. Okafor lay in the sun for two hours until a group of workers removed him to the hospital.

All around him men were "groaning and crying." Chikelu Eluke was one of the men who fell near him with a shot in his leg.[141] After the policemen had left some miners came out of hiding to help but fled when a second group of policemen came.

But despite the sheer terror of the police attack the miners refocused on their protest. Rather than evacuate Iva Valley the workers fled back into the mines, more

**Table 7.1** List of Dead Miners, Towns and Occupations, November 1949, Iva Valley Shooting

| Names | Home Towns | Occupations |
|---|---|---|
| 1. Livinus Okechukwuma | Ohi, Owerri | Machine Man |
| 2. Ngwu Nwafor | Ngwo, Udi | Tubman |
| 3. Agu Ede | Enugu, Ngwo | Machine Man |
| 4. Okafor Ageni | Umuabi, Udi | Tubman |
| 5. Thomas Chukwu | Ubahu, Okigwe | Machine Man |
| 6. Jonathan Ezeani | Uboji, Ngwo | Railman |
| 7. Ani Amu | Ajukwu Eke,[a] Udi | Hewer |
| 8. Onoh Onyia | Enugu, Ngwo | Tubman |
| 9. Nnaji Nwachukwu | Amaigbo, Owerri[b] | Screen Labourer |
| 10. Simeon Nwachukwu | Ubaha, Mbutu Owerri | Machine Man |
| 11. James Ekeowa | Nkanu, Udi | Clip Operator |
| 12. Sunday Anyasodo | Obazu, Mbieri Owerri | Hewer |
| 13. Felix Nnaji | Agbani, Udi | Apprentice Electrician |
| 14. Andrew Okonkwo | Owa, Udi | Hewer |
| 15. William Nwehu | Amuzi, Bende | Engine Driver |
| 16. Augustina Aniwoke | Owa, Udi | Hewer |
| 17. Ogbonnia Chime | Ihe, Awgu | Machine Man |
| 18. Moses Ikegbu | Amaimo, Owerri | Machine Man |
| 19. Nwachukwu Ugwu | Akagbe, Udi | Machine Man |
| 20. Nduaguba Eze | Owa, Udi | Tubman[c] |
| 21 Ani | Amankwo Ngwo, Udi | Hewer |
| | | |

[a]Ananaba, *Trade Union Movement in Nigeria* says he's from Akukwu Ebe, Udi., 108.

[b]Ananaba says he's from Ndembara Amaimo, Owerri.

[c]Onogbo Achogbuo lists only a name. The occupation is from Ananaba, p. 108 *Iva Valley Tragedy: A Memorable Incident in Nigerian National and Trade Union History,* Enugu: The Continental Press, n.d.

terrified than ever that government/management would make a lockout. Given the brutality of the state's response, they refused to relinquish the only leverage they had—the control over the workplace, the source of the coal. As this was groundnut season, the strike jeopardized Britain's access to Nigeria's valuable bumper groundnut crop at a time of desperately short dollar supplies. In the ensuing weeks, they continued their go slow, further aggravating the state's attempts to restore normal production conditions.

## THE SOUTHEASTERN CITIES ERUPT: ZIKISM AND POPULAR PROTEST

When the news spread to Enugu, Port Harcourt, Onitsha, and Calabar the cities erupted. From November 18 to 26 a wave of demonstrations swept the eastern provinces and quickly deteriorated into urban riots. The targets and composition of the crowds suggested that issues broader than the shooting had generated their anger. In furious outrage market women and casual urban workers attacked the most obvious target of imperial rule—the expatriate firms that had squeezed the country during and after the war. Several more would die in these protests. To the chagrin of officials, the uprisings gave the Zikists a platform to rally the "dangerous classes"—casual workers, market boys, the unemployed, and discontented traders. At first it appeared that the state had blundered into the type of urban insurrection that nearly toppled the colonial state in the Caribbean in the late 1930s, the insurrection that all Colonial Office labor policy had sought to deter. But in this case the outburst collapsed under the swift, brutal response of colonial police.[142]

The popular response to the shooting was almost immediate and became increasingly politicized as the Zikists moved to the forefront of organizing mass demonstrations. The targets and locations of the demonstrations and composition of the crowds acknowledged that the incident had ignited deep-seated grievances about declining wages, high prices, and the stranglehold that the expatriate firms continued to have over the Nigerian economy. The targets of the demonstrations were the expatriate firms and many were looted and burned. All occurred in the five largest cities in the east—Enugu, Aba, Umuahia, Port Harcourt, Onitsha, and Calabar.[143] According to one Zikist, Mokwugo Okoye, eastern chapters were largely composed of market women and casual urban workers attached to the markets, the groups directly affected by the policies of expatriate firms.[144]

In all cities the Zikists played key roles both in organizing the demonstrations and in delivering political speeches linking the massacre with generalized grievances against British colonial rule. S.O. Masi, Margaret Ekpo, J.A. Wachukwu, and Francis I. Nzimiro were named in police reports of incidents in the area.[145] Eyewitness accounts of the actions of these Zikists suggest that while leading the demonstrations, they also were fearful of the lawlessness of the urban "mob" which they tenuously controlled.

The shooting also galvanized the more moderate sectors of nationalist movement as well. In fact, it helped to abate a crisis that had occurred in the unity of the movement which had begun to break down into contentious regional/ethnic parties. Eighteen leaders of the divided nationalist movement met in Lagos and established the National Emergency Committee to investigate the shooting and to also explore the possibilities of establishing a consolidated national political party.[146] Nduka Eze, Zikist trade union organizer of the United African Company, remarked in his unpublished manuscript:

> The radicals and the moderates, the revolutionaries and the stooges, the bourgeoisie and the workers, sank their difference and remembered the word—"Nigeria" and rose in revolt against the evil and inhumanity.[147]

A similar rapprochement also occurred in the trade union movement. The National Labour Committee, formed from the militant Nigerian National Federation of Labour

(NNFL) and the more moderate elements in Trade Union Congress, was established as an affiliate of the National Emergency Committee.[148] Both groups, while attempting a coalition, incorporated all the contradictions that had split both the political and trade union organizations in Nigeria. Within days delegations of prominent nationalists representing all the major factions of the nationalist movement arrived in Enugu and attempted to position themselves as representatives of the miners or as intermediaries between the workers and the state. A thorough examination of this interaction between militant workers and largely moderate nationalist politicians requires further research and oral documentation. However, the tensions between them and the workers were even sharper than those between the union leadership and the hewers. Initially, the delegations cautioned the miners against resuming work. But by the twenty-seventh they were advising a return to normalcy.[149] Nonetheless, the miners continued their "go slow" throughout the month of December.

The NEC and Igbo State Union (a coalition of urban improvement unions) delegations gathered evidence from a broad spectrum of people involved in the affair and agreed to serve as counsel for the miners during the government investigations. Initially, the nationalist press was virulent in its condemnation of the government's version of the shooting, but the declaration of a state of emergency quieted their attacks. This restriction of civil liberties opened the Labour government to further attack by both the nationalist movement and the opposition in Parliament.[150]

## THE INTERNATIONAL RESPONSE

The international reaction was similarly immediate. The timing could not be more embarrassing to the Labour Party under pressure from both the United States and the Soviet Union to quickly dissolve its empire. As luck would have it, their nemesis, the Igbo nationalist, Nnamdi Azikiwe was on a speaking tour in the United States. He used the event to generate outrage against the colonialists and for Nigerian independence among the African American community.

Azikiwe found a warm reception among the African American left, particularly the members of the African Aid Committee of the Council of African Affairs, W.E.B. Du Bois and Paul Robeson condemned the British, and noted that the blood of slaughtered African coal miners lay squarely at the foot of these imperialists. Du Bois responded to an appeal from the Nigerian National Federation of Labor (NNFL) and gave them a $200 check for the Enugu mine workers.[151] Du Bois wrote, in his note to the NNFL:

> A tangible token of the concern of progressive Americans over the inhuman and shocking answer of the Nigerian authorities to the rightful demands of African workers for a decent living wage.[152]

The League Against Imperialism, a Fabian socialist organization, demonstrated in London against Chief Commissioner Pyke-Nott, who was on a speaking tour. Miners locals in Scotland, Wales, and England voiced their protest.[153]

## THE STATE RESPONSE: THE COMMISSION HEARINGS AS "THEATRE"

On November 28 the Colonial Office appointed a commission of investigation which included two British and two African judges. The chair, W.J. Fitzgerald, was former Chief Justice in Palestine where he had recently served on a commission to Enquire on Local Administration of Jerusalem.[154] The other was P.W. Williams, representative of Wigan in the House of Commons and legal advisor to the National Union of Mineworkers. The two African members, S.O. Quashie-Idun of the Gold Coast and N.A. Ademola of Nigeria, sat on the supreme court of their respective countries.[155] Despite protests by socialist and communist MPs, no British or Nigerian trade unionists were selected.

The Commission convened on December 12 amidst a state of emergency and continued worker protest. Zikists were actively proselytizing and the miners were only producing at 70 percent capacity.[156] Ojiyi was still struggling against the dissidents who now claimed that he was responsible for the massacre. Attendance at the hearing became a litmus test for authenticity as nationalists made the pilgrimage to see the miners and offer assistance. As many were lawyers, they represented the union and its dissidents, as well as both the National Emergency Committee and the National Labour Committee of Nigeria and the Cameroons.[157]

The hearings became a microcosm of the contradictions in colonial society. Nationalists used them as a platform to attack the Nigerian government for its failure to offer a suitable program of decolonization. Some, like A.A. Adio-Moses the trade unionist, gave a pointed criticism of the trade union legislation. The government witnesses argued that the shootings, though regrettable, were a justifiable response to the dangerous radicalization of the nationalist movement. The testimony of one government intelligence officer alleged evidence of "terrorist" groups.[158]

## NATIONALISM AND WORKERS' STRUGGLES IN POSTWAR NIGERIA

The Fitzgerald Commission Report was a broad critique of the Nigerian government's constitutional proposals as well as its labor policy.[159] It was such a scathing critique that the Colonial Office authorized the unusual printing of a rebuttal by the Governor of Nigeria. Predictably, the most severe critiques focused on the Nigerian workers' movement in general and Ojiyi in particular.[160]

The shooting demonstrated the difficulties that the state confronted when it attempted to control workers who did not accept the parameters of industrial struggle created in England. The postwar period of industrial unrests suggests that although the labor reforms were essentially developed to contain worker protest, workers' leaders were capable of using them to negotiate on behalf of their members. The state's distinction between an industrial issue and a political issue proved difficult for the state itself to determine. On the other hand, the colliery workers through their history of struggle with their employer, the state, instinctively understood the political nature of the capitalist workplace.

As this study ends we see how much the miners' movement changed over the thirty-six years of the industry and yet how little had changed in the state and management's ability to manage and control it. The work of David Smock chronicles another decade—the 1960s—of conflict between labor and management at the mines and within the labor movement itself.[161] Nonetheless, several officials were subjected to sharp questioning and subsequent criticism for their handling of the crisis. One, J.G. Pyke-Nott, the Chief Commissioner, Eastern Provinces, came under fire for authorizing the armed removal of the explosives and rejecting offers for mediation by the Department of Labour advisors. As a military man, Pyke-Nott handled the industrial dispute as a threat to internal peace, a conclusion reflected in the critical questioning by the commissioners. The others, R. Bracegirdle, the unpopular manager, and F.S. Philip, Senior Superintendent of Police, were severely criticized for making crucial errors that either exacerbated the severity of the crisis or, in the case of Philip, for panicking in the midst of the crisis.[162]

The testimony and questioning at the hearings were fascinating examples of the subtle power shifts in the interactions between Nigerians imbued with a sense of eminent political change and British investigators begrudgingly adjusting to the new realities. Nduka Eze, the Zikist trade unionist, was subjected to hostile questioning that challenged his integrity as a leader. The same manipulative "demagogue"–illiterate worker paradigm that shaped the solicitor general's reaction to Ojiyi was clear: "you are not interested in the workers at all, you are using them for your own political ends."[163] Eze replied, "That is your own personal opinion." Some of the harshest criticism came from moderate/conservative Africans Quashie-Idun and Rotimi Williams, who used this as an opportunity to chastise Eze for his political views and ridiculed him—"What do you call Imperialists? Are you confused? Are you sure you know the meaning of Imperialists?"[164]

The hearings lasted until January 5 and the report was made public the following June. The Colonial Office had considerable consternation about the response to its contents and debated the propriety of releasing the report amidst the continued political tension in Nigeria.[165] Specifically, the Colonial Office was concerned with the attack on Chief Commissioner Pyke-Nott to whom it attributed the decision to remove the explosives "at all cost." Because of the serious nature of this critique, the Colonial Office took the unusual opportunity to allow the Governor to write a defense which was published with the report. The Colonial Office also judged Philip to be dangerously unstable and judged him to be "a sick man," "unfit medically for further service in the tropics" and feared that the victims could quite possibly win a civil action against him in the courts.[166] It therefore suggested that the government award compensation to the relatives of those killed.[167] Bracegirdle was similarly considered to be a liability and a colonial official who proved unable to exercise the most skillful judgment in managing colonial workers. They suggested that "it was of the first importance that he should cease to have executive responsibility."[168] He had been secreted out of Nigena, never to appear again as a colonial civil servant.

The report is an astounding outline of a particular proposal for decolonization and one perspective of the role of workers and trade unions in the process of development. It made a generalized critique of trade union leadership throughout Nigeria, arguing that unions' main function should be economistic issues, "when the leaders stray from this they betray their responsibilities."[169] Its most fundamental comments ranged far beyond the massacre itself and ventured into the political realm. The report made broad comments on the Nigerian government's plans for political change, the current state of Nigerian trade unions and its leaders, and made recommendations for labor reform at the colliery and throughout Nigeria as well as political reform. It noted that West Africa's strategic importance during World War II had encouraged political activism because it "assumed a temporary importance out of proportion to its peace time place in the British Empire."[170] Its general assessment of the Nigerian government was that it had failed to propose progressive political reforms that would capture the imagination of the population. Similarly, it criticized the colliery management for being similarly outdated in its framework for industrial relations. At the core of the Commission's critique was its determination that the state's characterization of the industrial dispute as a political one was fatally erroneous. In treating a simple industrial protest as a threat to the public order the Chief Commissioner had unleashed unnecessary force on unarmed miners.[171]

Predictably, the report leveled its harshest criticisms at the "rascal Ojiyi" who it accused of misleading the workers, fomenting discontent, and being guilty of financial impropriety regarding the 1947 levy.[172] It had little sympathy for his allegation that the union dissidents fomented much of the unrest in the industry and their impact on the context in which he formed the workers' grievances.

The Commission's critique of Ojiyi was used by both the state and the union dissidents to deal the final blow to his leadership. The Coal Board used it to expel Ojiyi from his post as General Secretary of the CWU and banned him from all colliery installations and mines. The dissidents then formed a rival union, the Nigerian Coal Miners' Union, which was dominated by artisans, clerks, and foremen. By November 1950 the CWU was dead and, for the final time, its recognition withdrawn.[173] The state's plan was to reconstruct the colliery labor movement through the transformation of the union. Subsequently, a delegation of labor relations experts and mine managers were sent to the colliery from England to restore normal operations.[174] But Ojiyi remained as an encumbrance. Dissidents failed to have him convicted of misappropriation of funds in a court case because they had no legal standing since they had ceased to be members of the CWU. However, the government used the 1947 levy to bring Ojiyi and his executive up on criminal charges for fraud and conspiracy to steal funds. This time they succeeded and Ojiyi was convicted and given a harsh sentence of four and a half years which he served in Kaduna.[175] By the time he was released in February 1953, a new union leadership had emerged but the union still did not function as "responsibly" as the state had planned. The NCMU hired as its General Secretary a left-wing nationalist leader with links to Michael Imoudu, leader of the railway workers and member of the World Federation of Trade Unions. The colliery workers continued to block the government's best-laid plans and plunged the industry into several more decades of militant worker protest. It was remarkable that despite their tumultuous history the industry's managers still refused to see them as industrial men. The comments of the chair of the new Nigerian Coal Corporation are instructive. The old assumptions about the "primitive" nature of the miners still persisted. It was virtually impossible for them to be acknowledged as industrial men thirty-six years later.

> It is a fact that mining is not a traditional form of employment and the older men especially are peasants who do mining. They have a peasant's outlook and are concerned with putting away money against drought, famine, pestilence and war. They still do not realise that they are in a steady job. This makes them contemptuous of welfare, except the shops, and they openly say that it should all be stopped and the cost added to their wages. This is an attitude not easily understood by well-meaning advisers from overseas who think that an extension of welfare is needed to bring about industrial peace.[176]

## NOTES

1. Testimony of M. Ogbonna, 3rd Class Constable, Iva Valley Detachment, "Enquiry into the Disorders in the Eastern Provinces of Nigerias: Proceedings of the Commission," Mimeograph, Vol. 2, London, 1950 (Hereafter "Proceedings"), 805.

2. CO 537/4727 "Political Intelligence Reports 1948–1949," Secret 28 Nigeria. Political Summary of December 1948.

3. "Proceedings," 541.

4. For a discussion of the "ritualistic" role of industrial relations in mediating the contradictions between labor and capital, see Chapter 7, "Conflict and Accommodation: The Dialectics of Industrial Relations," Richard Hyman, *Industrial Relations: A Marxist Introduction* (London, 1975), 184–203.

5. Ibid.

6. Despite the importance of the shooting in nationalist mythology there are only two major published accounts of the shooting. The most prominent is Agwu Akpala's "Background to the Enugu Shooting Incident." See also S.O. Jaja, "The Enugu Colliery Massacre in Retrospect: An Episode in British Administration of Nigeria," *Journal of the Historical Society of Nigeria*, 2, 3–4 (December 1982-June 1983):86–106.

7. Gt. Britain, Colonial Office, *Report of the Commission of Enquiry into the Disorders in the Eastern Provinces of Nigeria*, Col. No 256. London, 1950 (Hereafter Fitzgerald Commission).

8. A census in 1945 claimed that of a colliery workforce of 6,800 only 2,081 lived in non-government quarters in Enugu, 1,640 in Colliery quarters and the remaining 3,100 lived in nearby villages. NIGCOAL 2/1/138, Local Authority, "Census of Enugu," 1945. This was conducted by the local authority in 1945. I thank Dr. P.E.H. Hair for allowing me to use his copy.

9. UDDIST 9/1/1/ "Annual Report 1946—Udi Division."

10. Coleman, *Nigeria* 253–254.

11. Sklar, *Nigerian Political Parties*, 52 ff; J. Coleman, *Nigeria*, 249ff.

12. "Zik" had a problematic relationship with these young men. He appeared to be too moderate to the most activist members and he assiduously distanced himself from them publicly as he negotiated with the colonial government.

13. *Sklar, Nigerian Political Parties* 72–75; Olusanya, *The Second World War and Politics in Nigeria, 1939–1953* (London, 1973), 114–15.

14. For an excellent history of the ideological development of the movement see Ehiedu E.G. Iweriebor, *Radical Politics in Nigeria 1945–1950: The Significance of the Zikist Movement*, (Zaria, Nigeria, 1996).

15. CO537/4631, "Report by Norman Smith, 30 November 1949."

16. For details see "Proceedings," 507 ff.

17. Enugu Government Colliery, "Annual Report for the Year Ending 1946."

18. Akpala, "Background to the Shooting Incident," 351.

19. Powell Duffryn, "Characteristics of the Coal," Table D-XXXVI.

20. The government proposed mass literacy in which rather basic reading skills were taught. The nationalists demanded formal primary and secondary education, which they felt would better prepare the people for independence.

21. UDDIST 9/1/1/, "Annual Report 1947—Udi Division." Both colliers resident in the villages and those who boarded in town held regular meetings to discuss their contributions to the school. P. 2/1/3, DO Udi to Colliery Manager, 12 February 1946.

22. Bracegirdle was apparently quite unpopular with his senior staff. After the shooting, the governor mentioned ... "had the Colliery been a commercial undertaking it is probable that it would have parted company with Bracegirdle long ago." CO537/5800 Governor Macpherson to Andrew B. Cohen, Colonial Office, 13 April 1950.

23. The railway workers struck because of a racist supervisor. Many of these men were from the British working class, the group often classified as "Second Class Europeans" (See Map, Chapter 3). Colonial jobs gave them more income than they could earn at home and they clearly relished the power they could exert over African men, whom they considered their inferiors. Decolonization hit them hard and they desperately tried to retain the types of arbitrary power they formerly held when the legal apparatus to preserve this was dissolving.

24. Sir Arthur Richards was the Governor of Nigeria. Nationalists objected to a number of provisions of the Richards Constitution, including the fact that it was introduced without any consultation with the people. They were particularly incensed that it did not give elected political representation to Nigerians in the legislature. Moreover, it allowed chiefs and emirs of the old "native authority" system to hold positions. It encouraged a split between the two nationalist power groupings, one, in the west of predominantly Yoruba-speaking peoples and the other, to the east of the Igbo. For a discussion of the controversy see Coleman, *Nigeria*, Chapter 12.

25. Ibid., 289.

26. P.E.H. Hair, "Enugu: An Industrial Urban Community in Nigeria 1914–1954," *Report of the Annual Conference-Sociology Section*, West African Institute of Social and Economic Research, Ibadan, University College, March 1953, 164.

27. Coleman, *Nigeria* 292.

28. See Powell Duffryn, "Characteristics of the Coal," D-138, Interview with Eze Ozogwu, 2 June 1975.

29. David Smock Papers, Jacob A. Diewait, typescript response to questions, mimeograph, n.d.

30. Documents in the PRO show how confused they were even at the Colonial Office level about nationalists' ideologies. I.e., Zik, himself. See C.O.537/4727 Political Intelligence Reports 1948–49; CO537/5807 "The Zikist Movement" 1949–1950.

31. P. 2/1/3, Fitzgerald Commission Representations, Attachment III, R. Bracegirdle to L.T. Chubb, Sec. Eastern Provinces, 15 September 1945.

32. P. 2/1/3 E.R. Chadwick to L.T. Chubb, 7 March 1946.

33. Ibid, D.P.J. O'Connor to L.T. Chubb, 11 March 1946.

34. *Fitzgerald Commission*, 35.

35. Akpala "Background to the Shooting Incident," 351.

36. Unrest among ex-servicemen began in 1946 when they demanded better conditions of life and payment. The contrast between their living conditions and those of Europeans increased their ire. Great Britain, *Report of the Commission of Enquiry into Disturbances in the Gold Coast, 1948*. Colonial No. 123.

37. NIGCOAL 1/1/36, Manager to Engineers, 11 September 1945.

38. In 1947 the senior clerk claimed that timekeepers were angry because ex-servicemen were given inflated grades without the requisite qualifications. NIGCOAL 1/1/22, F.O. Erinoso, to Colliery Manager, 11 August 1947.

39. Sklar, *Nigerian Political Parties*, 75; Olusanya, *The Second World War*, 116.

40. 22 August 1977, Roy Adams to Jeff Haydu Internet Exchange on H-Labour, posted 21 August 1997.

41. Ojiyi's personal papers are replete with internal memos between expatriate supervisors, the manager, and state officials trying to develop strategies to punish him for his trade union activities. See NIGCOAL P 2/1/1 (New Number).

42. NCCF P.2/1/1, Ojiyi to Colliery Manager, 12 March 1946.

43. P. 2/1/1, Ojiyi to CM 1 April 1946.

44. P.1/3, Ojiyi for the Colliery Workers, 10 November 1947.

45. P. 1/3 Ibid.

46. Akpala, "Background to the Shooting Incident," 354.

47. NIGCOAL 1/1/21, CWU to Manager, 24 September 1945.

48. NCCF P. 2/1/3 District Officer to Resident, 7 March 1946; Resident to District Officer, 11 March 1946.

49. Akpala, "Background," 355.

50. Douglass, "Pit talk," 311.

51. Ananaba mentions that Ojiyi trained the men in this tactic for three weeks in the 1947 dispute; Ananaba, *Trade Union Movement in Nigeria*, 101.

52. Sir W. Harragin, *Report of the Commission on the Civil Services of British West Africa, 1945–1946*, No. 209 (London: HMSO for the British Colonial Office, 1947).

53. Nigeria, *Report on Unestablished and Daily-rated Government Servants*, Sessional Paper No. 8 of 1947, Lagos: Government Printer, March 1947. Unestablished staff were daily paid laborers.

54. NNAE, P. 2/1/1, Ojiyi to Manager, 1 April 1946.

55. P. 1/3 Ojiyi to CM, 10 August 1947.

56. Akpala, "Background," 355.

57. Conciliation is a form of statute-regulated bargaining in which the two parties, labor and capital, meet with an impartial conciliator to resolve their difficulties. The Labour Department, however, was hardly an impartial participant in the dispute since it was so instrumental in expelling the union.

58. NCCF, P. 1/3/1, R. Bracegirdle, "Report on Trades Dispute at the Colliery—1947," 10 January 1948.

59. The best treatment of the most prominent of these strikes is by Timothy Oberst in his doctoral dissertation; "Cost of Living and Strikes in British Africa, c 1939–1948: Imperial Policy and the Impact of the Second World War," Ph.D. Diss., Columbia University, 1991.

60. This discussion is from the actual text of the agreement, NCCF P. 1/3, "Memorandum of Agreement—1947," 22 December 1947.

61. David Smock Papers, Interview with H.J. Honey, Macclesfield, Cheshire, England, 7 December 1961, Testimony of Robert Curry, "Proceedings," v. I, p. 316; Akpala, "Background to the Shooting Incident," 358.

62. For a study of the colliery see Ian Phimister, *Wangi Kolia: Coal, Capital and Labour in Colonial Zimbabwe 1894–1954* (Harare, 1994).

63. This was an industrial application of what Cooper called "the demagogue-mass connection." Frederick Cooper, *Decolonization*, 254.

64. Testimony of Robert Curry, "Proceedings," v.I, 93.

65. Akpala, "Background to the Shooting Incident," 356–57.

66. NCCF P. 1/3/1, Manager Comment, 10 January 1948.

67. P. 1/3, "Memorandum of Agreement, 22 December 1947."

68. This was included in a report by T.M. Cowan of the British Ministry of Labor on negotiations between government and its employees in which he feared that trade union leaders might be forced to use "aggressive tactics" to secure what he considered to be "unreasonable demands." *Report on Methods of Negotiation between Government and Government Employees on Questions affecting Conditions of Service in Industrial Departments*," as cited in Ananaba, *The Trade Union Movement*, 71.

69. P. 1/3/1, Passmore, Acting CM to C.W.U., 27 July 1948; Saint to Cook, 9 April 1948; "Petition for Regrading by Machine Drivers," 2 August 1948; Ugwu, Runners Group to CM, 21 December 1948.

70. David Smock Papers, Interview with H.J. Honey, Macclesfield, Cheshire, England, 7 December 1961.

71. P. 1/3/1, Coals to Chief Secretary, 5 March 1948.

72. P. 2/1/3, Attachment XIII, All Sectional Meetings to CM, 22 October 1948.

73. This group included a number of employees several of whom had been accused of bribery and corruption during the 1930s interpreter crisis. C.P. Morris (Timekeeper), A.E. Nwachukwu (Electrician), B. Anyasado (Timekeeper), G.B. Tasker (Electrician), G. Njeze (Mine Examiner), A.I. Okpokwu (Native Foreman), Eze Ozo-Ugwu, H. Okoro (Surface Headman). P. 2/1/3, Attachment XIII, to CM from All Sectional Meetings, 22 October 1948; NIGCOAL 1/1/21, R.W.H. Saint, "Minutes of Meeting," 11 November 1948.

74. *Fitzgerald Commission*, 31.

75. *Report of the Commission into the Cost of Living in the Colony and Protectorate of Nigeria*, Colonial Office No. 204 (London: HMSO, 1946).

76. The Harragin Commission report recommended that government set up advisory councils to counsel government on general issues concerning civil servants. Cowan's investigation suggested that the government establish national Whitley Councils as bodies to discuss general principles "governing conditions of service like recruitment, hours of work, promotions, discipline." Ananaba, *Trade Union Movement*, 72.

77. Jeff Haydu in an exchange with Roy Adams on H-Labor, 25 August 1997. For Haydu's argument see *Making American Industry Safe for Democracy: Comparative Perspectives*

*on the State and Employee Representation in the Era of World War I* (Illinois, 1997). Haydu argues that they also effectively privileged trade unions over more radical forms of workers' representation.

78. *Report of the Methods of Negotiation between the Government and Government Employees on Questions Affecting Conditions of Service in Industrial Departments* (Lagos, 1948).

79. Rob Davies, "The Class Character of South Africa's Industrial Conciliation Legislation," in *Essays in Southern African Labour History*, Eddie Webster, ed. (Johannesburg, 1978), 79.

80. Ananaba, *The Trade Union Movement*, 75–76; Cohen *Labour and Politics*, 75–76.

81. Testimony of Sir Hugh Foote, Governor of Nigeria, "Proceedings," v. I, 7.

82. Ibid.

83. Yesufu, *An Introduction to Industrial Relations in Nigeria*, 51.

84. *Fitzgerald Commission*, 21–22.

85. Ibid.

86. David Smock, "From Village to Trade Union in Africa," Ph.D. Diss., Cornell University, 1964, 142.

87. P. 2/1, "Minutes of the Meeting of the CWU Executive with Manager, 17 May 1949."

88. Ibid.

89. Akpala, "African Labour Productivity," 239.

90. Ibid., 299.

91. P. 2/1, "Minutes of the Meeting, 17 May 1949."

92. *Fitzgerald Commission*, 26.

93. Ibid.

94. P. 2/1, Labour Officer to Labour Commissioner, 17 May 1949.

95. P. 2/1, "Minutes of the Whitley Council, 12 July 1949."

96. P. 2/1, CM to Chief Secretary, 10 November 1949; *Fitzgerald Commission*, 28.

97. P. 2/1, Code Telegram from Chief Secretary to CM, n.d.; CM to Chief Secretary, 9 November 1949; CM to Chief Secretary, 10 November 1949.

98. P. 2/1, CM to Chief Secretary, 12 November 1949.

99. The Powell Duffryn Technical Services firm had been commissioned by the Colonial Secretary to conduct an extensive investigation of the technical and personnel problems of the coal industry. Its report is a detailed description of the industry's operations. See Powell Duffryn Technical Services, "First Report on the Government Colliery, Enugu," 1948.

100. Powell Duffryn Technical Services, H. 8–9.

101. P. 2/1, CM to Chief Secretary, 14 November 1949.

102. P. 2/ No. 1111, "Minutes of the Meeting at Government Lodge, 16 July 1950."

103. *Fitzgerald Commission*, 36–37.

104. David Smock Papers, Interview with H.J. Honey, Macclesfield, Cheshire, England, 7 December 1961.

105. *Fitzgerald Commission*, 36.

106. Ibid., 33.

107. Ibid., 34; *The Times of London*, 6 January 1950.

108. ONDIST 12/1/1563, Local Authority, "Account of the Colliery Strike"; "Statement by A.J.W. Clarke, Assistant District Officer, Udi," 2 December 1949.

109. Interview with Alice Afameufuna, Tinker's Corner, Enugu, 26 July 1975.

110. "Sitting on a man" is a traditional form of women's protests in Igbo villages in which the women of a market grouping surround the house of a man who has committed an of-

fense against women and make scurrilous comments and songs. Sometimes they beat down his house using large sticks. The 1929 Aba Women's Riots followed this format but were actually a protest against the corruption of the unpopular warrant chiefs and an attempt to institute taxation in the east. From the description of the singing and jovial mood of the crowd surrounding the manager's house it appears that this was the case. See Judith Van Allen, "'Sitting on a Man': Colonialism and the Lost Political Institutions of Igbo Women," *Canadian Journal of African Studies*, 6, 2 (1972): 165–81.

111. Ondist 12/1/1562, Local Authority, Enugu, "Account of the Colliery Strike."

112. The article in *New Africa* claimed that the miners were owed additional back pay because of illegal rostering. The Fitzgerald Commission reserved special comments for the paper, blaming the article for spreading misinformation which fanned the crisis. *Fitzgerald Commission*, 10.

113. Interview with Alice Afamuefuna, 26 July 1975.

114. "Proceedings of the Commission," and *Fitzgerald Commission*.

115. Interview with Emanuel Okafor, Uwani, Enugu, 10 July 1975. Interview with Peter Afamuefuna, Tinker's Corner, Enugu, 26 July 1975.

116. Testimony of J.E. Nzerogu, Screen Foreman; "Proceedings," 763.

117. Ibid., 761.

118. "Proceedings," 519.

119. Testimony of A. Okolie, Lance Corporal Police Force, "Proceedings," 775.

120. Ibid., 782.

121. Ibid.

122. Testimony of E.J.R. Ormiston, Senior Assistant Superintendent of Police, Enugu, "Proceedings," 435.

123. Philip's testimony is an excellent example of the hysterical response of a colonial policeman acting from his instincts and misinterpreting the demeanor and intent of an African crowd. See "Proceedings," 452–88.

124. The presence of weapons was challenged by many witnesses. I have included it here because it is part of the testimony and because it attests to the state of mind of the officers. See testimony of Philip above.

125. Philip, "Proceedings," 485.

126. Interview with Emmanuel Okafor.

127. Philip, "Proceedings," 460.

128. Philip was challenged in this characterization by Quashie-Idon, a lawyer for the men. "Proceedings," quote from Philip testimony, 483.

129. Ibid., 457.

130. Ibid., 477.

131. This dialogue is based on the Proceedings of the commission of investigation, the *Fitzgerald Commission*.

132. "Proceedings," 412.

133. When questioned by H.O. Davies as to how six men could have been shot in the back, Philip said that a ricocheting bullet could strike another person. Philip, 488.

134. "Proceedings," 541.

135. Philip, 458.

136. Emmanuel Okafor, a blacksmith, Uwani, Enugu, 10 July 1975.

137. Phillip, 476.

138. Interview with Emmanuel Okafor.

139. Interview with Isaiah Ojiyi, Amawbia, Awka, 27 July 1975.

140. Interview with Onovo Ana, Akegbe Ugwu, Enugu, 30 July 1975.

141. Interview with Chikelu Eluke, Ugbo' dogwu, Enugu, 5 August 1975.

142. For eyewitness accounts of these incidents see "Proceedings," 542–682.

143. In Calabar the ethnic divisions between the Igbo urban working class and the Efik former slaveowners led to a wave of ethnic violence immediately following the shooting. The Ekpo Society joined police in dispersing the predominantly Igbo demonstrations. Anti-Igbo violence continued for several days in December. *The Times*, 19 December 1949.

144. Interview with Mokwugo Okoye, East Central Broadcasting Layout, Enugu, 16 July 1975.

145. *Fitzgerald Commission*, 41–49; Mokwugo Okoye, 16 July 1975.

146. Ananaba, Trade union movement Nigerian Political Parties, 109; Sklar, 77.

147. Nduka Eze, "Memoirs of a Crusader," (typewritten) as cited in *Nigerian Political Parties* Sklar, 77.

148. According to Sklar, the NEC included from the NCNC, K.O. Mbadiwe, F.U. Anyiam, Oged Macaulay, A.K. Blankson, Mbonu Ojike; from the Zikist movement, Mokwugo Okoye; from the Northern National Movement, Dr. Akinola Maja, F.R.A. Williams, Oba Samuel Akisanya, H.O. Davis, and J. Akanni Doherty. Trade unionists who were members included P.O. Balonwu, and A.A. Adio-Moses. Undetermined affiliation: S.O. Gbadamosi, Odemo of Ishara, O.A. Thomas, G.B. Okeke, M.A. Ogun, N. Okoro, and Dr. I. Olorun-Nimbe (expelled from the NCNC in 1948). Ananaba, 109; Sklar, *Nigerian Political Parties*, 78n.

149. ONDIST 12/1/1564, "Minutes of Meeting between Lagos Delegates and Udi Clan Councillors, 27 November 1949."

150. Great Britain, 38th Parliament, *Hansard's Parliamentary Debates* (Commons), v. 470, 7 December 1949, 1866–68.

151. "African Aid Committee Sends Help to Nigerian Strike Victims," *New Africa*, 9, 1 (January 1950).

152. Ibid.

153. The African-American press also carried reports on the shooting. See "Wild Riots Sweep Nigeria, Police Kill Four," *The Pittsburgh Courier*, 10 December 1949; "18 Killed in African Riot," *Amsterdam News*, 26 November 1949. For Parliamentary Debates see *Hansards* V. 470, 38th Parliament 1948–49, 21 November–16 December 1949.

154. Anthony Kirk-Greene, *Biographical Dictionary of the British Colonial Service, 1939–1966* (London, 1991).

155. *The Times*, 28 November 1949.

156. ONDIST 12/1/1564, Colliery Manager to Chief Secretary, 7 December 1949.

157. For the CWU there was M.O. Ajegbo, G.C. Nkemena, and G.C.M. Onyuike. Charles D. Onyeama, son of Chief Onyeama, represented the union dissidents. F.R.A. Williams, H.O. Davies, H.U. Kaine, J.A. Chukwu, and G.C. Nonyelu represented the National Emergency Committee. See, *Fitzgerald Commission*, 4–5.

158. *Fitzgerald*, 34.

159. The chairman, W.J. Fitzgerald, was president of the Lands Tribunal and had served in the colonial legal service in Nigeria, Northern Rhodesia, and Palestine. *The Times*, 28 November 1949.

160. One of the unfortunate aspects of the event is the prominence given to this official report by historians of the period. The commission "Proceedings" give a more complex picture of evolving events and suggest that Ojiyi may indeed have been correct in his interpretation of the Trade Union Ordinance's position on rostering. "Proceedings."

161. David Smock, "Village to Trade Union"; *Conflict and Control in an African Trade Union: A Study of the Nigerian Coal Miners' Union* (Stanford, 1969). Both emphasize the period after 1950 and focus on the centralization of power in the union. Smock includes a formidable historical section in the thesis though not in the book.

162. For both see "Proceedings."

163. Ibid., 749.

164. Ibid., 752.

165. The Colonial Office debate about the publication of the report is in C.O. 537/5794, /5795, /5796, /5797. One particularly unsettling development had been a series of tense demonstrations by ex-servicemen in several cities in eastern Nigeria. Several had bordered on insurrection. See Geoffrey Nwaka, "Rebellion in Umuahia, 1950–1951: Ex-servicemen and Anti-colonial Protest in Eastern Nigeria," *Transafrican Journal of History*, Vol 16 (1987): 47–62.

166. C.O. 537/5799, Minutes, Andrew Cohen to W.C. Johnson, Sir C. Jeffries, Sir T. Lloyd.

167. "Notes of a Meeting Held on 21 April to Discuss the Fitzgerald Report."

168. Ibid.

169. *Fitzgerald Commission*, 14.

170. Ibid., 11.

171. Ibid., 101.

172. Ibid., 25.

173. David Smock, "From Village to Trade Union," 145.

174. One of the labor experts, H.J. Honey, objected to the Commission critique of Ojiyi and tried to give a more balanced perspective of the crisis. Perhaps for this reason he was removed from Enugu relatively soon after his opinions became known. P.2, No. 111 "Minutes of the Meeting held in the Senior Labour Officer's Office on Friday 16 June 1950." "Minutes of a Meeting Held at Government Lodge," 16 June 1950.

175. David Smock Papers, Interview with Okwudili Ojiyi, Amawbia, Awka, 3 October 1962.

176. New No. P. 2, Acting Chairman, Nigerian Coal Corporation, "Secret: Labour Relations at Enugu Collieries," 29 May 1951.

# CONCLUSION:
# WORK, CLASS, AND
# IDENTITY IN IGBOLAND

The first part of this study documented the construction of colonial labor relations in a state industry. The British charged into Igboland and created the first group of workers from the vanquished. But gradually Igbo men set the parameters of what they would and would not do, even within a system of exploitative structures in the workplace. Some were slaves, for whom wage labor was a prelude to emancipation, and others were free. But both were conscripted by the dragnet of forced labor. The second part of the study, from the late 1930s, describes the gradual erosion of the colonial labor process. Strikes over dignity—the slapping of a worker by a white boss, the insistence of respectful forms of address (the end of "pick boy")—all were markers that the old racist forms of authority were no longer tenable in the workplace.

The narrative ended with the Iva Valley shooting which was in many ways an inevitable result of a conventional fiction: that there was a clear distinction between economic and political disputes in a colony. The crucial difficulty was how to define this distinction. When pressed to do so, as in November of 1949, few officials in authority were able to determine when a "labor" dispute had become a threat to political stability. In fact, this distinction, which became a mantra of the Colonial Office social reforms during the war, was the articulation of a political position to moderate the activism of colonial workers and insulate them from nationalists. Such moderation was especially important at a time when the state could not differentiate a "safe" nationalist from a communist fellow traveler. The difficulty in the industrial/political distinction was that it was antithetical to the industry's history. In Nigeria as in most African colonies, the state was too dominant as an employer to make this analytical distinction a reality. From the foundational years of the industry the Nigerian state had acted as if colliery labor were political and Enugu mine workers understood this reality early and manipulated it. And it was incredibly naïve for officials to assume that government employees wouldn't understand the political nature of their protest.

In fact, the system of labor recruitment used in 1914—forced labor—was called "political labor." It was the state that introduced capitalist production relations into the area. The chief architect, Lord Lugard, explicitly crafted a paternalistic role for the state which intentionally introduced what he considered to be a superior labor system. Brushing aside the apparent contradiction of recruiting "free" labor using "forced" means, Lugard established a managerial structure in which political officials consistently intruded into industrial affairs. Intimate connections were similarly made between the purveyors of "customary" law, the warrant "chiefs" and later the village councilors and the industry. This, consequently, entangled the industry's concerns within the lower echelons of the colonial state.

The workers usually recognized the political impact of their grievances and always realized that the center of industrial authority lay not with the management but with the state. They were propelled by a strong concept of social justice with a definition of workers' rights and entitlements. As state workers this concept related to the ways that they conceptualized the responsibilities of political authorities and leaders. Some of this was rooted in Igbo concepts of the responsibility of leaders; others in new ideas that they had crafted from their understanding of western democratic forms. Their expectations of the state's responsibilities came from their experience with its frequent interventions which brought this or the other national official from Lagos in times of industrial crisis. Workers understood the bureaucratic hierarchy of the state and often took their grievances to the highest level—violating the chain of command. Usually they did not see the manager as the person who had the power to deal with their issues and often treated him with contempt.

By the inter-war period they were acutely aware of their power to summon officials from the highest echelons of the colonial state to tend to their complaints. It did not take long before their protests used petitions to government as a pivotal strategy. These petitions articulated a discourse through which we can glimpse the elements of a model of the state as perceived by African workers. The use of these documents suggests an important means to determine the political sensitivities of African workers that may be more useful than the usual search for explicit connections between labor and the nationalist movement. Planted within workers' petitions, the grievances, the demands, and the expectations is a philosophy of political authority held by broad sectors of the men.

The men assumed the state had responsibility for the well-being of its employees. It had claimed to bring "civilization," "enlightenment," and "progress" to Igboland and the men evaluated the conditions under which they worked and lived against this promise. These expectations became a yardstick which shaped their protests as they assumed the responsibility for improving their villages and communities. The income they earned was not simply used for subsistence, it was "banked" for the future in the education of their children, the improvement of health care facilities, and the introduction of modern sanitary conditions. It was also used in more established ways—to assume the highest ranks of title societies, to expand the household through polygyny, and to create a modern "Big Compound." All of these social uses of mining income transformed the meaning of masculinity, giving it complexity and fluidity. When officials called the men "coal gentlemen" they were describing a type of manhood linked to the industry and the "modernity" it fostered.

The British never seemed to respect or to recognize the complexity of Igbo governing traditions and organizations and the roles that these men played within them. By the late thirties the Colonial Office acknowledged that the best way of containing colonial workers' unrest was to develop industrial disputes procedures that acknowledged that workers had a right to some form of representation. But workers spent the remainder of the colonial period fighting over the form and degree of autonomy that these organizations were allowed to have. Initially there were the *Nzuko* but their militance and secretiveness made officials wary. Then management appointed Representative Councils, but the old *Nzuko* leaders seized their leadership and they remained disruptive. Thirdly were the state-mandated trade unions which were initially controlled by parasitic sectors—"boss boys," interpreters, foremen, and later Ojiyi. But as soon as the men began to use the new unions, recognition was withdrawn and a new representative committee was formed with members based on clan and job category. The men boycotted them. Finally, the state restored the union but restructured it in a way that institutionalized divisions among workers and especially emphasized the autonomy of hewers. The consequences were the November tragedy.

Similarly, officials failed to recognize the role that hewers played before the Bulkeley Award in organizing work to produce the output reflected in output statistics before 1938. When management dismantled the hewers' work-group the industry was never again able to achieve these levels of production. But the most tragic example of this arrogance was Curry's reorganization of the Colliery Workers Union following an organizational model quite alien to the associational culture of Igbo society. The consequences of this error were the destruction of centralized negotiations between workers and management and the hewers' autonomous strategy of protest.

Officials also underestimated the workers' understanding of their conditions of work and pay and saw them as easily victimized by unscrupulous leaders. Ojiyi was maligned in the *Fitzgerald Commission Report* and singled out for especially severe censure in its aftermath. Sending a trade unionist to four years in prison for a financial infraction was a fairly typical example of the types of state-orchestrated repression that stifled trade union development in Africa. But Ojiyi retained his indomitable spirit. A local Enugu newspaper in 1975 reported on yet another petition which he sent to Queen Elizabeth to secure the missing arrears that caused the 1949 sit-in.

The Colonial Office had a model of social policy that it tried to implement from the late thirties. It sought to order society around a disciplined working class and to intervene both in the workplace and home to insure social control. But the workers had their own ideas about reform. These were articulated in their grievances, petitions, actions, and the initiatives they took in developing their villages. Their modes of struggle were very progressive, involving support from lawyers and professional letter writers and implied a self-image deserving of rights.

There is the imprint of the coal mines on the urban identity of Enugu and the rural identity of the Agbaja villages. Senior men in Agbaja villages eagerly recall

their experiences in the mines and proudly speak of the importance of the industry in the social and economic development of the area. In the thirties, Croasdale
had warned government not to invest in the urban camps lest they encourage the
creation of militant mining villages as existed in England and Wales. The men were
more suited to rural life, which, he apparently assumed, brought more quiescence.
The role of Agbaja's miners in the history of the industry suggests that he was
wrong.

Finally, this study wanted to retrieve Nigerian miners from the domination of
nationalist historiography. While it is true that most Nigerians see the massacre as
the birth date of Nigerian nationalism, it is also true that they base their understanding of this event on the interpretations of the *Fitzgerald Commission Report*.
As nationalist icons, the dead miners become but a backdrop for the more dynamic
drama of nationalist politics, a fate so amply suggested in the politician's performance at the Commission hearings. This project suggests that if labor history is
only a backdrop for the narrative of the emergence of the independent state, it will
be difficult to understand the deep contradictions that so penalize contemporary
Africa.

# BIBLIOGRAPHY

**INTERVIEWS**

Afameufuna, Alice, Tinker's Corner, Enugu, 26 July 1975.
Afameufuna, Peter, Tinker's Corner, Enugu, 26 July 1975.
Agu, Josiah, Enugu, 22 May 1975.
Akpala, Agwu, London, 14 February 1975.
Alo, James, Okwojo, Ngwo, 6 June 1975.
Amahalu, Gabriel, Forest Hill Camp, Enugu, 17 July 1975.
Aneke, Samuel, Obinagu, Udi, 28 May 1975.
Anyasado, B.U., Mbieri, Owerri, 23 July 1975.
Ana, Onovo, Akegbe Ugwu, Enugu, 30 July 1975.
Brodrick, Thomas Osanogoze, Enugu, 16 July 1999.
Chiegwu, Anieke, Umuagba, Owa Imezi, Udi 6 and 7 July 1975.
Chime, Samuel, Awka, 27 June 1975.
Chukwuani, Chief Nwafor, Enugu, 15 June 1975.
Chukwuani, Prince Harry, Ozalla, 18 July 1999.
Cohen, Robin, London, 1 May 1975.
Ekwereonye, Joseph, Enugu, 15 July 1975.
Eluke, Chikelu, Ugbo'dogwu, Enugu, 5 August 1975.
Ephraim Ene, Nnamani Onovo, Nwolie Nnamuchi, Nnaaji Ogbodo, Akegbe Ukwu, 20
        August 1986.
Ene, Robert, Obinagu Udi, 4 June 1975.
Eze, Johnson, Obinagu Udi, 4 June 1975.
Igbodiegwu, Philip, Iva Valley, Enugu, 17 July 1975.
Iwuagwu, Daniel, Enugu, 3 July 1975.
Iwuagwu, Shedrack, Asata, Enugu, 12 July 1975.
Madubuegwu, Chivulu, Umuagba Owa, 3 June 1975.
Mbalemlu, Gabriel, Michael Nwakuache, and Clement Egbogimba, Ugwu Alfred, 5 July
        1975.
Mokoro, Osakwe, 8 July 1975 and Clement Ude, 9 July 1975, Ugwu Aaron, Enugu.
Morris, Charles, Ogbete, Enugu, 19 June 1975.
Nicholson, Marjorie, TUC Library, 1 October 1974, London.
Nnandi, Gabriel, Nsude, Udi, 7 August 1975.

Noisike, Thomas, Agbaja, Udi Division, Enugu, 7 June 1975.
Nwimoh, Edward, Awka, 19 July 1975.
Nwodo, Mazi Anyionovo, Uhuona, Ugbawka, 18 August 1988.
Ocam, E.C.N., Enugu, 31 July 1975.
Ochin, Joseph W., Uwani, Enugu, 9 July 1975.
Ogbodo, James, Obuofia, Akagbe, 2 June 1975.
Ohale, J.K., Amawom, Owerri, 9 August 1975.
Ojiyi, Isaiah O., Amawbia, Awka, 27 July 1975.
Okafor, Emmanuel, Uwani, Enugu, 10 July 1975.
Okoye, Mokwugo, East Central Broadcasting Layout, 16 July 1975.
Okpokwu, Joseph, Aboh, Ngwo, 5 June 1975.
Ona, Onovo, Akagbe Ugwu, 30 July 1975.
Onoh, Samuel N., Ngwo Etiti, Nigeria, 9 August 1975.
Onuora, Benjamin, Awka, 7 June 1975.
Onia, Mark, Uwani Ugoji, Ngwo, 9 December 1991.
Osakwe, Mokoro, Aaron Camp, Enugu, 8 July 1975.
Ozoani, Onoh, Ameke, Ngwo, 18 November 1991.
Ozobu, Chief Thomas, Imezi, Owa, Udi, 21 June 1975.
Ozogwu, Eze, Amankwo, Udi, 2 June 1975.
Ude, Clement, Aaron Camp, Enugu, 9 July 1975.
Ude, David, Amokwe, Udi, 7 August 1975.
Ude, Augustine, Umuaga, Udi, 5 August 1975.
Ude, C.O. Amokwe, Udi, 23 February 1972.

## ARCHIVAL SOURCES

### NIGERIA

### Nigeria National Archives, Enugu (NNAE)

CSE Series, 1914–1950. Secretariat, Southern Provinces. Includes Intelligence Reports of the Igbo Clans and Onitsha Province Annual Reports, 1921–1925.
Hair, P.E.H., Enugu: An African City, Report. Mimeographed. 1954.
LAE Series, 1930–1941. Continuation of SME Series. Local Authority, Enugu. Many files were damaged.
MINLOC Series. Udi (Enugu) Coal Mines, 1910–1920.
NIGCOAL/CHQ Series, 1921–1951. Nigerian Coal Corporation Files.
ONDIST Series, 1930–1938. Intelligence Reports.
ONPROF Series, 1928–1950. Office of the Resident of Onitsha Province. The Nomenclature of these records has changed several times. It includes Enugu division reports as well as provincial reports.
SME Series, 1930–1941. Local Authority, Enugu. Includes township reports.
UDDIST Series, 1934–1950. Udi Divisional Files. Includes Udi Division Annual Reports.

### National Archives Ibadan, Ibadan University

CSO 26/1 09253/V.I. Onyeama: Recognition as Paramount Chief of Abaja Tribe, Subsidy of.

## Nigerian Coal Corporation Headquarters, Enugu

P. Series, [Formerly NCC (Sec)] 1930–1951. Personnel Files of the Enugu Colliery and, after 1950, the Nigerian Coal Corporation.

## Federal Ministry of Labour Archives, Yaba, Lagos

No. 3, Vol. 5 to 9. Series, 1938–1943. Udi Colliery, Quarterly Report and Staff Welfare Officer's Quarterly Report.
No. 3/S. 2, 1943–1946. Colliery Manager's Quarterly Reports.

## GREAT BRITAIN
## Public Records Office (PRO), London. Colonial Office Series

CO 96/734. Gold Coast, 1937–1938.
CO 323. Labour Conditions in the Colonies. Proposed Departmental Committee, 1931. Proceedings, 1931–1941.
CO 537. Coal: Labour Relations at Enugu Colliery. MPGG129(11) Enugu Ngwu, 1917–1919 (Map).
CO 554. West Africa, 1937–1940.
CO 583. Nigeria. General Correspondence, 1914–1946.
CO 657/2. Nigerian Railway. Administrative Report, 1916–1919.
CO 741/1. Nigerian Railway. Minutes of Official Meetings, 1912–1922.
CO 859. Social Services. Labour. Colonial Labour Committee, 1939.
CO 888/1. Colonial Labour Committee. Papers, 1931–1941.
CO 888/2. Colonial Labour Advisory Committee. Papers and Minutes, 1942–1943.

## Church Missionary Society Archives, University of Birmingham

A2, A3, A9.
AF 35/49 G3A3.
CMS G3A3 Niger Mission 1913.
G3A3.

## Colonial Records Project, Rhodes House, Oxford University

Mss. Afr. s. 1117 Orde Browne, Granville, St. George. Personal Papers.
Mss. Afr. s. 3754 Adams, Lt. Gerald, "Miner and Executioner" in *Five Nigerian Tales*.
Mss. Afr. s. 1133. Dalgliesh, Andrew. "Visit to Nigeria for Industrial Relations," Typescript, 1950.
Mss. Afr. s. 1134. Mellor, A.R.I., "U.A.C. Labour Policy in Nigeria with Reference to the Report of the Commission of Enquiry into the Disorders at Enugu, 1949," London, 31 July 1950.
Mss. Afr. s. 571. Patton, J. Esquire. "Life in Nigeria as a Railway Pioneer, 1914–1927."
Mss. Afr. s. 1123. Ponsonby, Sir Charles Edward. "Miscellaneous Notes and Reports on Labour Unrest in Eastern Nigeria," 1950.
Mss. Afr. s. 1318 (1) Roberts, R.A. Papers.

Mss. Afr. s. 1507 Ministry of Information. 26 Photos with Captains of Model Village, Udi. Siding April 1943.
Mss. Brit. Emp. s. 16–24 Papers of British and Foreign Antislavery, and Aborigines Protective Society.
Mss. Brit. Emp. s. 25.K20 League of Colored Peoples.
Mss. Brit. Emp. s. 74. Lugard, Sir Frederick. "Correspondence and Papers about Building of the Baro-Kano Railway and Railway to Udi Coalfield."

### Crown Agents, London

PHOTO 61. Nigerian Railway, Port Harcourt to Udi Coalfield. Photographic Album, circa 1915.

### Royal Commonwealth Society, London

*Annual Report for the Colliery Department, 1938–1939.* Legislative Council, Sessional Papers, No. 9, 1940.
*Nigerian Railway and Udi Colliery Administrative Report, 1914–1937.*

### British Library of Political and Economic Science, London School of Economics

Papers of E.D. Morel. Individual Correspondence, 1914–1924.
Passfield Papers. Field Notes. Nigeria, 1934–1940.

### PERSONAL COLLECTION OF DAVID SMOCK

### Methodist Church, Overseas Division (Methodist Missionary Society), London

Richardson, Mrs. A.H., "Account of the Pioneer Work in the Agbani Area of Nigeria undertaken by the Rev. Arthur Humphrey Richardson of the Primitive Methodist Missionary Society 1916–1920." Unpublished manuscript. London, 1976.

### Modern Records Project, University of Warwick, Coventry England

British Trade Union Congress Reports.

### PERSONAL COLLECTION OF P.E.H. HAIR

C.H. Croasdale, "Report on the Enugu Colliery," 1938.

### OFFICIAL PUBLICATIONS

### NIGERIA

*Commission of Enquiry Appointed to Inquire into the Disturbances in the Calabar and Owerri Province.* Lagos: Government Printing Office, December 1929.

Department of Labour Annual Report. *Sessional Papers of the Legislative Council, 1942–1951.*

Financial Secretary. *Report on the Accounts and Finances for the Years 1943–1950.*

Jones, G.I. *Report on the Position, Status and Influence of Chiefs and Natural Rulers in the Eastern Region of Nigeria.* Enugu: Government Printing Office, 1958.

*The Laws of Nigeria.* Containing Ordinances in Force the First Day of May, 1923 and the Principal Imperial Statutes, Orders in Council, Letters, Patent and Royal Relating to Nigeria. Revised Edition. Vol. I. Lagos: Government Printer, 1923. Appendix. 1930, 1932, 1934, 1935, 1936, 1938, 1939, 1940, 1941.

*Ministry of Labour Quarterly Review, 1960–1970.*

Nigerian Coal Corporation Ordinance, Nigerian Coal Corporation, No. 19 of 1950.

Nigerian Legislative Council, Sir Hugh Clifford. G.C.M.C. Address of the Governor. Lagos: Government Printers, 1926.

Report of the Methods of Negotiations Between the Government and Government Employees on Questions Affecting Conditions of Service in Industrial Departments. Lagos, Government Printers, 1948.

Report on Unestablished and Daily-rated Government Servants, Sessional Paper No. 8 of 1947. Lagos: Government Printers, March 1947.

## GREAT BRITAIN

Colonial Office. *Labour Administration in the Colonial Territories 1944–1950.*

Col. No. 275. London: His Majesty's Stationery Office., 1951.

———. *Enquiry into the Cost of Living in the Colony and Protectorate of Nigeria.* Col. No. 204. London: His Majesty's Stationery Office, 1946. [Tudor Davies Commission]

———. "Enquiry into the Disorders in the Eastern Provinces of Nigeria: Proceedings of the Commission." Vols. 1–2. London: His Majesty's Stationery Office, 1950. Mimeographed.

———. *Labour Supervision in the Colonial Empire, 1937–1943.* Col. No. 185. London: His Majesty's Stationery Office, 1943.

———. *Memorandum on Colonial Mining Policy.* London: His Majesty's Stationery Office, 1946.

———. *Report of the Commission of Enquiry into the Disorders in the Eastern Provinces of Nigeria.* Col. No. 256. London: His Majesty's Stationery Office, 1950. [Fitzgerald Commission]

———. *Report of the Commission of Enquiry Into the Disturbances in the Gold Coast,* 1948. Colonial No. 231 (1948) [Watson Commission].

———. *Report of the Commission on the Civil Services of British West Africa, 1945–1946.* Col. No. 209. London: His Majesty's Stationery Office, No. 209 (1947). [Harragin Commission]

Mineral Survey Report. Colonial Reports. Misc. 1908–1912.

Ministry of Information. Reference Division. "Labour. West Africa." 29 January 1946. Mimeographed.

———. "Labour Supervision in the Colonies." With Appendix on "Industrial Welfare at Enugu Colliery, Nigeria." 24 January 1944. Mimeographed.

Orde Browne, Granville St. John. *Labour Conditions in West Africa,* Cmd. 6277. London: His Majesty's Stationery Office, 1941.

Ormsby-Gore, Hon. W.G.A. (MP). "Report on Visit to West Africa in 1926." *Parliamentary Papers* 9: 211–29.

Parliament. *Hansard's Parliamentary Debates* (Commons), 1914–1951.

Powell Duffryn Technical Services. "First Report to the Under-Secretary of State for the Colonies, Colonial Office, Dover House, Whitehall S. W. 1., on the Government Colliery, Enugu, The Characteristics of the Coal Produced and the Investigation into the Other Coal and Lignite Resources." London, 1948. Mimeographed.

## SECONDARY SOURCES

Achebe, Chinua. *Things Fall Apart*. London: Fawcett Crest, 1959.

Achogbuo, Onogbo. *Iva Valley Tragedy: A Memorable Incident in Nigerian National and Trade Union History,* Enugu: The Continental Press, n.d.

Adas, Michael. *Machines as Measure of Men: Science, Technology and Ideologies of Western Dominance*. Ithaca: Cornell University Press, 1989.

Adewoye, Omoniyi. *The Judicial System in Southern Nigeria, 1854–1954: Law and Justice in a Dependency*. Atlantic Highlands, NJ: Humanities Press, 1977.

Adi, Hakim. *West Africans in Britain, 1900–1960: Nationalism, Pan-Africanism and Communism*. London: Lawrence and Wisehart, 1998.

Afigbo, A.E. "Anthropology and Colonial Administration in South-Eastern Nigeria, 1891–1939." *Journal of the Historical Society of Nigeria* 8, 1 (December 1975): 19–35.

———— ed. *Groundwork of Igbo History, Ethno Historical Studies Series 1,* Lagos: Vista, 1991.

————. *Ropes of Sand: Studies in Igbo History and Culture*. Lagos: University of Nigeria Press, 1981.

————. "Southeastern Nigeria in the 19th Century." In *History of West Africa*. 2d ed. Vol. 2, edited by J.F.A. Ajayi and M. Crowder. New York: Columbia University Press, 1974.

————. *The Warrant Chiefs: Indirect Rule in Southeastern Nigeria, 1891–1929*. London: Longman, 1972.

————, ed. *The Image of the Igbo*. Ethno Historical Series 2, Lagos: Vista, 1991.

Agwuna, Igwe Osita, H.R.H. Iguaro. *Obu Ofo Nri Royal Documents*. Vol. 2, no. 11. Enugu: The Reveille Printing and Publishing, 1972.

Ajayi, J.F.A., and Michael Crowder, eds. *History of West Africa*. England: Longman, 1974.

Akpala, Agwu. "African Labour Productivity—A Reappraisal," *African Quarterly* 12, 3 (1972): 233–51.

————. "Background to the Enugu Colliery Shooting Incident in 1949." *Journal of the Historical Society of Nigeria*. 3, 2 (1965): 335–64.

————. *Managing Industrial Relations in Nigeria (Case Study of Nigerian Coal Industry.)* Lagos: Modern Graphics Systems Ltd. 1984.

————. "Problems of Initiating Industrial Labour in Pre-Industrial Communities." *Cahiers d'Etudes Africains* 12, 46 (1972): 291–301.

————. *The Prospects of Small Trade Unions in Nigeria*. Enugu: 1963.

Alagoa, Ebiegber Joe. *The Small Brave City-State:* A History of Nembe-Brass in the Niger Delta. Ibadan: Ibadan University Press, 1964.

Alexander, Peter, and Richard Halpern, eds. *Racializing Class, Classifying Race: Labour and Difference in Britain, the USA and Africa*. New York: St. Martin's Press, 2000.

Amadiume, Ifi. *Male Daughters and Female Husbands: Gender and Sex in an African Society.* London: Zed Publishers, 1987.

Ananaba, Wogu. *The Trade Union Movement in Africa: Promise and Performance.* New York: St. Martin's Press, 1979.

——. *The Trade Union Movement in Nigeria.* New York: Africana Publishing Corporation, 1969.

Anene, J.C. *Southern Nigeria in Transition: 1885–1906.* Cambridge: Cambridge University Press, 1966.

Aniakor, Chike C. "Igbo Life, World View, and Cosmology." *Genéve-Afrique* 21, 1 (1988).

Arua, A.O. *A Short History of Ohafia.* Enugu, 1952.

Atkins, Keletso. *The Moon Is Dead! Give Us Our Money!: The Cultural Origins of an African Work Ethic, Natal, South Africa, 1843–1900.* Portsmouth: Heinemann Publishers, 1993.

——. "'Kaffir Time': Preindustrial Temporal Concepts and Labour Discipline in Nineteenth Century Colonial Natal." *Journal of African History* 29 (1988): 229–44.

Bain, A.D.N. "The Nigerian Coalfield, Sec. 1, Enugu Area." *Geological Survey of Nigeria* 6 (1924).

Barrow, W.L. "Rural-Urban Alliance and Reciprocity in Africa." *Canadian Journal of African Studies* vol. 5.3. (1971): 307–25.

Basden, G.T. *Among the Ibos of Southern Nigeria.* London: Seely, Service and Company, 1921.

——. *Niger Ibos.* London: Frank Cass and Company, 1966.

Bauer, P.T. *West African Trade: A Study in Competition, Oligopoly and Monopoly in a Changing Economy.* New York: Augustus M. Kelley, 1967.

Beik, Mildred Allen. *The Miners of Windber: The Struggles of New Immigrants for Unionization, 1890's–1930's.* University Park: Pennsylvania State University Press, 1996.

Berg, Elliott, and Jeffrey Butler. "Trade Unions." In *Political Parties and National Integration in Tropical Africa,* edited by James Coleman and Carl G. Rosberg, 340–81. Berkeley: University of California Press, 1964.

Berman, Bruce. "Bureaucracy and Incumbent Violence: Colonial Administration and the Origins of the 'Mau Mau' Emergency." In *The Unhappy Valley: Conflict in Kenya and Africa.* Bk 2, *Violence and Ethnicity,* eds. Bruce Berman and John Lonsdale, 227–65. London/Ohio: James Currey, 1992.

Beverly, W.A. *Military Report on Southern Nigeria, 1908.* 2 vols. London: n.p., 1908.

Black, Henry C. *Black's Law Dictionary.* 5th ed. St. Paul, MN: West Publishing Company, 1979.

Bozzoli, Belinda, and Peter Delius, eds. "History in South Africa," a special issue of *Radical History Review,* 46/47 (Winter 1990).

Braverman, Harry. *Labor and Monopoly Capital: The Degradation of Work in the Twentieth Century.* New York: Monthly Review Press, 1974.

Brett, E.A. *Colonialism and Underdevelopment in East Africa.* New York: Nok Publishers, 1973.

Brown, Carolyn A., "Becoming 'Men,' Becoming 'Workers': Race, Gender and Workplace Struggle in the Nigerian Coal Industry, 1937–49"; in Peter Alexander and Rick Halpern, eds., *Racializing Class, Classifying Race: Labour and Difference in Britain, the USA and Africa,* New York: St. Martin's Press, Inc., 2000, 168–192.

——. "The Dialectic of Colonial Labour Control: Class Struggles in the Nigerian Coal Industry, 1941–1949," *Journal of Asian and African Studies* 23 (1988): 32–59.

———. "Testing the Boundaries of Marginality: Twentieth-Century Slavery and Emancipation Struggles in Nkanu, Northern Igboland, 1920–1929." *Journal of African History* 37 (1996): 51–80.

Bulman, H.F., and R.A.S. Redmayne. *Colliery Working and Management.* London: Crosby Lockwood and Son, 1896.

Burawoy, Michael. *The Politics of Production: Factory Regimes Under Capitalism and Socialism.* London: Verso Books, 1985.

———. *The Colour of Class in the Copper Mines.* Manchester: Manchester University Press, 1972.

Campbell, Allan, and Fred Reid. "The Independent Collier in Scotland." In *The Independent Collier: The Coal Miner as Archetypal Proletarian Reconsidered,* edited by Royden Harrison, 54–74. London and Sussex: Harvester Press, 1978.

Channock, Martin. *Law, Custom and Social Order: The Colonial Experience in Malawi and Zambia.* Cambridge: Cambridge University Press, 1985.

"The Coal Resources of the British Colonies and Protectorates." *The Imperial Institute Bulletin* 10 (1912): 435–43.

Cohen, Robin. *Labour and Politics in Nigeria, 1945–1971.* London: Heinemann Educational Books, 1974.

———. "Nigeria's Labour Leader No. 1: Notes for a Biographical Study of M.A.O. Imoudu." *Journal of the Historical Society of Nigeria* 5, 2 (1970): 303–08.

———. "Resistance and Hidden Forms of Consciousness among African Workers." *Review of African Political Economy* 19 (1980): 8–22.

Cole, Herbert M., and Chike C. Aniakor. *Igbo Arts: Community and Cosmos.* Los Angeles: Museum of Cultural History, 1984.

Coleman, James S. *Nigeria: Background to Nationalism.* Los Angeles and Berkeley: University of California Press, 1958.

———., and Carl Rosberg, eds. *Political Parties and National Integration in Tropical Africa.* Los Angeles and Berkeley: University of California Press, 1964.

Colls, Robert. *The Pitmen of the Northern Coalfield: Work, Culture, and Protest, 1790–1850.* Manchester: Manchester University Press, 1987.

Connell, Robert W. *Masculinities.* Berkeley and Los Angeles: University of California Press, 1995.

Cookey, Sylvannus J. "An Igbo Slave Story of the 19th Century and its Implications," *Ikenga* 1, 2 (1972): 1–9.

Cooper, Frederick. *Decolonization and African Society: The Labor Question in French and British Africa.* Cambridge: Cambridge University Press, 1996.

———. "Colonizing Time: Work Rhythms and Labor Conflict in Colonial Mombasa." In *Colonialism and Culture,* edited by Nicholas B. Dirks. Ann Arbor: The University of Michigan Press, 1992.

———. "From Free Labor to Family Allowances: Labor and African Society in Colonial Discourse." *American Ethnologist* 16, 4 (1989): 745–65.

———. *On the African Waterfront: Urban Disorder and the Transformation of Work in Colonial Mombasa.* New Haven: Yale University Press, 1987.

———. "Work, Class, and Empire: An African Historian's Retrospective on E. P. Thompson." *Social History* 20, 2 (May 1995): 235–41.

———. "Urban Space, Industrial Time, and Wage Labor in Africa." In *The Struggle for the City: Migrant Labor, Capital, and the State in Urban Africa,* Frederick Cooper ed., 7–50. Beverly Hills: Sage Press, 1983.

Cornwall, Andrea, and Nancy Lindsfarne, "Dislocating Masculinity: Gender, Power, and Anthropology." In *Dislocating Masculinity: Comparative Ethnographies,* A. Cornwall and N. Lindsfarne, eds. London: Routledge, 1994.

Cowen, Michael, and Nicholas Westcott. "British Imperial Economic Policy During the War." In *Africa and the Second World War,* David Killingray and Richard Rathbone eds., 21–67. London: Macmillan, 1986.

Crisp, Jeff. *The Story of An African Working Class: Ghanaian Miners' Struggles, 1870–1980.* London: Zed Publishers, 1984.

Crowder, Michael. *West Africa Under Colonial Rule.* Evanston, IL: Northwestern University Press, 1968.

———. "The 1939–1945 War and West Africa." In *History of West Africa.* Vol. 2, Michael Crowder and J.F.A. Ajayi, eds 596–621. London: Longman Group, 1974.

Curtin, Phillip. *The Image of Africa: British Ideas and Action, 1780–1850.* Vol. 2. Madison: University of Wisconsin Press, 1973.

———. "Medical Knowledge and Urban Planning in Tropical Africa." *American Historical Review* 90 (1985): 594–613.

Daunton, M.J. "Down the Pit: Work in the Great Northern and South Wales Coal Fields, 1870–1914." *Economic History Review,* 2d ser., 34, 4 (November 1981): 578–97.

Davies, Ioan. *African Trade Unions.* London: Penguin Publishers, 1966.

Dike, Azuka A. *The Resilience of Igbo Culture: A Case Study of Awka Town.* Enugu: Fourth Dimension Publishers, 1985.

Dike, K. Onwuka. *Trade and Politics in the Niger Delta 1830–1885: An Introduction to the Economic and Political History of Nigeria.* Oxford: Clarendon Press, 1956.

———, and Felicia Ekejiuba. "Change and Persistence in Aro Oral History," *Journal of African Studies* 3, 3 (1976): 277–96.

Dix, Keith. *What's a Coal Miner to Do? The Mechanization of Coal Mining.* Pittsburgh: University of Pittsburgh Press, 1988.

Douglass, Dave. "Pit Talk in County Durham." In *Miners, Quarrymen and Saltworkers History Workshop Series,* Raphael Samuel, ed., 297–348. London: Routledge and Kegan Paul, 1977.

———. "The Durham Pitman." In *Miners, Quarrymen and Saltworkers History Workshop Series,* Raphael Samuel ed., 205–95. London: Routledge and Kegan Paul, 1977.

Dubow, Saul. "Race, Civilization, and Culture: The Elaboration of Segregationist Discourse In the Inter-War Years." In *The Politics of Race, Class, and Ethnicity in Twentieth Century South Africa,* Shula Marks and Stanley Trapido, eds., 71–94. New York: Longman, 1987.

Echenberg, Myron. *Colonial Conscripts: The Tirailluers Senegalais in French West Africa, 1857–1960.* Portsmouth: Heinemann Educational Books, 1991.

———. "'*Morts pour la France*': The African Soldier in France During the Second World War," *Journal of African History* 26 (1985): 363–80.

Edwards, Paul, ed. *Equiano's Travels.* London: Heinemann Educational Books, 1967.

Egboh, Edmund. "Labour Relations in Nigeria: The Development of Joint Consultative and Negotiating Machinery 1940–1964." *Genevé-Africa* 11, 1 (1972): 52–73.

Ekechi, Felix. *Missionary Enterprise and Rivalry in Igboland 1857–1914.* London: Frank Cass, 1971.

Ekejiuba, Felicia O. "The Aro System of Trade in the Nineteenth Century, Part I." *Ikenga* 1, 1 (1972): 11–26.

———. "The Aro System of Trade in the Nineteenth Century, Part II." *Ikenga* 1, 2 (1972): 10–21.

Ekundare, R. Olufemi. *An Economic History of Nigeria, 1860–1960.* New York: Africana Publishing, 1973.

Eltis, David, Stephen D. Behrendt, David Richardson, Herbert Klein, eds. *The Trans-Atlantic Slave Trade: A Database on CD-ROM.* Cambridge: Cambridge University Press, 1999.

Enechukwu, Anayo. *The History of Nkanu.* Enugu: Kaufhof Publishers, 1993.

Fanon, Frantz. *The Wretched of the Earth.* New York: Grove Press, 1963.

First, Ruth. *Black Gold: The Mozambican Miner, Proletarian and Peasant,* New York: St. Martin's Press, 1983.

Flint, John E. *Sir George Goldie and the Making of Nigeria.* London: Oxford University Press, 1960.

Forde, Daryll, and G.I. Jones. *The Ibo and Ibibio-Speaking People of South Eastern Nigeria Part III.* Ethnographic Survey of Africa. London: International African Institute, 1962.

———, and Richenda Scott, eds. *The Economics of a Tropical Dependency.* London: Faber and Faber, 1946.

Frank, David. "The Country of Coal." *Labour/Le Travail* 21 (Spring 1988): 233–242.

Freund, Bill. *The African Worker.* Cambridge: Cambridge University Press, 1988.

———. *Capital and Labour in the Nigerian Tin Mines.* Atlantic Highlands, NJ: Humanities Press, 1981.

———. "Labour Migration to the Northern Nigerian Tin Mines." *Journal of African History* 22 (1981): 73–84.

Gailey, Harry A. *The Road to Aba: A Study of British Administrative Policy in Eastern Nigeria.* New York: New York University Press, 1970.

Gilmore, David G. *Manhood in the Making: Cultural Concepts of Masculinity.* New Haven: Yale University Press, 1990.

Goodrich, Carter. *The Miner's Freedom.* Boston: Marshall Jones, 1925.

Green, Margaret M. *Land Tenure in an Ibo Village.* London: Percy Lund, Humphries, 1974.

Grier, Beverly. "Invisible Hand: The Political Economy of Child Labour in Colonial Africa." *Journal of Southern African Studies* 20, 1 (1994): 27–52.

Grillo, Ralph D. *African Studies Series 10: African Railwaymen.* London: Cambridge University Press, 1973.

———. *Race, Class and Militancy.* New York: Chandler Publishing Company, 1974.

Grove, A.T. "Soil Erosion and Population Problems in South-East Nigeria." *Geographical Journal* 117, 3 (1951): 291–306.

Gupta, Partha S. *Imperialism and the British Labour Movement, 1914–1964.* New York: Holmes and Meier, 1975.

Gutkind, Peter. *The Emergent African Proletariat.* Centre for Developing-Area Studies, Occasional Paper Series, No. 8. Montreal, Canada: McGill University, 1974.

———, Robin Cohen, and Jean Copans, eds. *African Labor History.* Beverly Hills: Sage Publications, 1978.

———, Robin Cohen, and P. Brazier, eds. *Peasants and Proletarians: The Struggles of Third World Workers.* New York: Monthly Review, 1970.

Gutman, Herbert. *Work, Culture and Society in Industrializing America.* New York: Vintage Books, 1977.

Guy, Jeff. "Analyzing Pre-Capitalist Societies." *Journal of South African Studies* 14, 1 (October 1987): 30–42.

———. "Gender Oppression in Southern African Societies." In *Women and Gender in Southern Africa to 1945,* Cheryl Walker ed., 33–47. Capetown: David Phillips, 1991.

Guyer, J.I. "Wealth in People and Self-Realization in Equatorial Africa." *Man* n.s., 28 (1993): 243–65.

Hailey, Lord. *Native Administration in the British African Territories. Part 3, West Africa: Nigeria, Gold Coast, Sierra Leone, Gambia.* London: His Majesty's Stationery Office, 1951.

Harries, Patrick. *Work, Culture, and Identity: Migrant Laborers in Mozambique and South Africa, 1860–1910.* Portsmouth, NH: Heinemann.

Harris, J.R. "Skills, Coal, and British Industry in the Eighteenth Century." *History* 61, 202 (June 1976):

Harris, J.S. "Some Aspects of Slavery in Southeastern Nigeria." *Journal of Negro History* 27 (1942): 37–54.

Harrison, Roydon, ed. *The Independent Collier: The Coal Miner as Archetypal Proletarian Reconsidered.* Sussex: Harvester, 1978.

Haydu, Jeffrey. *Making American Industry Safe for Democracy: Comparative Perspectives on the State and Employee Representation in the Era of World War I.* Champain-Urbana: University of Illinois Press, 1977.

Haywood, Colonel A. *The History of the Royal West Africa Frontier Force.* London: Aldershot, Gale and Polden, 1964.

Henderson, Ian. "Early African Leadership: The Copperbelt Disturbances of 1935 and 1950." *Journal of Southern African Studies* 2 (1973): 83–97.

Henderson, Richard N. *The King in Every Man: Evolutionary Trends in Onitsha Society and Culture.* New Haven: Yale University Press, 1972.

Henige, David. *Oral Historiography.* New York: Longman, 1982.

Higgenson, John. *A Working Class in the Making: Belgian Colonial Labor Policy, Private Enterprise, and the African Mineworker, 1907–1951.* Madison: University of Wisconsin Press, 1989.

Hill, Robert. *Marcus Garvey and the Universal Negro Improvement Association Papers,* Berkeley: University of California Press, 1983–2000, 9 vols.

Hobsbawm, Eric, and Terence Ranger, eds. *The Invention of Tradition.* Cambridge: Cambridge University Press, 1983.

Hodder, Barry W., and Ukwu I. Ukwu, eds. *Markets in West Africa.* Ibadan: Ibadan University Press, 1969.

Hodgkin, Thomas. *Nationalism in Colonial Africa.* New York: New York University Press, 1963.

Hogendorn, Jan S. *Nigerian Groundnut Exports.* Zaria: Ahmadu Bello University Press and Oxford University Press, 1978.

Holbrook, Wendell P. "British Propaganda and the Mobilization of the Gold Coast War Effort, 1939–45," *Journal of African History,* 26, 4, 1985.

Hopkins, Anthony G. *An Economic History of West Africa.* New York: Columbia University Press, 1975.

Horton, W.G.R. "From Fishing Village to City-State: A Social History of New Calabar." In *Man in Africa,* Mary Douglas and Phyllis M. Kabery, eds., 38–60. Garden City, NY: Doubleday, 1971.

———. "God, Man, and the Land in a Northern Ibo Village-Group." *Africa* 26 (1956): 17–28.

———. "The *Ohu* System of Slavery in a Northern Ibo Village Group." *Africa* 24 (1954): 311–36.

Huessler, Robert. *Yesterday's Rulers: The Making of the British Colonial Service.* Syracuse, NY: Syracuse University Press, 1963.

Hyman, Richard. *Marxism and the Sociology of Trade Unions.* London: Pluto Press, 1971.

———. *Industrial Relations: A Marxist Introduction.* London: The Macmillan Press, 1975.

"The Influence of International Labour Conventions on Nigerian Labour Legislation." *International Labour Review* 82, 1 (1960): 26–43.

Ikime, Obaro. *Niger Delta Rivalry: Itesekiri-Urhobo Relations and the European Presence 1884–1936.* New York: Humanities Press, 1969.

Iliffe, John. "A History of the Dockworkers of Dar es Salaam." *Tanzanian Notes and Records.* 71 (1971).

Isichei, Elizabeth. *A History of Nigeria.* New York: Longman, 1983.

———. *A History of the Igbo People.* London: The Macmillan Press, 1976.

———. *The Ibo People and the Europeans: The Genesis of a Relationship to 1906.* New York: St. Martin's Press, 1973.

———. *Igbo Worlds: An Anthology of Oral Histories and Historical Description.* Philadelphia: Institute for the Study of Human Issues, 1978.

Iweriebor, Ehiedu. *Radical Politics in Nigeria, 1945–1950: The Significance of the Zikist Movement.* Zaria: Ahmadu Bello Press, 1996.

Jaja, S.O. "The Enugu Colliery Massacre in Retrospect: An Episode in British Administration of Nigeria." *Journal of the Historical Society of Nigeria* 2, 3–4 (December 1982–June 1983): 86–106.

Jones, G.I. "Dual Organization in Ibo Social Structure." *Africa* 19 (1949): 113–154.

———. "Chieftaincy in the Former Eastern Region of Nigeria." In *West African Chiefs: Their Changing Status Under Colonial Rule and Independence,* Michael Crowder and Obaro Ikime eds., 312–24. Ife-Ife, Nigeria: University of Ife Press, 1970.

———. "Ecology and Social Structure Among the Northeastern Ibo." *Africa* 31, 2 (1961): 117–34.

———. "Ibo Land Tenure." *Africa* 19 (1949): 309–23.

———. "Native and Trade Currencies in Southern Nigeria During the 18th and 19th Centuries." *Africa* 28, 1 (1958): 43–53.

———. *The Trading States of the Oil Rivers.* Oxford: Oxford University Press, 1963.

Jones-Quartey, K.A.B. *A Life of Azikiwe.* London: C. Nicholls and Company, 1965.

July, Robert. *The Origins of Modern African Thought.* New York, 1967.

King, Anthony D. *Urbanism, Colonialism and the World Economy: Cultural and Spatial Foundations of the World Urban System.* London: Routledge Press, 1990.

Kirk-Greene, Anthony. *Biographical Dictionary of the British Colonial Service, 1939–1966.* London: Hans Zell, 1991.

Klubock, Thomas. *Contested Communities: Class, Gender and Politics in Chile's El Teniente Copper Mine, 1904–1951.* Durham: Duke University Press, 1998.

Koelle, Sigismund Wilhelm. *Polyglotta Africana.* London: Church Missionary House, 1854.

Ladell, W.S.S. "Applied Physiology in Nigeria." *The West African Medical Journal* Vol. I (new series). (March 1952): 35–37.

———. "Some Physiological Observations on West African Coal Miners." *British Journal of Industrial Medicine* 5, 16 (1948): 16–20.

Laslett, John H.M. ed., *The United Mine Workers of America: A Model of Industrial Solidarity?* University Park: The Pennsylvania State University Press, 1996.

Lenin, V.I. *On Trade Unions.* Moscow: Progress Publishers, 1965.

———. *The Collected Works of V. I. Lenin, Vol. 3: The Development of Capitalism in Russia.* Moscow: Progress Publishers, 1964.

Lewis, Arthur. *Labour in the West Indies: The Birth of a Worker's Movement.* London: New Beacon Books, 1977.

Lewis, David Levering, *W.E.B. Du Bois: The Fight for Equality and the American Century, 1919–1963.* New York: Henry Holt, 2000.

Lewis, Jon, "South African Labor History: A Historiographical Assessment." In Belinda Bozolli and Peter Delius, eds. "History in South Africa," a special issue of *Radical History Review* 46/47: 213–35.

Lewis, William Roger. *Imperialism at Bay: The United States and the Decolonization of the British Empire, 1941–1954.* New York: Oxford University Press, 1978.

"The Lignite Deposits of Nigeria." *Imperial Institute Bulletin* 21 (1923): 325–48.

Little, Kenneth. *West African Urbanization.* New York: Cambridge University Press, 1965.

Lindsay, Lisa A. "Domesticity and Difference: Male Breadwinners, Working Women and Colonial Citizenship in the 1945 Nigerian General Strike." *American Historical Review* 104, 3 (June 1999): 783–812.

Long, Prisilla. *Where the Sun Never Shines: A History of America's Bloody Coal Industry.* New York: Paragon House, 1991.

Lovejoy, Paul. *Transformations in Slavery: A History of Slavery in Africa.* Cambridge: Cambridge University Press, 1983.

———, and David Richardson. "Trust, Pawnship and Atlantic History: The Institutional Foundations of the Old Calabar Slave Trade." *American Historical Review* 104, 2 (April 1999): 333–55.

Lugard, Frederick. *The Dual Mandate in British Tropical Africa.* Hamden, Connecticut: Archeon Books, 1965.

———. Foreword to *The African Labourer,* Granville St. George Orde Browne. New York: Barnes and Noble, 1967.

———. *The Political Memorandum: Revision of Instructions of Political Officers on Subjects Chiefly Political and Administrative, 1913–1918.* 3d ed. London: Frank Cass, 1970.

Mabongunje, Akin L. *Urbanization in Nigeria.* New York: Africana Publishing Corporation, 1968.

Mafeje, Archie. "The Ideology of 'Tribalism'." *Journal of Modern African Studies* 9, 2 (1971): 253–61.

Mamdani, Mahmood. *Citizen and Subject: Contemporary Africa and the Legacy of Late Colonialism.* Princeton: Princeton University Press, 1996.

Mann, Kristin. *Marrying Well: Marriage, Status, and Social Change Among the Educated Elite in Colonial Lagos.* Cambridge: Cambridge University Press, 1985.

———. "The Rise of Taiwo Olowo: Law, Accumulation, and Mobility in Early Colonial Lagos." In *Law and Colonial Africa,* Richard Roberts and Kristin Mann, eds. Portsmouth, NH: Heinemann Press, 1991.

Manning, Patrick. *Slavery and African Life: Occidental, Oriental, and African Slave Trades.* Cambridge: Cambridge University Press, 1990.

Mars, J. "The Monetary and Banking System and the Loan Market of Nigeria." In *Mining, Commerce, and Finance in Nigeria,* Margery Perham, ed. Vol. 2. London: Farber, 1948.

Marx, Karl. *Capital: The Critique of Political Economy,* Eric Hobsbawn, ed. Vol. I–III. New York: International Publishers, 1972.

———. *Precapitalist Economic Formations.* New York: International Publishers, 1965.

Mason, Michael. "Working on the Railways: Forced Labor in Northern Nigeria, 1907–1912." In *African Labour History,* Peter Gutkind, Robert Cohen, and Jean Copans, eds., 56–79. Beverly Hills: Sage Publications, 1978.

McClintock, Anne. *Imperial Leather: Race, Gender, and Sexuality in the Colonial Contest.* London: Routledge Press, 1995.

Meek, C.K. *Law and Authority in a Nigerian Tribe: A Study in Indirect Rule.* New York: Barnes and Noble, 1937.

Miers, Suzanne, and Richard Roberts, eds. *The End of Slavery in Africa.* Madison: University of Wisconsin Press, 1988.

Morgan, Kenneth O. *Labour in Power: 1945–1951.* Oxford: Clarendon Press, 1984.

Morgan, W.B., and J.C. Pugh. *West Africa.* London: Metheun, 1969.

Moodie, Dunbar, and Vivienne Ndatshe. *Going for the Gold: Men, Mines, and Migration.* Los Angeles: University of California Press, 1994.

Moore, Barrington. *Social Origins of Dictatorship and Democracy: Lord and Peasant in the Making of the Modern World.* Boston: Beacon Press, 1966.

Moorsom, Richard. "Underdevelopment, Contract Labor and Workers' Consciousness in Namibia, 1915–1972." *Journal of Southern African Studies* 4, 1 (1977): 52–87.

Morrison, J.H. "Early Tin Production and Nigerian Labour on the Jos Plateau, 1906–1921." *Canadian Journal of African Studies* 11, 2 (1977): 205–16.

Mudimbe, V.Y. *The Invention of Africa: Gnosis, Philosophy, and the Order of Knowledge.* Bloomington and Indianapolis: University of Indiana Press, 1988.

Naneen, Benedict. "Itinerant Gold Mines: Prostitution in the Cross River Basin of Nigeria, 1930–1950." *African Studies Review* 34, 2 (September, 1991): 57–79.

"The New Coalfield in West Africa." *Imperial Institute Bulletin* 14 (1916): 369–78.

Nkrumah, Kwame. *Revolutionary Path.* New York: International Publishers, 1973.

Northrup, David. "The Compatibility of the Slave and Palm Oil Trades in the Bight of Biafra." *Journal of African History* 17, 3 (1976): 353–64.

———. *Trade Without Rulers: Pre-Colonial Economic Development in South Eastern Nigeria.* Oxford Studies in African Affairs. Oxford: Clarendon Press, 1978.

Nsugbe, Phillip O. *Ohaffia: A Matrilineal Ibo People.* Oxford: Clarendon Press, 1974.

Nwabara, S.N. *Iboland: A Century of Contact with Britain, 1860–1960.* Atlantic Highlands, NJ: Humanities Press, 1978.

Nwachukwu-Ogedengbe, K. "Slavery in Nineteenth Century Aboh." In *Slavery in Africa,* Suzanne Miers and Igor Kopytoff, eds., 133–154. Madison: University of Wisconsin Press, 1977.

Nwaguru, J.E.N. *Aba and British Rule.* Enugu, Nigeria: Santana Press, 1973.

Nwaka, Geoffrey I. "Rebellion in Umuahia, 1950–1951: Ex-servicemen and Anti-colonial Protest in Eastern Nigeria," *Transafrican Journal of History,* Vol. 16 (1987): 47–62.

Nwala, T. Uzodinma. *Igbo Philosophy.* Lagos, Nigeria: Literamed, 1985.

Nzimiro, Ikenna. *Studies in Ibo Political Systems: Chieftaincy and Politics in Four Niger States.* London: Frank Cass, 1972.

Oberst, Timothy. "Transport Workers, Strikes and the 'Imperial Response': Africa and the Post-World War II Conjuncture." *African Studies Review* 31, 1 (1988): 117–34.

Offodile, E.P. Oyeaka. "Growth and Influence of Tribal Unions." *West African Review* (August 1947): 937–41.

Ofonogoro, Walter Ibekwe. *The Currency Revolution in Southern Nigeria, 1880–1948,* Occasional Paper No. 14, African Studies Center, Los Angeles: University of California, July 1966.

Oguagha, Phillip A., and Alex I. Ikpoko. *History and Ethnoarchaeology in Eastern Nigeria: A Study of Igbo-Igala Relations with Special Reference to Anambra Valley.* Cambridge Monographs in African Archaeology, 7, Oxford, 1984.

Ohadike, D.C. "The Influenza Pandemic of 1918–1919 and the Spread of Cassava Cultivation on the Lower Niger: A Study in Historical Linkages." *Journal of African History* 22 (1981): 379–91.

Ojiyi, Okwudili. *The British Political Shooting of the Nigerian Coalminers in November 18, 1949.* Onitsha: Goodway Printing Press, 1965.

Olusanya, J.O. *The Second World War and Politics in Nigeria, 1939–1953.* London: Evans Bros., 1973.

Omu, Fred I.A. *Press and Politics in Nigeria, 1880–1937.* Atlantic Highlands, NJ: Humanities Press, 1978.

Onyeama, Dillibe. *Chief Onyeama: A Story of an African God.* Enugu: Delta Publishers, 1982.

Onyemelukwe, C.C. *Problems of Industrial Planning and Management in Nigeria.* New York: Columbia University Press, 1966.

Orde Browne, Granville St. John. *The African Labourer.* New York: Barnes and Noble, 1967.

Orizu, A.A. Nwafor. *Without Bitterness: Western Nations in Post-War Africa.* New York: Creative Age Press, Inc., 1944.

Osuntokun, Akinjide. *Nigeria in the First World War.* Atlantic Highlands, NJ: Humanities Press, 1979.

———. "Disaffection and Revolts in Nigeria During the First World War, 1914–1918." *Canadian Journal of African Studies* 5, 2 (1971).

Ottenberg, Simon. *Leadership and Authority in an African Tribe.* Seattle: University of Washington Press, 1971.

Oyemakinde, Wale. "Michael Imoudu and the Emergence of Militant Trade Unionism in Nigeria, 1940–1942." *Journal of the Historical Society of Nigeria* 7, 3 (December 1974): 541–61.

———. "The Pullen Marketing Scheme: A Trial in Food Price Control in Nigeria, 1941–47." *Journal of the Historical Society of Nigeria* 6 (1973): 413–23.

———. "The Nigerian General Strike of 1945." *Journal of the Historical Society of Nigeria* 7, 4 (June 1975): 693–771.

Parker, R.A.C. *The Second World War: A Short History.* Oxford: Oxford University Press, 1977.

Parpart, Jane. *Capital and Labor on the African Copperbelt.* Philadelphia: Temple University Press, 1983.

Perham, Margery. *Mining, Commerce, and Finance in Nigeria.* Vol. 2. London: Farber Company, 1948.

———. *Native Administration in Nigeria.* Oxford: Oxford University Press, 1937.

———. *The Native Economies of Nigeria.* London: Farber Company, 1946.

———. *Ten Africans.* 2d ed. Evanston, IL: Northwestern University Press, 1963.

———, and Frederick Lugard. *Lugard: The Years of Authority, 1898–1945.* London: Collins Publishing Company, 1960.

———, and Mary Bull, eds. *The Diaries of Lord Lugard.* Vol. 1–4. Evanston, IL: Northwestern University Press, 1963.

————, ed. *The Diaries of Lord Lugard.* Vol. 5. Evanston, IL: Northwestern University Press, 1963.

Perrings, Charles. *Black Mineworkers in Central Africa: Industrial Strategies and the Evolution of an African Proletariat in the Copperbelt 1911–41.* London: Heinemann, 1979.

————. "Consciousness, Conflict, and Proletarianization: An Assessment of the 1935 Mineworkers' Strike on the Northern Rhodesian Copperbelt." *Journal of Southern African Studies* 4, 1 (1977).

Phillips, Anne. *The Enigma of Colonialism: British Policy in West Africa.* London: James Curry, 1989.

Phimister, Ian. "Lashers and Leviathan: The 1954 Coalminers' Strike in Colonial Zimbabwe." *International Review of Social History* 39 (1994): 165–96.

————. "Wage Earners and Political Protest in Colonial Africa: The Case of the Copperbelt," *African Affairs* 57 (1973): 288–99.

————. *Wangi Kolia: Coal, Capital and Labour in Colonial Zimbabwe 1894–1954.* Harare, Zimbabwe: Baobab Books, 1994.

Post, Ken. *"Arise Ye Starvlings": The Jamaican Labour Rebellion of 1938 and Its Aftermath.* The Hague: Nijhoff, 1978.

————. "The Politics of Protest in Jamaica: Some Problems of Analysis and Conceptualization." In *Peasants and Proletarians: The Struggles of Third World Workers,* Peter Gutkind, Robin Cohen, and P. Brazier, eds. New York: Monthly Review, 1970.

Rathbone, Richard, and Shula Marks, eds. *Industrialization and Social Change in South Africa.* New York: Longman, 1982.

Ray, D.W. "The Takoradi Route: Roosevelt's Pre-war Venture Beyond the Western Hemisphere," *Journal of American History,* LXII, 2 (September 1975).

Rodney, Walter. *How Europe Underdeveloped Africa.* Washington DC: Howard University Press, 1974.

Roper, J.I. *Labour Problems in West Africa.* London: Penguin Books, 1958.

Sandbrook, Richard, and Robin Cohen, eds. *The Development of an African Working Class: Studies in Class Formation and Action.* Toronto: University of Toronto Press, 1975.

Sandoval, Alonso de, S.J. *De Instauranda Aeethopun Salute.* Bogotá: Empresa Nacional de Publicaciones, 1956 (a reissue of Naturaleza ... de Todos Etiopes, Sevilla: Francisco de Lira, 1627).

Saul, John. *The State and Revolution in East Africa.* New York: Monthly Review Press, 1979.

Scott, Joan. *Gender and the Politics of History.* New York: Columbia University Press, 1988.

Sembene, Ousmane. *God's Bits of Wood.* New York: Doubleday, 1962.

Shaw, Thurston. *Igbo Ukwu.* Chicago: Northwestern University Press, 1970.

Singh, Makhan. *History of Kenya's Trade Union Movement.* Nairobi: East African Publishing House, 1969.

Sinha Mrinalini, *Colonial Masculinity: The "Manly" Englishman and the "Effeminate" Bengali in the late 19th Century.* Manchester: Manchester University Press, 1995.

Sklar, Richard. *Corporate Power in an African State.* Berkeley: University of California Press, 1975.

————. *Nigerian Political Parties: Power in an Emergent African Nation.* New Jersey: Princeton University Press, 1963.

Smock, David. "Changing Political Processes Among the Agbaja," *Africa* 38, 3 (1960): 281–92.

———. *Conflict and Control in an African Trade Union: A Study of the Nigerian Coal Miners' Union.* Stanford: Hoover Institute Press, 1969.

———, and Audrey Smock. "Ethnicity and Attitudes Toward Development in Nigeria." *The Journal of Developing Areas* 3 (1969): 499–512.

Spitzer, Leo, and LaRay Denzer. "I.T.A. Wallace-Johnson and the West African Youth League." *International Journal of African Historical Studies* 6, 3 (1973): 413–52.

Stamp, Dudley. "Land Utilization and Soil Erosion in Nigeria." *Geographical Review* 28, 1 (January 1938): 33–45.

Stavenhagen, Rodolfo. *Social Classes in Agrarian Societies.* New York: Anchor Press, 1975.

Stecopoulos, Harry, and Michael Uebel, eds. *Race and the Subject of Masculinities.* Durham: Duke University Press, 1997.

Stevenson, R.F. *Population and Political Systems in Tropical Africa.* New York: Columbia University Press, 1968.

Stracham, I.C.F. *Coal Mining Practice.* Vol. 1. New York: The Caxton Publishing Company, 1958.

Supple, Barry. *The History of the British Coal Industry. Vol. 4, 1913–1946: The Political Economy of Decline.* Oxford: Clarendon Press, 1987.

Swanson, Maynard W. "The Sanitation Syndrome: Bubonic Plague and Urban Native Policy in the Cape Colony, 1900–1909." *Journal of African History* 18, 3 (1977): 387–410.

Szentes, Tomas. *The Political Economy of Underdevelopment.* Translated by I. Veges and A. Gardiner. Budapest: Akademiai Kiado, 1971.

Talbot, P. Amaury. *The Peoples of Southern Nigeria.* 4 vols. London: Frank Cass, 1969.

Tamuno, T.N. *The Evolution of the Nigerian State.* New York: Humanities Press, 1972.

———. "The Genesis of the Nigerian Railway, II" *Nigeria Magazine* 84 (1965): 31–43.

Thomas, Northcott W. *Anthropological Report on the Igbo-Speaking Peoples of Nigeria.* 4 vols. London: Harrison and Sons, 1914.

Thomas, Roger. "Forced Labour in British West Africa: The Case of the Northern Territories of the Gold Coast, 1906–27." *Journal of African History* 14 (1973): 79–103.

Thompson, E.P. *The Making of the English Working Class.* New York: Vintage Books, 1963.

———. "Time, Work-Discipline, and Industrial Capitalism." *Past and Present* 28 (1967): 56–97.

Tignor, Robert L. "Colonial Chiefs in Chiefless Societies." *Journal of Modern African Studies* 9, 3 (1971): 339–59.

Tokunboh, M.A. *Labour Movement in Nigeria: Past and Present.* Lagos: Literamed Publications, 1985.

Tosh, John. "What Should Historians Do with Masculinity? Reflections on Nineteenth-Century Britain." *History Workshop Journal* 38 (1994): 185–202.

———. "The Old Adam and the New Man: Emerging Themes in the History of English Masculinities 1750–1850." In *English Masculinities 1660–1850,* Tim Hitchcock and Michele Cohen, eds. 217–38. London: Longman, 1999.

Uchendu, Victor. "Slaves and Slavery in Igboland, Nigeria." In *Slavery in Africa,* in Suzanne Miers and Igor Kopytoff, eds., 121–54. Madison: University of Wisconsin Press, 1977.

———. *The Igbo of Southeast Nigeria.* New York: Holt, Rinehart and Winston, 1965.

Ukwu, Ukwu I.T. "The Development of Trade and Marketing in Iboland." *Journal of the Historical Society of Nigeria* 3, 4 (1967): 647–62.

Usoro, Eno J. *The Nigerian Oil Palm Industry.* Ibadan: Ibadan University Press, 1974.

Van Allen, Judith. "'Sitting on a Man': Colonialism and the Lost Political Instutitions of Igbo Women." *Canadian Journal of African Studies* 62, (1972): 165–81.

Van Onselen, Charles. *Chibaro: African Mine Labour in Southern Rhodesia, 1900–1933.* London: Pluto Press, 1976.

———. *New Babylon. Vol. 1: Studies in the Social and Economic History of Witwatersrand, 1886–1914.* New York: Longman, 1982.

———. *New Babylon Vol. 2: Studies in the Social and Economic History of Witwatersrand, 1886–1914.* New York: Longman, 1982.

———. "Worker Consciousness in Black Miners: Southern Rhodesia, 1900–1920." *Journal of African History* 14, 2 (1973): 237–55.

———. "The 1912 Wankie Colliery Strike." *Journal of African History* 15, 2 (1974):

Wallace, Anthony F.C. *St. Clair: A Nineteenth-Century Coal Town's Experience with a Disaster-Prone Industry.* Ithaca: Cornell University Press, 1987.

Wallerstein, Immanuel. "Voluntary Associations." In *Political Parties and National Integration in Tropical Africa,* edited by James S. Coleman and Carl Rosberg, 318–39. Berkeley: University of California Press, 1964.

Warren, W.M. "Urban Real Wages and the Nigerian Trade Union Movement, 1939–1960," *Economic Development and Cultural Change,* 15 (1966): 21–36.

Waterman, Peter, and Peter Gutkind, eds. *African Social Studies: A Radical Reader.* New York: Monthly Review Press, 1977.

Webster, Edie, ed. *Essays in Southern African Labour History.* Johannesburg: Ravan Press, 1978.

Weiler, Peter. "Forming Responsible Trade Unions: The Colonial Office, Colonial Labor, and the Trades Union Congress." *Radical History Review* 28–30 (1984):367–392.

White, Luise. *All the Comforts of Home.* Chicago: University of Chicago Press, 1990.

Wilkenson, Rupert. *The Prefects: British Leadership and the Public School Tradition.* London: Oxford University Press, 1965.

Willian, Brian. *Sol Plaatje: South African Nationalist, 1876–1932.* Berkeley: University of California Press, 1984.

———. "An African in Kimberly: Sol T. Plaatje, 1894–1898." In *Industrialization and Social Change in Africa,* edited by Richard Rathbone and Shula Marks, 238–58. London: Longman Press, 1982.

Wilson, Francis. *Labour in the South African Gold Mines 1911–1969.* London: Cambridge University Press, 1972.

Woodis, Jack. *Africa: The Lion Awakes.* London: Lawrence and Wishart, 1961.

———. *The Mask is Off! An Examination of the Activities of Trade Union Advisers in the British Colonies.* London: Thames Publications, 1954.

Yesufu, T.M. *An Introduction to Industrial Relations in Nigeria.* Oxford: Oxford University Press, 1962.

Young, Crawford. *The African Colonial State in Comparative Perspective.* New Haven: Yale University Press, 1994.

Zola, Émile. *Germinal.* New York: Penguin Books, 1954.

Zimbalist, Andrew, ed. *Case Studies on the Labor Process.* New York: Monthly Review Press, 1979.

## UNPUBLISHED SOURCES

Agu, J.O. "A Review of Labour Relations in the Nigerian Coal Industry." Enugu, Nigerian Coal Corporation, 1962. Mimeographed.

Akpala, Agwu. "Industrial Relations in an African Enterprise: A Case Study of the Nigerian Coal Mining Industry." Department of Business Administration, University of Nigeria, Enugu Campus, August 1970.

Brown, Carolyn. "History of the Development of Workers' Consciousness of the Coal Miners at Enugu Government Colliery, Nigeria, 1914–1950." Ph.D. diss., Columbia University, 1985.

Cohen, Robin. "The Making of a West African Working Class." Paper for the Canadian Association of African Studies Conference, 27 February 1974.

———. "Trade Unions and the Military in Africa: The Nigerian Case." Paper presented at the fifteenth annual meeting of the African Studies Association, Philadelphia, November 1972.

Cooper, Frederick, "Rethinking Social Policy: Colonial Bureaucrats and African Labour in the age of Decolonization," unpublished paper, 1990.

Gbanite, Michael E. "Third World Urbanisation: Enugu, Nigeria." Ph.D. diss., New School for Social History, New York, 1978.

Hair, P.E.H. "Enugu: An Industrial Urban Community in Nigeria 1914–1953." *Report of the Annual Conference-Sociology Section.* West African Institute of Social and Economic Research, Ibadan, University College, 143–67.

Harniet-Sievers, Axel. "Repercussions of Pre-Colonial Slavery in Contemporary Local Politics: The Case of Nike, Enugu State, Nigeria," unpublished paper presented at "Repercussions of the Atlantic Slave Trade: The Bight of Biafra and the African Diaspora." Nike Lake, Enugu, Nigeria, 10–14 July 2000.

Lindsay, Lisa A. "Shunting Among Masculine Ideals: The Nigerian Railway Men in the Colonial Era." Paper presented at the thirty-eighth annual meeting of the African Studies Association, Orlando, Florida, 1995.

Mgboh, Felix C. "Biography of Chief Onyeama." Research paper of History-Civics, Alvan Ikoku College of Education, Owerri, Nigeria, 1980.

Oberst, Timothy. "Cost of Living and Strikes in British Africa, c. 1939–1948: Imperial Policy and the Impact of the Second World War." Ph.D. diss., Columbia University, 1991.

Ofonagoro, Walter Ibekwe. "The Opening Up of Southern Nigeria to British Trade and Its Consequences: Economic and Social History, 1881–1916," Ph.D. diss., Columbia University, 1971.

Ogbu, E.N. "Examples of Resistance to the Colonial Rule in the Former Eastern Region of Nigeria from 1890–1960." Ibadan: University of Ibadan, 1972.

Okolo, Mabel Ifejika. "A History of Eke Community 1800–1993" Unpublished interviews, Owerri, 1979.

Perrings, Charles. "Black Workers in Industry: Union Miniere du Haut Katanga, 1911–1931." Seminar paper, Institute for African Studies, University of Zambia, 1974.

Ray, Deborah W. "Pan American Airways and the Trans-African Air Base Program of World War II" Ph.D. diss., New York University, 1973.

Sandbrook, Richard. "The Political Potential of African Urban Workers." Paper prepared for delivery to the joint meeting of the African and Latin American Studies Associations, Houston, Texas, 2–6 November 1977.

Smock, David. "From Village to Trade Union in Africa." Ph.D. diss., Cornell University, 1964.

Uzeochi, Innocent. "The Social and Political Impact of the Eastern Nigerian Railway on Udi Division, 1913–1945." Ph.D. diss., Kent State University, 1985.

Van Onselen, Charles. "Black Labour in Central African Industry: A Critical Essay on the Historiography and Sociology of Rhodesia." Seminar paper, Institute of Commonwealth Studies, University of London, 1974.

———. "The Randlords and Rotgut, 1886–1903." Paper for seminar, The Societies of Southern Africa in the 19th and 20th Centuries, Institute of Commonwealth Studies, University of London, May 1975.

# INDEX

**About the Author**

CAROLYN A. BROWN is an Associate Professor of History at Rutgers University where she is also the Director of the Center for African Studies. In addition to her work on Nigerian coal miners, she has published articles that examine the relationship between African labor processes in the colonial workplace and African working-class masculinity.